NATIVE LAND TALK

RE-MAPPING THE TRANSNATIONAL

A Dartmouth Series in American Studies

SERIES EDITOR
Donald E. Pease
Avalon Foundation Chair of Humanities
Founding Director of the Futures of American Studies Institute
Dartmouth College

The emergence of Transnational American Studies in the wake of the Cold War marks the most significant reconfiguration of American Studies since its inception. The shock waves generated by a newly globalized world order demanded an understanding of America's embeddedness within global and local processes rather than scholarly reaffirmations of its splendid isolation. The series Re-Mapping the Transnational seeks to foster the cross-national dialogues needed to sustain the vitality of this emergent field. To advance a truly comparativist understanding of this scholarly endeavor, Dartmouth College Press welcomes monographs from scholars both inside and outside the United States.

For a complete list of books available in this series, see www.upne.com.

Yael Ben-zvi, *Native Land Talk: Indigenous and Arrivant Rights Theories*
Joanne Chassot, *Ghosts of the African Diaspora: Re-Visioning History, Memory, and Identity*
Samuele F. S. Pardini, *In the Name of the Mother: Italian Americans, African Americans, and Modernity from Booker T. Washington to Bruce Springsteen*
Sonja Schillings, *Enemies of All Humankind: Fictions of Legitimate Violence*
Günter H. Lenz, edited by Reinhard Isensee, Klaus J. Milich, Donald E. Pease, John Carlos Rowe, *A Critical History of the New American Studies, 1970–1990*
Helmbrecht Breinig, *Hemispheric Imaginations: North American Fictions of Latin America*
Jimmy Fazzino, *World Beats: Beat Generation Writing and the Worlding of U.S. Literature*
Zachary McCleod Hutchins, editor, *Community without Consent: New Perspectives on the Stamp Act*
Kate A. Baldwin, *The Racial Imaginary of the Cold War Kitchen: From Sokol'niki Park to Chicago's South Side*
Yuan Shu and Donald E. Pease, *American Studies as Transnational Practice: Turning toward the Transpacific*
Melissa M. Adams-Campbell, *New World Courtships: Transatlantic Alternatives to Companionate Marriage*

YAEL BEN-ZVI

NATIVE LAND TALK

Indigenous and Arrivant Rights Theories

DARTMOUTH COLLEGE PRESS
HANOVER, NEW HAMPSHIRE

Dartmouth College Press
An imprint of University Press of New England
www.upne.com

Manufactured in the United States of America
Typeset in Sabon and Scala Sans Pro by Integrated Publishing Solutions

Research for this book was supported by the Israel Science Foundation (grant #272/07).

Library of Congress Cataloging-in-Publication Data available upon request
Hardcover ISBN: 978-1-5126-0145-9
Paperback ISBN: 978-1-5126-0146-6
Ebook ISBN: 978-1-5126-0147-3

5 4 3 2 1

in loving memory
of my brother Dani
and
for Yael Ronen
who gives me
the present
by the handful

CONTENTS

ACKNOWLEDGMENTS

Nothing about this book came easy, and I'm grateful to the people who helped make it happen. This study is a remote reincarnation of ideas that first emerged during my PhD work at Stanford University, and I thank Ramón Saldívar, David Palumbo-Liu, Priscilla Wald, and Sylvia Yanagisako, who encouraged me to consider the fuller implications of my interests. V. Y. Mudimbe promised to convert me, and in some senses he did.

Although this book was conceived and written later, its guiding questions were inspired by the enriching intellectual community I was fortunate to share with my fellow graduate students, especially in writing groups with Lisa Arellano, Raúl Coronado, Nicole Fleetwood, and Mishuana Goeman, as we mutually tended to one another's work and grew as scholars. Over several years, conversations with them and with Evelyn Alsultany, Manishita Dass, Shona Jackson, Bakirathi Mani, Celine Parreñas-Shimizu, and Beth Piatote shaped my sense of the real-life implications of academic work.

My understanding of history's complex ties to life evolved by talking with Khalil Barhoum, the late Ghaida Firestone, Bryce Giddens, and Rachelle Marshall. I thank Phillip Round and Hilary Wyss for an American Antiquarian Society workshop that highlighted the multiple conditions under which texts are created, circulated, transmitted, erased, reclaimed, and preserved. It broadened and refined my approach to the texts I discuss here. I'm grateful to Lisa Brooks for her helpful insights at an early stage.

Don Pease actively encouraged my work over time and read and responded to chapter drafts. Richard Pult of UPNE has been consistently patient and encouraging along this journey. Mark Rifkin reviewed the manuscript, generously shared his profound understanding of all it had and hadn't done, and suggested what I could do to fulfill its potentials. This book would not have been the same without their support.

Barbara Hochman's mentorship, unfailing friendship, humor, and honesty were invaluable to this project from inception to completion. Shona Jackson's research has always been worlds apart from mine yet eerily close. As I was working on this book our friendship deepened and she is an intellectual inspiration. Catherine Rottenberg has been a great colleague and friend through thick and thin—involved, resourceful, and generous. Barbara,

Shona, and Catherine read whatever I asked them to, and their combined responses were the best blend I could have hoped for.

Faith Damon Davison generously shared her knowledge and work, read and responded to a draft of chapter 2, and answered many questions. She told me that Owaneco sent the pipe to London, and it was a pleasure to eventually find and share with her the elusive 1704 *Monthly Mercury* piece about it. Colleen O'Brien read a draft of chapter 5 and suggested directions for further development. Audra Simpson read a draft of the introduction and helped me rethink some of my assumptions.

In the preliminary research stages, Liza Futerman, Orly Perez, and Danielle Rubin diligently read eighteenth- and nineteenth-century newspapers, and their work contributed immensely to this book.

An earlier version of chapter 1 appeared in *Early American Literature* 48, no. 2 (2013). I thank *EAL*'s editor Sandra Gustafson for her support.

Aviv Ronen good-heartedly resolved all kinds of challenges, especially whenever anything had to be charted, mapped, measured, or calculated, or when technical problems came up.

Yael Ronen's love sustains me, and this book would have never been written without her. Among other things, she's been teaching me how to tell stories while keeping an eye on the bigger picture.

NOTE ON TERMINOLOGY

The terms *arrivant* and *Indigenous peoples* are explained in the introduction.

When referring to particular *Indigenous polities* or their members, I use specific names (e.g., Seneca, Mohegan). Such names often have more than one version, and I have tried to use designations consistently without suggesting that any particular version is more authentic than others. When used as singular nouns, such specific names often refer both to the homeland and to the community, and signify a polity. When referring to a number of people, I use plural nouns (e.g., Cherokees).

I use *Native(s)* or *Native American(s)* in general references that do not specify a particular polity. The term *Indian* refers to settlers' representations of Indigenous peoples.

I follow eighteenth-century capitalization in distinguishing the *Native rights* that Native Americans claimed from the *native Rights* that settlers claimed. The lowercase terms *native right* and *native title* refer to settlers' constructions of *Indians'* extinguishable, transferable entitlements.

US Indian affairs is a category of US policy and governance; it does not suggest the mutual relations that the term *US-Indian* (or *settler-Indigenous*) *relations* connotes.

The terms *America* and *American* refer to the continent rather than to the United States in order not to conflate US sovereignty with America's geopolitical identity.

I use *Indigenous Africans* and *native Africans* for polities or people born there.

NATIVE LAND TALK

INTRODUCTION

DISCUSSIONS OF RIGHTS OFTEN centralize the state. The history of usage recorded in the *Oxford English Dictionary*'s definition of the noun right highlights law, justice, possession, and action—categories that have often reinforced states' power to confer, protect, regulate, limit, or deny rights.[1] It is therefore not surprising that scholars have explored and questioned the state's role in forming conventional understandings of rights. Hannah Arendt simultaneously critiqued and contributed to this view of rights in *Origins of Totalitarianism*. Arendt analyzed Europe's interwar period and the Second World War as the epoch when states—acting in the name of nations —appropriated to themselves the power to confer rights. By so doing, states usurped the Enlightenment political philosophy that promised all men an inalienable entitlement by birth to freedoms defined as natural rights. With this usurpation the states that Arendt studied conditioned the "right to have rights" on national membership, rendered national minorities stateless, and redefined statelessness as rightlessness.[2] In a series of lectures entitled *Society Must Be Defended*, Michel Foucault considered the histories of European monarchies in order to explore the genealogy of states' power to confer rights. He asserted that the primary signification of "right" was a "vehicle" for the "relations of domination" that organize "multiple subjugations . . . within the social body." From this perspective, Foucault defined the rights of subjects or citizens as effects of sovereign power. Rights legitimize the sovereign by "mask[ing]" the relations of domination that undergird sovereignty, "replac[ing]" them with the "legitimate rights of the sovereign" and "the legal obligation to obey" it.[3] The history of rights thus seems to be synonymous with the history of states.

Native Land Talk tells a different story, focusing primarily on the mobilization of rights theories in resistance to state authority by people(s) who, as far as the state was concerned, could at best enjoy meager liberties that the state subordinated to its own power. To appreciate these forms of resistance this book detaches the concept *rights* from normative state protocols and defines it instead as the power to choose, shape, or determine the epistemological and practical groundings within which people(s) are embedded and through which they interact with others. This definition is necessarily partial and tentative because in the absence of a definite structure such as that which states aspire to create, freedom refers to potentialities of choice, thought, and action rather than to predetermined forms of entitlement. Of the potentially vast fields that this definition opens, *Native Land Talk* concentrates on rights claims that were predicated on birthplaces and therefore produced complex representations of native status.

During the nineteenth century, in the midst of struggles over freedom and belonging, birthplace emerged as the focal point of rights claims in the United States. Native American and African American writers and spokespersons challenged settlers' rights claims that attempted to justify and naturalize the dispossession, disenfranchisement, and objectification of Indigenous and black communities, persons, and aspirations. They resisted settler constructions of rights by articulating political philosophies that exceeded settler thought. However, despite the often incompatible conceptual worlds on which they drew, members of all these groups referred to their nativities —albeit in divergent locales, from Indigenous homelands through the African-diasporic Americas to places defined by the expanding bounds of the settler regime—to support their competing rights claims. Violent struggles over the meanings of freedom and belonging were undergirded, in other words, by tacit agreement that birthplace was an indispensable element in the production of political empowerment.

Settlers imagined England as their native land as long as they accepted Britain's imperial domination of American soil. They began to shift their claimed birthplaces to North America when they wished to portray their independent regime as the single legitimate political power in the newly defined territorial scope of the United States. Indigenous peoples refuted settler claims by mobilizing spatially grounded political histories and philosophies that undermined settler expansionist aspirations, and African-descended people invoked varied birthplaces to argue that the transatlantic slave trade did not extinguish their inherent entitlement to freedom. First-generation immigrants, however, refrained from invoking birthplaces in support of their rights claims because their expatriate births carried little cultural capital in a settler state that sought to establish its "foundational claims" to Indigenous peoples' homelands by representing settlers' right to that soil as axiomatic.[4]

Native status—a composite construct encompassing a broad range of significations that invest birthplace with meanings—played a central role in debates regarding freedom and entitlement across vast epistemological and geopolitical spectrums at least since the early eighteenth century. In 1700, Mohegan leaders Owaneco and Ben Uncas disputed Connecticut's claims to Mohegan lands on which settlers established Colchester by arguing for their "native Right which hath been of ansiant [ancient] standing,"[5] thus subverting the English monarchy's expansionist royal realm that circumscribed and threatened to dispossess the Mohegan. Settlers, basing their entitlement to American lands on royal claims, argued that their rights emanated from London. At the dawn of the Revolutionary era, Connecticut's House of Representatives resolved that settlers should enjoy the rights "of Freeborn Englishmen . . . as fully and amply as if they and every [one] of them were born within the realm of England."[6] Benjamin Franklin also stated that the English Crown should "grant a Continuance of [English] Right" to settlers and "their Posterity born in" the colonies.[7] Similarly to settlers' claims for the liberties that non-American birthplaces authorized, ex-slave Olaudah Equiano regarded his successful purchase of his freedom as a reclamation of his "original free African state," although at that point he had been away from his claimed native place for most of his life.[8]

The multiplicity of birthplaces that eighteenth-century rights claims fostered was replaced in the nineteenth century with a more consolidated sense of American births as settlers and African Americans increasingly attached their rights claims to births on lands that the United States defined as its national soil. Free black abolitionist David Walker critiqued African Americans who "have left their native land and home and gone away to Africa" because, he insisted, the United States was "as much ours as it is the whites[']."[9] A decade later, white US citizens who formed a nativist organization they called the Native American Association told Congress that foreigners could not attain the same "perfection of political knowledge" as the "native of the soil."[10] As the century drew to a close, Frederick Douglass echoed Walker's rejection of African American mass emigration to Africa, their presumed native land, by embracing a view of nativism similar to that expressed by the white Native American Association—a view in which birthplace shaped human capacities. "All this native land talk is nonsense," he wrote to refute the claim that Africa was African Americans' only native land. But Douglass did not completely abandon the logic of native status; he asserted that "[t]he native land of the American negro is America. His bones, his muscles, his sinews, are all American."[11] Douglass's simultaneous critique of "native land talk" as "nonsense" and affirmation that "America" was the "native land of the American negro" testify to the enduring power and tensions through which birthplace became the most significant anchor of rights in the expanding region that the United States claimed as its own during the nineteenth century.[12]

The struggles that set these assertions apart illustrate a central premise of this book: that rights discourses are shaped by violence. Foucault writes that "right, peace, and laws were born in the blood and mud of battles," but the constitutive violence that shaped the perceptions of rights discussed below had multiple forms.[13] The three texts that often figure as milestones in the evolution of rights—the United States' Declaration of Independence (1776), France's Declaration of the Rights of Man and of the Citizen (1789), and the United Nations' Universal Declaration of Human Rights (1948)—materialized in the wake of the violent histories that made each of them necessary. But while research on this evolution is often framed within strictly Eurocentric scopes, this book expands and reorients the violent conditions from which ideas of freedom and belonging emerged by centralizing the resistance of Indigenous and African-descended people(s) to Eurocentric imperial and colonial violence. It thus unsettles the tendency in scholarship on eighteenth-century North America to limit the history of rights to the founding of the United States. Whether that founding is interpreted as anti-colonial liberation or as complex reproduction of colonization intertwined with certain departures from British governance, it is often considered to require analyses based on Eurocentric politics and law as though this is the definitive, exclusive perspective from which rights can be studied.[14]

In challenging this assumption, this book draws on non-Eurocentric analyses of human rights, which provide a new angle from which to understand North American settler colonialism and the violence that facilitated it between the late eighteenth and early nineteenth centuries.[15] But whereas such studies often focus on the twentieth and twenty-first centuries, *Native Land Talk* explores an earlier history of violent struggles over the meanings of freedom. The focal point of that older violence was native status, a historically malleable construct that was a fundamental, constitutive element of multiple formulations of freedom, belonging, and rights in eighteenth- and nineteenth-century North America. As I suggest above, permutations of native status extended well beyond Indigenous peoples' claims. However, the settler colonial geopolitical obsession with native status that made such permutations meaningful meant that native status was always imagined in relation to the prior rights that Indigenous peoples represented.[16]

What can we learn about freedom, belonging, and rights from the very people(s) who protested settler colonial efforts to subjugate and dispossess them? Why does it matter that the colonized and the enslaved were theorizing rights simultaneously with settlers? How and why have peoples' claimed relationships to land, particularly by birth, become crucial to ideas of freedom? By asking these questions this book joins a growing number of works that critique liberalism's imperial legacies as it redefines the role of Indigenous philosophies in the rise of rights theories, considers the significance of slavery's diasporas for the idea that freedom had to be grounded in particular spatial locales, and expands the temporal dimensions through which to chart the impact of imperial liberalism and its critiques on geopolitical realities.

Native Land Talk argues that expressions of freedom and belonging by the colonized, the enslaved, and ex-slaves were not merely marginal commentaries on hegemonic constructs of entitlement. The rights theories that mobilized resistance to the settler regime were crucial aspects of emergent rights discourses in the period under study. This argument is a corollary of the idea that rights emerge from violent collisions, and it undermines portrayals of states as the purveyors of entitlement. Rights theories that Indigenous and African-descended people(s) articulated and honed in resistance to settler impositions during the United States' founding and the antebellum period scrutinized native status and centralized inhabitation-based freedoms. Such freedoms question state monopolies over rights and space and discard the uniform generalizations of *human* and *rights* undergirding universal human rights. Whereas civil and human rights offer finite sets of freedoms, equal statuses, and entitlements whose applicability either depends on a centralized, normative authority or promises to transcend specific geopolitical conditions, inhabitation-based rights emphasize localized conditions and practices that produce historically specific forms of knowledge and agency. Indigenous and African-descended inhabitation-based rights claims challenged the settler's role as the quintessential rights-bearing subject, the tacit protagonist of state and human rights. In analyzing these processes, *Native Land Talk* bridges Indigenous studies, African American studies, and settler colonial studies by exploring the historical legacies of struggles over the political significance of belonging, attachment to land, indigeneity, and diaspora.

Native Land Talk's major intellectual-political purpose is to centralize theorizations of human capacities and agency that critique the racialized subject-object relations, progressive historical frameworks, and expansionist spatial aspirations that naturalize settler colonial power. It focuses primarily on the period between the 1760s' inception of settler revolutionary thought and the 1840s' formulation of Manifest Destiny. In the last decades of this period, Indigenous peoples, the enslaved, and ex-slaves theorized rights against the backdrop of two forced migration projects that targeted them in an attempt to establish the United States as the exclusive native land of white settlers. Indian removal was the better known of these projects because the US government fully endorsed and executed it, compelling and forcing Indigenous peoples to exchange their homelands with distant places under settlers' territorial control. African colonization was a lesser-known, simultaneous project whose advocates agitated for the presumed "return" of African Americans to Africa, which they presented as the only native land that African Americans could ever have.[17] Both projects were central to the mid-nineteenth-century formation of Manifest Destiny. They helped settlers to fortify their "foundational claims" by redefining dispossession and disenfranchisement as the particular historical lots of Indigenous and African-descended people(s) that derived necessarily from Native and African American births and were incompatible with human or civil rights. Indian removal and African colonization symbolically displaced the peoples they targeted onto eliminatory temporal dimensions where they would presumably cease to have meaningful historical existence.[18] Indian removal confined Indians to the past through the trope of inevitable disappearance, while African colonization removed African Americans to an abstract, timeless Africa that seemed antithetical to Eurocentric progress.[19]

Native Land Talk explores a tripartite power relation that calls attention to the mutual exclusions by which two central binaries that compartmentalize American studies operate: the Native/settler binary that guides work on the dispossession of Indigenous peoples in settler colonial and Native American studies, and the black/white or black/nonblack binaries that inspire antiracist work in African American studies. Each binary serves as a critical focal point in its respective field, but their simultaneous separate developments tend to obfuscate an integrated critique of settler colonialism and enslavement and to preclude elaborate analyses of solidarities between Native American and African American struggles. The Native/settler binary is associated most prominently with Patrick Wolfe's field-shaping work on settler colonialism, and it highlights attempts by settler regimes to establish themselves through the elimination of Native polities. Wolfe explains this double effort in terms of the "zero-sum logic" that drives settler regimes, and which those regimes try to "repudiat[e]." In the United States, he adds, such repudiation operates through affirmations of the black/white binary that attempt to obliterate the "Native/settler one."[20] In Wolfe's influential analysis the black/white binary functions almost as a smokescreen that prevents us from seeing the systematic violence by which the US settler colonial regime carries out its eliminatory project.

Indeed, the black/white or black/nonblack binaries often naturalize US sovereignty over Indigenous peoples' lands by representing the discrimination of African Americans as the effect of "internal colonialism," as Jodi A. Byrd shows. This logic tacitly domesticates Indigenous peoples as racial minorities within the United States as it seeks to establish cross-racial equality within it rather than subvert US authority over that space.[21] Yet the black/white or black/nonblack binaries address significant, unresolved historical and contemporary injustices, and some scholars of African American studies claim that the focus on sovereignty in Native-settler relations may preclude analyses of the political aspirations of African-descended people. Iyko Day calls for replacing such mutual obliterations by multidimensional analyses of "the dialectics of settler colonial capitalism" that develop through both "colonial land and enslaved labor."[22]

The bifurcation of settler oppression and resistance to it, which resulted in the Native/settler and black/white binaries, is not new. When I started formulating this project, I hoped to find solidarity between African American and Native American resistances to the white settler regime. I eventually realized that the logic of the mutually exclusive binaries was consolidated in the period I study. Both groups struggled separately against the settler regime as though the other disenfranchised or colonized group was inconsequential to the outcomes of these struggles. Many of the African-descended writers I discuss endorsed imperialism as the foundation of their geopolitical interventions and tried to nativize themselves in America as settlers entitled to Indigenous peoples' lands within imperial political logics. In the process, they presupposed that Indians would soon disappear to facilitate imperialist progress. At the same time, almost all the Native American writers or spokespersons discussed here refused to acknowledge that African-descended people had any geopolitical stakes in America. Even when they admitted that white settlers' presence was an irreversible fact—one that they had to take into account in formulating any geopolitical vision—they almost never perceived African-descended people as political entities to be reckoned with. By demanding separately that the oppressive settler regime respect their rights, African Americans and Native Americans fortified binaries that the settler regime also wished to maintain in order to secure itself from joint African American and Native American resistance.

Beyond the disappointment raised by these findings, they shed light on the difficulties that Tiya Miles and Sharon P. Holland address in their works on shared African American and Native Americans histories and experiences. These difficulties operate through ambiguous oscillations between solidarity that may enable freedom from white settler domination and the persistence of racist legacies that complicate such aspirations.[23] Such ambiguities are often displaced by scholarship that highlights *either* the Native/settler *or* the black/white (or black/nonblack) binary as though considering them together may threaten the liberatory project that the separate study of each binary promises.

Native Land Talk intervenes in these problematics by positioning native status as a multifaceted category that shifted shapes as it traveled violently among the rights theories that Native Americans, African Americans, and white settlers developed. Its turbulent permutations impacted the diverse manners by which settlers converted colonized Indigenous homelands into slave-labored national soil, the formative process that shaped the US settler regime. This focus on native status highlights the centrality of *both* the colonization of Indigenous peoples and the enslavement of African-descended people to the settler project. In formulating this idea I draw on J. Kēhaulani Kauanui's recent argument regarding the centrality of the Native/settler binary to settler colonial studies. Kauanui asserts that indigeneity is "a counterpart analytic to settler colonialism," so that "any meaningful engagement with theories of settler colonialism . . . necessarily needs to tend to the question of indigeneity." She bases this assertion on the argument that "indigeneity" is "enduring"—both in the sense that "indigenous peoples exist, resist, and persist" and because "settler colonialism is a structure that endures indigeneity, as it holds out against it."[24]

In light of Kauanui's argument, this book claims that US settler colonialism endures *both* indigeneity and the disenfranchisement that slavery's history represents; settlers validated what they perceived as their rightful inheritance of Indigenous peoples' lands by imposing the doctrine of *partus sequitur ventrem* on the slaves who worked those lands and whose labor and traffic fortified the settler economy. *Partus sequitur ventrem* decreed that any child born to a female slave would inherit nothing but her enslaved condition. It thus excluded the enslaved from human inheritance by turning them into a form of heritable property modeled on livestock.[25] In Saidiya Hartman's words, slavery created "negative inheritance"—an idea I trace below to William Blackstone's term, "a negative kind of birthright."[26] Hartman explains that "[s]lavery made your mother into a myth, banished your father's name, and exiled your siblings to far corners of the earth" so that "[t]he only sure inheritance passed from one generation to the next was this loss."[27] This multigenerational loss was crucial in ensuring settlers' gainful, positive inheritance of Indigenous peoples' homelands. It enabled settlers to bypass the biblical and Lockean property doctrines by which the land belonged to its cultivators and claim ownership and inheritance rights in slave-cultivated Indigenous lands.

The violence that establishes and maintains the settler regime, and which that regime disavows in order to legitimize itself, is crucial for rethinking the relations between the two binaries. Settler colonial studies scholar Lorenzo Veracini prioritizes the Native/settler binary, focusing on the genocidal invasion of Indigenous peoples' lands as the major form of violence whose disavowal serves settlers' self-nativization—the joint cause and effect of the settler regime's legitimacy.[28] Veracini's analysis obfuscates the violence that sustained slavery and thereby facilitated the settler economy in North America. In imagining America as vacant, available virgin soil, settlers disavowed the violence of conquest by which their regime established them on that soil. Slavery was also indispensable for the settler economy, and its impact stretched from New England's shipping interests to Southern plantations. Settler fantasies of the free yeoman farmer substituted this reality with a narrative of benevolent cultivation, and in the Revolutionary era settlers complained that slavery was an English imposition. If we examine the settler regime through the perspective of disavowed violence, colonization and enslavement emerge as the two major aspects of its historical development.

Native Land Talk intervenes in analyses of resistance to imperial liberalism in three ways. First, although scholarship on imperial liberalism tells a more diverse history of rights than accounts of imperial and settler formulations do, studies of imperial liberalism rarely analyze Indigenous political philosophies. In *The Many-Headed Hydra* (2000), Peter Linebaugh and Marcus Rediker identify "dispossessed commoners, transported felons, indentured servants, religious radicals, pirates, urban laborers, soldiers, sailors, and African slaves" as the sources of revolutionary thought in the Atlantic world. They discuss Indigenous peoples as objects of this process whose lands facilitated British imperial expansion and who had to be converted to Christianity while their "classless, stateless, egalitarian societies . . . inflamed the collective imagination of Europe."[29] But *The Many-Headed Hydra* does not mention any instance in which Native Americans contributed actively to revolutionary thought—either collectively or as individuals. Somewhat similarly, in *The Intimacies of Four Continents* (2015), her study of the geopolitical conditions in which liberalism thrived, Lisa Lowe acknowledges Indigenous peoples and settler colonialism as constitutive elements of the complex histories she analyzes, but her book's focus on British archives and labor-motivated migrations limits its discussion of Indigenous topics.[30] Such omissions certainly do not result from the wish to exclude Indigenous peoples from the narratives of imperial liberalism. Rather, they may be explained by the constraints that archives and archival work present. *Native*

Land Talk corrects such omissions by centralizing Indigenous peoples' active contributions to the development of rights discourses.

Second, studies of imperial liberalism often attend to slavery by focusing on the diasporic conditions that shaped the experiences of slaves and ex-slaves, thereby neglecting the functions of spatiality in works by African-diasporic writers. Linebaugh and Rediker portray ex-slaves and free blacks —whose revolutionary struggles led them to such places as "Sierra Leone, London, Dublin, Nova Scotia, Bermuda, eastern Florida, the Bahamas, Jamaica, the Mosquito Shore, and Belize"—as "real citizens of the world," or "'cosmopolitan' . . . in the original meaning of the word" and thus as harbingers of "modern pan-Africanism."[31] Susan Buck-Morss analyzes the emergence of Haitian revolutionary universalism in similar terms, arguing that "the discontinuities of history" enable "people whose culture has been strained to the breaking point" to "give expression to a humanity that goes beyond cultural limits."[32] Analyses that focus on diasporic uprootedness —the idea that, as Ashraf H. A. Rushdy writes, diaspora "is necessarily attuned to the ways identities are constituted in spaces not bound by the borders of the nation-state"—tend to translate it into ideals of universal humanity that transcend the particularities of spatialized belonging.[33] Such representations of African-descended people as eternally deterritorialized cosmopolitans diverts attention from their multiple re-rooting projects and therefore cannot explain Walker's and Douglass's interpretations of the consequences of their US nativities.

Third, *Native Land Talk* intervenes in the temporality of belatedness that characterizes analyses of imperial liberalism whose critical studies often work as efforts to unmask and return repressed imperial motivations, forms, and purposes to the liberalisms they have spawned. Uday Singh Mehta's pioneering *Liberalism and Empire* (1999) affirms and elaborates on the "denied link" between the two components of his title in contemporary political theory; Lowe connects "the traditional texts of liberalism with the colonial archive from which it is customarily separated"; and two of Walter D. Mignolo's book titles illuminate the "darker side[s]" of the "Renaissance" and "Western modernity," respectively.[34] Mignolo distinguishes the European "control of knowledge" that shaped the Renaissance and Enlightenment from the present in which "everyone is speaking," thus marginalizing pre-twentieth-century contestations of Eurocentric claims.[35] Similarly, S. James Anaya discusses Indigenous peoples' contributions to "international human rights law" as an emergent phenomenon he dates to the late twentieth century.[36] And Ronald Niezen writes that Indigenous peoples "lack[ed] . . . awareness" of "the widespread, almost global nature of the crises they faced" until "the 1960s and 1970s." He adds that "[u]ntil the mid-twentieth century there was also an absence of international forums to which such grievances could be addressed"—although "the British Empire did create an opportunity for redress through appeal to the monarch in London"—and that "such initiatives were taken by Canadian Indians and the New Zealand Maori beginning in the mid-nineteenth century."[37] In such formulations, temporal and theoretical distances separate the past in which imperial liberalism was first practiced in the colonies from present decolonizing efforts that scholarly projects support.[38]

However, many of the texts I study address the global conditions of imperial oppression. Olaudah Equiano, for example, spoke in the name of "those who are called barbarians" (see chapter 1), and Indigenous peoples began going to England's court earlier than Niezen suggests. In chapter 2, I discuss Mohegan "Native rights," in the context of which the first Mohegan delegation visited London in 1736. Representatives of other Indigenous polities went to London on diplomatic trips earlier. Belatedness is also belied by eighteenth- and nineteenth-century writers who—aware of their marginalization by the settler regime—anticipated the future recuperation of their political views. In 1772 the young Mohegan teacher Joseph Johnson addressed an imagined future reader in his diary. "What think you," he wrote, "who ever, here after may peruse these Lines[?] . . . [W]hat impression think you, was left upon my heart?"[39] Johnson referred to his spiritual experiences, which his Christian mentor Eleazar Wheelock expected him to contrast with his Mohegan upbringing, and in this apostrophe addressed a future reader who might better understand his experiences as Christian Mohegan. David Walker anticipated a broader-scale appreciation of African American leaders whose thought and acts white settlers failed to appreciate. "When the Lord shall raise up coloured historians in succeeding generations," he wrote, such historians would "present the crimes of this nation, to the then gazing world" and "do justice to the name of Bishop [Richard] Allen, of Philadelphia."[40] Johnson and Walker critiqued the settler regime's political temporalities, which excluded their voices from the present moments in which they spoke.

Arrivants, Indigenous Peoples, and Settlers

The categories *arrivants*, *Indigenous peoples*, and *settlers* index the spatial dynamics that undergird the stories of freedom and subjugation that *Native Land Talk* tells. All but *settler* are of contemporary coinage, and I use them anachronistically because the texts I read anticipate their current significations. These anachronisms question the belatedness thesis and emphasize the decolonizing possibilities that past texts encapsulate. *Arrivant*, the least familiar term in English, points to the radical deterritorializations that facilitated transatlantic slavery from its inception throughout its history and that shaped its aftermaths in the post-emancipation struggles of African-descended peoples in the Americas. Caribbean writer Edward Kamau Brathwaite coined the English term *arrivant* in his 1973 poetry project, *The Arrivants: A New World Trilogy*, and Byrd borrowed Brathwaite's word to refer to "people forced into the Americas through the violence of European and Anglo-European colonialism and imperialism." Byrd uses *arrivant* to signal the differential relations to space characterizing Indigenous peoples' and African Americans' realities, and this category facilitates her critique of interpretations of African American oppression as "internal colonialism."[41]

I follow Byrd's usage of *arrivants*, alongside *Indigenous peoples* and *settlers*, in order to examine "the degree to which" members of these groups have differentially "functioned within" and "resisted" the "historical project of the colonization of the 'New World.'"[42] However, I depart from Byrd's analysis by reinvesting this term with Brathwaite's constructions of complex tensions between rootedness and diaspora, pasts and presents. The poems of the three books he collected in *The Arrivants* shuttle painfully among pre- and post-slavery Africa as a site of bloody betrayals and fantasies of redemption, Caribbean islands that were reshaped by slavery and in its wake, and US and European cities that accentuate the diasporic experiences of Afro Caribbean exiles, travelers, and migrants. The epigraph in *The Arrivants* uses the titular phrase in reference to Africans who "came" to Jamaica as slaves, distinguishing them from those who were "born" in, and therefore "belongs" to, Jamaica rather than Africa.[43] However, Brathwaite's poems blur this distinction by mixing multiple temporal and spatial elements of identity and belonging and by repositioning departures, returns, and arrivals within ever-shifting, nonlinear, open-ended historical narratives. The last section of Brathwaite's book, entitled "Beginning," undermines the idea of linear progress as it ends with an incomplete vision of emergence from and into presumably infinite, potentially creative ruins. It ends as the dawn rises "over shattered homes," "musty ghettos," and "men" who are "making / with their / rhythms some- / thing torn / and new"[44] These, the book's last words, are not followed by a full stop, and thus constitute an open ending that merges old ruptures with new directions as "rhythms" flow in both directions.

Uncertainties such as those with which Brathwaite invests *The Arrivants* shaped the experiences of many African-descended writers whose texts I read. Racist disenfranchisement destabilized their sociopolitical positions even if they were nominally free because they were entitled to no citizenship, their activities were monitored by an explicitly racist legal regime, and they could be kidnapped into slavery. Whereas Caribbean arrivants used the postcolonial era to reposition themselves as self-nativized settlers, as Shona N. Jackson shows, this process was not as feasible in the United States.[45] Especially prior to the Fourteenth Amendment, the category "native" was already occupied by settlers who attempted to racialize it exclusively as white in order to naturalize their dispossession of Indigenous peoples. Thus, although the African-descended writers whose works I read tried to nativize themselves and thereby gain recognition as settlers, their efforts were consistently countered by a racist regime that limited self-nativization to voluntary white settlers. Chapters 1, 3, and 5 portray the efforts of African-descended writers to root themselves and their communities in spaces of freedom and entitlement where they would be able to overcome the legacies of slavery that the term *arrivant* suggests. However, their dissimilar efforts were framed by the idea that the perils of arrivant status were multigenerational, as Brathwaite's poetry and Hartman's work also suggest. In addition, the term *arrivant* is broad enough to encompass enslaved and free African Americans as well as those who, like Equiano, fall outside the contemporary label African American that connotes actual or prospective US citizenship.

The term *Indigenous peoples*, which emerged at the end of the nineteenth century and was pluralized in the twentieth century, is also used anachronistically here.[46] The term *native* was far more common in the period I study; William Apess, the most prolific published Native American author in the nineteenth century, preferred it to "Indian."[47] However, the texts I discuss anticipate contemporary conceptualizations of indigeneity as a dynamic, international position of resistance to settler colonialism and state orders. They fit Taiaiake Alfred and Jeff Corntassel's definition of "indigenousness" as "oppositional, place-based existence" and "consciousness of being in struggle against the dispossessing and demeaning fact of colonization by foreign peoples."[48] In addition, this book's focus on native status and the texts it analyzes render the term *native* so ambiguous that it cannot be applied consistently to any single group. Settlers used the term for themselves (initially as native Englishmen, then as native Americans) in order to naturalize their claims to Indigenous peoples' homelands, and arrivants also utilized the category "native" in order to claim their entitlement to freedom and belonging in America and sometimes also in Africa.[49] My usage here differs from Jackson's distinction between "native" as a "fixed category" and the "more fluid process of belonging" that she terms "indigeneity" because in the texts I study *native* often appears as the fluid, violently appropriated category, so I use *Indigenous peoples* to denote an irreproducible relationship to ancestral lands fostered through multigenerational inhabitation.[50] As much as the coveted label *native* seemed to guarantee certain freedoms, it was an intensively embattled category to an extent that no single instance of its usage can reveal. As I show below, this English word was rooted in a history of subjugation from which settlers tried to liberate themselves by adapting it to colonial circumstances and by imposing it on Indigenous peoples and arrivants.

Texts

The indigenous and arrivant theories of birth, belonging, and rights studied here were produced under duress and in hostile conditions as settlers established their own rights claims violently at the expense of Indigenous peoples and arrivants. Many of the texts I read were created in direct response to settler pressures—as petitions, memorials, or answers to settler projects and propositions. My archive comprises books, pamphlets, newspaper articles, petitions, letters, speeches, and US records of negotiations with indigenous polities. Some of these texts were written in English by published authors such as Olaudah Equiano, Mohegan leader and minister Samson Occom, and African American abolitionist David Walker, or were edited and published by Cherokee Elias Boudinot in the *Cherokee Phoenix*. Others were written by less well-known black activists or spoken by Indigenous ones in various languages. In the process of translation and transcription, settlers often reshaped the latter texts to make them palatable for settler audiences.

The complex conditions under which these texts were produced and preserved mean that the key terms of this book—*native*, *rights*, *belonging*—often function as imperfect approximations for terms in indigenous languages that were no simple equivalents of these English words.[51] However, editorial and translational practices do not hinder the analyses that this book offers. *Native Land Talk* focuses on the messy, uneven, cacophonous development of rights discourses in English out of multiple sources, languages, and epistemologies. It is not guided by a quest for original purity, but seeks instead to explore the conditions under which rights theories emerged from violent contests over human agency and the geopolitical conditions that facilitated or curbed it.

With the exception of Equiano's and Walker's books, and articles from the *Cherokee Phoenix*, most of the Native American and African American texts I discuss are available as fragments in settler publications that circulated through imperial and settler print networks.[52] Even the *Cherokee Phoenix* relied on those networks for its survival. Settlers fragmented Indigenous and arrivant rights theories and political philosophies as though they could be made intelligible only if their fuller, more coherent philosophical functions were denied. The broader print networks and published works within which those fragments were read followed the conventional documentary politics that Christopher Hager discusses, by which texts "usually overrepresented the experiences of powerful, well-educated people" and thus marginalized the voices of those whom elite writers and publishers represented as objects of their own texts.[53] Such fragmentations complemented settlers' efforts to minoritize and fracture Indigenous and arrivant sociopolitical visions, and particularly their investments in decolonization, unsettlement, and resettlement projects that undermined settler hegemony. In addition to fragmenting texts and discourses, settlers appropriated the fragments into anthropological and other discourses that objectified the agentive subjects who produced their sources.[54] Settlers' publishing and political networks marginalized women's voices, so most of the voices I discuss are men's. The relatively few female contributors whose voices reach us through these networks include Cherokee leader Nanyehi (Nancy Ward), Seneca elders whose words US officials recorded anonymously, and African American abolitionist Maria Stewart. Settler fragmentations of Indigenous and arrivant texts and their concomitant marginalization of female voices were part of broader efforts to fragment the communities and homelands within which these texts were produced and for whom they spoke.

As a literary form, the fragment constitutes a counternarrative to settlers' self-fashioning as self-sufficient, coherent rights-bearing subjects empowered to delimit, distribute, and exercise entitlements. Settler colonial ideologies and policies positioned the settler as the quintessential rights-bearing possessive individual, a complete human whole by contrast to which slaves could be defined as fractions of persons and Indians could be perceived as eternally vanishing. Thus, this book reconstructs fragmented rights claims into fuller critiques of the settler colonial project without assuming that such reconstructions can ever approximate some pristine historic authenticity. It seeks instead to map a more complex terrain of rights theories than conventional histories portray. I contextualize these fragments of Native American and African American expressions by considering contemporaneous discussions of native status in US newspapers and pamphlets. These organs of settler expression often marginalized non-settler voices not only through oblivion (the most prevalent tactic), but also through exoticizing, sensationalist representations of Indians and through the relegation of references to African Americans primarily to advertisements for the sales or attempted recaptures of slaves. Analyses of these settler texts provide occasions for reflecting on the manners whereby native status operated in US public discourse. The next section clarifies the relations among the disparate political projects that all the texts examined here articulated.

Settlement, Unsettlement, and Resettlement

The Indigenous and arrivant rights theories I analyze facilitated resistance to the white settler regime as they were used to mobilize unsettlement and resettlement: initiatives of geopolitical reorganization that proffered epistemological and ontological rearrangements of the relations among people(s), space, and the temporal frames by which history is perceived and lived. On the most general level, *unsettlement* refers to Indigenous peoples' efforts to reconstitute and redefine their relationships with their homelands in order to enable their communities to flourish in the wake of European colonization. *Resettlement* refers to arrivants' attempts to reconfigure the imperial relations that disenfranchised and dehumanized them, in ways that would be conducive to emancipation. *Settlement* is founded on a radical objectification of space as territory, a conquerable domain that can be "owned, distributed, mapped, calculated, bordered and controlled."[55]

I discuss unsettlement by drawing on Anna Brickhouse's analysis of this term, which comprises "concrete attempt[s] to annihilate or otherwise put an end to a European colony, or to forestall or eliminate future colonial projects." Brickhouse studies unsettlement through an earlier historical narrative than those I explore (and she traces it to its later afterlives): the efforts of the sixteenth-century "Algonquian-speaking Indian"—whom Spanish colonizers named Don Luis de Valesco—to frustrate Spanish colonization. Brickhouse argues that unsettlement "signals not merely the contingency and noninevitability but the glaring incompleteness of the history of the New World as we currently know and write it."[56] This sense of incompleteness is crucial here as well because the Indigenous unsettlement projects I study—although formulated when settlement seemed much more established than it might have been in sixteenth-century North America—emerge from the conviction that as strong as the settler regime may seem, its establishment is never complete. Its illusory completeness derives from the spatial configuration of conquerable territory as the stage on which history unfolds, but it is simultaneously undermined by what Kauanui calls "enduring indigeneity."[57]

Unsettlement projects attempt to dethrone imperialism from its hegemonic position as the dominant organizing logic of human-spatial relations. Conversely, resettlement projects are founded on the acceptance of imperialism as an inescapable if not inevitable historical framework that needs to be negotiated to facilitate emancipation but which cannot be fully replaced because the uprooting of millions of Africans reshaped Africa and the Americas so drastically that recuperative reversals must necessarily be utopian.[58] So whereas unsettlement projects were based on replacing the geopolitical conditions in the region claimed by the settler regime as its own, resettlement projects tried to reform the settler regime by exposing its arbitrary, contradictory logic of entitlement and the systematic disenfranchisement that enabled it. Despite these distinctions, both unsettlement and resettlement intervene in settler colonialism by exposing the foundational, ongoing violence through which it establishes its authority. Such authority depends on settler colonialism's successful efforts to efface the violent history by which it was established and by which it perpetuates itself.[59] Unsettlement and resettlement initiatives insist on the need to represent and redress this ongoing history.

The differential relations to the land that unsettlement and resettlement represent are reflected in the texts I study as well as in contemporary scholarship in Native American and African American studies. Indigenous unsettlement projects were based on reaffirmations of interactive, interdependent human-spatial relations that encapsulate and produce history.[60] This distinction undergirds much of the discussions in the chapters dedicated to Indigenous rights claims (chapters 2, 4, and 6), although chapters 1 and 2 also highlight complex interactions between unsettlement and resettlement. Taiaiake Alfred explains that Indigenous attachment to the homeland is based on "stewardship" through which Indigenous peoples maintain what he defines as their "special responsibilities within the areas they occupy."[61] Alfred therefore argues that the term *sovereignty*—a focal point of Eurocentric governance—is incompatible with Native politics because unlike "state sovereignty doctrines," which are "rooted in notions of dominion," "indigenous concepts of political relations" are "rooted in notions of freedom, respect, and autonomy."[62] Lisa Brooks and Glen Coulthard theorize these relations through their respective conceptualizations of the "common pot" and "grounded normativity." Brooks uses the term "common pot" to refer to a "cooperative, interdependent" sociopolitical space in which the land "requires participation from all its interwoven inhabitants" whom it "nourishes" and "sustain[s]."[63] Interdependent participation is also central to Coulthard's definition of "grounded normativity" as a foundation of Indigenous "struggles" that are "not only for land," but "also deeply informed" by the land. Coulthard defines the land as "a mode of reciprocal relationship" that "ought to teach us about living our lives in relation to one another and our surroundings in a respectful, nondominating and nonexploitative way."[64] Native American scholarship on land extends well beyond these writers to numerous analyses of cultures, literatures, politics, and histories.[65]

Whereas space in Native American texts is often contextualized by relations of sustenance and their colonial disruptions, in African American scholarship and writings space tends to connote confining mechanisms that require emancipatory actions. For example, Rashad Shabazz uses the term "spatialized blackness" to analyze "how mechanisms of constraint" and "systems of control" create "a prison-like environment."[66] A similar sense of resistance to spatial confinement seems to motivate Thadious M. Davis's argument that under white supremacism "the place of blacks" was "narrower, contained, and limited," and Davis works toward an "idea of space as interactive and constitutive . . . of a black public sphere as political counternarrative" to white supremacism.[67]

In the arrivant texts discussed here, these dynamics were almost invariably contextualized by the adoption of imperialist geopolitics—minus advocacy for the transatlantic slave trade—as the normative, singularly authoritative framework of politics and history. This choice facilitated arrivants' self-nativization projects, by which they sought to redefine themselves as settlers, and suggests that they also adopted settlers' objectification of space as territory. However, since slavery operated through the conversion of space into a confining mechanism of oppression, arrivants who asserted their rights to slave-labored lands partially critiqued the spatial constructs that made territory possible. Moreover, by claiming that their landed rights stemmed from slavery's history on American soil they undermined the idea that rights derived from states. Their critiques of landed entitlement contributed tremendously to geopolitical constructions of freedom because they insisted that neither subjugation nor liberty could be experienced unless they were embedded in particular spatial realities. Through this vision, arrivant texts advocated the resettlement of the United States in the service of a more egalitarian settler regime.

I define Indigenous and arrivant interventions in rights discourses as responses, the rhetorical structures that facilitated grievances, resistance, and negotiation. Indigenous and arrivant rights claims resisted settler oppressions, settlers redefined their entitlements in response to such resistance, and members of all these groups did so by embedding their claims in incompatible spatio-historical visions. Daniel Heath Justice identifies response as the underlying activity that maintains Indigenous peoplehood. Since the "ground is always shifting," he writes, "the people are always responding to change within and without, [and] new challenges require new or revised responses."[68] In this formulation, response facilitates unstable, antifoundationalist interactions contingent upon particular developments of human agency and relationships. Analogous contingencies shaped the discursive relations among Indigenous peoples, arrivants, and settlers, so it makes sense to consider them as complex structures of responses that did not produce a "peoplehood" but rather questioned and undermined settlers' motivation to eliminate, subjugate, contain, and minoritize Indigenous peoples and arrivants.

This antifoundationalist conceptualization of response disrupts hegemonic portrayals of the colonial encounter that pit Europeans as possessors of religious, political, economic, and scientific knowledge against presumably epistemologically destitute Indigenous peoples and arrivants whose historical roles are reduced to the passive consumers and objects of colonial discourse. Settler discourses were shaped by communication with Indigenous peoples and arrivants to the same extent that Indigenous and arrivant discourses were shaped by communication with the settler regime. *Native Land Talk* approaches the question of historical precedence by adopting Audra Simpson's understanding of indigeneity as an entity that "must know itself [politically] as having been in place prior to" colonization while simultaneously recognizing that it "is made in its present form" through the "matrices" of settlement and its forms of knowledge.[69] Such double temporal movements help us remember that Indigenous peoples' and arrivants' responses to settler claims were anything but mere reactions triggered by presumably original settler initiatives. Instead, such responses mobilized and reconstituted philosophies that they rechanneled into new and ongoing struggles against settler oppression.[70]

Simpson's negotiation of past and present constructs partially parallels discussions of rupture and continuity in African-descended cultures and resistance. Hartman writes that the enslaved "sustained, amended, and abandoned the customs, manners, and proclivities of the Old World," "created a new language out of the languages they had known and the languages foisted upon them," and "danced old dances for new purposes." She defines their "separation from and clinging to the Old World" as "Cleavage" that connects as it disjoins and "gives rise not only to dispossession but as well to a new set of possibilities."[71] And David Scott approaches similar issues through the debate between advocates of the "retentionist" and "creationist" models of cultural production. Whereas the former argue that the horrors of slavery failed to prevent the enslaved from importing and drawing on African cultures in the Americas, the latter claim that since African cultural formations could not have survived those horrors, any facet of diasporic African culture must have emerged in the Americas independently of African pasts.[72] Scott problematizes this distinction by arguing that evaluations of diasporic African modernity should not focus on "whether the colonized accommodated or resisted" colonization as though these two options existed independently of colonial realities. Instead, Scott suggests that we should examine "how colonial power transformed the ground on which accommodation and resistance was possible" and "how colonial power reshaped or reorganized the conceptual and institutional conditions of possibility of social action and its understanding."[73] Both Indigenous unsettlement projects and arrivant resettlement ones responded to the transformations of the "grounds" on which settlers, Indigenous peoples, and arrivants acted, and their responses were simultaneously indispensable to these transformations. Settlers tried to erase these multivocal, multidimensional processes by establishing their sovereignty as axiomatic, exclusive, and absolute, and they manipulated the idea of birth—through and well beyond *partus sequitur ventrem*—to do so. The following three sections elaborate on these manipulations, because understanding the violent genealogies of settler rights claims is necessary for contextualizing the Indigenous and arrivant rights claims that this book studies. Following these three sections I offer an alternative contextualization of rights discourses beyond settler forms and the state formations that naturalize them.

The Violence of Settler Rights

The figure of the *native* is at the core of this book's exploration of the violent processes that shaped rights through struggles among settlers, Indigenous peoples, and arrivants. In telling its history here, I emphasize the torturous dynamics by which Europeans and settlers tried to figure and control the precise relations between freedom and space. In the English tradition that settlers utilized to establish their regime, *native* was a Janus-faced figure because localized birth could symbolize either empowerment or subjugation. Raymond Williams relates the "opposite senses and tones" of the word *native* to "positive" patriotism and "negative" inferiority and traces the latter to *nativus*—native's etymological origin that signified "bondman or villein, born in bondage."[74] In English imperial discourses this was the model for the colonized native and for the exiled slave. Mahmood Mamdani represents the "colonized . . . native" as "pinned down, localized, thrown out of civilization as an outcast, confined to custom, and then defined as its product."[75] Settlers imagined slaves in similar terms, and the history of *nativus* enables us to trace the colonized native to Renaissance and Enlightenment interpretations of England's medieval past.

The thirteenth-century treatise *Bracton on the Laws and Customs of England* (attributed to the English judge Henry of Bratton) uses "bondsman," "villein," and "nativus" interchangeably to denote the inherited unfreedom of landless peasants.[76] Four centuries later the scholar Henry Spelman, who initiated the legal study of feudalism in England, defined the *nativus* as a slave by birth who was confined permanently to his lord's land. In Spelman's Latin usage, the phrase *native land* does not suggest a place of inalienable affirmative belonging, but signifies the violent subjugation that binds unfree peasants to the land they must inhabit and cultivate.[77] Renaissance English dictionaries support this sense by glossing the Latin *nativo habendo*—a writ for apprehending runaway bondmen and -women who were confined permanently and heritably to their lords' lands.[78] This is the history behind the *OED*'s listing of the earliest denotation of the noun *native* as "a person born in bondage; a person born to servants, tenants, etc., and inheriting their status."[79]

The duality of *native* was mirrored in its contemporary concept *birthright*, a foundation of English subjection that justified both privilege and subjugation. But whereas the polarized senses of *native* were applied to mutually exclusive social groups by endowing them with either the patriotism or the inferiority that Williams identifies, English *birthright* connoted an ambiguity that was the lot of every English subject. British historian and legal writer Francis Plowden explained in 1784 that "every British subject born" was simultaneously "debtor" and "creditor" of the monarch, so English birthright—correspondingly with English subjection—was simultaneously limiting and privileging. The English subject owed "faith, fidelity, fealty, loyalty, ligeance or allegiance" to "his sovereign and the state" and was entitled in return to "the benefit and protection of the king, laws, and constitution."[80] North American settler colonialism evolved by dividing ambiguous birthright into mutually exclusive, inherent, heritable conditions that endowed some natives with the patriotic pole of William's definition, and therefore destined them to freedom, and others with its inferiority, which destined them to lifelong subjugation. Through this polarization, settlers sought to relegate Indigenous peoples and arrivants to negative birthright that would justify their dispossession and dehumanization.

I adapt the phrase *negative birthright* from the Enlightenment's most prominent English jurist, William Blackstone, who referred to slavery as "a negative kind of birthright," and I extend it to explain the rationale for settlers' dispossession of Indigenous peoples as well.[81] Blackstone's definition of slavery as a "negative kind of birthright" within a broader feudalist history—including the *nativus*—enabled him to frame English liberties in contrast to colonial subjugation. Tracing these developments requires a reassessment of feudalism's impact on settler colonialism, which corrects the exceptionalist thesis by which settler freedoms seemed to have developed thanks to the availability of abundant lands, which were unencumbered by a feudal past.[82]

An influential recent reiteration of this thesis appears in Saskia Sassen's *Territory, Authority, Rights*, which argues that "[w]hile wealth in England had been grounded in landownership," a presumed "abundance of land" made feudal landholding "impractical in the colonies," and therefore the "general disposition" of colonial landholding tended "toward utility more than privilege."[83] The idea is not new; indeed, the myth of a classless US society has long rested on it. However, analyses of settler colonialism and slavery prove it wrong because Indigenous and arrivant experiences of settlers' dispossessive, disenfranchising, and expansive mechanisms show that US cultural and economic capital was significantly "grounded" in an elaborate system of "landownership" that turned Indigenous homelands into available, "abundant" resources for settlers at the expense of both Indigenous peoples whose homelands became scarce and endangered and arrivants for whom these lands were meant to be punitive, subjugating spaces.[84]

Medieval historians critiqued feudalism as a vague, misleading concept that Spelman and other Renaissance and Enlightenment writers introduced in order to serve their reductive historical narratives. In 1974, historian Elizabeth A. R. Brown argued that "feudalism" should be abandoned as an analytical historical category and replaced with careful attention to the diverse processes it masked.[85] Two decades later Susan Reynolds followed up with a detailed examination of several medieval societies whose complexities exceeded feudalist assumptions.[86] In 2008, Kathleen Davis analyzed feudalism's ties to imperialism and slavery, reiterated that "there simply never was a 'Feudal Middle Ages,'" and argued that Enlightenment liberals fabricated it in order to theorize "sovereignty and subjection at crucial moments of empire, slavery, and colonialism." Davis asserts that French and English thinkers envisioned individual entitlement through its contrast with *both* an imagined feudal past *and* contemporaneous discourses of slavery and colonialism.[87] Feudalism, slavery, and colonization were thus mutually constitutive sites in the production and stabilization of un/freedom, dis/possession, and dis/enfranchisement.

This claim begs larger questions regarding the direction of intellectual exchange between Europe and America. America has long been viewed as a "crucial laboratory for Enlightenment thought," as though ideas that emerged in Europe were first tested in the colonies and then refined in Europe.[88] Sassen's discussion of American history fits this model by representing America as the place where European ideas of territory, authority, and rights could be realized and tested. Similarly, geographer Stuart Elden argues that America's presumable discovery was the condition of possibility for the rise of *territory* as a central concept of Eurocentric geopolitics that redefined "the relation between place and power."[89] He states that the concepts *territory* and *sovereignty* were not produced on a preexisting European model, but that new European "ideas" and "techniques" were tested in "the New World" and "then carried back to Europe."[90] By contrast, Jennifer Greeson argues that "the European conquest of the American hemisphere and development of the Atlantic slave system provided the necessary preconditions for the subsequent intellectual innovations of the Enlightenment era."[91] But the processes charted here, by which the rights-bearing subject became imaginable thanks not only to settler colonialism, but also to Indigenous and arrivant resistance to settlers' claimed sovereignty, show that imagining transatlantic exchanges without the contributions of both Indigenous peoples and arrivants is necessarily partial. While the bulk of this book focuses on these contributions to rights discourses, the next section explores American feudalist thought—the consequences of which led Indigenous peoples and arrivants to action.

American Histories of Feudalist Birthrights

Positive and negative birthrights expanded with the English empire—the former provided English subjects with legally protected freedoms in a growing royal realm, and the latter allowed them to enjoy the lands and labor of Indigenous peoples and arrivants in that realm.[92] Imperial jurists and writers extended positive birthright by redefining English birthright as a *portable* power that Englishmen could carry with them over geographic distances. This portability made settlers the model rights-bearing subjects. The settler was so crucial to the history of rights that influential Enlightenment texts—from Locke's *Two Treatises of Government* to the US Declaration of Independence—turned it into the epitome of the possessive individual, rights-bearing subject whose liberty was measured by his ability voluntarily to accumulate and alienate possessions across geographic distances.[93] However, English birthright was neither exclusive nor superior nor prior to Indigenous and arrivant rights claims. I frame this discussion of feudalist birthrights within settler constructions of entitlement and oppression in order to clarify the conditions under which Indigenous peoples and arrivants asserted their freedoms in resistance to settler violence.

In 1606, King James's charter for Virginia constituted settlers' positive portable birthrights by extending English birthright across the Atlantic, so that any English subject who "shall dwell and inhabit" in the colony "shall have and enjoy all liberties, franchises, and immunities, within any of our other dominions . . . as if they had been abiding and born" in England.[94] Two years later, settlers affirmed their portable positive birthrights by imposing a feudalist ritual called subinfeudation on Powhatan, leader of the Algonquian-speaking confederacy whose homeland they redefined as Virginia's Tidewater region.[95] Subinfeudation was a feudalist procedure that legalized the settlers' desire to represent Powhatan as lacking any political history or prior attachment to his own homeland. Through this procedure a superior lord grants land to an inferior who thereby becomes his vassal and holds the land under his lord. Subinfeudation became the dominant logic by which settlers positioned themselves as superior landlords empowered to grant lands to Indigenous peoples. It is affirmed whenever US lands are presented as undisputed national soil as though Indigenous peoples must hold their lands under US authority. Subinfeudation is therefore a significant factor in settlers' disavowal of settler colonialism's founding violence: instead of conquering the land, they imagine themselves as lords empowered to allot it. Powhatan initially indulged the colonists' wish to subinfeudate him, but when they wanted to conclude the ceremony by crowning him, he refused to kneel and thus prevented them from consummating the ritual. When settlers realized that they could not persuade Powhatan to kneel, they resorted to "leaning hard on his shoulders" in order to crown him, thereby exposing the very founding violence that the ceremony was meant to conceal.[96] Powhatan's minimal physical resistance—similar to the unsettlement and resettlement projects discussed below—forced this revelation.

Contemporaneous judicial and theoretical developments across the Atlantic substantiated settlers' positive birthrights. Sir Edward Coke's decision in *Calvin's Case* (1608) made English subjects' inheritance rights commensurate with the royal realm so that English birthright would support an expanding empire.[97] This principle opened up a new way of imagining the subject as bearer of rights who possessed his entitlement as inherent property within the royal realm. Coke's decision achieved this effect, ironically, despite his suspicion of territorial attachment—a suspicion that may be traced to the feudalist connotations of spatialized belonging, because Coke explained positive birthright in somatic rather than territorial terms. He wrote, "As the ligatures or strings do knit together the joints of all the parts of the body, so doth ligeance join together the Sovereign and all his subjects."[98] He distanced his birthright theory explicitly from territorial concerns by arguing that the "natural born subject" is produced by "neither the climate nor the soil" because "natural legiance" "is not circumscribed within any place."[99] This theorization of subjection clarifies that Coke perceived spatial attachment as antithetical to civil liberties.

Coke's deterritorialized birthright, Virginia's dispossessive subinfeudation ritual, and the slaves' spatial oppression enabled settlers to define their own freedoms in contrast to feudalist legacies. The settler regime created an analogy between American lands and African-descended slaves by imagining both as correspondingly wild. This analogy facilitated the dispossession of Indigenous peoples, who were symbolically removed from the land that was reinterpreted as the foundation of settlers' slave-holding and -trading economy. Whereas settlers imagined Indigenous peoples' presumed wildness as incompatible with cultivation, they portrayed Africans' putative wildness as conducive to agricultural development and argued that Africans were uniquely fit for working American lands. By attaching "wild" slaves to wild, "bare Land" as complementary means for gaining profit, settlers reproduced the feudalist idea of the *nativus*'s inherited, permanent, subjugating attachment to land. One major difference between villeins and slaves was that whereas the former inherited their condition patrilineally and were therefore considered fully human, *partus sequitur ventrem* meant that the latter inherited it matrilineally and were thereby owned as livestock.

The first English colonial slave code, Barbados's 1661 "Act for the better ordering and governing of Negroes," defined slaves as "an heathenish brutish and an uncertaine dangerous kinde of people."[100] Seven years later, Barbados invoked slaves' "barbarous, wild and savage nature" to justify its continued legislations of slavery.[101] The Barbados assembly asserted that "without [slave] labour and service we should be utterly unable to manage our Plantations," and it entrenched the analogy between American lands and African labor by declaring slaves "real estate" for inheritance purposes. This law was meant to prevent the undesired scenario in which slaveholders' heirs may inherit "bare Land, without Negroes to manure [it]" in case the land and the slaves would descend to different heirs.[102] Similar laws in Virginia and other North American colonies demonstrate the extent to which both Indigenous peoples and slave labor functioned as the joint foundations of the settler regime. Settler perceptions of the relations between African-descended people and the colonized land led them to force slaves into an oppressive "intimacy" with the environment that attempted to prohibit slaves from developing any empowering sense of spatial attachment.[103]

The oppressive territorialization that negative birthright symbolized was accompanied by an empowering interpretation of territorialized positive birthright that enabled settlers to imagine America as the space of their own liberation. Coke's somatic birthright was therefore replaced with one that signified territorial control and helped distinguish settlers' positive birthrights from the negative birthrights that they attributed to Indigenous peoples and arrivants. In 1722 the Privy Council ruled that "as the law is the birthright of every subject, so wherever they go, they carry their law with them" and thereby confirmed John Locke's earlier idea that territorialized portable birthright was indispensable for colonization.[104] Locke was invested personally in the colonial enterprise; in his *Two Treatises of Government* (1689) and *The Fundamental Constitutions of Carolina* (1669) he positioned portable positive birthright and negative birthright as mutually constitutive elements of English colonization. He contributed immensely both to the extension of negative birthright to Indigenous peoples and arrivants and to the portability of settlers' positive birthright.[105]

Locke's *Two Treatises* defends universal positive birthright by arguing that "[e]very Man is born with a double right"—that being "*A Right of Freedom to his Person*" and "*A Right*, before any other Man, to *inherit*, with his Brethren, his Fathers Goods."[106] However, in the *Fundamental Constitutions* Locke reveals the limits of this universalism as he creates a rigidly stratified, exclusive colonial organization that merges the twin sites of negative birthright—England's feudalist past and the colonial present—into foils for the rights-bearing liberal subject. In the feudalist, slaveholding colonial society that Locke planned for Carolina, absentee "lords proprietors" and their subordinate "landgraves" and "cassiques" rule over "commoners" and "leet-men," who occupy settlers' lowest social rungs. A landgrave himself, Locke modeled the leet-men on the *nativus* by stipulating that the children of these lowly settlers would inherit their parents' condition, which would bar them from "go[ing] off from the land of their particular lord, and live any-where else."[107] He planned that such "leet-men" would be English settlers with negative birthrights, but this construction subverted settlers' attempt to define their exclusive entitlement in contrast to Indigenous peoples and arrivants. The plan proved unsustainable when colonists "revolted and overthrew [Locke's] constitution" in 1719.[108] But while the *Fundamental Constitutions* failed to legislate settler subjugation, it succeeded in legislating slavery by endowing slaveholders with "absolute power and authority" over their slaves. This idea is mirrored by inversion in the *Two Treatises*'s definition of universal positive birthright as inalienable "Freedom from Absolute, Arbitrary Power."[109] In both texts, Locke conceptualizes rights by using the same words: the "Absolute, Arbitrary Power" from which the bearer of positive birthright must be free is the capacity that grants slaveholders authority over their slaves.[110]

In the late eighteenth century, Blackstone used the jurisprudential traditions of feudalism, empire, and slavery to further territorialize Englishmen's positive birthright by contrast to slaves' negative birthright in a manner that anticipated the patriotic connotations of Williams's definition of *native*. Blackstone defined English law as the liberating "birthright of every [English] subject" and England itself as the "only" land "in the universe" constituted to provide "political or civil liberty" and claimed that the "spirit of liberty" is "rooted even in our very soil."[111] To defend this territorialized freedom he considered the Atlantic voyages of "a slave or a negro" arriving in England—a scene he discussed twice in the *Commentaries* as he worked on the relations between post-feudalist English liberty and feudalist colonial law. He declared "that a slave or a negro, the moment he lands in England, falls under the protection of the laws, and with regard to all natural rights becomes *eo instanti* a freeman." The language ironically reveals the complete subjection of the newly constituted "freeman" to the land and its law as the "slave or . . . negro" involuntarily "falls" and "becomes" what the laws dictate without exercising any agency. The "slave or . . . negro" is thus still defined by spatial prescriptions of freedom and subjugation.[112]

To support the idea that slaves could be emancipated by setting foot on England's land, Blackstone referred to two court decisions in which Justice John Holt judged that "as soon as a negro comes into *England*, he becomes free: One may be a villein in *England*, but not a slave."[113] In both Blackstone's citation and Holt's decisions, the "negro" has no control over his or her fate.[114] Instead of portable positive birthright, the "negro" enjoys temporary protection as the feudalist term "villein" partially suspends his or her "negative kind of birthright" and replaces it with a feudalist English category. So while English soil is represented here as an environment that cannot tolerate feudalist colonial inventions, it is saturated with its own feudalist legacies that serve as partial placeholders for colonial ones. This portrayal suggests that English law imagined slaves' negative birthrights as always already portable, as though they were first transferred from Africa's coast to the Americas and then carried to England where they were translated into the feudalist "villein." By contrast to this process, the next section considers settlers' liberating, portable positive birthright and its consequences for settlers' perceptions of spatial attachment.

Settler Rights and the Portability of Native Status

Prior to the Revolutionary era, settlers argued that their rights emanated from England's monarch. They endorsed the legal fiction of expansive English births, which allowed English subjects to carry their birthrights everywhere within the royal realm. Even those who were born in the colonies and never visited England imagined that their "essential" "native Rights" were English constructs that their colonial experiences could augment but not undermine. In 1755, Pennsylvania assembly member Benjamin Franklin responded to Governor John Penn's tax plan by stating that "Freeborn Subjects of England do not lose their essential Rights by removing into the King's Plantations." He claimed that by "extending the British Dominions at the Hazard of their Lives and Fortunes, and encreasing the Power, Wealth and Commerce of their Mother Country," settlers gain "particular Privileges" that are "added to their native Rights, for their Encouragement in so useful and meritorious an Undertaking."[115] In 1774, Connecticut settlers responded to Britain's Coercive Acts (which they termed Intolerable Acts) by claiming "the rights, privileges, and immunities of Freeborn Englishmen ... as fully and amply as if they and every of them [*sic*] were born within the realm of England."[116] This discourse survived beyond 1776.[117] But during the Revolutionary era, settlers also began to protest the ambiguity of English birthright and specifically portrayed subjection to the king as a form of negative birthright. They rejected their subjection to the king as a form of "slavery" and argued that no particular government or territorial domain could limit their universal natural rights.[118]

However, even as settlers fantasized on portable rights that would transcend any particular region, they held on to the idea that the "native"—defined in relation to specific place—was the quintessential locus of entitlement. In an overlooked text, Thomas Jefferson imagined that he could reconstitute international relations by centralizing the traveling settler as the normative rights-bearing subject. In July 1785, while serving as US minister to France, Jefferson drafted a proposal for an international treaty that would make portable positive birthright the foundation of states' treatments of one another's citizens. The proposal never matured to an actual treaty, which might explain its scholarly neglect.[119] However, the proposal is a significant milestone in the construction of settlers as the model rights-bearing subjects because it offered to internationalize privileging, portable native status by liberating its place-based logic from any particular locality. The proposal suggested that travelers to any signatory polity should be able to enjoy rights there equal to those that the "native citizen or subject" of that polity are entitled to.[120] The treaty would have obliged its signatories to accept each other's traveling members as equal to their own members without naturalizing these visitors and without requiring them to forego any privileges in their home country.

This proposal sought to project settlers' privileging self-nativization on colonized land unto the European international arena as its normative order of individuals' international rights. The proposed internationalization of portable positive birthright was a radical expression of a broader discursive project by which settlers sought to replace English forms of entitlement and allegiance with a new order of rights, based on the dynamics of settler native status, to fit their new independence from Britain. It tried to liberate the native from the circumscribed, inalienable nativity of the *nativus* and provide an expansive, portable, alienable nativity immune to subjugation by retaining the positive birthright that facilitated what would later be defined as territorial birthright citizenship while substituting its specific territorialization with portability.[121]

Jefferson's treaty would have enabled "citizens or subjects" of any signatory nation to travel to the countries of the other signatories and enjoy there the same rights to which the "citizen or subject" who is "native" of that country was entitled. It would have allowed citizens of each party to the treaty who "shall be travelling or sojourning" in the jurisdiction of another party to "be considered to every intent and purpose as members of the nation where they are" and to "be entitled to the same protection, the same privileges, immunities, capacities, advantages and rights of every possible species or description, which the subjects or citizens natives of the same place shall at the same time be entitled to."[122] The treaty would have allowed its signatories "mutual[ly]" to "adopt" the "citizens or subjects" of other parties for as long as such adopted foreign nationals would choose to remain in the adopting country without being naturalized there and without hurting their privileges in their countries of origin. This noncommitting appropriation of space-specific rights extends settlers' view of their entitlement to Indigenous peoples' homelands to their intervention in a European international order.

Jefferson's proposal replaced the phrase that colonists used to claim English rights—"as if they were born in England"—with the spatially nonspecific phrase "as if he were a native." Jefferson repeated that phrase three times, thereby turning generalized native status into the backbone of the entire proposal. This phrase generalizes the condition of the self-nativizing settler and distributes it internationally as the new foundation for potentially unbound civil rights. Although his proposal never materialized, its constitutive logic was arguably translated into the international prominence that several settler regimes enjoy. Scott Lauria Morgensen argues that "while settler colonialism may appear to be contained within settler states, its actions are inherently transnational" because "settler states and societies define and lead the economics and laws that articulate a globalized world with ongoing, naturalized colonization."[123]

Property was central to this process because the logic of alienable possession structures settler entitlement and self-nativization. Jefferson's traveling settler would enjoy the right to "property in places within the jurisdiction or possession of" signatory nations "as if he were a native citizen or subject of the same country."[124] The Jeffersonian fantasy thus reflects and responds to settler constructions of liberty as a function of both freedom to migrate and landed possessions. Expanded spatially beyond any particular place, nativity becomes both indispensable and disposable in this fantasy of universal freedom. The proposal's striking combination of fantasy and ambivalence might explain why scholars have barely discussed it, but its value lies precisely in its ability to reveal the acute problem that spatial attachment signified in the early republic and the simultaneous force that the category "native" held as a necessary component of entitlement.[125] Against this backdrop of settler rights the next section elaborates on *Native Land Talk*'s approach to rights.

Unsettling Rights

Morgensen's idea that settler regimes have succeeded in shaping international political protocols, as well as the construction of the settler as the quintessential rights-bearing subject, invite us to envision rights outside of the settler ethos and its Eurocentric universalist assumptions. I began this introduction with an open-ended, necessarily tentative and partial definition of rights that replaces state authority with non-statist approaches to imagining the possibilities of human actions. Such open-endedness draws on critiques of the Eurocentric ideal of universal human rights that is often accepted as the normative framework for considering rights beyond the particularistic authorities of individual nation- (and settler-) states. This open-endedness runs counter to efforts to create "another canon" of human rights, such as José-Manuel Barreto's recovery of a "theory of human rights that emerged in the context of history of the modern colonization of the world and the struggles against imperial violence."[126] Instead, *Native Land Talk* highlights theories whose particular temporal and spatial groundings resist the idea of universal authority that the term *canon* evokes. Thanks to such groundings, human agency interacts with its enabling environmental conditions, thereby becoming meaningful in local, specific ways that resist Eurocentric definitions of universal rights.

The universality of human rights is often perceived as its main virtue, and its expansion as the normative framework for historical progress. Proponents of this narrative often locate the emergence of human rights in the European Enlightenment and name the US and French Revolutions, as well as the United Nations' Universal Declaration of Human Rights, as the most important milestones in its evolution.[127] From this position of endorsing universality, even diverse, inclusive views of human rights limit the sources of this discourse to Babylonian, Greek, Roman, biblical, Confucian, Hinduist, Buddhist, and Islamic texts.[128] However, even such inclusive genealogies rarely imagine that pre-twentieth-century sub-Saharan Africans and Indigenous peoples in the Americas had anything to contribute to conceptualizations of human rights. This selective, progressive teleology tacitly suggests that imperial oppression was a worthy price to pay for the eventual fruition of human rights.

However, when we define rights theories as necessary components of violent conquest and conflict, we must recognize their centrality to any power dynamics. *Native Land Talk* focuses on the rights theories of some of those peoples who were either excluded from the progressive narratives of universal human rights or presented as their (perhaps ungrateful) recipients. This focus critiques representations of rights theories as a unified discourse that emerged from a limited number of cultural sites through written texts that led to the formulation of several categories of rights seemingly stored in a finite (albeit historically adaptive) reservoir that can be applied uniformly to any human inhabitant of the world. It therefore does not discuss universal human rights that seem to be divisible into, for example, "human dignity," "civil liberties and other liberal rights," "political, social, and economic equity," and "cultural rights" that support "communal and national solidarity."[129] This conventional framework of universal human rights positions the state, as Makau Mutua argues, as "the guarantor and subject of human rights" and the human—presumably the citizen—as "the individual egoist at the center of the moral universe."[130] As the above discussion shows, this "egoist" was modeled on the *settler* as rights-carrier whose freedom is defined by contrast to localized obligations. The fictional, generalized "native" that Jefferson envisioned, who could enjoy the rights of privileged natives wherever he chose to travel, is, in other words, the ideal individual endowed with human rights that presumably lack any cultural, geopolitical, or historical particularities.

Critical analyses of universal human rights emphasize that liberalism continues to be authorized by its imperial legacies and that imperial assumptions about peoples, histories, and futures still shape the international frameworks that seek to globalize rights norms. Barreto explains that human rights can no longer "be based . . . in a priori universal geopolitics and history" and positions the "voices that testified to the struggles against slavery, racial domination and the colonial enterprise" as crucial for this history.[131] Such deconstruction of European universalism has long guided the works of Sylvia Wynter, who positions contemporary concerns within the history of Eurocentric thought. Wynter argues that our storytelling capacities make us human, and she explains Eurocentric theological, biological, and economic histories as particular stories that produced a specific "genre" of the human that Europe's geopolitical power universalized. Struggles for liberation must therefore mobilize alternative stories and genres as no single narrative or style can claim absolute superiority.[132] The rights theories analyzed below present non-Eurocentric expressions of humanness facilitated by awareness and negotiations of the specific spatial and temporal conditions in which it is grounded.

Native Land Talk's critique of universalism also draws on Mignolo's theorizations of "pluriversality" or "diversality" as correctives to faith in universality, which globalizes single uniform protocols of being in the world.[133] Mignolo's discussion of the history and consequences of universal human rights focuses on birth; analyzing the assertion that "all men (and women)" are "born equal," he argues that this formulation disguises the unacknowledged implication that "men and women are all born equal but they do not remain equal the rest of their lives" because equality is granted or denied based "on the place" of one's birth.[134] Mignolo attributes these double movements of exclusive universality to the simultaneous development of the categories "human" and "rights" by "European humanists of the fifteenth and sixteenth centuries" who used these categories to distinguish themselves "from co-existing communities they perceived as a threat, challenge, or enemies."[135] In the process, they suppressed "the body" and "its geo-historical location."[136]

Native Land Talk counters Jefferson's attempt to liberate the generalized native's body from any particular geohistorical location by emphasizing the role of inhabitation—a concept comprising diverse practices by which bodies become embedded in space and time—in the construction of non-Eurocentric, spatially and historically particularist rights theories. Chapter 1 focuses on Olaudah Equiano's *Interesting Narrative*, which became the center of debates regarding its author's native status. The chapter analyzes Equiano's complex protest of arrivants' negative birthright and contextualizes it within his attempts to recuperate the native status of exiled and would-be exiled Africans and to assert their right to inhabit the world as Indigenous Africans. Equiano frames his critique of negative birthright within a broader analysis of the inconsistencies that shape liberal imperialism. He develops resettlement plans that open up uncertain beneficial futures that fluctuate between a sense of reformed, inclusive universalism and a commitment to pluriversalism. Equiano's resettlement plans, and his entire book, are framed by his acceptance of imperialism as the only possible framework of global geopolitics, and he attempts to reform imperial rule instead of imagining its overthrow. Although Equiano's narrative and resettlement plans are almost wholly external to the United States, his insistence that resettlement needs to accommodate imperialism and his idea that a recuperative native status would enable arrivants' emancipation provide a useful, elaborate background for subsequent discussions of arrivants' rights claims in the United States. Like his African American counterparts, Equiano works within imperialist constructs and from this vantage point attempts to reconceive native status in order to reform imperial geopolitics. His *Interesting Narrative* critiques the reduction of Africans and other peoples whom Europeans defined as barbarians into objects of imperial history; from this position he mounts his vision of reformed imperialism that would ensure a more viable future of global prosperity.

Whereas chapter 1 discusses struggles for Indigenous rights from an arrivant perspective, chapter 2 concerns Indigenous peoples' efforts to overcome the dispossession that threatened to render their homelands unsustainable.

It examines what I define as the eighteenth-century discourse of Mohegan rights in texts representing the works of three Mohegan leaders: Owaneco, Samson Occom, and Joseph Johnson. Early in the century, Owaneco resisted settlers' attempts to dispossess Mohegan by presenting its precolonial history; later, Occom and Johnson reconsidered the consequences of precolonial and colonial histories as they worked on a resettling-unsettlement plan in order to help Mohegan and other Indigenous polities flourish. Owaneco, Occom, and Johnson used irony to negotiate settlers' denials of Mohegan rights, and irony structured the re/unsettlement project on which the two latter men worked—and which culminated in the establishment of Brothertown on Oneida land. These complex, ironic negotiations of resettlement and unsettlement were necessitated by settlers' negations of Mohegan political past, present, and future. Through them, Occom and Johnson scrutinized the geopolitical and epistemological foundations of Mohegan rights and envisioned a multilayered inhabitation network that connected Mohegan to Oneida lands despite the geographic distance and settlements that separated them.

The first two chapters focus on attempts to construct spatial certainties as stable foundations of rights discourses through Equiano's sense of an "original free African state" and the Mohegan discourse of Native rights. In both cases such certainty was rooted in assertions of attachment to Indigenous homelands. By contrast, chapter 3 focuses on the uncertainties that arrivants and settlers expressed regarding the spatial parameters of freedom. It juxtaposes three seemingly unrelated discourses: Revolutionary-era abolitionist petitions by enslaved and free blacks, advertisements that slaveholders placed in newspapers in order to capture fugitive slaves, and settlers' protests of Britain's impressment policies in the years that led up to the War of 1812. By examining the functions of nativity across these discourses I highlight arrivants' contributions to representations of the settler as the quintessential rights-bearing subject. At a time when settlers thought that voluntary travel was the best tool for maintaining their freedom, arrivants argued that permanent settlement could affirm their own nativities as those of settlers and thus protect them from enslavement. This chapter analyzes the fluctuations of nativity between its negative and positive poles and shows that territorial expansion over Indigenous peoples' lands enabled white US settlers to resolve these tensions and liberate themselves from the legacies of negative birthright.

While settler authorities tried to render unintelligible the arrivant rights claims discussed in chapter 3, chapter 4 focuses on the geopolitical visions that Indigenous polities presented to US officials in the late eighteenth century. The geopolitical positions of Indigenous peoples on the land prevented the United States from ignoring Indigenous geopolitics, and the chapter explores the conflicting geopolitical visions that the settler regime and Indigenous unsettlement proposals represented. I read records of treaty negotiations between the United States and Indigenous polities in order to examine how their incompatible rights claims responded to each other. The chapter traces two later doctrines of US Indian policy—impossibility and allotment—to their early manifestations at the inception of US Indian affairs and analyzes them as crucial to settlers' construction of US sovereignty as an exclusive, absolute, and axiomatic power. Next to these doctrines the chapter discusses the geopolitical visions that Indigenous peoples presented to US officials in order to unsettle that sovereignty by confronting it with decolonizing inhabitation practices and embodied spatial relations. By following the course of negotiations from an initial condition of relative US weakness and Indigenous military might to changed geopolitical circumstances in which the United States perceived itself as the powerful owner of Indigenous peoples' homelands, the chapter considers the geopolitical implications of loss and defeat, and their potential uses for unsettlement initiatives.

While chapter 4 highlights settlers' responses to and negotiations of Indigenous peoples' geopolitics, chapter 5 illustrates arrivant efforts to establish an emergent geopolitical resettlement program within reformed parameters of the settler state. The chapter focuses on the intensive self-nativization initiatives that African Americans embarked on in resistance to African colonization, a process they grounded within a rehistoricization of slavery and its consequences. Whereas slave law excluded the enslaved from the human orders of inheritance that structure historical descent in property-oriented settler regimes, arrivants reinterpreted slavery's history in order to claim the expanding scope of US soil as their patrimony. They did so by arguing that the blood of their enslaved ancestors, which saturated that soil, naturalized their claims to it, and they sometimes argued that slavery's coercive history produced stronger, more historically valid entitlement than the voluntary migration that constituted the settler as the quintessential rights-bearing subject. By analyzing the trope of ancestral blood in US soil this chapter discusses arrivant attempts to nativize themselves as settlers and the function of the black/white binary in this process.

Whereas chapter 5 demonstrates how arrivants revised US property orders by inserting their history into that of the settler regime, chapter 6 focuses on Cherokee and Muscogee unsettlement projects that replaced settler understandings of temporality and spatiality with radically incompatible configurations of historic, ongoing inhabitation practices. In an interlude between these chapters, I juxtapose ancestral blood with ancestral graves in order to explore the broader contexts within which these elements of

African American and Native American resistance to settler colonialism circulate.

Chapter 6 emphasizes the distinctions between settlers' expansive territoriality and progressive temporality, on the one hand, and Cherokee and Muscogee interwoven, multilayered temporalities and inhabitation practices, on the other. The chapter focuses on the struggle against Indian removal, and analyzes the small-scale spatialities and complex temporalities that Cherokee and Muscogee writers and spokespersons mobilized in resistance to removal. The focal point of these spatialities and temporalities was ancestral graves, a category I compare and contrast to arrivant discourses of ancestral blood. Chapters 5 and 6 thus provide two comparable, yet highly discrepant theories of the relevance of past deaths in the production of present and future rights: one that ties arrivants to the settler regime, and another that insists on Indigenous peoples' detachment from it. Both chapters concern the freedom to inhabit and maintain multilayered temporalities and spatialities that the settler regime seeks to replace with its teleological narrative of national progress.

[1]

EQUIANO'S NATIVITY

The Interesting Narrative of the Life of Olaudah Equiano, or Gustavus Vassa, the African (1789–94) is an impassioned survivor's appeal for the abolition of slavery.[1] This highly politicized autobiography establishes its subject's authority by unfolding his tumultuous personal trajectory—from the bountiful childhood of an Indigenous "Eboe" African through enslavement in Africa, the Middle Passage, Caribbean slavery, and emancipation—and culminates in his abolitionist work in Britain.[2] In the late twentieth century, Olaudah Equiano's Eboe African nativity led scholars to hail the book as an unparalleled first-person account of the Middle Passage from the perspective of a slave. Scholars imagined Equiano's African birth as the foundation of entitled selfhood violated by slavery. However, this unanimously appreciative reception soured after Vincent Carretta discovered baptismal and naval records that list Equiano's birthplace as Carolina.[3] The ensuing debate—much like the earlier consensus—positioned birthplace as the major constitutive element of authenticity, identity, and cultural value. The new information led some scholars, who now believed Equiano was born to slavery in America, to interpret his birth through Orlando Patterson's influential "social death" thesis. In Patterson's analysis, slaves experienced a radical "loss of native status" that dooms them to "natal alienation," which turns them into "genealogical isolate[s]" deprived of "all 'rights' or claims of birth."[4]

Patterson's discussion of "natal alienation" is based on the presupposition that natality necessarily founds entitlement, an idea that resists the logic of slavery by denying the possibility of negative birthright. However, a more multifaceted interpretation, capturing the subjugating as well as the emancipatory connotations of native status, is required in order to understand both the scholarly debate regarding Equiano's nativity and Equiano's representations of natality. The debate has been shaped by conflicting interpretations of

Equiano's baptismal record, which reads, "Gustavus Vassa a Black born in Carolina 12 years old."[5] While many scholars have accepted this document as historically valid, Cathy Davidson compares it with adjacent entries in the same baptismal record, which feature parental names and birthdates rather than races or overseas birthplaces. Given this discrepancy she denounces the record's "erasure" of Equiano's "black and/or African parentage," its "exorcism" of his "non-Christian past," and its validation of "natal alienation."[6] Her analysis of the rhetorical problems plaguing the putatively objective record argues for the primacy of Equiano's volition and voice over the discourses that oppressed him. A similar interest in the perspectives of the enslaved motivates Stephanie Smallwood's study of perceptions of African births among eighteenth-century slaves and slaveholders. Smallwood argues that African nativities were "stigma[tized]" as unintelligible, antihistorical signs of "ignorance and inexperience," which explains why Equiano might have preferred to claim a Carolina birth.[7] Both Armstrong and Smallwood alert us to the possibility that contemporary appraisals of nativity may not be sensitive enough to the eighteenth-century challenges that Equiano faced.

This chapter analyzes Equiano's nativity as a significant discursive construct that should not be reduced to the binary logic of historical truth. It argues that the complexity of Equiano's nativity stems from his textual attempts to liberate himself from the constraints of disenfranchisement by claiming the status and agency of an Indigenous African in order to use his historic situation as the condition from which to envision a reformed imperial order. *The Interesting Narrative* challenges the Eurocentric construction of "negro," which denotes natural slavery, by reframing nativity within a liberating Indigenous vision for global reform that Equiano positions as a more reliable ground for egalitarian human rights than Eurocentric thought. Equiano formulates his vision of global reform within imperial geopolitics in order to reform the very imperialism that led to slavery. He thereby develops a diasporic Indigenous ethic through which he intervenes in imperial geopolitics. Indigeneity functions in his narrative both as pristine formation of pre-imperial freedom and as a category by which to imagine non-Eurocentric solidarity among geographically distant peoples. This diasporic Indigenous ethic, like the entire narrative, is structured by tensions between positive and negative birthrights, Indigenous and arrivant rights, Christian universalism, and pluriversally oriented conceptions of global freedom and equality. While some critics prioritized Equiano's commitment to either an English identity or an African one, and others have stressed his hybridity,[8] the classificatory logic of identity politics hinders us from appreciating the *Interesting Narrative*'s investment in the internal tensions of what Equiano presents as imperial-oriented Indigenous politics.

Equiano's intervention in imperial constructions of native status stems from his intensive exploration of the ideas of universal freedom and equality. He tries to recuperate universalism from its Eurocentric constraints and redefine it under terms that would ensure global respect for diverse manifestations of human thought and action. Such redefined universalism would render meaningless the discursive practices by which imperial Eurocentrism has established the colonized native. Equiano appropriates one of the earliest terms in the Eurocentric lexicon of inferior otherness, *barbarian*, and defamiliarizes it in order to recast global geopolitics in a manner that would render slavery intolerable and illegitimate. He utilizes the position he claims as exiled Indigenous Eboe African to offer a diasporic Indigenous ethics by which to establish an alternative order of "universal good" (*IN* 234).

Equiano mounts his diasporic Indigenous critique of Eurocentric racism through an ironic exploration of the category "barbarian," whose history linked such labels as "Ethiopian" and "Indian" and made them equally available for slave-trading and -holding Eurocentric regimes. Equiano affirms his commitment to an inclusive, pluriversal idea of human rights by aligning himself with his African or Eboe "countrymen" as well as with a broader spectrum of "those who are called barbarians"—a category that brings together the "Samaide" and the "Hottentot," two peoples that Eurocentric geopolitics posited as exotic subhumans occupying the northern and southern margins of a hierarchic, geopolitically divided human and semi-human global population (*IN* 43, 205, 109). This inclusive perspective recasts the world's population as a community united by horizontal, nonhierarchic relations that challenge Eurocentric constructions of a vertical, hierarchic global order where non-European peoples are subordinated to ideals of property and mastery.[9] Equiano's vision seeks to transform imperial relations by ensuring that the ideal of mutual global benefit encompasses all peoples. In order to achieve this geopolitical transformation, he proposes a number of resettlement projects that reposition colonized natives as fully historical subjects whose pasts, presents, and futures are crucial to a complete understanding of human realities.

This chapter begins with the category "barbarian" as the structural foundation of Equiano's diasporic Indigenous ethics. Equiano manipulates the term's origins in the hierarchic interpretation of linguistic differences to critique the gulf between Eurocentric universalism's moral claims and its disastrous practices. Through Equiano's investment in imperial geopolitics I explore his construction of Indigenous African freedom and the legal discourses that render it oxymoronic. The chapter then moves from law to proto-ethnographic representations of Africans that constituted the colonized native as an object of European knowledge excluded from human history. Equiano positions Indigenous Africans as early practitioners of Judeo-Christian principles in order to reinsert them as equal humans into the history that reduced them to subhuman status. He does so by simultaneously localizing and globalizing biblical ethics as a viable alternative to Eurocentric universalism. The following section reads Equiano's representations of climate and land as crucial aspects of native status in a book that focuses primarily on the sea. Tensions between sea and land as spaces that enable or constrain freedom are central to Equiano's reorganization of diasporic Indigenous politics. This analysis of the land is the backdrop against which I read Equiano's three resettlement plans, to which the remainder of the chapter is dedicated and which bridge precolonial indigeneity with arrivant realities.

The first resettlement plan is formulated in Equiano's attempt to recreate an Indigenous African community in Central America with Mosquito cooperation. This project failed because it was embedded in colonial slavery, and its failure led Equiano to plan Africa's post-slavery future. His second resettlement proposal attempts to establish slave-free trade relations between England and Africa. Like his first resettlement project, this too is based on the idea that a geopolitics of justice can be achieved only if communities can inhabit their homelands safely—whether such homelands are original or are adopted ones to which these communities had been invited by the land's Indigenous inhabitants. I conclude with Equiano's imagined return to his African "estate" as a site of an alternative Enlightenment. These resettlement visions that begin in the Americas and then center on Africa position imperial relations as the necessary context for formulating emancipatory possibilities, an idea central to the arrivant discourses discussed in chapters 3 and 5.

Barbarian Histories

The *Interesting Narrative* refers to indigeneity by engaging the now familiar language of birth and nativity, the intertwined historic legacies of barbarism and slavery, and the idea of global solidarity. The "barbarian" functions as the theoretical foundation from which all these meanings emerge and to which they respond. Equiano presents the barbarian as the major construct of the dehumanized colonized native produced by Eurocentric universalism and he explores this category in order to critique the legacies of negative birthright.

Equiano refers to himself recurrently as "African," but he replaces this label twice when he describes his conversion to Christianity ("Now the Ethiopian was willing to be saved by Jesus Christ" [IN 190]), and upon signing his 1788 petition to Queen Charlotte as "The oppressed Ethiopian" (*IN* 232). V. Y. Mudimbe explains that classical Greek myths presented Ethiopians as "the 'first of all humans,'" who were therefore named "autochthonous" and considered to be "the first to be taught how to honor the gods" and enjoy "a state of freedom and of peace with one another." However, as Mudimbe shows, Greek discourse on Africa gradually shifted from such representations to portrayals of Ethiopians as "savage[s]" whose "ways of living" "display the nature of wild beasts" by "contrast" to Greek "customs." This focus on a wildness that contrasts with the Greek home was the conceptual foundation of the Greek terms *barbaroi* and *agriori* which refer to that which is barbarian, "wild," and "savage."[10] Greek distinctions between foreign-speaking barbarians and domestic Greek-speaking persons depended on the "accident of birth," but this idea was paradoxical, as Pagden explains: "for the Greeks . . . birth could never be a matter of accident" because it was crucial in delimiting the boundaries between the "superior" and inferior, the "truly human" and those whom Aristotle defined as natural slaves.[11]

This history enables us to glimpse the earlier genealogies that supported binary English birthright. The Aristotelian idea of a world organized by the hierarchies of rule and submission—within which "natural master" and "natural slave" were mutually exclusive, mutually constitutive categories—facilitated Renaissance extensions of the "barbarian" to what Pagden terms "those who neither subscribed to European religious views, nor lived their lives according to European social norms."[12] In this context the Greek "Ethiopian" became the model for Spanish constructions of Indigenous peoples in the Americas. Pagden writes that Spanish colonizer and historian Gonzalo Fernández de Oviedo y Valdés first identified "Indians" with "the 'Ethiopians'" of Greek thought. Imperial policy consolidated this analogy in 1493 when Pope Alexander VI allowed Spain to enslave Indigenous peoples in the Americas in order to equate Spain's imperial powers in America with those of Portugal in Africa.[13] Spain's eventual replacement of Indian slaves with African ones ended this shared conceptual history that Equiano partially revives in the *Interesting Narrative*.

The "barbarian" was crucial to the early modern evolution of Eurocentric imperial law and its rights discourses. The early sixteenth-century English theologian John Mair, who directly impacted Spanish thought by educating Spanish theologians such as Francisco de Vitoria, argued that "by nature, the barbarians and slaves are the same."[14] In the mid-sixteenth century the barbarian became a fixture of imperial policies when Spain's King Charles V convened the Valladolid debates in order to shape imperial governance. Juan Ginés de Sepúlveda defined Indians as the "barbarian" "natural slave[s]" of their new Spanish masters, while his opponent Bartolomé de Las Casas—whom Paolo G. Carozza calls "the midwife of modern human rights talk"[15]—used the universalist argument of creation "in God's image" to argue that since Indigenous peoples were capable "of attaining Christ's kingdom" they were evidently not destined to perpetual slavery.[16] Las Casas could imagine the future conversion of "barbarians" into equality with Europeans precisely because he viewed them, as Walter Mignolo writes, as "those who 'lacked' something in the area of government, . . . knowledge, . . . [and] religion."[17] Unlike Sepúlveda, Las Casas argued that Spain's imperial responsibilities required that Spanish authorities provide for such lack, and he used the term *barbarians* ironically to refer to the Spanish conquistadors whose actions violated his ideal of civilized behavior.[18]

Equiano's Barbarians

Equiano's rejection of Eurocentric norms is encapsulated in his lexical preference of *African*, *native*, and *barbarian* over *negro*. He often uses the three former terms in reference to universal equality and reserves *negro*, which colonial slave law and British legal doctrine conflate with *slave*, for his critique of racial hierarchies.[19] He thus liberates *African*, *native*, and *barbarian* from Eurocentric classifications and subverts the distinction between civilized Britons and barbarous Africans. Responding tacitly to Aristotle's representation of barbarians as natural slaves, and to the conventional association of barbarity with nakedness and lack,[20] Equiano reminds his English readers that their own ancestors—"the Aborigines of Britain"—were once as "barbarous" as contemporaneous "Africans" seem to them (*IN* 45, 233). Of these four terms, Equiano uses *barbarian* ironically by appropriating it to critique Eurocentric imperialism. Equiano manipulates the barbarian's etymological reference to speakers of languages other than Greek in order to use it as a site of pluriversality that appreciates rather than seeks to extinguish a multiplicity of perspectives and expressions. He also relates this distinction between African practice and English faith to his inversion of the category "barbarian" by writing that when the English crewmembers onboard the vessel he had worked on refused to share his Christian enthusiasm, he "became a barbarian to them in talking of the love of Christ" (*IN* 191). Yet he also deploys "barbarian" as a site of inhumane cruelty by arguing that slaveholders engage in acts of "barbarity" (*IN* 109).

The power of Equiano's malleable "barbarian" stands out in comparison to its usage by his contemporary, the African-descended poet Phillis Wheatley, who used the term in responding to a proposal by English theologian Samuel Hopkins that she join missionaries to Africa. Wheatley rejected Hopkins's offer by imagining the burden she would be on the missionaries who will have to "carry [her] So long a voyage." She further hypothesized that "[u]pon my arrival, how like a Barbarian Should I look to the Natives; I can promise that my tongue shall be quiet for . . . being an utter stranger to the Language of Anamaboe." Wheatley clarified that she was joking by adding, "Now to be serious, this undertaking appears too hazardous," and she mentioned her lack of eligibility, her reluctance to leave her "British & American Friends," and her unfamiliarity with "those Missionaries" she would have joined.[21] In this context her reference to herself as potential "Barbarian" reproduces the conventional deployment of the domestic/foreign binary as the axis on which the meaning of "barbarian" turns, as her joking fear of looking like a "Barbarian" to the "Natives" reaffirms her belonging to the cultural milieu of her "British & American Friends."[22]

Next to Wheatley's conventional uses of *barbarian*, Equiano's fluctuations between Eurocentric conventions and their subversions stand out. Another instance of such fluctuations is his treatment of the relations among individuals and communities. On the one hand, Equiano portrays African societies through representations of freedom and action that are incompatible with the possessive individual. Such portrayals, as I show below, center on commitments to communal well-being and may thus be interpreted as reflections of "communitism," the concept that Indigenous studies scholar Jace Weaver coined to refer to action motivated by responsibility for the welfare of the entire community.[23] On the other hand, Equiano profited from possessive individualism, which enabled him to buy his freedom and become a pre-Franklinian model of the self-made man, as Carretta argues.[24] This tension between possessive individualism and communities that is formative of the book is absent from, for example, the contemporaneous narrative of Venture Smith, an ex-slave whose dictated autobiography, *Narrative of the Life and Adventures of Venture* (1798), consistently centralizes self-possession.[25]

We may consider the "communitist" aspects of Equiano's *Interesting Narrative* in the context of African philosophies, thanks to a brief essay in which Mudimbe distinguishes the "unconstrained and uncontextualized 'I'" of Western philosophy from a "more communal" "African mode" of thought that "emphasizes an 'I' that is always connected to and in relationship with others." Whereas Western and British philosophy understands "human freedom" "as a means for mastering the 'other,'" Mudimbe writes, what he calls the "African model" of liberty centralizes "a human being who is free and at the same time highly dependent upon others, on the memory of the past, and on the objective reality of nature and the universe."[26] With this distinction in mind I define Equiano's project as an imaginative diasporic extension of "communitism" onto a global scale. Equiano's ideas regarding Africa, the Indigenous discourse in which he engages, and his investment in imperial reform emerge out of tensions not only with "memories and experiences of the indigenous cultures of Africa," as James Sidbury argues, but also with English and colonial cultures.[27] These tensions necessitate his "re-invent[ion]," as Hazel Carby writes, of the African subject "as the bearer of a valuable and valued perspective and knowledge for his contemporary readership," but they simultaneously found his imperial position.[28]

Ironic Inversions and Appropriations

Such tensions are crucial to Equiano's entire imperial-based critique of the Eurocentric discourses that justify and naturalize slavery. He responds to the heritable fixity of English birthrights by contrasting it with the precarity and mutability of "African" freedom that enables the "free born" African subject to be enslaved without completely losing a sense of valuable social selfhood and without becoming a "genealogical isolate" defined by "natal alienation." Equiano argues that his early enslavement within African communities did not obliterate his sense of inherent African freedom. He represents slavery in Africa as an almost egalitarian institution, where slaves are distinguished from slaveholders only by being prohibited from eating "with those who were free born" (IN 40).[29] This formulation captures the distance between perceptions of native status in English traditions and in the Eboe legacies Equiano represents. While English social stratification was grounded in the fixity of heritable positions, the African who was born free loses this status once he is enslaved, but Equiano suggests this loss may be temporary because it depends on mutable social circumstances rather than on fixed imperial categories like race.

The *Interesting Narrative* argues that the power dynamics of African slavery depend on experience rather than birth, so slaves may enjoy a more varied range of historical and political options. After leading his readers through various stages of his African bondage to his arrival at the home of an African slaveholding family that treats him almost like a son, Equiano reflects on his condition as a qualified form of freedom that injures his "love of liberty" in one sense alone: observing the taboo on joint meals, he is "mortified" by his fear of "eat[ing] with the free-born children" who befriend him (IN 48–49). This fear naturalizes his enslavement by suggesting that he has lost his previous "free born" status, yet his "love of liberty" functions tacitly as an equally natural, inherent affective property that precedes this loss and survives it. Inherited social conditions, in other words, are vulnerable to subsequent transformations, although they are protected by the ostensibly natural "love of liberty" that remains unaltered despite changing historical circumstances. The idea of enduring inherent entitlement denaturalizes colonial constructions of slavery as a permanent heritable condition and implicitly critiques the reduction of Africans to objects of imperial trade.

Equiano constantly negotiates the distinctions between colonial and "African" discourses of slavery and freedom. When he uses possessive individualism to his own advantage in 1766 by purchasing his freedom, Equiano defines his new condition in terms of English law by celebrating his new interpellation as "freeman" (IN 138). As I showed in the introduction, Blackstone qualified the liberty of ex-slaves whose racialized negative birthrights prevented them from completely enjoying English subjects' positive birthrights. When Blackstone wrote that upon arrival in England the "slave or a negro" may still be bound to his master's will, he defined the racial limits of imperial English liberty and naturalized the lingering negative birthright of newly emancipated freemen.[30]

In this context, Equiano uses the term *freeman* almost ironically while acknowledging his master's "right" to his services by narrating how, following his emancipation, he had agreed to postpone his desired trip to London in order to continue working for his former master in the Caribbean. But Equiano augments the racially limited freedom of the English category "freeman" by grounding it in his "original free African state" (IN 138), which functions as an alternative source of affirmative power that precedes English law and may therefore overcome its paradoxes. Reflecting on his decision to continue working for his former master, Equiano writes: "being *as in my original free African state*, I embarked upon the Nancy," his former master's vessel (ibid. [my italics]). As this formulation indicates, Equiano's decision is not bound by English law but is enabled by what he presents as a foundational African liberty that he may still access across the Atlantic. However, having witnessed multiple instances in which free arrivants were kidnapped into slavery, Equiano understands Blackstone's qualifications of the "liberty" that English law may accord the "free negro," which, especially in the colonies, "is but nominal" (IN 122). Equiano uses his "original free African state" as an unambiguous alternative to nominal liberty; it failed him only when the logic of affirmative communal attachment on which it rests was violated at his initial abduction in Africa.

Equiano extends his critique of slavery beyond his personal history and develops a broader attack on Eurocentric justice by reading slave law. He uses the gaps between nominal designations and ethical commitments to challenge Eurocentric norms. Focusing on violence against slaves, Equiano discusses Barbados's 1688 "Act for the governing of Negroes" that justified the killing and maiming of resistant slaves and fined slaveholders who willfully murdered their "Negro or other Slave" out of "bloody-mindedness, or cruel intention."[31] Equiano argues that the distinction between these crimes, the law's defense of slaveholders, and its monetary appraisal of their violence exemplify the savagery of enslavement. But since he writes for an English audience taught to view the law as a protective mechanism, he makes the point by mobilizing the hypothetical perspectives of those excluded from the protection of English law. He asks rhetorically whether "the assembly which enacted" Barbados's Act do not "deserve the appellation of savages and brutes rather than of Christians and men?" (IN 109). He undermines Eurocentric racism by adding that the "cruelty" of the Act "would disgrace an assembly of those who are called barbarians; and for its injustice and *insanity* [the act] would shock the morality and common sense of a Samaide or a Hottentot" (ibid. [italics in original]). This rhetoric stretches moral judgment beyond Eurocentric norms by imagining a global justice system guided by inhabitants of the northern and southern ends of Eurocentric geopolitics. It emphasizes Europe's distance and isolation from a broader human field of potential Christian love, exposes the violent limits of Enlightenment universalism, and calls for global fraternity to replace Eurocentric oppression.

The reference to the "common sense of a Samaide or a Hottentot" (Sami and Khoikhoi in current parlance) inverts the inherent dehumanization of such phrases as Blackstone's "a slave or a negro" and responds, as Carretta suggests, to Oliver Goldsmith's classification of the "Samoids" as groups dwelling "round the polar regions." Goldsmith used geopolitics to literalize barbarian lack and affirm its scientific validity by representing the "Samoids" as incompletely human. "In proportion as we approach towards the north pole," Goldsmith wrote, "the size of the natives appear to diminish, growing less and less as we advance higher, till we come to those latitudes that are destitute of all inhabitants altogether."[32] Goldsmith's theory of the geographic distribution of human populations was based on an absolute vanishing point toward which certain Indigenous peoples gradually recede. Hottentots were similarly assigned a peripheral geopolitical existence at "the most southern part of Africa."[33] Equiano critiques these perceptions of a peripheral, diminishing humanity by arguing that the perspectives of nominal barbarians emphasize Europe's distance and isolation from a broader human field and are thus necessary for exposing the violent limits of Eurocentric universalism. The next section continues to explore Equiano's reformulations of the barbarian by focusing on the natural history discourse of manners-and-customs descriptions, which he critiques using biblical morality.

The Manners and Customs of Indigenous Christianity

Equiano's descriptions of Eboe culture and of his enslavement in Africa comprise complex adaptations and revisions of contemporaneous Anglophone depictions of Africa.[34] This portion of his book became a major site of the debate concerning Equiano's nativity because scholars used it to investigate whether his knowledge of Africa reflected a native's experience or was a mere regurgitation of oral and printed accounts. However, by focusing on the discursive logic of these descriptions rather than their factual implications, we can see how Equiano challenges English conventions by engaging them. He does so by reproducing the colonial proto-ethnographic genre of manners-and-customs descriptions, the normative lens through which European readers have been accustomed to view colonized peoples, but he revises this genre in order to present Christianity as a universal, anti-Eurocentric foundation of human history.

This focus revises prevalent interpretations of Christianity's role in the *Interesting Narrative*. Since Christianity has often been understood as the proper content of white English civilization, Equiano's conversion appears to affirm his assimilation and thus either to invalidate postcolonial readings of his work or to exemplify his postcolonial hybridity.[35] Several critics have worked against such analyses. Srivinas Aravamudan suggests that we need "an expanded understanding" of religion to appreciate the *Interesting Narrative*; Joanna Brooks rejects "the conceptual reduction" of "conversion to cultural or racial assimilation or even to hybridity" and argues that Equiano's conversion does not disavow his claimed African identity but constitutes an act of "self-determination"; and Eileen Razzari Elrod writes that Equiano uses the Bible to position Eboe culture "at the very heart of the dominant religious tradition."[36] Equiano uses Christianity to reposition Eboe within meaningful human history in resistance to Eurocentric erasures and exclusions. Even more significantly, his uses of the Bible enable him to position Eboe ethics as historically prior to English Christianity.

The *Interesting Narrative* intertwines the Bible with Eboe culture and thus translates the colonial category "native" into an affirmative site of originary Christianity that rehistoricizes the Eboe. Manners-and-customs descriptions were a major colonial means for producing the dehistoricized otherness of colonized natives. As Mary Louise Pratt writes, this genre abstracted and homogenized human populations by representing their histories in "a timeless present tense" where "particular historical event[s]" exemplified "pregiven custom[s] or trait[s]" rather than agentive developments.[37] Equiano's use of manners and customs seems to approximate what Audra Simpson calls "ethnographic refusal," which rejects the reduction of Indigenous polities to timeless "cultures," but whereas Simpson critiques *culture* as a dehistoricized, depoliticized category, Equiano uses what we may call the cultural facets of Eboe life to rehistoricize it.[38] In this revisionist history, references to the Bible support Equiano's assertions of Eboes' full humanity, which is defined by his adaptation of Christianity to this geopolitical purpose.

Equiano locates his homeland in Christian history by dating his African nativity to "the year 1745" (IN 32), by claiming a "strong analogy" between "the manners and customs of my countrymen, and those of the Jews" of "Genesis," and by suggesting that "one people had sprung from the other" (IN 43–44). Throughout the first chapter of the *Interesting Narrative*, Equiano highlights his attachment to his native valley, "Essaka," and negates slavery's natal alienation by claiming an enduring nativity that the Middle Passage could not obliterate. In addition, he reinvests the colonial category "the natives" with meanings that exceed colonial stereotypes, as he does with "barbarian." Roxann Wheeler traces Equiano's analogy between Africans and biblical peoples to other eighteenth-century texts—particularly abolitionist ones—and writes that the "comparison attempts to use Jews as a bridge between Africans and Europeans."[39] But Equiano insisted that Africans had been practicing biblical traditions *prior* to the writing of the New Testament and before the ancestors of his English readers converted to Christianity. Thus, his religious history uses Africans to bridge the gap between Genesis's Abrahamic lineage and newly converted Europeans. From this vantage point, his idea of an "original free African state" does not reflect the isolation of Africans from human or divine law, but testifies to their status as recipients of divine protection that transcends the human laws that violate what he represents as universal Christian morals. Equiano supports this idea and critiques colonizing knowledge about non-alphabetic African societies when he states that upon first reading the Bible he found "the laws and rules of my country written almost exactly" there (IN 92). He thus represents his African childhood as proto-Christian anticipation of his conversion as an adult.

The Bible is the source of Equiano's production of manners-and-customs descriptions because reading it "tended to impress our manners and customs more deeply on my memory" (IN 92). Equiano therefore tacitly represents conversion as a recovery of earlier Eboe experiences rather than a departure from Eboe life and asserts that he "was from early years a predestinarian" (IN 119). He "reduplicate[es]" biblical "salvation history"[40] as part of his quest for global Christian justice within the revisionist history that frames his individual spiritual struggle. By associating the origins of Christianity with Africa *at Europe's expense*, Equiano refutes the prevalent eighteenth-century claim that slavery under Christian masters was preferable to heathen life in Africa because it allowed Africans to enjoy the spiritual virtues of Christian society.[41]

Equiano critiques this idea by claiming that colonial Christianity is "nominal"—a word he uses three times in the book to mark superficial or hypocritical commitments. First, he employs it to assert Eboe independence: "our subjection to the king of Benin was little more than nominal" (*IN* 32). Second, he articulates his outrage at the reduction of people to marketable commodities: "O, ye nominal Christians! might not an African ask you, learned you this from your God?" (*IN* 61). And finally, he charts the Caribbean limitations of "negro" freedom, which "is but nominal" (*IN* 122). Together, these statements constitute the "African" or "Eboe" as exclusive site of authentic liberty, whose implicitly original Christianity was violated by slavery's constitution of the essentially unfree "negro." The authenticity he claims here does not refer to some pristine, uncontaminated past, but rather stands for commitment to ethical action based on a revisionist history of the past.

Equiano constructs an Indigenous Christian ethic that denaturalizes Europe's claimed monopoly on Christianity, rejects colonial legal manipulations of Christianity, and roots Christian ethics in the everyday life of Indigenous Eboes. By identifying biblical norms with the "laws and rules of [his] country," Equiano points to a normative ethic that requires the replacement of colonizing law with universal justice. These moral issues are developed further in Equiano's geopolitical constructions of freedom and slavery.

Geopolitics

Naval settings dominate the *Interesting Narrative*, and relations between sea, land, and people shape its geopolitical investment in imperial slavery. The book highlights fluctuations between land-based ideas of indigeneity and the sea that molds arrivant experiences. Equiano tries to replace the tumultuous experiences of arrivant lives with a reaffirmed attachment to the land that the slave trade violates. The prominence of marine settings begins with the Atlantic Ocean, as Equiano narrates the Middle Passage, and continues with his subsequent marine career as slave and freeman. However, this prominence becomes an indispensable threshold through which Equiano envisions landed spatial relations anew and formulates resettlement projects to mitigate transatlantic slavery. To understand this facet of the text we need to complement the oppressive uses of the land in the feudalist tradition of negative birthright with Renaissance political theory in which oceans figured as focal points of debates regarding global freedom precisely because they facilitated Europe's enslaving imperial expansion.

In the wake of Portuguese attempts to monopolize naval access to Africa and Asia, the Dutch jurist Hugo Grotius theorized the sea as the spatial realm of universal human freedom in contrast to landed geopolitical constraints and prohibitions. Grotius developed this analysis of marine politics in *Mare Liberum* (*The Free Sea*) (1609), which distinguishes conquerable land—a passive domain that may be delimited, settled, and dominated—from the free sea, an inexhaustible resource open to all because it defies exclusive dominion. Grotius argued that "the consent of all mankind" exempts the sea "from propriety," allowing anyone to navigate or fish it precisely because no one can claim exclusive possession of it.[42] This interpretation clashed with the Atlantic Ocean's facilitation of the slave trade and imperial domination, and with British jurist John Selden's *Mare Clausum* (The closed sea) (1636), by presenting the sea as exhaustible, divisible, appropriable domain. Selden's theory served British interests by defining "the British Sea" as an expanding naval domain that stretched to America's shores.[43] The *Interesting Narrative* seems attentive to these debates and their violent consequences as it highlights the oppressive and liberating potentialities of both sea and land.[44]

First, Eboe land is an idyllic pre-slavery space where agricultural labor maintains harmonious, mutually nurturing relations between land and people. The entire Eboe community cultivates the "uncommonly rich and fruitful" land, and Eboes "have no beggars" because "every one, even the children and women, . . . contributes something to the common stock" (*IN* 38). This bountiful land is protected by Eboes' distance from trade routes; their home valley, Essaka, is located "in one of the most remote" areas of the African "interior" beyond European travel and exploration (*IN* 32). These descriptions as well as Equiano's insistence that Eboes "are unacquainted with idleness" (*IN* 38) together create a counternarrative to the very British imperial discourse from which Equiano borrows to construct his portrayals of Africa. That imperial discourse constitutes Africa, and particularly its interior, as the negative pole of "binary geographies" in which Africa's putative backwardness emphasizes European progress, but Equiano translates Africa's presumed alterity into moral superiority. Geographer John Agnew explains that binary geographies were instrumental for the emergence of a fixed, hierarchic "geopolitical imagination" that distinguished the African climate and the "idleness" it seemed to induce in Africans from European "industry and innovation."[45] This expression of environmental determinism helped exclude Africa from the progressive political and historical order associated with Lockean possessive-individual labor, trade routes, private property, and civil government. Equiano must subvert this environmental determinism in order to represent an Africa that may be conducive to abolitionist resettlement efforts so that he would be able to refute slavery's negative birthright regime and recuperate the indigenous African status he claims.

To expose the fallacies of imperial liberalism, Equiano critiqued Lockean economy and governance by associating it with slavery. "[Y]ou assert that [slaves] are incapable of learning," he writes, addressing a British audience reared on imperial discourse that contends "their [slaves'] minds are . . . a barren soil or moor" on which "culture would be lost," as though "they came from a climate, where nature (though prodigal of her bounties in a degree unknown to yourselves) has left man alone scant and unfinished, and incapable of enjoying the treasures she has poured out for him!" (*IN* 111–12). The contrast between these charges and Equiano's earlier description of plentiful Eboe life in Essaka clarifies that the dehumanization of Africans stems from Eurocentric discourse rather than African realities. The reference to a "man" who is "left . . . alone scant and unfinished" alludes simultaneously to Goldsmith's racist depiction of the Samoids and, more tacitly, to the possessive individual whose human integrity depends on private property. The reference to "barren . . . moor" indexes domestic British geography and thus highlights the distance between British imagination and African realities.[46]

By placing Eboe "bounties" and "treasures" beyond European knowledge, Equiano challenges the hierarchic Eurocentric order that distinguishes lands, climates, and populations from one another. The wealth and fertility of Africa's soil become a metaphor for the strength and creativity of African minds while Equiano simultaneously implies that pluriversal "learning" and "culture" may be more valid than Eurocentric universal exclusions. This process resists Eurocentric constructions of America and Africa as places defined by degrading wildness or savagery. Whereas the discourse of natural history developed by such writers as Buffon and the Abbè Raynal attributed degradation to America's physical climate and soil, Equiano roots degradation in the social and cultural climate of enslaving colonization, thus tacitly freeing the land from such negative connotations. When "a British seaman" protects him from violent robbery, for instance, Equiano writes that his protector's "heart had not been debauched by a West India climate" (*IN* 108). Equiano responds to Eurocentric "binary geographies" by insisting that societies are shaped by human agency rather than by the degrading spatial conditions imagined by environmental determinists.

This is the backdrop for Equiano's first resettlement project, which he develops in relation to his involvement in "cultivating a plantation at Jamaica and the Musquito Shore" (*IN* 202) in the hope that cooperation among African and central American Indigenous peoples may ameliorate the evils of colonial slavery. This project is facilitated by slavery's economy—it begins when Equiano buys slaves for the plantation—but he simultaneously tries to mitigate slavery's imposition of negative birthright by choosing his "own countrymen" in order to reassemble a Native African community in America (IN 205, 211). That such communal rehabilitation can be attempted within slavery may sound counterintuitive, but Equiano attempts to reconstruct an Indigenous environment that would replace colonial hierarchies with reciprocal, nonexploitative partnership. Rather than invading or expropriating Indigenous space, Equiano and his employer, Dr. Charles Irving, tell the "native Indians" that they "come to dwell amongst them" and, in doing so, tacitly accept Indigenous governance. Musquito leaders acknowledge this initiative and invite Equiano to choose a plantation site from various prospective locations on their homeland (IN 205).

As Nicholas Rogers shows, mutual interest in preventing Spanish colonization motivated cooperation between the English and the Musquito Indians.[47] Lisa Lowe writes that Musquito relations to slavery were more complex than Equiano suggests, because "Mosquitos were occasionally captured along with African slaves and sold in Jamaica, while they too often raided and traded African slaves." Lowe's analysis of this part of the text prioritizes the Native/settler binary. She argues that Equiano's narrated experiences allegorize "the degree to which liberal abolition reiterates settler colonialism, erasing indigenous difference."[48] Lowe refers particularly to Equiano's emphasis on the similarities between Musquito and African practices. Equiano likens Musquito musical instruments with "those of any other sable people," finds similarities between Musquito and Eboe dance, and appreciates the Musquito community's voluntary help in building houses for the new plantation, "exactly like the Africans" would have done (IN 209, 206). However, David Kazanjian explains "Equiano's complex understanding of Indian and African affiliation" by the fact that "the Miskitos were well known at the time as an Afro-Indian people."[49] It seems, then, that in this case the Native/settler binary does not recuperate an obliterated history but performs its own erasures.

Instead of arguing over these categories it might be more productive to place this part of the *Interesting Narrative* in the context of Equiano's broader search for non-Eurocentric foundations for global human relations and his critical engagement with the "barbarians" and natural slaves that justified Eurocentric genocidal racism. From this perspective we might appreciate Equiano's attempt to redefine the common ground among "those who are called barbarian." Equiano's emphasis on similarities may be read as an attempt to revise a host of imperial constructs, including settler colonialism, slavery, and the conditions by which various non-European people(s) could relate to one another. Equiano's erasure of differences between arrivants and Indigenous peoples in the Americas bridges the gaps that imperial interests have created between these people(s) and enables him to affirm that arrivants' "original free African state" may survive the Middle Passage.

This reconfiguration of the colonial enterprise is conditioned by a revised perception of the land and the social relations it supports. Although Equiano represents Musquito land as unimproved wilderness whose planting necessitates the replacement of its "woods" with "different kinds of vegetables," and although this wilderness threatens the colonial project, such threats are associated neither with Musquitos nor with slaves. And although the woods reverberate with the "hideous roaring" of "wild beasts," "none of them ever hurt" the colonists, "except [for] poisonous snakes," whose "bite . . . the Doctor used to cure" (*IN* 205). This is a far cry from colonial perceptions of wild carnivorous animals as quintessentially harmful creatures that had to be destroyed so that wild land could be improved. Colonial Virginia, for example, repeatedly enacted laws that rewarded colonists (and Indigenous people) for killing wolves in order to protect colonial cattle.[50] By contrast to the Virginia legislature's view of the local fauna as a potentially unsettling threat to the colonial project, Equiano presents it as an acceptable part of his resettlement scheme.

Equiano's non-Eurocentric resettlement model differs from two prevalent discursive constructs by which Eurocentric writers registered their discontent with the imperial practices that enabled their works: Mary Louise Pratt calls one of these modes "anti-conquest," and Renato Rosaldo defines the other as "imperialist nostalgia." Pratt defines the "anti-conquest" as "a utopian, innocent vision of European global authority," by which natural history writers imagined they could take "possession" of colonized spaces, peoples, and species "without subjugation and violence," as though the discursive practices by which they translated lived experiences into objects of science were neither violent nor crucial for solidifying imperial domination.[51] Rosaldo explains "imperialist nostalgia" as the experience of those "agents of colonialism" who "mourn the passing of what they themselves have transformed" and thus deny their own responsibility for the consequences of imperial violence.[52] Pratt and Rosaldo study these modes of imperial thought by focusing on writers who were committed to Eurocentric universalism and its progressive schemes. By contrast, Equiano's resettlement project attempts to recuperate the mutually nourishing relations between land and people that he uses to portray Eboe life and that colonization threatens to annihilate.

This resettlement project was short lived, because the nominal Christianity that characterized the European members of the resettled community introduced into it the Eurocentric vices that Equiano sought to overcome.

Instead of offering an alternative sociopolitical order that would replace slaveholding colonization, the Musquito Coast gradually became a place of white "heathenism" because the whites, Equiano charges, were not "more pious than th[e] unenlightened Indians." At this point Equiano actually differentiates Musquitos from Eboes by attributing to the former no distinct spiritual order within which the settlement could have thrived. In the absence of such order, the plantation community lost its sense of time and history, and Equiano deserted it when he realized the white people around him could not tell "one day from another" (*IN* 210, 206–7). By highlighting the temporal aspect of this spatial venture, Equiano represents European colonization as a project that defies both religious ethics and the foundations of Christian and human history. In representing the failure of this resettlement project, Equiano attributes dehumanized historical degradation to the colonial impulse rather than to Indigenous peoples or arrivants. Finally, the site of his resettlement project is reshaped by the conventional plantation slavery that overtakes it. Equiano writes that following his desertion of the place, the "white overseer" who had replaced him abused the Native African slaves he had purchased, and they eventually died while trying to escape the plantation, which was thus left "uncultivated" (*IN* 217–18).

This chain of events seems to reaffirm the colonial convention that slave codes promoted: that the cultivation of plantations in the Americas could not be done without slaves. However, Equiano formulates the founding and eventual failure of this project by revising colonial relations between land and people, and he attributes that failure to the social and legal climate that cultivates slavery and to European colonists' lack of responsibility for land and people. This failure led Equiano back to Africa as a site of resettlement that would abolish slavery rather than ameliorate it.

Africa's Future

Equiano eventually abandoned colonial slavery and moved to London, where he promoted abolitionism and turned his resettlement plans toward Africa. In 1787 he worked for the establishment of Sierra Leone, but he was deprived of his position in that enterprise after protesting against the racist policies that guided it. This experience might have led him to look more intensively for nonracist resettlement that would enable him to develop the sociopolitical reform to which he was committed.

To prepare for Africa's post-slavery future, Equiano advocates the replacement of the slave trade with benign mercantile relations between Africa and England. This resettlement project would focus on transforming the routes and commodities that define imperial trade and would reinstate

Africans as Indigenous peoples who would remain in Africa and thus avoid the fate of arrivants. Equiano imagined this project as part of a reformed, beneficial British imperial domination. To make this proposal palatable to English readers, Equiano argues that abolition would serve British economic interests and promises that Britain would continue to profit from its slave-free imperial power. In this cyclical project, Britain would extract resources from Africa, process them in England, and sell the finished products in Africa. Consequently, Africans would become "civilized" by consuming English goods (*IN* 235).[53] The project therefore tacitly accepts a definition of barbarism as a condition of lack that the goods of British civilization may undo, yet Equiano structures the proposal to subvert such perceptions.

Like Equiano's manners-and-customs description, this offer has been read as a capitulation to English colonial discourse. Wheeler translates this argument to "what we would now call imperial colonialism" and compares it to "current government and World Bank" projects, while Tanya Caldwell states that this proposal "reveals the thoroughly European nature of his mind" in that Equiano "proposes strengthening the system of which he is part by offering up Africa to the forces of British trade."[54] But the condition of possibility for this proposal reveals much more: such trade can only materialize, Equiano states, if "the blacks were permitted to remain in their own country" (*IN* 235). If we examine this proposal as a subaltern response to the effects of colonial history, we can see Equiano negotiating for the one crucial condition that would ensure abolition of the transatlantic slave trade within a system of imperial constraints. The core of his resettlement project is Indigenous African rootedness. With this focus in mind it is possible to frame Equiano's proposal in terms of the moral principles he advocates in other parts of the book, including communal well-being, affirmative attachment to land, and the global protection of exploited peoples within a new geopolitical order that would prevent the inherent dehumanization of Eurocentric universalism.

Equiano first worked on this proposal by intervening in England's imperial policy. He published the proposal in a letter to Charles Jenkinson, Lord Hawkesbury, president of the Board of Trade, on March 13, 1788, as the Privy Council's Board of Trade was reviewing the slave trade. Having submitted a request to testify before the board, and been denied, Equiano sought a way to make his voice heard. At the end of that month he published another version of this proposal, in the *Public Advertiser*.[55] Finally, he included a third version of the proposal in his *Interesting Narrative*.[56] The most significant differences among these versions are in pronoun usage; in the earliest one, Equiano writes as a former government official who mediates the distance between the ancient "aborigines of Britain" and contemporaneous Native Africans by identifying with the former, whom he calls "our Forefathers" (*IN* 335).[57] In the two subsequent versions, he utilizes his public role as African-descended activist and refers to Britain's ancient Aboriginal peoples in the third person, as "their forefathers" (*IN* 233). Such shifts, which are paralleled in the manners-and-customs descriptions of his book, testify to the difficulty of presenting African pasts and futures in a world dominated by slavery and its imposition of the category "negro"; they suggest the limits of Equiano's geopolitical vision, as though he worked within the framework of imperial policy because he could not imagine that this framework could be overcome or replaced by an alternative order. His use of the mercantile civilizing mission parallels his use of the Bible: in both cases he appropriates global imperial aspirations for economic and religious domination in order to promote the extension of human equality and freedom beyond the limits of Eurocentric thought.

The most intriguing aspect of this process is Equiano's use of Africans' exclusion from free market relations—ostensibly the core of their status as "barbarians"—to support his proposal. "There are no Book or outstanding Debts," Equiano writes about Africa in the two versions he omits from his book; "[t]he Word Credit is not to be found in the African Dictionary" (*IN* 335). This reassuring statement begins by affirming the absence of literacy, which his readers may expect, but Equiano then twists this colonial convention to imply that the economic order of African societies may offer a stable alternative to European ones. Equiano's invocation of the "African dictionary" debunks the idea of African epistemological destitution and affirms a pluriversal view of human values. To emphasize the false foundations of Eurocentric racism, Equiano manipulates the idea of barbarian lack and reduces civilization to the production, marketing, and consumption of clothing. This tactic facilitates his proposal (in all three versions) that the slave trade be replaced by a clothing trade that would meet the needs of both British manufacturers and African consumers. To erode the hierarchies between civilizing producers and would-be civilized consumers, Equiano stresses mutual benefit. His proposal, he writes both in the *Interesting Narrative* and in the *Public Advertiser*, "opens up a most immense, glorious, and happy prospect—the clothing, &c. of a continent ten thousand miles in circumference, and immensely rich in productions of every denomination in return for manufactures" (*IN* 235). This promotional text inverts assumptions of barbarian nakedness by engaging them. It represents Africa as an "immensely rich" region interested in seeing a "return" for its participation in imperial projects rather than as passive recipient or victim of British enterprise.[58]

Equiano establishes the economic profitability of his proposal by arguing that the value of "the manufacturing interest is equal, if not superior, to the landed interest" (*IN* 234) and highlights Africa's size as a potentially immense plantation-free market for British goods. The single condition for his proposal—that Africans be "permitted to remain in their own country"—highlights their ownership of the land, which suggests self-determination even as they would become consumers of English commodities. This idea undergirds Equiano's argument that the "abolition of slavery" would be a "universal good," based on the idea that each region would enjoy its own form of locally specific "good" (ibid.).

Like Equiano's discussion of Barbados's slave law, all three versions of his mercantile proposal contrast such "universal good" to slavery's "barbarity" (*IN* 234). By invoking the commodities manufactured exclusively for enslavement—"neck-yokes, collars, chains, hand-cuffs, leg-bolts, drags, thumb-screws, iron-muzzles, and coffins; cats, scourges, and other instruments of torture"—Equiano distinguishes malicious commerce from benevolent one and correlates this distinction with his earlier differentiation between "landed" and "manufacturing" interests (ibid.). Most English manufacturers, he states, should "unit[e] in the cause" of abolition because those engaged in manufacturing tools of torture subvert the presumably universalizing spirit of free trade. This vision represents universal benefit as historical inevitability necessitated by the idea of universal reason: "In a short time one sentiment alone will prevail," Equiano writes, "from motives of interest as well as justice and humanity" (ibid.). This reference to universal reason leads Equiano to consider Eurocentrism as a mistake that allows its followers to omit the interests and worldviews of Africans from global affairs despite their numerical majority: "Europe contains one hundred and twenty millions of inhabitants," Equiano asserts, in order to ask rhetorically, "How many millions doth Africa contain?" (ibid.). While the immediate context for this comparison is potential market size, the question also implies that geopolitical divisions must not obstruct pluriversal human rights. The focus on populations counted by the millions suggests that numerical plurality requires plural interpretations of human possibilities. This question parallels Equiano's earlier invocation of the "shock" that Barbados's slave law would induce in "a Samaide and a Hottentot." I now turn to Equiano's last resettlement plan; in it, he imagined his own return to Essaka, which he represented as his native valley.

Hosting Britons in Africa

Between June 1788 and 1790, following the publication of both Equiano's proposal for slave-free trade relations and his book, as well as the parliamentary discussions that led to the passage of the Slave Trade Regulation

Act limiting the number of slaves per voyage, Equiano continued to advocate for reorganized imperial relations.[59] He published letters expressing his gratefulness to members of Parliament and subscribers to his book, whom he aspired to host in his African "estate." Like the former plan, which was contingent upon the condition that Africans would "remain in their own country" (*IN* 235), this one depends on Equiano's restoration to his "lost estate."[60] This individualized resettlement fantasy promises to reconcile property relations with generous communal attachment and turns Equiano's English guests into consumers of African produce, in contrast to the larger-scale conversion of Africans into consumers of English goods. Rather than the source of raw material in need of English manufacturers, Africa becomes the origin of a new, liberating Enlightenment within its future reciprocal relations with England. In the first version of this text, addressed to the Senate and published in the *Public Advertiser* on June 19, 1788, Equiano promises to entertain his visiting senators with "a libation of pure virgin palm-wine" and monumentalize them by "erect[ing] two altar[s]—one to Pity—the other to Freedom—to perpetuate their benevolence to my countrymen" (*IN* 340). Here the returning African host and his English guests use African raw materials to reshape Africa's cultural memory and landscape in honor of English abolitionists.

The second version of this fantasy, published in the *Cambridge Chronicle* on August 1, 1789, expands Equiano's role as the host who shapes his guests' African experiences. In addition to entertaining his visitors with "the richest [African] produce," Equiano promises to "burn a certain kind of tree that would afford us a light, as clear and brilliant as the virtues of my guests."[61] This African source of new enhanced "light" refutes perceptions of a benighted Africa in need of European enlightenment. By conditioning this idea on his "restor[ation]" to his "lost estate," Equiano emphasizes the history that robbed him of his "original free African state" and turned him into an arrivant. He expresses his desire to regain the liberating status of an Indigenous African by redefining his "native country" as both his origin and a destination where he would welcome his readers as visitors rather than invaders. The third version of this vision (published in the *Aris's Birmingham Gazette* on June 28, 1790 and addressed to subscribers to his book) reproduces this formulation (*IN* 352).

How seriously should we take such promises by an Englishman of African descent who never returned to Africa and eventually bequeathed his estate in England to his English-born daughters? John Bugg reads Equiano's fantasy as a rhetorical ploy designed to "defuse the trouble" that an outspoken African-descended activist might have caused an English audience.[62] But Equiano performs this hospitality as a token of gratitude *following* his encounters with his addressees. Had Equiano believed there was "trouble" to "defuse" by such performance, he should have considered this prior to his speaking engagements rather than in their wake. Whereas Bugg reads Equiano as a person who "[s]elf-consciously theatricaliz[es] himself" after having "learned . . . how much public approbation this familiarized exoticism might generate," I suggest that this performance of African native status exceeds self-exoticization. Like the Mohegan Samson Occom, who was "quite Willing to become a Gazing Stock, yea even a Laughing Stock" during his fundraising tour of Britain *on the condition that* such sacrifice would promote the education of Native children,[63] Equiano might have accepted the exoticization that a British audience imposed on him in order to promote his abolitionist cause. The question here is what constitutes exoticism, and who evaluates it. Occom suggested that he could not avoid it because British audiences read him as exotic regardless of his actions, and the same might be true of Equiano's reception as well.

Equiano's performance parallels his acceptance of the generic conventions of manners-and-customs descriptions and his offering up of Africa for English trade. He addresses a self-consciously diasporic vision to the powers that shape the diasporas that produced him, and yet he promises an African Enlightenment that would emerge spontaneously from Africa's soil and be directed by an Indigenous African no longer constrained by English law. Instead of dismissing Equiano's expressions of back-to-Africa sentiments as mere rhetoric, we may consider the conditions under which he recurrently worked on these plans and kept offering them to his readers. He attempted to rechart geopolitical relations by overcoming the legacies of negative birthright that his readers believed were the natural historical lot of African "barbarians." Within this reality, Equiano worked on the fault lines between the possibilities he offered and the convictions and expectations of his readers.

The next chapter moves from Equiano's imagined Africa to Mohegan, an Indigenous homeland in present-day Connecticut. Equiano's contemporary Mohegans tried to distinguish their indigeneity from the conditions of arrivants in resistance to settlers' arguments that marriages with members of settler and arrivant populations had already or would soon annihilate Mohegan as an Indigenous polity and extinguish any Native rights Mohegans might have held. Despite the contrast between Equiano's attempt to fuse the predicaments of Indigenous peoples and arrivants in order to propose a future pluriversal equality and Mohegans' attempts to exclude arrivants from their communities, Equiano's Mohegan contemporaries shared with him a perception of resettlement as a strategy for mitigating the horrific consequences of the imperial invasions that threatened their homeland. However, whereas Equiano's resettlement projects attempted to redeem African-descended people from the fate of arrivants by protecting their Indigenous inhabitance rights, Samson Occom and Joseph Johnson—the Mohegans who helped realize the resettlement project that resulted in the establishment of Brothertown—envisioned it simultaneously as a project that would unsettle imperial power over their communities.

[2]

MOHEGAN NATIVE RIGHTS

OLAUDAH EQUIANO'S LONG-TERM attempts to realize what he called his "original free African state" within imperial parameters partially resembled settlers' claimed entitlement to the rights of freeborn English subjects. But while Equiano clarified that full recovery of such a "state" would be best achieved through inhabitation in a post-slavery Africa, settlers saw their portable positive birthrights as commensurate with the British Empire. From the early days of English colonization and well into the Revolutionary era, settlers used *Calvin's Case* to claim their portable positive birthrights, which were often rooted in fictional English births. In 1662, Connecticut's royal charter promised that all English persons who would settle there and all their children who "shall happen to be born there" would "enjoy all liberties and immunities of free and natural [English] subjects . . . as if they and every one of them were born within the realm of England."[1] A century later, Connecticut settlers responded to Britain's 1774 Coercive Acts by claiming "the rights, privileges, and immunities of Freeborn Englishmen . . . as fully and amply as if they and every of them [*sic*] were born within the realm of England."[2]

During this hundred-year period, as Connecticut settlers continued to imagine English births as their sources of entitlement in America, they learned of a local, anti-imperial logic of Indigenous rights that was rooted in attachment to, responsibilities for, and protection of Indigenous homelands from settler encroachments. One of the earliest Anglophone discourses of Indigenous rights to which settlers were exposed developed in Mohegan, which had been threatened by settler expansion since the establishment of Connecticut in the 1630s. This chapter analyzes that discourse by focusing on its emergence in texts representing the words and actions of Mohegan sachem Owaneco (1640–c.1712) and its subsequent development in texts by the Mohegan ministers, teachers, and leaders Samson Occum (1723–92) and Joseph Johnson (1751–c.1777). This discourse and the Mohegan struggles in which it emerged crystallized its discrepancy with English birthright theories, which depended on the objectification of colonized land through which royal sovereignty was extended over vast geographic regions. Conversely, the Mohegan Native rights discourse that links Owaneco, Occom, and Johnson—like all the rights claims of Indigenous peoples discussed in this book—emphasized particularistic spatial locales with which the people maintained interdependent relations. Such interdependence meant that neither the land nor the people were a fixed given because both existed as interactive, meaningful entities through ongoing practices that preceded colonization and that had to be maintained despite colonization in order to protect forms of inhabitation that produced peoplehood.

For Owaneco, Occom, and Johnson, freedom could not be detached from inhabitation because it was a function of attachment to the communal birthplace. By making this argument in resistance to colonial dispossession, they turned Mohegan into a prominent site where simultaneous, relational, contradictory rights discourses developed through violent conflicts prior to the US, French, and Haitian revolutions. In the written Anglophone archive representing these processes, the Mohegan words that Owaneco spoke and that settlers rendered in English appear rudimentary next to Occom's and Johnson's elaborate English texts on Mohegan past, present, and future. I therefore focus primarily on the work of the latter two men and treat the former as important predecessor.

Mohegan's situation vis-à-vis the settler project explains why this polity provides a glimpse into an early shift in Anglophone discussions of rights. Mohegan was allied with the New England colonies and fought on their side in the Pequot War (1638), and its leaders represented themselves as equal partners of the English. Such equality was supported by the idea that Mohegan political freedoms could not be subsumed under English discursive conventions because they had emerged from Mohegans' relations to their homeland.[3] In 1704, struggles over that homeland and the freedoms it supported made Mohegan the first Indigenous people to challenge an English colony's claim to its land by petitioning the English Crown. Seven decades later the protracted legal battle of the Mohegan land case ended with England's validation of Connecticut's claim to Mohegan lands.[4] England thus upheld settlers' demotion of Mohegan native title to an inferior foundation of proprietorship dwarfed by the "radical" or "paramount" title of the Crown to which every other claim was necessarily subordinated.[5] Even when settlers recognized Mohegan prior rights to its homeland, they perceived these rights as extinguishable and anticipated the tribe's eventual disappearance—either spontaneously or through the admission of free blacks as equal members that would enable settlers to claim that Mohegan ceased to exist as a Native community.[6] In 1662, following the restoration of the English monarchy, Connecticut settlers secured King Charles II's royal charter, which gave Connecticut a territory that included all of Mohegan's ancestral lands and vast western regions reaching as far as the Pacific Ocean.[7] Thus, by the early 1770s, the Mohegan land case was a top-priority item on the tribe's agenda, whereas Connecticut saw it as an almost negligible annoyance and focused instead on competing with Pennsylvania over the Wyoming Valley. Connecticut settlers and officials argued that the royal charter gave them a large portion of Pennsylvania and purchased Wyoming Valley lands from Native sellers, while claiming exclusive right to the land. They represented Indians as rightless communities, foreign to the English knowledge that established entitlement, in order to reduce Indigenous relation to the land to an extinguishable condition.[8]

Under the charter, settlers established and expanded New London, Norwich, and Colchester into Mohegan planting, fishing, and hunting grounds that previous agreements and treaties had reserved or entrusted for Mohegan's exclusive use.[9] Mohegan sachems Uncas and his son Owaneco tried to protect tribal lands by entrusting and selling portions both to their Pequot War ally Major John Mason and to the colony in the hope of controlling colonial access to the land, while settlers argued that such cessions entitled them to the tribe's lands.[10] By the late eighteenth century, following significant settler expansion into the Mohegan homeland, and especially following Mohegan's legal defeat in London, Johnson and Occom had started working on the resettlement project that led to the founding of Brothertown on Oneida land.

Whereas arrivant resettlement projects such as Equiano's were framed within imperial parameters, Brothertown encompassed a resettlement mechanism within a larger unsettlement vision. While it drew on settlers' economic and racial norms, Brothertown was facilitated by spatial practices of Oneida, Mohegan, and other Indigenous peoples. Most importantly, the Brothertown project should not be understood as an abandonment of Mohegan, because the unsettlement aspects of its founding included ongoing relations with Mohegan. Brothertown was established through a complex, highly ironic process of voluntary removal. Occom and Johnson embarked on this project because they were convinced that settler encroachments in New England posed serious threats to the survival of Indigenous polities. The policies of eliminatory settler colonialism curbed Mohegan's inhabitation practices, and Occom's and Johnson's work suggests that they turned to planned diaspora as the means for reestablishing such spatial communal responsibilities and protecting them from settler control. Occom's and Johnson's work on Brothertown critiqued settlers' dichotomous view of Native spatiality, which contrasted intensive attachment to particular places with absolute nomadism devoid of any settled practice. Settlers viewed both images as symptoms of savagery and used them to justify dispossession and removal; Occom and Johnson formulated the Brothertown project in resistance to these ideologies. They envisioned the relations between Indigenous communities in New England and those that relocated to Oneida as a dynamic form of self-determination that refuted both nomadism and the idea of fixed, ahistorical attachment to land.

By framing the Brothertown project as voluntary removal, Occom and Johnson responded ironically to settlers' perceptions of Indians. Like Equiano's redeployments of the barbarian, their engagement with settler spatial discourses, including the prediction of Natives' imminent disappearance, was highly ironic. This irony was necessary because Mohegan rights clashed with Anglophone imperial discourse that denied the existence of Mohegan knowledge. Irony enabled Mohegan leaders to intervene in settler discourses without embracing their presuppositions. Settler encroachments were based on the idea that Eurocentric epistemologies were the only tool by which Indigenous peoples may be known and governed, so Mohegans had to invest in ironic representations of their rights and the knowledge systems in which they were embedded. It is also ironic that Mohegan, which formulated an early Anglophone discourse of Indigenous rights, was also the polity whose leaders had to turn to resettlement to save their people from settlers' elimination efforts. This chapter thus examines the ironies, reversals, and inconsistencies by which Mohegan Native rights developed in the eighteenth century.

These ironies, then, were necessitated by settlers' violent self-representations as carriers of portable English birthright on Mohegan land, and by their insistence that Indians lacked any form of entitlement, knowledge, or history that did not derive from settler discourses. The creative irony that Occom and Johnson used to elaborate on the idea of Mohegan Native rights enabled them to formulate the significance of spatial and temporal conditions of inhabitation and belonging that settler thought denied systematically. These spatial and temporal conditions tied unsettlement to resettlement in the Brothertown project, which could not be realized without settler approval. I argue that the discourse of Mohegan Native rights, which resulted in Brothertown's founding, illustrates how resettlement might potentially unsettle the colonial project by questioning the very terms of spatial belonging that settler colonialism imposes, including the confining attachment and forced migrations through which negative birthright has been imposed on Indigenous peoples and arrivants. This chapter thus oscillates between settler limitations and ironic Mohegan inversions and potentialities.

Occom's and Johnson's responses to the Crown's 1773 decision in the Mohegan land case illustrate the functions and necessity of irony in their resistance to settler power. Occom interpreted the decision with a bleak tautology: "the Poor Indians will never Stand a good Chance with the English, in their Land Controversies," he wrote, "because they are very Poor." He clarifies that poverty extends from economic to educational assets by asserting that besides having "no Money, . . . the Indians have no Learning, no Wit no Couning the English have all."[11] "Poor Indians" was a central trope of British missionary literature that helped mobilize support for Indian conversion, and Laura Stevens shows that it shaped the structures of feeling on which British imperialism developed.[12] Interpreting an earlier instance in which Occom used the "poor Indians" trope, Stevens writes that Occom's irony "detached the term from the compassion that originally produced it" and "reveal[ed] the abysmal treatment that such pity symbolized."[13] In the context of the land case, however, this irony rang louder because the British justified their efforts to dispossess Indigenous peoples by representing them as always already poor materially and intellectually. The "English ha[d] all," in other words, because the imperial system ensured their own enrichment at the expense of Indigenous peoples and arrivants.

In February 1774, Johnson concluded that "unless the Indians use proper Endeavours, to keep in Possession of their Native Liberty, in short time they will unavoidably be involved in that wretched state of perfect slavery, which every rational being dreads." He explained the Brothertown project as the means to prevent such "perfect slavery" by offering to "lead" his "poor Brethren in New England . . . out of Bondage . . . to a land of Liberty."[14] While Occom's "poor Indian" was an easily identifiable British trope, Johnson's "Native Liberty" suggests two simultaneous sources. On the one hand, the term resounded in revolutionary texts, yet on the other, "Native Liberty" was also embedded in an older discourse of Mohegan Native rights. Laura Murray interprets it as "some kind of basic indigenous right or custom," which harnesses the "rhetoric of colonial dissent,"[15] and Lisa Brooks substantiates the first part of Murray's interpretation by tracing "Native rights" to a 1700 text in which Owaneco and his brother Ben are reported to have complained of settler encroachments.[16] Below, I read that 1700 text as the origin of the written Anglophone discourse of Mohegan Native rights.

The irony of Johnson's "Native Liberty" lies in his insistence that the protection of Indigenous peoples' rights—especially self-determining inhabitation in the particular places that define their polities—required resettlement because these places have become lands of "Bondage." If Indigenous peoples stayed home in what has become New England, Johnson warned, settlers would try to reduce them to the condition of arrivants in order to appropriate the category "native" to themselves. It is even more ironic that when settlers needed the support of Indigenous people such as Johnson, they appropriated Indigenous rights discourses such as that which developed in Mohegan. During the Revolutionary War, settlers expected Johnson to help them secure Haudenosaunee (Iroquois) neutrality, casting their claims in the mold of Native grievances as though this rhetoric would persuade Johnson to serve colonial interests. By using this rhetorical tactic settlers who dispossessed Indigenous peoples expected them to sympathize with their own claimed dispossession. In January 1776, the New Hampshire assembly issued an official recommendation to assist Johnson's travels to the Haudenosaunee and protested King George III's efforts "to strip the Inhabitants of the Colonies of their native Rights & Privileges, and thereby to take . . . the produce of our Lands, our Trade and Fisheries from us" (*TDG* 279). Land and fishing rights were a persistent item on the political agendas of Indigenous peoples in New England because settlers targeted these sources of Indigenous livelihood. A month later, George Washington wrote Johnson that the British "want to rob us of our Lands and our Homes"—again, employing rhetoric that Indigenous peoples used in their grievances and protests of settlers' dispossessive policies (*TDG* 281). Alan Taylor writes that the United States "hastened the dispossession of Indians and prolonged the enslavement of African Americans" in this period.[17] Settlers' claims for their native status in America fueled this development ideologically.

This chapter focuses on multidirectional, prevalent ironies that structured the petitional texts I analyze here. This category includes texts written as petitions to settler and imperial authorities as well as works that utilized the generic conventions by which petitions become intelligible as entreaties for urgently needed assistance under oppression. Petitions are subaltern documents whose subversive potential may "give way," as Lisa Brooks writes, "to satirical protest."[18] Their constitutive ironies stem from inherent tensions between deference and subversion: petitions must explicitly defer to hegemonic power while their writers present themselves as possessors of knowledge to which those in power are oblivious. Petitions thus have an instructional function that subverts dominant assumptions about knowledge and power. This function is often referenced by the verb *show*, which petitioners use to introduce their addressees to what they present as important yet repressed or disavowed truths. Thus, petitioners become bearers of uncommon knowledge because their addressees are initially ignorant of the urgent information they reveal. Petitions thus open up an instructional space that becomes ironic in the case of Indigenous petitions to colonial authorities.

Yet in juxtaposing the petitional texts that articulate the eighteenth-century discourse of Mohegan Native rights we must distinguish Owaneco's words that colonists translated and transcribed from the letters, journal entries, and of course, petitions that Occom and Johnson wrote without settler mediation. David Murray warns that the complexity of Native-English collaborations —such as those that enable Owaneco's claims to reach us—produces uncertainty regarding the precise involvement of Indigenous leaders who did not write English in the texts that claim to represent their words.[19] However, the translated texts that record Owaneco's words and deeds provide powerful precedents for considering Occom's and Johnson's texts within a broader discourse of Mohegan Native rights. Settlers' involvement in the production of texts associated with Mohegan does not necessarily discredit early Anglophone Mohegan expression.

Owaneco's, Occom's, and Johnson's texts teach their readers of Mohegan Native rights and articulate a nexus of birth, land, and freedom that subverts settler constructions of knowledge, history, property, and governance. Their writings offer a theory of inhabitation, attachment, and entitlement that redefines rootedness and diaspora in resistance to imperial orders by stressing temporal and spatial openness, continuation, and mobility. Rootedness in these texts is not a passive feature of life on ancestral homelands but a function of the responsibilities that accompany active inhabitation of the land.

The following sections begin with a discussion of Owaneco's early eighteenth-century formulations of Mohegan Native rights and the ironies that he employed to assert them in the face of Britain's imperial expansion. Then I discuss Occom's assertions of Mohegan knowledge as an epistemological foundation of rights that exists independently of settler claims. The chapter then examines the ironic trope of ancestral ignorance, which Johnson and Occom used in order to present the discrepancies and unintelligibilities between the struggle for Mohegan rights and settler encroachments. The chapter concludes with the ironies of resettlement and unsettlement in the inception of the project that created Brothertown.

However, before proceeding I would like to clarify that the ironic resistance presented by the Mohegan discourse of Native rights had one notable exception because in resistance to settler impositions, Mohegan leaders obeyed settlers' racial classifications. Settlers argued that arrivants' status as equal members of Indigenous communities justified settler possession of Indigenous lands. This argument proved an effective tool of Native dispossession in New England in the eighteenth and nineteenth centuries, and Occom responded to it officially at least twice. In 1773 he "spearheaded a Mohegan drive to expel any Indian women" who married non-Indians and "exclude the children of Negroes from inheritance rights in tribal property"; in 1789 he tried again to "exclude blacks from the Mohegan tribal registers."[20] Brothertown "denied membership" to people "of African American ancestry" from its inception;[21] its "agreements" with Oneida "barred the children of African-Americans or African-Native unions from land rights at Brothertown."[22] Mohegan and Brothertown thus offer explicit illustrations of settler pressures that effectively frustrated Indigenous-arrivant solidarities. This history enables us to interpret the mutually exclusive and exclusionary Native/settler and black/white binaries as products of the settler regime's divide-and-conquer approach to Indigenous and arrivant struggles against settler authority. Of all the writers and spokespersons discussed in this book, only Equiano articulated visions of Indigenous and arrivant solidarity that would potentially undermine that authority.

Mohegan vs. Colonial Native Rights

In protecting Mohegan "Native rights," Mohegan leaders countered the settler concepts of "native right" and "native title," which the imperial regime formulated as inferior to its monarch's "paramount" title. Settlers' claim for royal right to Indigenous peoples' homelands rested on a feudalist legal fiction that Blackstone defined as the "fundamental maxim and necessary principle" of all English property law, by which "the king is the universal lord and original proprietor of all the lands in his kingdom," which meant that no one could hold land anywhere in the royal realm unless the monarch granted them that right.[23] This legal fiction made feudalism foundational to English liberty; while in England proper it had primarily symbolic functions, in the colonies it had an immense impact on Indigenous peoples because it produced what political scientist Fae Korsmo calls a "colonial mythology" that bound "newcomers to the territory" at Indigenous peoples' expense and later facilitated what political scientist Taiaiake Alfred dubs "the myth of state sovereignty."[24] This process enabled English settlers to impose negative birthright on Indigenous peoples.

This legal fiction meant that once the kingdom had expanded to Indigenous peoples' homelands, such expansion necessarily subjected those lands to royal sovereignty. British law subordinated to itself any claim that preceded, challenged, or negated that sovereignty and demoted any other title to a weaker right whose respect depended on royal generosity. So while the term *native title* may seem like a translation of positive birthright in favor of Indigenous peoples, it was actually used to impose an extinguishable and therefore inherently negative birthright on Indians. Elizabeth Povinelli explains that native title was both alien to Indigenous peoples' conceptualizations of entitlement and far more limited than "the radical title the Crown claims at the moment of colonization."[25] Legal scholar Samantha Hepburn shows the significance of this logic for imperial expansion: "if the Crown was presumed to occupy the position of paramount lord," she writes, "it would hold complete ownership over all land *to the exclusion of any other*."[26] Next to such "complete ownership," legal scholar Gordon Bennett adds, native title is reduced to a "right of occupancy" whose "survival" depends on the Crown's "continued goodwill."[27]

Since the seventeenth century, Mohegan treaties and grievances fractured colonial discourse by distinguishing the inferior colonial constructs *native title* or *native right* from Mohegan-defined "Native rights" that challenged settler claims by mobilizing an independent discourse. Extant documents suggest that Owaneco might have been the first to make this claim in a written English text. In 1684, he tried to protect a portion of the tribe's homeland by transferring "any right" to it "unto ye Mohegen Indians," so that "neither I nor my son, nor any under him shall at any time make sale of any part thereof."[28] Owaneco must have understood settlers' faith in the idea that sachems were empowered to grant tribal lands, as he used settler legal forms to affirm tribal responsibility for Mohegan land. His phrase "any right" seems potentially to include both settler-defined property rights and the communal import of self-determination to which he would later refer by a phrase that settler interpreters would render as "Native rights." Five years later, Owaneco used "Native Right" in an English document that confirmed his father Uncas's post–Pequot War grant to Connecticut in the 1638 Treaty of Hartford. That treaty between Connecticut, the Narragansett, and the Mohegan was formulated in the service of settler interest and did not mention rights of Indigenous peoples, so "Native rights" appeared in it ironically—but the irony was at Mohegan's expense. Owaneco declared that he had "freely Given . . . all [his] Native Right" to Pequot land within the "Bounds of Stonington" to settler Samuel Mason and declared that he did not transfer such rights to another settler, George Denison.[29] This double affirmation and denial of two settlers' claims to Pequot or Mohegan land fits settler perceptions of native right as transferable title whose major function was to justify settler claims. Both the earlier deed and its confirmation are based on the idea that the right to Pequot land was transferred to the Native polities who conquered the Pequot in order to enable them to give it to settlers. "Native right" here is an extinguishable, alienable commodity that served settlers' interests. It is ironic precisely because it denies that Indigenous peoples' rights can exist independently of settler constructs.

A decade later, in 1700, Owaneco recontextualized this phrase and began redirecting the ironies of settler-Indigenous relations. Colonial officials examined Mohegan complaints about the establishment of Colchester on Mohegan lands and reported that when Owaneco and his brother Ben presented their grievances, they referred to their rights three times. First, the report mentions "that the whole grant of the said township is their proper Right and therefore ought not to be taken from them." By contrast to transferable native title, this "proper Right" is structured as the inalienable foundation of Mohegan existence. Then Owaneco and Ben explained that such inalienable rights preceded colonization, by protesting that Mohegans are "Injured in their just rights and possessions" because Colchester's settlers deny "their native Right which hath been of ansiant [ancient] standing."[30]

Owaneco's and Ben's differentiation between the rights that settlers may claim and precolonial Mohegan rights is the beginning of explicit disassociation between Native rights and colonial forms. Lisa Brooks argues that this document represents Indigenous rights as holding "greater weight" than colonial claims.[31] This "weight" stems from a particular perception of history that mobilizes precolonial knowledge and materiality to counter the shorter spans of settlers' historical positions vis-à-vis Indigenous peoples in the Americas. The "ansiant standing" of "native Right" positions that right beyond settler politics in a discursive tradition that settlers cannot interrupt. Owaneco developed this idea further in a 1703 letter he addressed to advocate Nicholas Hallam as Mohegan decided to address its grievances directly to England. The letter acquaints Queen Anne with "our Hereditary Right to ye Soyll and Royalltys of our Dominion & Territorys before the English came into ye Country," thus reproducing settler constructions of priority, inheritance, royalty, "dominion," and territory in order to claim enduring precolonial rights. But it departs from settler concepts in substantiating the 1700 claim to "native Right . . . of ansiant standing" within Mohegan history. Owaneco explains that "all due Loyallty & Obedience by our people is not conferred on us by the English, but by ye Gods" who "gave us a Token as an Earnest & pledge of our Happy Reign here."[32]

To substantiate this exclusive entitlement, Owaneco indicates that it is materialized in a "Strange Pipe"—which he (probably with the interpreter's clarifications) describes as "being like Ivory, with two Stemms to the Boll in ye Middle"—that Mohegans found long ago in their homeland on the "Beach at Seabrook."[33] The pipe is "strange" in the sense of irreproducible uniqueness, and Owaneco argues that it provides "Sufficient Evidence" for Mohegan's special relationship to its homeland. Owaneco adds that the pipe is a "strange Wonderment" that was "not made by Man" and that Mohegans have continuously "kept [it] choicer than Gold from Generation to Generation" since they first found it. Thus, the pipe represents the long history of continuous Mohegan inhabitation and attachment to its homeland. Owaneco clarifies that the pipe represents a logical order and foundation of rights that is distinct from English forms, saying that Mohegan has recently kept "A Bible and Sword" that King Charles II gave the tribe "in ye Treasury as choice as we do ye aforesaid Gods Pipe."[34]

Owaneco's pipe thus represents a historical order of no lesser validity but of much longer history than that symbolized by the English Bible and royal power. This history tacitly challenges the two influential sources of English rights vis-à-vis Indigenous peoples: the Bible, with which the divine source of the pipe competes for authority, and John Locke's theory of property, which excludes the "Indian" from history and governance. Whereas the Bible's power stems from its reproducibility and communicability, through which multiple communities across historical and spatial distances may claim it as their own originary narrative, the pipe signifies the exclusive belonging of a particular people to its specific homeland. From this perspective, the most important detail about the pipe is the place where it was found, because its localization encapsulates the rights it symbolizes or protects. Whereas the settler as possessive individual carries his rights over the regions he traverses, the pipe encapsulates Mohegans' irreproducible rights in and to their homeland.

Several months after Owaneco dictated this letter to Hallam and asked him to present it to England's Commissioners of Trade and Plantations, a London newspaper reported that "after he had given the Letter to Mr. *Hallum*, and before the latter set out for *England*," Owaneco "was reduced to so great Want, that in a Melancholly Fit he brought his Pipe to him and told him, That since his Land was all taken from him, he would keep his Pipe (the vain Ensign of Royalty) no longer, and he might take it over with him to *England* for a Token of the Distress he was in, so Mr. *Hallum* brought it over with him."[35]

By giving the pipe in protest to Hallam and asking him to take it to London, Owaneco reaffirmed its role as symbol of Mohegan rights and used it ironically to signify settler disregard of those rights. The same object that had previously symbolized Mohegan Native rights now equally symbolizes their loss, and Owaneco forces the English monarchs to recognize those rights by holding the "Token" that validates them. We have no direct access to Owaneco's words during the period in which he acquainted the English court with the pipe and then gave them the pipe itself, but the irony of his actions is hard to miss. Owaneco gives away that which by definition is inalienable and nontransferable, a pipe that represents the permanence of Mohegan's right to its homeland precisely because it represents the polity's long history on that land. He thus does what should have been impossible and inconceivable had Mohegans been able to protect their homeland against imperial powers and clarifies that the very gift encapsulates settlers' threat to Mohegan rights.

The logic of rights that the pipe represents contrasts sharply with English constructions of entitlement and landownership as products of royal will performed in language and recorded in writing. By giving it to Hallam, Owaneco suggests that the text of the letter he dictated is insufficient and that its textuality pales next to the historic materiality represented by the pipe. The logic of Mohegan rights expressed through the pipe also clashes with Locke's influential theory of property in *Two Treatises of Government* (1689), whose foundation is the objectification of land as worthless, passive means that must be subdued in order to produce property relations and monetary value. In Locke's theory, historical development depends on agricultural labor and trade by which farming landowners convert the soil's corruptible produce into durable currency and accumulate private property under the protection of civil government. Therefore, land that has yet to be connected to trade networks has neither value nor history.[36] Locke asks rhetorically, "What would a Man value . . . an Hundred Thousand Acres of excellent *Land*," even if it were "cultivated" and "stocked . . . with Cattle, in the middle of the in-land Parts of *America*, where he had no hopes of Commerce with other Parts of the World, to draw *Money* to him by the Sale of the Product? It would not be worth the inclosing."[37]

In the *Two Treatises*, Locke uses America to dramatize the history that leads to the creation of civil government. "In the beginning," he writes famously, "all the World was *America*, and more so than that is now; for no such thing as *Money* was any where known" (*TT* 319). Since America's past is the cradle of history, the Indigenous peoples who inhabit it must give way to the empires that supplant them in order for history to proceed. What Owaneco represents as Mohegan history thus has no role to play in the future, and Native poverty is not an effect of colonization but an originary condition that renders Indigenous attachment to the land either meaningless or degrading. Given "something that hath the *Use and Value of Money*," Locke writes, any "Man," including the hitherto destitute, "wild *Indian*," as Locke calls the abstract Indigenous person, "will begin presently to *enlarge his Possessions*" (*TT* 319, 305). In this absolutist historical logic, Locke assures his readers that "the Condition of Humane Life . . . necessarily introduces *private Possessions*" whose "*Preservation*" requires civil governments (*TT* 310, 368). Under this historical thesis, which enjoyed immense popularity in eighteenth- and nineteenth-century settler regimes, neither the rights not the polity that the pipe supported could exist.

The perspective of the mediated Mohegan cosmology that speaks to us through Owaneco's translated words—written less than two decades following the publication of Locke's famous works—shows that the Lockean logic of property and history fails to respect materially grounded entitlement to and responsibility for non-commodified land. The sharp contrast between Lockean thought and Owaneco's mediated representations of the pipe necessitates irony as the only means by which these two oppositional systems can be brought to bear on each other. Since the import of Owaneco's words was diametrically opposed to settler rights discourses, he could include their claims to power within his own speech only by subverting the foundations of his own rights in protest.

Settlers used Locke to refute Mohegan claims, but they failed to appreciate the ironies that undergirded those claims and represented them instead as unsuccessful imitations of English rights theories. One of the earliest writers to use Locke's *Two Treatises* in British America was John Bulkley, who happened to be one of the original proprietors of Colchester, whose establishment on Mohegan land had triggered the land case.[38] In 1725, Bulkley published a treatise on native rights that drew on Locke's theory of property in the *Two Treatises* in order to refute the idea of Native rights. Positioning Indian lives in a Lockean "state of nature," Bulkley reduces their "good right or title" to "here and there a *few spots*" that "they had separated and enclosed from the rest of the Country" and argues that Mohegan lacked "*any Established, Settled, common Law*" to regulate and protect any property its members might have had.[39] He quotes Locke to portray Indigenous peoples as ignorant even of the "*Law of Nature*" that governs the "*State of Nature*" in which they presumably live. Denying Native history, Bulkley writes that any "*Shadow*" of "*Civil Policy*" currently present among Indigenous peoples was "assumed by them . . . from an Humor *of conformity to us* their New Neighbours." Since the Natives of his text lack knowledge, law, and meaningful history, Bulkley argues that the idea of "*Native Right*" is "but a meer [*sic*] *Chimera of Fiction*."[40] Bulkley clarifies that the idea of Indigenous rights contradicts the very structure of knowledge on which his treatise is founded. Because Indigenous peoples have not "*Settled their Bounds* and the terms of *each Community* respectively"—i.e., because their entitlement is not based on enclosure—"all their Rights or Properties instantly become so Perplext and in the Dark that nothing can be Known or Determin'd upon them, and consequently *no good Title* possibly founded on them."[41]

This is a reminder that rights claims are always embedded in value systems. Whereas Locke argued that American lands "would not be worth the inclosing," Bulkley writes that Indigenous peoples' failure to enclose lands refutes their rights claims; both texts of imperial liberalism represent Indigenous value systems as lack of knowledge. Locke links property to knowledge in the *Two Treatises* and in *An Essay concerning Human Understanding* (1690), where he represents lack of possessions and learning as the fundamental condition of "Indian" life. Locke's theory is premised on the distinction between an individual subject ("Man") and the environment that allows that "Man" to acquire property and knowledge by "mixing" his powers (of labor or reflection) with the objects or impressions that populate his surroundings (TT 306).[42] Early in the *Essay*, Locke uses this distinction between Man and environment to define understanding as ownership's condition of possibility: "it is the *Understanding* that sets Man above the rest of sensible Beings, and gives him all the Advantage and Dominion, which he has over them" (EC 43). "Indians," for Locke, are "rational creatures" who have yet to "mix" their labor or reflection significantly with the environment, which they can thus neither own nor fully comprehend. Ostensibly ignorant of the value of money and stripped of communal relations, Locke's "*Indian*" has neither a right to America's lands nor any meaningful history or social existence (TT 316).

Locke solidifies the analogy between lack of property and lack of knowledge by classifying Indigenous peoples among "*Children, Ideots, Savages,* and the grossly *Illiterate*" (EC 64), who are considered to be incapable of self-government, so that the Crown's "radical title" can extend to their homelands uninterruptedly. Locke quotes colonial travel literature to link this idea to Indigenous peoples' ostensible lack of innate moral values. "They have not so much as a Name for God. . . . No Acknowledgment of any God, no Religion, no Worship," Locke writes of the "*Caribes*," of a "People in *Peru*," and of the "*Tououpinambos*" (EC 71).[43] Against this intellectual background, Occom began to discuss Mohegan knowledge, which later founded his ironic representations of Mohegans' ignorant ancestors.

Occom's Early Assertions of Mohegan Knowledge

In her sensitive analysis of Occom's petitions, Caroline Wigginton characterizes them as "concrete moments of intellectual sovereignty," and Occom achieves such "moments" by tying Mohegan intellectual traditions to Mohegan land claims.[44] One of Occom's earliest petitions (1764) addresses Sir William Johnson, the Crown's superintendent of Indian Affairs, to protest multidirectional colonial infringements of Mohegan rights. The land case was still dragging on and Mohegan leadership and communal life were divided between rival factions that disagreed over the best way to respond to Connecticut's pressures. Occom represents himself and his co-petitioners as those "few" who "[s]tand between the two parties" in an attempt to replace internal conflict with resistance to settler efforts to "render us as Cyphers in our own land" (CW 145).[45] The term *cyphers* targets colonial attempts to impose the feudalist landholding hierarchy on Mohegan. Within the colonial order, Mohegans who have neither bought nor received the land from the king may occupy any of the inferior ranks by which feudalism establishes a landlord's authority. They may be subinfeudated as vassals under a superior land-granting lord (see introduction), they may be tenants at will who may remain on lands defined retrospectively as Crown property as long as the Crown suffers them to do so (see chapter 6), or they may be serfs whose status is defined by forced attachment to a particular plot of land owned by their lord (see chapter 3). Occom rejects such feudalization of Mohegan rights by grounding tribal entitlement in a political tradition that preceded colonization.

"We have a Law and a Custom to make a Sachem over us Without the help of any People or Nation in the World," Occom writes Sir William Johnson, "and When he makes himself ^unworthy^ of his Station we put him down—ourselves" (CW 145).[46] Insisting that Mohegan political and legal traditions validate tribal land rights, and vice versa, Occom undermines colonial claims by asking "from whence [has Connecticut] got that Power or Whither they Can Maintain such Power Justly over us" (ibid.). Occom and his co-petitioners assert Mohegan independence of "any People or Nation," refuting English claims to exclusive rights over Mohegan lands and thus invalidating Connecticut's claims. The petitioners argue that the only source of leaders' power is communal responsibility for land and people, so any leader who neglects this responsibility is disqualified. Rhetorically asking "[w]ither it woud not be as well for ^us^ to be Without Sachem as With in Time to Come" (ibid.), they assert the independence of communal will and judgment over any single leader the colony might support or manipulate.

Occom's contributions to Mohegan leadership soon met with the censure of the settler religious establishment. In 1765, missionary officials forced Occom to apologize for his involvement in the land case, and in 1766 they sent him on a two-year fundraising tour of England that effectively removed him from intervening locally in the case. Occom wrote an ironic apology and continued his involvement in the land case from England.[47] But following his 1764 petition to Sir William Johnson that had earned him at least part of that censure, Occom did not write such direct public political statements until the 1770s; then, he would develop the ironic ancestral ignorance trope in contrast to his earlier investment in the assertion of Mohegan knowledge. However, his prospective son-in-law Joseph Johnson had begun developing that ironic trope even earlier, so I now turn to Johnson's writings from the late 1760s and early 1770s.

Memory and Forgetfulness in Oneida

Like Occom, Johnson spent years doing missionary work away from home, and these experiences proved crucial for both men's development of the resettlement/unsettlement project that materialized in Brothertown. Johnson developed his theory of attachment to Mohegan within a complex nexus of memory, forgetfulness, and ignorance over the distance between Mohegan and Oneida that enabled him to experience how the settler regime tried to replace Indigenous peoples' rootedness with diasporic longings. The relations between Algonquian and Haudenosaunee peoples that facilitated the founding of Brothertown can be neither subsumed under the category of Indian removal nor attributed exclusively to the missionary networks established by Occom's and Johnson's mentor, Eleazar Wheelock. Lisa Brooks shows that when Occom first arrived in Oneida in 1761 as a graduate of Wheelock, his visit served to continue older alliances rather than create new ones *ex nihilo*.[48] Wheelock was probably both unaware and uninterested in this history or its significance even though his own pedagogical institution, Moor's Indian Charity School, was a meeting place for Algonquian and Haudenosaunee students.[49] Wheelock was not interested in Indigenous histories or epistemologies; he expected his educational work to "purge all the Indian" out of his students and turn them into "Englishm[e]n."[50] But the Brothertown project and the missionary work that led to it were grounded in ideas of historical continuities that refuted settler constructions of Indigenous spatial practices and their past, present, and future import. Such continuities informed Johnson's perception of his role as missionary in ways that Wheelock could not anticipate.

Beginning in 1766, Johnson's career as a young missionary teacher gradually exposed him to the potential power of communal action that settler infringements had significantly disrupted in Mohegan. In the letters he sends to Wheelock from Oneida, the teenage Johnson formulates the origins of what he would later call "Native Liberty" and relates this process to systems of knowledge that debunk Wheelock's and Locke's convictions regarding Indians' intellectual deficiency. In 1767 the fifteen-year-old Johnson writes Wheelock that the Oneidas are "very kind" to him—"all that they have," he explains, "is free to me as one Born and brought up in the house" (TDG 64). His mission to Oneida provided Johnson with an experience of hospitable Indigenous sociality, which his letters portray as a corrective experience that enabled him—perhaps more freely than at home—to learn the value of maintaining Indigenous epistemologies and practices. Johnson's missionary experiences thus inverted the core assumptions of English missionary projects—that Indians were destitute intellectually and spiritually, and that only Christian teachings could remedy their deficiencies. This discrepancy between Johnson's education and his experiences might have triggered his development of ironic resistance to settler claims.

Wheelock refused to accept such experiences and fostered systematic pedagogical disappointment with his Native students by requiring them to perform humiliating confessional rituals.[51] In December 1768, the seventeen-year-old Johnson volunteered such a performance when his social life in Oneida clashed with Wheelock's teachings. Johnson wrote that he had "been guilty of the most heinous Sins" by having "indulged myself in Brutish Ease whilst in the wilderness" (*TDG* 76). The next day, missionary Samuel Kirkland informed Wheelock that Johnson seemed tired of "puritanic *Relig[ion]*" and had "turn'd pagan for about a week—painted, sung, danc'd—drank and whor'd it, w[ith] some of the savage Indians he could find." Kirkland used the occasion to ask Wheelock to stop sending Indian schoolteachers because they may be possessed by the "Indian Devil."[52] When Johnson refers to his acts as "heinous Sins" he seems to accept Wheelock's dichotomy of Indian vices and English virtues, but he complicates it by augmenting this confession with that which he offered to his hosts.

By contrast to Wheelock's demand for constant acknowledgment of sins, the Oneida provide forgiveness through oblivion and thus associate ignorance with benevolence. "I publicly made Confession as is their Custom," Johnson writes, and "they promised as it were to Bury in Oblivion and let things be as if it never happened so" (*TDG* 76). Having lost face, fearing losing Wheelock's favor and perhaps already concerned about the loss of Mohegan lands back home, Johnson experiences Oneida as a recuperative, comforting social environment and expresses his wish to enjoy both Oneida and Protestant forms of absolution as he acknowledges non-Christian social healing processes. He presents Oneida ethics that utilize ignorance as a social mechanism through which the community takes responsibility for the welfare of its members. Johnson dubs this letter a "humble petition," focuses on the repentant pain of having sinned, and begs for Wheelock's "Incouragement." Knowing by experience that Wheelock rarely responds to his students' letters, Johnson adds that if Wheelock rejects this request he may be forced to "depart" from the colonial authority that Wheelock represents and seek the protection of Indigenous "Custom[s]" instead (ibid.).

By concurrently seeking Christian and Oneida forms of absolution, Johnson expresses his willingness to judge each value system in light of the other—an intellectual initiative that contradicts his education at Wheelock's school and facilitates his complex integration of Christianity with Indigenous ethics. This process leads him away from Wheelock, and in a subsequent letter, from 1769, Johnson petitioned his former teacher for liberty. "I came up to petition to you my Ever Hon[ore]d Benefactor," he writes, "that as my mind is wholly Bent from here, that thou would So much Condescend as to discharge one from Under you" (*TDG* 78). By arguing that his "mind is wholly Bent from here" Johnson suggests that minds orient themselves to spaces that ground their volition, moral choices, value systems, and beliefs. Johnson's language in this letter reproduces requests for relief from "guardians" in the petitions that Indigenous peoples in New England submitted to colonial authorities. Such petitions often exposed guardians' presumed benevolence as a pretense that barely disguised systematic exploitation of Indigenous resources.[53] In place of such oppressive guardianship Johnson asks Wheelock for forgetful forgiveness similar to that which he received in Oneida. "Be pleased to forgive what I have done and bury me in deep forgetfullness and Remember me no more," he writes, trying to educate his teacher in benevolent ignorant consolation (ibid.). In this context, Johnson developed the ancestral ignorance trope over the final years of his brief life.

Ignorance and Communal Responsibility in Johnson's Texts

One of Johnson's earliest references to ancestral ignorance appears in a February 1773 journal entry that includes his "fare well" sermon to Farmington, a Native town in Connecticut where he ran a school for Indigenous youths and preached to the community. In that sermon, Johnson exhorts his listeners to the Christian faith by assuming the voice of biblical prophets while developing his version of spiritual history: "This is the God whom Our fathers Disobeyed, & Provoked, and were Ignorant of, and are Destroyed" (TDG 166). By implicitly comparing his audience's ancestors to exiled Israelites, Johnson positions those ancestors as a dispossessed chosen people whose sins were punished by destruction that therefore manifests their destiny of eventual spiritual—and perhaps earthly—redemption. The charge of ignorance follows those of disobedience and provocation, suggesting that the former two charges may be read ironically, which would mean that the destruction of his listeners' ancestors was not justified. Johnson alludes to biblical injunctions against visiting the fathers' sins upon their sons and discusses ancestral ignorance as a crucial factor in the history of colonial dispossession, although he interprets past events and their present consequences differently in various texts by applying them to discrepant systems of accountability and agency.

For example, when several months later Johnson writes Connecticut governor Jonathan Trumbull requesting financial assistance to help defray the expenses of his school, he suggests that Indigenous peoples are responsible for their own dispossession by contrasting his present investment in Indigenous education with a past of ancestral sins that led to colonial disrespect of Indians. "My forefathers, the Natives of this land, brought this disrespect upon themselves," Johnson writes as he imagines colonial relations in similar terms to his relations with Wheelock. "When your forefathers intreated them as brothers, and . . . declared unto them the mind and will of God," he tells Trumbull, "they paid no regard" and consequently "these days many are walking in the same beaten track of their fore fathers, the Savages." Taking upon himself to confess what he represents as ancestral sins in order to gain settler absolution, he adds that "the Sins past which our fore fathers and we their children have Sinfully Committed, is the Cause of all these heavy Judgments, which my poor Nation is groaning & Sinking under" (*TDG* 185). This formulation casts ancestral adherence to Native tradition as ignorance, but by comparing it with the journal entry about God's punishment we can read it as Johnson's critique of colonists' meddling in the relationship between a chosen people and its God. The explicit import of Indian sin therefore disguises the tacit one of colonial sin that Johnson must not acknowledge when he petitions the colonial governor.

In subsequent texts Johnson clarifies that what the English perceived as ignorant Indian obstinacy was in fact a valid system of knowledge and values. As part of his "proper Endeavours" to deliver Indigenous peoples from "Bondage" in New England, Johnson appealed to Oneida leaders for land in January 1774 and explained his request by discussing the consequences of colonial dispossession. Having stated that "many" Natives in the region "are very poor, by reason of the Ignorance of our forefathers who are now dead" (*TDG* 206), Johnson presents that ignorance as the product of settlers' deliberate touting of alcohol. He portrays Mohegan's early colonial history as a time in which "our forefathers were blind, and ignorant, yea drowned in Spirituous Liquors," but then he clarifies that alcoholism as well as the blindness and ignorance that Locke and Bulkley represented as foundational conditions of Indian life were products of settler encroachments. He emphasizes that settler production of Indigenous ignorance was the major means of dispossession, writing that "the English stripped them, yea they as it were cut off their Right hands" (*TDG* 207). At this point Johnson shifts to the present and links ancestral ignorance to his own work: "and now we their Children just opening our Eyes, and having knowledge grafted . . . in our hearts, . . . or coming to our Senses, like one that has been drunk . . . we . . . perceive that we are stripped indeed, having nothing to help ourselves, and thus our English Brethren leaves us, and laugh" (ibid.).

Settlers such as Wheelock perceived Indians' Christian knowledge as a new endowment that would transform them into "Englishmen." Johnson augments this conventional Eurocentric perception, according to which Indians require the "graft[ing]" of European knowledge together with an independent, anticolonial intellectual awakening by which colonized people regain their senses after having lost them because of European liquor. He distances this recuperative process from settler initiatives both by portraying settlers as oppressors who originally caused ancestral ignorance and by emphasizing settler satisfaction with—and profit from—the consequences of that oppression. Johnson highlights settlers' unwillingness to acknowledge their responsibility for Indigenous dispossession in order to justify the Brothertown project. "So now brethren," he writes, "we leave the English those who have acted unjustly towards us in New England" and thus clarifies that the migration project is motivated not by the wish to abandon Mohegan but rather by the need to leave the settlers behind (*TDG* 207). The Brothertown project constitutes unsettlement in the sense of moving away from the region that settlers have tried to reshape to one that is still relatively free of settler interference.

In this context Johnson alludes to Psalms 137:5—"If I forget thee, O Jerusalem, let my right hand forget her cunning"[54]—and frames colonial dispossession as a sin against a sacred covenant between a people and the land that makes the resettlement/unsettlement project a spiritual necessity. Like the exiled Israelites who are ordered to sing and forget their loss in Psalms 137, Johnson suggests, the ancestors of his Indigenous audience were forced to forget their communal responsibilities and deny their collective memory. At the same time that Johnson presents Indigenous life in New England as "Bondage" and Oneida as "a land of Liberty" in his letter to Trumbull (*TDG* 225), his negotiations with the Oneida portray Algonquian homelands as the lost promised land of which Indigenous peoples have been dispossessed.[55] In this speech to Oneida leaders, Johnson's biblical constructions of exile stress that rootedness cannot be practiced responsibly under colonization and, thus, diaspora may be the means of renewing the spatial and communal responsibilities that settler colonialism disrupts.

The Oneida's response to Johnson offers an Indigenous vision of unity that heals the wounds of diaspora by assimilating Algonquian history into Oneida tribal memory: "We well remember what you said concerning the English, and we are sorry to hear the low Circumstances into which ye are involved in, owing to the Ignorance of your fore fathers" (*TDG* 218). Remembrance becomes a precondition for reunification that compensates for the loss of community and land; the Oneida leaders state, "We receive you into our Body as it were. Now we may say we have one head, one heart, and one Blood" (ibid.). This negotiation focuses on forging a new collective memory, a new language to articulate it, and a new homeland protected from colonialism by communal embodiment of the land.[56]

Oneida recognition of the ancestral ignorance that caused Mohegan hardships indicates that Johnson used this argument not merely as a rhetorical tactic for negotiating with settlers under unequal power relations. Rather, his relations with Indigenous peoples suggest that it was a substantial component of his historical and geopolitical view. The prominence of "ignorance" might be explained by Occom's later argument that the ancestors of contemporary Indigenous peoples assumed that the presence of settlers would not necessarily transform Indigenous ways of life (I discuss this idea below). In this sense, ancestral "ignorance" can be assessed only in retrospect, because it stemmed from unfamiliarity with settler practices. By fully understanding the historical difficulties facing Mohegan and other Indigenous peoples in their homelands, the Oneida may better protect Native newcomers from the threats of colonial expansion. The unsettling potential of the resettlement project lies in this retrospective attempt to interpret the past and look for liberating possibilities. The next section explores Occom's use of the ancestral ignorance trope.

Occom's History of Ancestral Ignorance and Colonial Sin

Other than the brief contrast between Indian lack of "Learning" and absolute English "Wit" in his response to Mohegan's 1773 legal defeat, Occom did not elaborate on the idea of ancestral ignorance until later. Prior to employing this aspect of Johnson's rhetoric, he focused on what he perceived as an English lack of humane religious knowledge. In an undated sermon written no earlier than 1774, Occom portrayed Indigenous Christianity ironically as ignorance.[57] Beginning with the words "When he drowned his Reason," the sermon first targets alcoholism—an enduring element of the anti-Native stereotyping that Johnson used to explain colonial production of ancestral ignorance. Reminding his audience that "Rational M[e]n" must control their actions, Occom discusses the prevalence of profanity "among the People Called Civilized Nations" and shifts his attention from Native alcoholism to "Universal" English practices of "Cursing Swearing and Profaining the name of God," defining these speech acts as the "mother Tongue" of "the White People." He portrays this knowledge as inherent to "White" culture by asking rhetorically, "[A]re there Schools Where they go to Learn this Language?" (CW 226–27).[58]

Occom states that "there is no Such Language among the Indians" and attributes this absence to ethical virtue. Developing the idea of Indigenous Christianity, he writes that the "perfect Heathenism" of Indigenous peoples includes "Very great Veneration for the Name of the great God." Occom warns "those that are Call'd Christians" that "these Heathen Indians" may yet "rise up against [them] at the last Day" (CW 227), and this idea would later be echoed in Equiano's apostrophe to "nominal Christians": "might not an African ask you, learned you this from your God?"[59] From this point on, Occom continued to refer ironically to the ignorance of Native ancestors in order to constitute "White" knowledge as moral depravity that drove colonial crimes. In doing so, he developed a theory of knowledge that contradicted Locke's assumption of Indian ignorance. Locke associated moral knowledge with the conditions that create civil society and therefore tacitly justified the colonization of those he defined as ignorant. Occom used the ancestral ignorance trope to target this link between epistemology and colonization in order to defend Indigenous rights.

Occom tied alcohol to ancestral ignorance in a 1780s petition from the "Montaukett Tribe" to "The State of New York" in which he invited state lawmakers to read a treaty between the respective ancestors of contemporary US citizens and of Montauketts.[60] The treaty limited the tribe's property rights, and the petition suggests that the Montaukett's agreement to these restrictions shows "a profound Ignorance in our fore Fathers," which means "that what little understanding they had was Drowned with hott Waters" while "the English took advantage of the Ignorance of our Fore Fathers" (CW 151). By simultaneously critiquing English denials of Indigenous knowledge and conceding the assumption of Indian ignorance, the petition highlights the immorality of English colonization. Occom packaged this apparent concession within an overriding sense of equality by alluding both to Matthew 7:12 ("all things whatsoever ye would that men should do to you, do ye even so to them") and to the Native ethic that Lisa Brooks calls the "common pot": he asked, "Would they be willing to be Servd so by us?" and "Were we Capable to use them So?" (ibid.). This rhetorical invocation of obligatory ethics helped Occom expose the criminal applications of English knowledge to imperial policies. As in his discussion of swearing, here too Occom refused to equate English culture with the absolute wisdom he lamented ironically in his 1773 response to the end of the land case.

To debunk settlers' absolutist claims, Occom positioned the various "tribes of Indians" whose grievances he wrote and others whose rights were similarly infringed by colonization within an integrative "Indian World" (CW 149) that prescribed the ethical norms of the "common pot," which visitors and latecomers should have respected. By framing his petitions in an Indigenous geopolitical context, Occom placed distinct grievances within a broad moral and historical reality that settlers denied. In a petition to Congress on behalf of the Brothertown community (c.1785) Occom recounted settlers' invasion of "this Great Indian World" as the cause of losses in land and livelihood. He portrayed settlers as knowledgeable agents who "found us very poor and wild and Ignorant," thereby bridging the temporal divide between the Brothertown Natives and their ancestors. This identification enabled Occom to understand that previous generations of Indigenous peoples had assumed they would "live always by hunting." Based on this assumption, and lacking knowledge regarding "the Value of Lands," the petitioners' "fore Fathers" had "Sold all their Country" and "were greatly under a mistake for now we find our selves Stript of all our Natural Priviledges" (ibid.).

The assumption that a hunting-based economy may endure indefinitely requires willful or unwitting ignorance of settler assessments of "the Value of Lands," and thus represents a distinct value system that validates Indigenous "Natural Priviledges." Occom's argument that "our Father[s] thought to live always by hunting" clashes with Locke's historical logic. Whereas Occom represents hunting as a durable source of livelihood that settlers should not have disrupted, Locke's theory requires its replacement with private property and money. Following Locke, colonists viewed subsistence hunting as part of a savage state of nature, and Occom reminded his audiences that Indigenous freedom and livelihood depended on noncolonial spatial practices, including subsistence hunting. Thus, the ancestral "mistake" to which he refers stems not from a faulty value system, but rather from colonial disruptions of an affirmative, community-nurturing value system: "for now we find our selves Stript of all our Natural Priviledges," Occom writes, conflating Indigenous land usage with rights so that the loss of the former necessarily impacts the latter. In addition, the verb *strip* negates settlers' assumption of original Indigenous nakedness that settler knowledge and conduct should clothe. Rights are thus embedded within an assertion of Indigenous peoples' precolonial practices.

The "Natural Priviledges" that Occom claimed in the Brothertown petition are synonymous with "Native rights" grounded in precolonial embeddedness in the land, an idea he expanded in the Montaukett petition. The history that the latter petition narrates begins with the decision of the "Great and good Spirit above" to "plant" Montaukett's "Fore-Fathers in this great Wilderness," but this event eludes historical memory: "when and how, none knows but himself" (CW 151). Like Owaneco's pipe, this divine order prioritizes spatial relations over the exact temporal measurements of Eurocentric history because the validity of political claims is grounded in space. The next item on the divine agenda was "to give us this great Continent," for which God had "fill'd this Indian World" abundantly with "Beasts, Fowls . . . and Fish" that should have enabled the Montaukett to "live always by hunting" (ibid.). Settlers' denial of Montaukett "Natural Priviledges" thus constitutes a blasphemous act. In this and other petitions, Occom's historical narrative begins prior to colonization in order to undermine the Eurocentric ideas that America's history commenced with European arrivals and that it should therefore be measured by European standards.

Gaps between Mohegan and colonial approaches to land, governance, and history led Occom to formulate a fuller critique of colonial oppression in May 1785, when he joined fellow Mohegans Henry Quaquaquid, Robert Ashpo, Phillip Cuish, Joseph Uppauquiyantup, and Isaac Uppauquiyantup in petitioning the Connecticut General Assembly regarding state limitations on Mohegan and Niantic fishing rights. Protesting the severity of state policies in comparison to the relative leniency of English colonial policies, they clarified that they demanded "not a Priviledge, which we never had before, but a Protection in our Natural Priviledges, which the King of Heaven gave to our Fathers and to their Children forever." Echoing Occom's earlier protest of the colony's attempt to reduce Mohegans to "Cyphers in our land," here too the petitioners considered the spatialization of oppression, asking, "Alas, where are we?" They named various conditions of oppression and claimed their incompatibility with Indigenous peoples' inhabitance of their homelands. "If we were slaves under tyrants, we must submit; if we were captives, we must be silent, and if we were strangers, we must be contented; or if we had forfeited our priviledges at your hands by any of our agreements we should have nothing to say." Of all these options, only the latter may fit the position of Indigenous peoples, and in rejecting its validity they countered earlier claims regarding ancestral ignorance. They affirmed Indigenous value systems by referring to Mohegan's non-Anglicized name, *Monooyauhegunnewuck*, and they positioned this self-affirmation by imagining "the various tribes of Indians, of this boundless continent," who may critique Mohegan's historical alliance with settlers in light of subsequent settler betrayals. "Will they not all cry out," the petitioners asked rhetorically, "mmauk, mmauk, these are the good that the Mohegan ever gloried and boasted of—" (CW 148). Joanna Brooks explains that *mmauk* refers to fish, so by using this word they positioned their source of livelihood of which settlers threatened to deprive them within a value system that exposed settler ignorance.[61] This inversion of ignorance from a property of Indigenous ancestors to a modifier of settler thought suggests that Mohegans' historical flaw was their past cooperation with settlers rather than their inability to comprehend settler truths.

This petition illustrates the continuums that link rootedness to diaspora, and resettlement to unsettlement. Occom submitted this petition to Connecticut officials while spending a year in Mohegan between two trips to Brothertown. These circumstances show that his attachment to Brothertown did not cancel his enduring sense of responsibility for Mohegan, and the petition's contextualization of local Indigenous-settler relations within a "boundless Continent" defined by Indigenous value systems and communication networks clarifies that international Indigenous relations may be far richer than settlers' imagination of Native existence. Such links among various regions in an "Indian World" were key to Occom's and Johnson's resistance to settler spatial divisions. The next section focuses on Johnson's representations of Mohegan as a focal point of both rootedness and diaspora, which further complicate the distinction between resettlement and unsettlement.

Rootedness and Diaspora in Mohegan

In 1772, Johnson wrote an apostrophe to Mohegan while he was teaching some fifty miles away in Farmington. The distance between Farmington and Mohegan was insignificant by comparison to the distances that Johnson had been traversing since his teenage stays at Oneida, and this short distance accentuates Johnson's insistence that neither estrangement nor attachment can be measured in miles. Johnson contemplated Mohegan while at Farmington, thus positioning physical and spiritual estrangement and attachment at the core of his perception of Mohegan. This apostrophe is the most poetic of Johnson's surviving works and the most intensive expression of his spatial thought. I quote the apostrophe in full because its complete poetic flow and internal conflicts are required for understanding how Johnson invests Mohegan with multiple meanings.

> Well I remember home—O mohegan O Mohegan—the time is long before I Shall be walking my wonted places which are on thee—once there I was but perhaps never again, but Still I remember thee—in you is lodged my father & Mother Dear—and my Beloved Sisters—and brothers—
>
> Keep them in thy womb O Mohegan, till thou dost hear the Voice of God—O Mohegan give up thy Dead—then no longer Prisoners Shall they be unto thee—the joyfull hour is Approaching. My Soul Come Meditate the Day and think how near it stands when you must leave—this house of Clay—and fly to Unknown Lands.—Hast[e] my beloved fetch my Soul up to thy blest aboad [abode] fly for my Spirit Longs to see—my Saviour—and my *God*—Mohegan is a lonesome place, oft have I sighed—but sighed in vain—desired, but desired in vain—Cast down—but no one to Comfort me—in destress—no one to relieve me—no friend to open my heart and vent my Sorrows—I opened my mouth to the open air—and told the Stones my Sorrow. Thus o Mohegan have you treated me—and thinkest thou—I can forget thee—or thy inhabitants—thinkest thou—or thine inhabiters that I am desireing to be on thee or with them—far far from me be such a thought—but Still there is a precious few in thee, which Causes my mind often to Meditate on thee—Perhaps in due time I may once more Come on thy borders—but first I have to go, to distant Lands; and far Country—and Differant Nations I have to walk through—before I see thee. Thus O Mohe-

> gan I must bid you farewell, and Shut the door of my Heart against thee—for I have a truer friend—to entertain in My Heart—So good night—. (TDG 160–61 [italics in original])

In the middle of this apostrophe Johnson incorporates parts of two hymns by Isaac Watts, the most prolific eighteenth-century hymnodist (the passage begins with "My Soul Come" and ends with "my *God*," excerpted from Watts's hymns 2:61 and 2:75). Watts dedicates these two hymns to death and the afterlife, next to which he represents worldly life as imprisonment in "flesh" and "tomb" without referring to any particular earthly place. The only specific location that Watts defines as "eternal home" is heaven, in 2:61. In 2:75 the dominant dimension is time; the speaker longs to die and enjoy "endless ages" in heaven.[62]

Johnson centralizes the longing and loathing that dominate Watts's hymns on Mohegan—his "wonted place" in contrast to Watts's "unknown lands" of heaven—and turns Mohegan into a "womb" that he hopes will protect his family, compared with Watts's "hollow gaping tomb" that imprisons the unredeemed dead. Johnson thus represents Mohegan as pregnant with a community to which it should eventually give birth, and he imagines his own wandering away from it as part of the gestation of this yet embryonic community. The unsettlement and resettlement project by which he distances himself from Mohegan and plans its eventual redemption would facilitate its communal rebirth and Johnson's aspired reunification with the Mohegan he vows not to forget.

By opening the apostrophe with "Well I remember home—O mohegan O Mohegan," Johnson alludes to Psalms 137:1 ("we wept, when we remembered Zion") and constitutes Mohegan as the promised land, its people as the chosen people, and his distance from it as biblical exile (TDG 160). Johnson also charges Mohegan with a lack of Christian faith, ending the apostrophe with a resolution to "Shut the door of my Heart against thee—for I have a truer friend—to entertain in My Heart" (TDG 161). These lines led Drew Lopenzina to suggest that Johnson "seeks a homeland of the heart" in "rejecti[on of] the geographical Mohegan," as Johnson's psychological restlessness turns exile into a personal emotional condition.[63] And Joanna Brooks argues that by "substituting 'Mohegan' for 'Jerusalem' as his spiritual and physical homeland" Johnson participates in the formulation of Indigenous Christianity that is "neither bound nor determined by Anglo-American orthodoxy."[64]

Analyses of the apostrophe have yet to consider its allusions to the Book of Lamentations and their relevance to Johnson's critique of colonization.[65] Like the double layers of his letter to Trumbull, Johnson's explicit rejection of Mohegan is intertwined with mourning over the effects of colonization that have driven him to seek temporary voluntary exile. The speaker of Lamentations 1 mourns the destruction of Jerusalem by addressing God and representing Jerusalem as a desolate widow lacking comforters; he conflates place and people and thus facilitates Johnson's exploration of the effects of colonization on Mohegan's attachment to ancestral soil. Johnson alludes to the opening of Lamentations 1:1 ("How doth the city sit solitary") in stating that "Mohegan is a lonesome place," but he shifts the biblical relations between God, speaker, and Jerusalem by attributing the sorrows of the latter to his own experiences of having "sighed in vain" and "desired in vain" with "no one to Comfort" or "relieve" him in his "destress" and "Sorrows."

As Wheelock's student, Johnson might have read John Calvin's commentaries on Lamentations 1, which refer to the absence of comforters in times of extreme sorrow by explaining that "when they who have had many friends, and thought that they would be always ready to bring them aid—when they see themselves forsaken, their sorrow becomes much more grievous."[66] Johnson's apostrophe roots Calvinist doctrine in localized Christian Indigenous experience while his "sorrow" stems from his explicit alienation from an unchristian Mohegan and motivates his reproach to Connecticut, Mohegan's former ally that dispossessed the tribe.[67] This reading is supported by Calvin's interpretation of voluntary exile, which fits the solution that Johnson eventually formulates as well as his current stay at Farmington.

Commenting on Lamentations 1:3 ("Judah is gone into captivity because of affliction, and . . . great servitude: she . . . findeth no rest: all her persecutors overtook her between the straits"), Calvin explains that "the Jews had . . . left their own country and fled to other countries, because they were subjected to miseries and cruel servitude" (*CPJ* 306). These words enable us to reposition Johnson's 1773 letter to Governor Trumbull of Connecticut—in which he stated that Indigenous peoples faced the risk of being reduced to a "wretched state of perfect slavery"—in the context of Johnson's intellectual background rather than in that of revolutionary discourse. Calvin emphasizes that voluntary exile results from particularly "barbarous" and "violent oppression" that forces people to perceive removal as "more tolerable than their condition in their own country" (*CPJ* 307). In Calvin's reading of Lamentations 1:3 and 1:8, voluntary exile precedes forced expulsion and both equally highlight the "contrast between the rest which had been promised to the Jews, and a wandering and vagrant exile" (*CPJ* 306, 319).

Lamentations 1:8 and 1:9 explain the punitive function of removal and exile ("Jerusalem hath grievously sinned; therefore she is removed"; "she remembereth not her last end; therefore she came down"). Johnson laments that Mohegan has yet to "hear the Voice of God," and he personalizes this sin by representing himself as its victim—"Thus o Mohegan have you treated me"—and yet he can neither "forget thee—or thy inhabitants" nor is he "desireing to be on thee or with them" (*TDG* 160). The combination of disappointment and commitment, alienation and enduring attachment, prompts Johnson to hope for an eventual return to Mohegan, and the "precious few" in it, when he "may once more Come on thy borders" following his prospective trips to "distant Lands; and far Country—and Differant Nations." Here, as well as in Occom's idea of a "great Indian World" or "boundless Continent" of Indigenous discourses, travel to distant regions facilitates a revised approach to Mohegan that can potentially redeem it from settler manipulations.

Johnson assesses the effects of colonization that reduced the community and its land to a fraction of their former dimensions and strength, and the phrase "precious few" refers to the survival of an uncorrupted core from which redemption may proceed. The word *precious* recurs in the King James Version of the Hebrew Bible, but only once does it refer to a community: "The precious sons of Zion, comparable to fine gold, how are they esteemed as earthen pitchers" (Lam. 4:2).[68] Although Calvin claims that the opening phrase of this verse refers to the degradation of the honorable elite (*CPJ* 457), and although the explicit import of Johnson's apostrophe may lead us to interpret his reference to the "precious few" as meaning a minority of Christian Mohegans, an anticolonial reading suggests that the "precious few" are the survivors of genocidal colonization that sought to fragment Mohegan's land and people.

Facing an ongoing history of colonial encroachments that he compares tacitly to biblical destruction, Johnson suggests that voluntary exile may be required in order eventually to enable his return to Mohegan when he would be capable of rehabilitating it. Since the biblical allusions position Johnson as a voice of the entire community (the "Jerusalem" or its people who have no comforter in Lamentations 1), his own wanderings become a synecdoche for the condition of Mohegan.

Yet the biblical speaker's address to God differs from Johnson's apostrophe to Mohegan. Calvin's commentaries on Lamentations 1:20 ("Behold, O Lord; for I am in distress") distinguish "the children of God" who turn to God in distress from the "ungodly" who "pour forth their complaints into the air" (*CPJ* 338). By contrast, Johnson's lack of comforters leads him to address Mohegan's "air" and "Stones": "no friend to open my heart and vent my Sorrows —I opened my mouth to the open air—and told the Stones my Sorrow." By "open[ing his] mouth to the open air" Johnson ostensibly reproduces ungodly complaints, but by telling "the Stones [his] Sorrow" and by addressing Mohegan directly and preaching to it about God, Johnson expresses communal sorrow over the loss of ancestral lands. Elsewhere in his texts, Johnson clarifies that "Native Liberty" is grounded in a complex idea of "Native home" (*TDG* 152) or "Native Place" (*TDG* 187), but colonial encroachments turn this grounding into a condition of immense sorrow that requires voluntary exile. The next section places these complexities of rootedness and exile in the context of the relations between Brothertown and Mohegan.

Double Rootedness in Brothertown and Mohegan

As the Crown confirmed Connecticut's claim to Mohegan land in 1773, Johnson's work stretched in three directions: teaching at Farmington, working on the Brothertown project, and helping to reorganize Mohegan following the legal defeat. In October 1773 a Mohegan delegation planned to address the Connecticut assembly regarding their remaining lands; Johnson could not join them because he had to travel to Oneida for negotiations. Instead, he wrote Governor Trumbull to support the stance of his fellow Mohegans and to request that proceeds from leasing Mohegan lands to colonists would "be paid to the Whole Tribe" to ensure that the entire community profits from its common lands even if settlers have transformed them to fit a monetary economy (*TDG* 197). In June 1774, Johnson petitioned the Connecticut assembly for reimbursement to defray his expenses during "all my travels up and down the Country since I have been Seeking the welfare of my dying Nation" (*TDG* 234). By signing the petition as "an Indian of the Mohegan Tribe" he tied himself to Mohegan while also working tirelessly on the resettlement project (ibid.). The assembly granted the petition, paying Johnson "Six pounds" for his "necessary preparations for the removal of sundry Indians out of this colony."[69] The colony imagined removals as one-way deal that would rid it of Indigenous peoples, but Johnson's "travels up and down the Country" failed to efface his attachment to Mohegan; rather, they were motivated by the need to conceptualize Indigenous inhabitation through the lens of diaspora in the wake of colonization.

Two days after writing Trumbull in October 1773, Johnson joined eight friends in Farmington and wrote their joint letter to "all our Indian Brethren, at Mohegan, Nihantuck, Pequtt, Stonington, Narraganset, and Montauk." The letter urged its addressees—all from the communities targeted by the Brothertown project—to "remember the [Mohawk] Affair" (an early name for the Brothertown project) and asked each community to "Send a Man" to "go with us, and Seek a Country for our Brethren" (*TDG* 198).[70] Rather than forgetting their ancestral homelands, the letter clarified that the project stemmed from, depended upon, and was crucial to long-term communal memory: "Let us consider of our Condition. Let us think of our Children.

Let us think of time to come. We mention these things to put you in Remembrance" (TDG 200). By appealing to its addressees' communal memory of the past and their present plan for a joint future, the letter suggested that Indigenous peoples' anticolonial struggles required interactions with diverse locales over time. Johnson and his friends prepared for the trip by asking that the women who remain in New England prepare "Yoke-hegg" for the road, invoking the continued communal sustenance they would need as they seek to expand their sense of home beyond settler definitions.[71]

Two days later Oneida delegates arrived at Johnson Hall, Sir William Johnson's home, to deliver an invitation to Joseph Johnson to meet them upon their return from their seasonal hunting trip, at which point they would "shew" (show) Johnson and his fellow Algonquians "a Place to settle on, which if they did not like, they would give them liberty to chuse a Place that might be more agreeable" (TDG 201). The generous promise was backed by evidence that the Oneidas had sufficient land to support communal hunting expeditions of the kind that Indigenous peoples in New England had long been forced to abandon. The following month, Johnson wrote his fiancé, Occom's daughter Tabitha, that "We have a large Tract of Land given us, and we have Liberty to chuse for ourselves, any where in the district of the Oniodas" (TDG 202). In January 1774, Johnson gave his first speech to the Oneidas, from which I quoted above, clarifying that the Algonquians who would come to dwell in Haudenosaunee country "as a younger Brother" would not be forsaking their own communities but rather abandoning the colonists (TDG 207).

In March 1775, Johnson traveled to Oneida again, accompanied by fewer men than he had hoped because settlers had on the eve of the Revolutionary War changed their minds regarding traveling Indians: "it seemed to me Matter of great Surprize," Johnson wrote, "that as the People of New England had got almost all our Lands from us, and thereby Oblig'd us to go else where, [they] Shoul'd want to Stop us now, when a Year ago they wanted to get rid of us" (TDG 255). Pressed to prove their loyalty, serve the colonists, and ensure Haudenosaunee neutrality, the prospective emigrants were forced to delay the project amid suspicions that they might be working for land-grabbing colonists. Johnson wrote the New York Congress in June 1775 that recent "false reports" alleged he had been "in pursuance of a design formed by the People of New England to settle in that Western Country" (TDG 265). Johnson's critique of settlers who attempted to appropriate and manipulate his work in the service of colonial expansion illustrates the hard work of formulating spatial dynamics that would not be appropriable by settler norms.

Colonial epistemologies rendered the Brothertown project unintelligible because settler logic could not contain the complex interactions of resettlement and unsettlement, which could potentially undermine settler disavowal of settler colonialism's founding violence. Traveling Natives who were engaged in initiatives of both resettlement and unsettlement potentials, in other words, destabilized settlers' efforts to determine their regime's spatial and temporal dimension. Johnson attempted partial emigration in March, but three months later he petitioned for passes to return to New England until safer times. Settlers granted his request the next day, but the following month Johnson headed northwest again as settlers compelled him to try to secure Oneida declarations of neutrality. Faced by accusations that he was a disguised loyalist, Johnson wrote the New York Congress again; he represented Mohegan as "my own native place" and ended the petition by referring to Mohegan again as "my native place" (*TDG* 266, 269).

The endurance of Mohegan as their "own native place" suggests that for Johnson, Occom, and Owaneco native status was a complex foundation of communitist responsibilities through which they questioned and critiqued settler conventions in order to resist settler infringements of their "Native rights." By positioning Mohegan "Native rights" as prior to settler formulations and beyond them, they tried to detach Mohegan—and, at times, a broader "Indian World"—from the stranglehold of negative birthright by which settlers sought to justify their dispossession of Indigenous peoples. This chapter focused on Mohegan inhabitance as a complex mode of spatial relations that required intensive negotiations between rootedness and diaspora because the settler regime disrupted more stable, volitional inhabitation patterns. The next chapter focuses on comparable uncertainties and fluctuations in arrivants' searches for emancipating inhabitation. It explores arrivants' resistance to negative birthright on the eve of the Revolutionary War and in its antebellum aftermath, and it positions such resistance in the context of settlers' efforts to liberate themselves from English birthright, which they increasingly perceived as inherently negative. Through these processes, arrivants and settlers scrutinized the spatial dimensions of freedom and bondage. Whereas this chapter showed that Mohegan presented settlers with an anticolonial theory of Native rights that was based in Mohegan and developed through complex relations among various spatial constructs, the arrivants discussed in the next chapter insisted that freedom had to be embedded in space—but this insistence was based on uncertainty in terms of which place would best serve their political aspirations. The next two chapters explore the slow process by which the concept of rights gradually became rooted in the expanding spatial terrain that the United States claimed as its national territory. As a result of this process, African colonization and Indian removal (discussed in chapters 5 and 6) were finally reformulated in the language of native status.

[3]

SPACES OF SLAVERY AND FREEDOM

OWANECO, SAMSON OCCOM, AND Joseph Johnson could mobilize Mohegan history to theorize Mohegan freedom and claim Mohegan rights because that history was rooted in spaces that signified Mohegan's political existence. However, transatlantic slavery radically stripped arrivant communities and individuals of spatio-political rootedness, binding them to settlers' slave law, which attempted to render unintelligible any freedom they might have theorized. Therefore, slaves and ex-slaves often formulated their rights claims in terms of slavery's law. To achieve emancipation they had to either break that law by escaping slavery, or engage that law by submitting petitions for freedom. While fugitive slaves were in constant danger of recapture, legal emancipation presumably secured ex-slaves' freedom, and slavery's history is dotted with both innumerable escapes and numerous petitions by which slaveholders, slaves, and free blacks asked legislative bodies to emancipate particular slaves.[1] While escapes were rarely rewarded, some of the petitions resulted in the manumission of certain slaves without challenging slavery as an institution. However, in January 1773, the free black Bostonian Felix Holbrook made history by submitting the first petition to ask for the liberation of a colony's entire slave population.[2] Subsequent petitions by Holbrook and others provide an unparalleled early glimpse into the textual development of arrivant rights discourses.

This chapter juxtaposes abolitionist arrivant petitions with an unlikely genre: newspaper advertisements that slaveholders placed in order to recapture fugitive slaves. The petitions sought to renegotiate the social order by rejecting the imposition of negative birthright through *partus sequitur ventrem*, which perpetuated slavery by decreeing that the children of female slaves would inherit nothing but the conditions of their mothers. By excluding slaves from the logic of human inheritance rights and classifying them instead as property, *partus sequitur ventrem* was meant to strip arrivants from the agentive belonging that spatio-political rootedness signified and to limit their existence to the objectified belonging that produced property. Fugitive slaves rejected negative birthright in practical terms and their escapes triggered ads that focused on reinstating that order. Differing in voice, authorship, and agenda, the petitions and the ads form contrastive genres that provide glimpses into slaves' and free blacks' performances and formulations of their liberties. Both genres show that arrivant rights claims scrutinized the complex links among freedom, inhabitance, and socio-spatial attachment.

Neither the petitions nor the advertisements take a single clear stance on the role of birthplace in determining rights, but in both, space and native status are crucial aspects of belonging, be it objectified or agentive. The petitions oscillate between alternative sites of freedom that often relate to actual or imagined birthplaces in Africa or the Americas, while the ads mention nativities irregularly alongside other identifiers such as scars or peculiarities of speech.[3] The juxtaposition of birthplace and scars in the ads is particularly instructive as references to the former read as claims for axiomatic negative birthright, a given that cannot be undermined, while the latter emphasize the intensive violence that had to be inflicted on the enslaved in order to maintain their negative birthright.

Both the escapes represented in the ads and the petitions challenge or utilize birthplaces to offer resettlement projects—whether small-scale, even individualized ones, as practiced by fugitives who redefined their places in the world, or broader ones, as the petitioners proposed to either settle Africa or resettle non-slaveholding American spaces. These resettlement projects position freedom as a function of inhabitation grounded in spatial rootedness and producing agentive belonging. Through both projects, arrivants unearthed and underlined the violence that serves as settler colonialism's condition of possibility and thereby challenged the foundational disavowal of violence by which settler regimes legitimize themselves (see introduction).

Understanding the role of slavery in US settler colonialism requires a recentralization of enslaving violence within the settler project, and I do this by juxtaposing the ads and the petitions with a third body of texts: settlers' protests of Britain's impressment policy, which extended the logic of negative birthright to settlers. The impressment crisis that culminated in the War of 1812 triggered settler theorizations of rights and freedom as antithetical to spatial attachment and stable inhabitance. Similarly to Jefferson's 1785 attempt to free rights-bearing subjects of space-specific inhabitance commitments, anti-impressment discourse associated territorial ties with feudalist negative birthright and measured freedom by individuals' ability to voluntarily detach themselves from any polity and assert their portable positive birthrights by moving elsewhere.

Anti-impressment discourse is related to slavery because settlers who opposed impressment compared it to slavery in order to distinguish their rights-bearing capacities from arrivants' objectifying spatial attachment. While settlers used slavery metaphorically to support their theorizations of spatial attachment as bondage, arrivants' histories of literal enslavement drove them to look for the emancipatory potentials of spatial attachment. References to birthplaces in slaveholders' ads often signal attempts to re-impose circumscribed nativity on fugitives—a particular form of negative birthright that confined slaves to the places where they were forced to labor and denied them the option of developing ways to inhabit the world, either through affirmative attachment to land or by exercising freedom of movement. Anti-impressment writers argued that *any* political claim based on birthplace enforced circumscribed nativity and was therefore inapplicable to settlers. They thus defined settlers as always ready to leave a former place of inhabitation and find their freedom elsewhere. Anti-impressment discourse shows that settler fantasies of resettlement focused on what Veracini defined as "emptiness"—on spaces that are always already imagined as available not only because they are presumably devoid of Indigenous peoples, but also because they lack any particular feature that may produce spatial attachment.[4]

Conversely, the arrivant resettlement projects examined here seek to redefine spatial attachment so that it would support liberty within a reparatory acknowledgment of imperial and colonial violence. Whereas the petitions have been analyzed primarily as imitations of revolutionary natural rights or as contributions to the democratic ethos of the United States, my focus on settler colonial dynamics and spatial emancipation sheds light on the relations between the texts I read and their contemporaneous abolitionist and revolutionary discourses. The geopolitical discrepancies between settler and arrivant texts complicate assumptions regarding arrivants' adoption of natural rights theories and their role within US democracy. By juxtaposing these three bodies of texts I argue that while settlers have been anxious to ensure slaves' negative birthright, and while this anxiety led them to prefer freedom of movement to stable inhabitation, free blacks associated rights-bearing subjecthood with settlement, and particularly with the kind of settlement that nativizes the settler and thereby naturalizes settlers' rights claims. In investigating the spatial parameters of freedom under imperial conditions, arrivants thus formulated settlements' relation to entitlement in terms of spatial attachment before settlers were willing to endow stable inhabitation with liberating consequences.

By relating these bodies of texts to each other, I rethink the spatial dimensions of freedom and of negative and positive birthrights. Together these bodies of texts expose the construction of arrivants' belonging as a fragile yet persistent and multifaceted element in the formation of entitlement in the United States. This chapter begins by discussing the petitions, developing an analysis of their geopolitics in order to unsettle the Eurocentric assumption that arrivant philosophies were imitating natural rights discourse. I then analyze the advertisements in order to complement the petitioners' representations of the spatial grounding of freedom with an analysis of slaveholders' perceptions of slave nativities. I conclude the chapter with a reading of anti-impressment discourse in order to place arrivant geopolitics in the context of settlers' suspicion of spatial attachment.

Petitioning for Freedom

Peter Holbrook's first petition, dated January 1773, addressed the Massachusetts governor and House of Representatives on behalf of "many Slaves" in the colony and asked colonial officials to "take their unhappy State and Condition" into "just Consideration."[5] Holbrook referred to Atlantic abolitionist discourse by appealing to "Humanity and Justice" and "bless[ing] God" for "lately put[ting] it into the Hearts of Multitudes on both sides of the Water, to bear our Burthens" (*DH* 6). Historians have read this and subsequent petitions as evidence that natural rights discourse circulated among arrivants, suggesting that this discursive formation originated in Eurocentric thought and then traveled unidirectionally to the sociopolitical margins of Europe's empires.[6] In her recent history of abolition, Manisha Sinha revises this historiographic convention, insisting on the centrality of African-descended peoples to abolitionist thought and practice. Sinha highlights African American abolitionists' commitment to an "ideal of an interracial democracy," arguing that they "question[ed]" dominant "revolutionary professions" and that, consequently, white revolutionaries "borrowed their ideas and words" in order to critique revolutionary colonial "democracy."[7] My analysis of the petitions (and of arrivant rights claims throughout this book) is similarly motivated by the need to understand the political discourses of African-descended writers on their own terms. However, it departs from Sinha's study by problematizing the relations of these discourses to US settler colonialism.

Holbrook's biblical reference to Galatians 6:2 ("Bear ye one another's burdens, and so fulfil the law of Christ") suggests that Eurocentric abolitionist discourse developed because some Europeans were willing imaginatively to "bear" slaves' burdens, to empathize with slaves by trying to approximate their perspectives, and to recognize slaves' experiences as sources of knowledge. Holbrook thus tacitly represents slavery as the cause of contemporaneous faith in natural rights. Holbrook's first petition presented the dehumanizing, disempowering destitution of the enslaved as the core of unfreedom. It tacitly protested the logic of *partus sequitur ventrem* by stating that neither "the Negroes," "nor their Children to all Generations, shall ever be able to do, or to possess and enjoy any Thing, no, not even *Life itself*, but in a Manner as the *Beasts that perish*" (DH 6). This portrayal of violent dehumanization implicitly asserted the existence of multigenerational slave communities, and Holbrook emphasized tensions between intelligible constructions of human lives and dehumanizing enslavement by presenting the latter as a serial deprivation of economic, kinship, and geopolitical power: "We have no property! We have no Wives! No Children! We have no City! No Country!" (ibid.). This sequence of lacks increases in scale and significance from the "property" that defines the possessive individual to the communal and geopolitical belonging by which kinship, inhabitation, and self-determination humanize individuals. The tension between the temporal perpetuation of slavery "to all generations" and the absence of politically meaningful slave community anticipates Orlando Patterson's "social death" thesis by critiquing the logic of *partus sequitur ventrem* as an order that attempts to evacuate life of any sociopolitical meaning.

Over the next year and a half Holbrook and his associates submitted five petitions on behalf of the colony's slaves.[8] Whereas their first petition proposed no specific action, in subsequent petitions Holbrook and his copetitioners began a serious investigation of the spatial grounding of freedom. After the colony tabled Holbrook's January 1773 petition, he joined Peter Bestes, Sambo Freeman, and Chester Joie in petitioning members of the colony's legislative assembly in April of the same year. Positioning their appeal within broader revolutionary and abolitionist projects, they declared, "The divine spirit of *freedom*, seems to fire every human breast on this continent, except such as are bribed to assist in executing" slavery. They supported this explicit association of liberty with America by critiquing settler geopolitics. Whereas English imperial thought portrayed Spanish colonization as the quintessence of cruel tyranny toward Indigenous peoples, the petitioners argued that Spain was a more humane enslaver than England. They centralized Spanish models of slavery and emancipation rather than Spain's treatment of Indigenous peoples, thus suggesting that imperial endeavors should be evaluated through their enslavement mechanisms. They claimed that although "the *Spaniards*" lack "those sublime ideas for freedom that English men have," Spanish colonizers recognized that they had "no right to all the services of their fellow-men . . . the *Africans*." Thus, without any reference to Spain's conquest of Indigenous peoples' lands, the petitioners informed their readers that Spanish colonizers "allow[ed]" slaves "one day in a week to work for themselves" so they could "earn money to purchase the residue of their time, which they have a right to demand in such portions as they are able to pay for" (DH 7). The petition accepts slavery's economic logic in order to open up a liberating space within it and in this sense foreshadows Equiano's early resettlement initiative on the Musquito Coast. But whereas Equiano formulates his project in the joint context of empire *and* Indigenous peoples' purported aspirations, these petitioners limit the evils of colonization to slavery.

Their reference to Spain's lack of "sublime ideas for freedom" indicates the petitioners' awareness of the black legend—the English discourse about Spanish imperial cruelties by which English imperialists and settlers could reassure themselves of their own moral superiority. The fact that the black legend focused primarily on genocidal policies toward Indigenous peoples indicates the petitioners' explicit choice in diverting the critique of colonialism from the genocidal dispossession of Indigenous peoples to that of the enslaved. This choice may suggest more than a lack of interest in Indigenous-arrivant solidarity on their part. The text's function as a petition to colonial authorities probably forced them to focus on their own grievances, and the reference to the black legend might indicate an attempt to appropriate English settlers' presumed interest in Spanish cruelties toward Indians in order to recruit support for slaves. In this sense the text may explain why, when Indigenous peoples and arrivants fought separately for their rights against the settler regime, they looked not for solidarity, but for distinct arguments. In the case of arrivants, such arguments enabled them to position themselves potentially as settlers who may yet replace their forced migration with a narrative of voluntary settlement. This and subsequent petitions show that arrivants' interactions with natural rights discourse was guided by their recognition of the settler as the rights-bearing subject and therefore their formulation of settlement as the framework for exercising freedom.

Holbrook, Bestes, Freeman, and Joie's reference to Spanish law coincided with Benjamin Rush's treatment of this subject in *Address to the Inhabitants of the British Settlements in America, upon Slave-Keeping* (1773), which urges colonists to abolish slavery and "entitle [the manumitted] to all the privileges of free-born British subjects." Rush supported this idea by quoting a letter by Granville Sharp that discussed the Spanish practice to which the petitioners referred.[9] But while Rush framed this reference to Spanish law within the tradition of English rights and proposed to declare emancipated slaves "free-born British subjects," the petitioners invoked an African horizon of entitlement beyond Europe and its American colonies. They presented their resettlement plan by asserting their "determin[ation]" to "leave the province . . . as soon as we can, from our joynt labours procure money to transport ourselves to some part of the Coast of *Africa*, where we propose a settlement" (DH 8). Their preference for Spain's law over British regulations facilitates a broader global examination of the places that may support their aspirations for freedom. Yet, they formulated this globality in imperial terms by overlooking the colonization of Indigenous peoples in the Americas as though both America and Africa were available for colonization. This, as Dorothy Porter writes, was "[p]ossibly the earliest" collectively written "request of slaves to return to Africa,"[10] and they formulated it by replacing the Spanish focus on slavery as denial of *temporal* freedom with an emphasis on freedom's spatial dimensions, articulated by their aspirations for volitional inhabitation in Africa. The "joynt labours" that the petition envisions reconstitute the community that Holbrook's first petition presented as impossible under slavery, and Africa emerges here as the only place where such a community may be able to support itself permanently.

These petitions had to revise settlers' natural rights discourse because it was predicated on white supremacism, possessive individualism, and metaphoric slavery—three issues that made natural rights inaccessible to arrivants. For example, James Otis's pamphlet *The Rights of the British Colonies Asserted and Proved* (1764) contributed prominently to settlers' natural rights discourse. Otis argued that settlers were entitled to both natural and civil rights and that this double entitlement protected them from slavery, which he defined metaphorically as a consequence of British tax policies. His critique of imperial policies replaced English writers' focus on the black legend and the abuse of Indigenous peoples with an emphasis on the misery that imperial regimes inflict on settlers. Prior to the Glorious Revolution, he asserted, all imperial European governments imposed "nothing but ill-usage, slavery and chains" on their colonists, and he warned that parliamentary policy may reinstate and aggravate this history.[11] Otis's pamphlet oscillates between universal natural rights ("all men . . . white or black" are "free born") and settlers' exclusive entitlement to "*more*" "rights, liberties and privileges" than other British subjects because of their larger contribution to the British economy (RBC 43, 37). He defined settlers as "freeborn *British white* subjects" and denounced their representation as "a compound mongrel mixture of *English*, *Indian*, and *Negro*" (RBC 36–37). Under this overarching white supremacism, the freedom to which the "law of nature" entitles "black" "men" becomes a metaphor, as the phrase *free born* applies metaphorically to blacks just as *slavery* applies metaphorically to the condition of settlers (RBC 43).

Otis depicted settlement as a heroic voluntary undertaking that distinguished settlers from arrivants. Quoting Grotius, he portrayed settlers as voluntary emigrants in search of a just government (RBC 39) and used this historical narrative to warn that Parliament's actions might drive "persecuted" settlers farther "into a more western wilderness, on the score of liberty, civil and religious, as many of our ancestors were, to these once inhospitable shores of America" (RBC 62). This idea positions settlers as rights-bearing subjects whose relation to space is contingent upon the jurisdictional orders they inhabit. This resettlement vision represents space as a hurdle to be overcome, a wilderness to be tamed, a metaphor like settlers' enslavement by the British Parliament rather than a particular terrain that may facilitate or limit specific human aspirations. However, once that space is redefined as a settler colonial regime its sheer size becomes a source of settlers' power. To support this idea, Otis emphasizes the absurd geopolitical perceptions of British officials who think of North American colonies as "a parcel of *little insignificant conquered islands*, [rather] than as a very extensive settlement on the continent" and suggests that settlers' freedom and superior whiteness derive from this deterministic geography (RBC 36–37).

Against this backdrop we may reconsider the extent to which the resettlement plan of Holbrook's second petition both reproduced and revised imperial assumptions. Metaphors of slavery in revolutionary speech prevented enslaved and free blacks from adopting settlers' natural rights discourse, and by revising it they scrutinized the spatial relations that concretized the discrepancies between figurative and literal enslavement. Holbrook's emergent spatial formulation of slavery and freedom reflects arrivants' need for an alternative vocabulary of entitlement befitting the lived realities of slaves and free blacks. They fulfilled this need by refashioning themselves through the wish to settle America. Their geopolitical intervention focused on stretching the historical imposition of settlers so it could accommodate their aspirations for freedom.

This idea crystallized in the third petition that Holbrook submitted, in June 1773, which intensified arrivant disavowal of Indigenous peoples' colonization in order to root arrivant freedom in America as new settlers. The fragment that remains of that petition shows that the petitioners introduced themselves as representing "all thous who . . . are held in a state of slavery, within the bowels of a free Country." Whether the "free Country" refers to Massachusetts, British North America, or the Americas, they portray freedom as an attribute of American space from which they are excluded despite their presence there. This idea supports their definition of liberty as a universal natural right. They declared that they had "a naturel right to be free" and own property, which they held "in comon with other men" and thus positioned themselves as equal to the settlers who enslaved them.[12] This argument attempts to replace *partus sequitur ventrem*'s objectifying belonging with a spatial principle of freedom that would apply equally to voluntary and forced contributors to the settler project. The Massachusetts House of Representatives probably read this petition later that month. The House Journal reports on a part of it that seems not to have survived, indicating that Holbrook and his co-petitioners may have asked to be "made Freemen of this Community; and that this Court would give and grant to them some Part of the unimproved Lands belonging to the Province, for a settlement."[13]

As these petitions show, between April and June 1773 Holbrook and his fellow petitioners consistently associated freedom with settlement, but they vacillated between Africa and Massachusetts as the best places to support their "freedom" and "natural rights." However, they insisted that the place of their liberation must be related to their histories. They represented neither place as unknown wilderness whose properties are meaningless next to the settlement project that would convert it, as Otis did, but rather proposed that resettlement required historical action based on acknowledgment of the violence and consequences of imperial slavery. Whereas in the second petition they had expressed their intention to fund their journey to Africa independently of the colony, in the third they placed themselves under colonial authority by asking the colony to provide a place of resettlement. They suggested that reversing forced migration projects might be beyond their power and so proposed to resettle the colony in a manner that would enable Massachusetts to reformulate its relation to its arrivant population beyond slavery. Under a slaveholding regime that deprived them of the right and means for executing their exodus, they affirmed New England's originary settler colonial myth but revised its focus on voluntary migration into the "wilderness" by requesting assistance in establishing their own settlement within the colony to which they were forcefully driven. Examining this recuperative proposal next to their earlier reference to Spanish colonization clarifies that the petitioners were attempting to redeem arrivants from their negative birthright while simultaneously redeeming the settler regime from its systematic founding violence toward arrivants.

Holbrook's fourth petition, submitted in May 1774 on behalf of "a Grate Number of Blackes of this Province," began by declaring the petitioners' "naturel right to our freedoms"—a right they supported by asserting that they were "a freeborn Pepel" who "have never forfeited this Blessing to aney compact or agreement whatever." They portrayed the slave trade and their enslavement as radical infringements of their inviolable right to freedom by writing that "we were unjustly dragged by the cruel hand of power from our dearest frinds," adding that "sum of us [were] stolen from the bosoms of our tender Prents and from a Populous Pleasant and plentiful country and Brought hither to be made slaves for life in a Christian land." They added that the slave trade's violent assault on the family was reproduced in America where "[o]ur children are also taken from us by force and sent maney miles from us." This juxtaposition of two forced migrations—one in Africa and the other in the British Empire—distinguishes Africa as a nurturing place that supports social and environmental agentive belonging ("Populous Pleasant and Plentiful Country") from America as unfamiliar, calculable, measured territory of bondage and separation ("maney miles"). Holbrook bridged these spatialities by referring to settlers' portrayals of the colonies as places of freedom, asking whether any positive law justified the enslavement of "our children for life when Born in a free Countrey." Following this critique, Holbrook asked the colony to emancipate all slaves at age twenty-one and thereby tried to make their legal nonpersonhood and the imposition of negative birthright temporary so that, like settlers, they too would be able to overcome it and reach the full-blown humanity of the adult rights-bearing subject (*DH* 8–9).

This petition offers a tacit resettlement plan whereby those slaves who would be manumitted at twenty-one and become equal citizens would necessitate a reorganization of the colony's sociopolitical reality. The appropriation of settler freedom constructs such as legal adulthood might have paved the way for the next petition, submitted in June 1774, in which the petitioners asked to "be liberated and made free men of this community, and be entitled to all the privileges and immunities of all its free and natural born subjects." They repeated their request for "unimproved land, belonging to the province, for a settlement" or, failing that, at least for "release . . . from bondage."[14]

By referencing African and American spaces inconsistently, these petitioners formulated freedom's spatial foundations independently of nativity yet in relation to their histories. When Holbrook submitted his first petition, an anonymous letter writer supported it in the *Massachusetts Spy* by considering freedom's spatial grounds and arguing that slavery violated the liberty that the Massachusetts charter promised in 1629. The writer quoted from the charter, which rejected feudalist social norms and extended portable positive birthright to all British subjects who "shall go to, and inhabit within the province, and every of their children born there, or on the seas in going thither."[15] He argued that the charter entitled anyone in this category to "all liberties and immunities of *free* and natural subjects of the realm of England." While the charter conditioned rights on birth by equating the freedom of those "born" in or en route to the colony with that of those born in England, the writer to the *Spy* replaced this condition with inhabitation. He suggested that once colonial rights are detached from the tacitly racial legal fiction of English birth they may encompass "all people who should *ever* inhabit within the province" and who should thus "enjoy the same *lib-*

erties and *privileges* as in England."[16] This shift in emphasis from portable positive birthright in the charter to residence attempts to overcome the feudalist logic of negative birthright that the charter presumably annihilated, but which continued to direct white supremacism. By framing the petition in the context of the 1629 charter the writer also distances the petition from revolutionary natural rights discourse and places it instead in the context of settler freedom.

Three years after Holbrook filed his last petition, Prince Hall, Lancaster Hill, Peter Bess, Brister Slenser, Jack Pierpont, Nero Funelo, Newport Sumner, and Job Look repeated similar arguments in a petition they submitted to Massachusetts General Court on January 13, 1777. Complaining of the state's failure to act on previous petitions, they asked to be "Restored to the Enjoyments of . . . the Naturel Right of all men—and their—Children who wher Born in this Land of Liberty may not be heald as Slaves after they arive at the age of Twenty one years."[17] Whereas this petition omits any explicit reference to African births, instead emphasizing the American births of African arrivants' descendants, a petition that Nero Brewster and other slaves submitted to the New Hampshire General Assembly in 1779 seems to be the first of this genre to use African nativity as a privileging identity category.

Chapter 2 shows how Occom and Johnson used ignorance ironically to discuss epistemological options that colonists refused or failed to recognize. Similarly to their arguments that Mohegan ancestral ignorance facilitated colonization, the New Hampshire petition submitted by "*Nero Brewster*, and others, natives of Africa" attributed ignorance to the Africans who collaborated with slave traders. Brewster and his fellow petitioners began with natural rights—"freedom is an inherent right of the human species"—and then used their African nativities to discuss slavery's violence. They blamed their capture in Africa on the "ignorance & brutish violence of their native countrymen" and the "sinister designs" of Europeans "who ought to have taught them better." They explained that as "children" deserving "protection" and "incapable of self-defence" they "were seized, imprisoned, and transported from their native country," where "ignorance and inchristianity prevailed," and were "born free to a country, where (tho' knowledge, christianity and freedom, are their boast) they are compelled, and their unhappy posterity, to drag on their lives in miserable servitude."[18] The phrase *borne free* (which they spelled "born free") contributes to an understanding of spatialized freedom that approximates Equiano's "original free African state" as well as Occom's and Johnson's ideas of Native rights that precede imperial conquest. By emphasizing that even during the Middle Passage they were free—in principle, though not in practice—they suggest that violence against "ignoran[t]" "[u]nchristian[s]" is a grave historical crime that settlers must redress.

Like Occom, Johnson, and Equiano, the petitioners held Europeans accountable for the ignorance of those exploited by imperial expansion, asserting that Europeans "ought to have taught [Africans] better." But whereas Occom, Johnson, and Equiano rooted Christian ethics in Indigenous epistemologies that demote Eurocentric thought to partial, provincial imagination, the New Hampshire petitioners highlighted the universal knowledge and validity of natural rights without linking those rights to an Indigenous African tradition. They argued that "the God of Nature gave them life and freedom" in Africa "upon terms of the most perfect equality with other men" before they were "born[e] free" to America. The petition represents scales of freedom in which the capture and transportation of the enslaved diminish their abilities to enjoy their liberties without completely obliterating their free selfhoods, in turn redefining their native status as though both forced and voluntary migrations can support portable positive birthright. Only when they arrived in America, the petitioners argued, did settlers' white supremacism deprive them of their positions as "free agents."

This portrayal of America as a place of bondage is particularly meaningful because the petition was submitted during the Revolutionary War. By asking "that the name of SLAVE may no more be heard in a land gloriously contending for the sweets of freedom," the petitioners appropriated revolutionary rhetoric to support their conflation of America with bondage and, in doing so, tacitly critiqued the assumption that they merely reproduced settler rights discourse. When they expressed their wish to contribute to a liberating war and suggested that their experiences have prepared them for this task, they redefined slavery as the condition of possibility for freedom struggles. "[G]ive us an opportunity," they asked, "of evincing to the world our love of freedom, by exerting ourselves in [America's] cause, in opposing the efforts of tyranny and oppression over the country in which we ourselves have been so injuriously enslaved."[19] They thus positioned themselves as the rightful subjects of revolutionary emancipatory projects and conditioned successful liberation on the recognition and cessation of violent enslavement.

Following the Revolutionary War, petitioners again used their African nativities as foundations of positive birthrights to promote resettlement there. A petition that Prince Hall and over seventy signatories submitted to Massachusetts General Court on January 4, 1787, formulated spatialized attachment and freedom in terms of native status and turned Africa into the exclusive source of their liberty, which could therefore not be enjoyed elsewhere. Tracing their history from the Middle Passage through American enslavement to Massachusetts's abolition of slavery, they equated life "in America" with "very disagreeable and disadvantageous circumstances." They identified Africa conversely as "our native country" in order to portray it as the only region where they could thrive, and they supported this view by arguing that its "warm climate" was "much more natural and agreeable to us" because "the God of nature has formed us" for it. They wished to "live among our equals" and be useful "to our brethren there" (*BP* 207–8). Slavery's history is indispensable to their liberatory project, as in previous petitions, but this petition invests their imagination of Africa as their "native country" with geographic determinism that the previous petitions lacked. It employs geographic determinism to refute the argument of slavery's legislators that Africans alone were fit to cultivate American lands (see introduction) by recasting African nativities as the foundation of sociopolitical recuperation rather than exploitation.

While the April 1773 proposal for an African settlement did not refer to the journey as a "return," the 1787 petition portrays the desired journey as a redemptive project by which the petitioners would overcome negative birthright, redeem the original liberties signified by their African births, and reclaim their "native country." This representation of "native country" did not necessarily depend on their actual birthplaces. As in Equiano's case, many of these birthplaces have not been recorded definitively or reliably in imperial archives. Documents show that Holbrook, who did not claim an African nativity, might have been born in Africa, whereas the birthplace of Hall, who called Africa his "native land," remains uncertain, and James Sidbury suggests that he might have been born in New England.[20] Yet both Holbrook and Hall argued that birthplace validated rights. Hall's petition used the term "native country" twice as a future destination to which petitioners "desire to return." The petitioners wrote that "the soil of our native country is good" for agricultural development and that "large tracts" of its "uncultivated lands . . . might be obtained, and would be freely given for those to settle upon, who shall be disposed to return to them" (*BP* 208). Unlike Brewster's New Hampshire petition, which first used the language of native status and confined it to the past, the resettlement project that this petition develops offers a new future-oriented theory of nativity that promises the restoration of lost liberties rather than their portability.

Return and African native status are thus made to fit a broader framework of settlement that imagines the availability of "uncultivated lands" that might be "freely given" to the settlers who are portrayed as returning Native Africans. Nativity therefore is not independent of settler identification but derives from it, as settlement is the only means by which the petitioners may reclaim their native entitlement to African lands. The relations between this resettlement plan and the settler regime it addresses underline the complexities of the petitioners' historical vision. They simultaneously recognized their dependence on settlement as the normative framework of historical agency and, particularly, on the US settler regime as a necessary model and support for further (re)settlement projects. The petitioners hoped to be "formed" into a "civil" and "religious" society in the United States and then to "remove to Africa, and settle" there, explaining that their American origins were particularly conducive of "inlightening and civilizing those [African] nations, who are now sunk in ignorance and barbarity." Africa functions here as an ambiguous origin-cum-destination that symbolizes past freedom and its future restoration, which depends on American "farming utensils" and "materials" without which the prospective emigrants would be unable to "build houses and mills" (*BP* 208). The African destination of "return" would materialize only if US aid could ensure successful resettlement. This intertwined historical vision explains the petitioners' subsequent uncertainty regarding the precise location of freedom.

The petition was "quickly buried in committee"[21] and ten months later Hall petitioned the state on behalf of taxpaying "freemen of this Commonwealth" who asserted their "right to enjoy the privileges of free men" (*DH* 19). This tautological claim for freedom replaces the racist tautologies that justified slavery—most prominently Blackstone's conflation of "a slave or a negro," in which the latter represents relative bondage even after emancipation. The tautology the petitioners use does not redefine freedom but rather appropriates to themselves settlers' freedom. Having faced racial segregation in Boston's "free schools," they asked the state to educate their children lest they grow "in ignorance in a land of gospel light" (ibid.). Slavery in a free country and ignorance in a Christian one represent the paradoxes that they hoped to overcome with the tautology of settler freedom. By requesting educational facilities the petitioners expressed their wish to be recognized as belonging to Massachusetts rather than as "natives" of Africa and again emphasized settler responsibility for their condition.

Joanna Brooks suggests that Hall's success in gaining official recognition for his Masonic African Lodge persuaded the petitioners to stay in America because they had established an "'African' cultural, political, and ritual space in America" that deferred their desired return to Africa.[22] This explanation contains symbolic attachment to Africa within civil attachment to the United States. "Sometime during the spring or summer of 1787," Brooks writes, "Prince Hall recognized that the welfare of Boston's black community rested immediately with its domestic political power."[23] But a juxtaposition of these petitions shows no clear telos from an earlier attachment to Africa to a maturation of ties to America. Hall and members of his lodge had already petitioned the state for recognition as loyal citizens several months prior to requesting an African return. In the fall of 1786 they offered to help the state suppress Shays' Rebellion and argued that their "fraternity" obliged them to be "peaceable subjects to the civil powers" where they resided and forbade their participation "in any plot of conspiracies against the state where we dwell" (*BP* 205).

The state rejected their offer. Emancipated yet disenfranchised, members of the African Lodge debated the foundations of belonging: Did social and geopolitical attachment stem from nativity, descent, or residence? Sidney Kaplan and Emma Nogrady Kaplan offer a telos opposite to that of Joanna Brooks by arguing that the state's rejection of their military assistance drove Hall and his fellow petitioners to consider moving to Africa.[24] As Richard S. Newman, Roy E. Finkenbine, and Douglass Mooney write, the "tension" between "domestic abolitionism and transatlantic emigration" was "never resolved during the early national period" when numerous arrivants "flirted with emigration schemes" while "remaining involved in black abolitionist movements."[25] These shifts represent one aspect of broader uncertainties regarding the locations, portability, and survival of arrivants' (desired) freedoms in the United States in the late eighteenth century. Such uncertainties stemmed at least partially from the difficult task of articulating a history of violence in a political culture that was predicated on its disavowal. As the undeniable violence of forced migration and unfreedom triggered multiperspectival approaches to origins and destinations, uncertainty regarding the precise parameters of historical change became central to the development of rights claims. The next section examines (dis)avowed violent histories and uncertainties regarding the spatial dimensions of freedom in slaveholders' advertisements of fugitive slaves. Whereas free blacks associated freedom with settlement that naturalized the settler, how did escapes from slavery impact representations of nativity and inhabitance?

Runaway Nativities

Slaveholders who advertised fugitive slaves invested their energies explicitly in defending the reduction of people to property, yet many ads also show that slaveholders had to acknowledge that the enslaved belonged affirmatively and agentively to communities and families that subverted slavery's social order. The ads therefore reveal complex gaps between slaveholders' and fugitives' perceptions of history and belonging. Therefore, while historians have read such ads for their statistical value as windows into lived realities under slavery, I read them—specifically, their treatments of native status—as complex evidence for the development of oppositional rights discourses within slavery.[26] By reading the ads against the grain and looking for how fugitive slaves might have perceived the freedom they sought, I partially follow David Waldstreicher's study of such ads, which interprets them as reflections of slaves' self-fashioning as con-men.[27] The following reading of the ads traces a fine line between slaveholders' interests—which the ads represent explicitly—and fugitive slaves' realities, which emerge implicitly in the ads because capturing a fugitive required slaveholders to imagine the fugitive's life beyond slavery. The ads therefore represent complex interpretations of arrivant freedom.

The ads convey slaveholders' anxieties over arrivants' uncontained presence in settler spaces and show how slavery reflected changing norms of inhabitation, belonging, and national identity. They represent slaveholders' attempts to restore the order of slavery over time and present it as the necessary structure of reality; they reveal the violence that maintained slavery; and they reflect slavery's contribution to settler colonial thought. For example, the ads show that between the eighteenth and nineteenth centuries, slaveholders' perceptions of slaves' domestic nativities shifted to accommodate settlers' changing attitudes regarding their own inhabitation of settled space. In the eighteenth century, slaveholders often used the pronominal phrase *this country born* in reference to American-born slaves, but in the nineteenth century they omitted the pronoun and defined such slaves as *country born*. In 1750, for instance, New Jersey slaveholder Wilson Hunt sought "a Negroe boy, named Peter, about 19 years of age, this country born."[28] The pronoun *this* highlights the contingency of spatial location and suggests that Peter might as well have been born elsewhere, as though nothing in particular sets "this country" apart from any other. Six decades later, North Carolina planter John Reed offered a reward for "ABEL, a country born Negro, about 15 or 16 years old."[29] This shift reflects the rise of what Mark Rifkin calls "settler common sense," through which settlers translated the processes of "elimination, replacement, and possession" of Indigenous peoples and lands into "geographies of everyday nonnative occupancy" that naturalized settlers' belonging to Indigenous homelands.[30]

In analyzing "settler common sense," Rifkin privileges the Native/settler binary over the black/white one, arguing that "the legalities of the settler-state shape everyday experiences of givenness for all nonnatives."[31] Slaveholders' omission of the pronoun *this* in references to slaves as "country born" supports Rifkin's emphasis on the settler regime's "givenness," but at the same time it suggests that this givenness was constructed through slavery. More significantly, the givenness suggested by the phrase "country born" reminds us that the term *nonnative* is itself rooted in a particular historical context. The position of slaves as "nonnative[s]" was structured by negative birthright, while settlers' occupation of that category (which they resisted through intensive self-nativization efforts) was derived from positive birthright. This history requires nuanced understandings of nonnativeness. The logic of the Barbados assembly's legislation of the shared "wild[ness]" that fitted slaves for Caribbean lands (see introduction) is echoed in "this country born," suggesting that settlers' relation to America was *un*stable, *non*-given, and contingent upon slaves' presence there. By contrast, the condition of *partus sequitur ventrem* and the definition of some slaves as real estate attempted to legislate slaves' forced presence in America, to make their presence there an unalterable given. When slaveholders referred to slaves simply as "country born," they replaced their own contingent presence there with an axiomatic one—this new givenness seems to have been facilitated by slavery, which mediated settlers' power over the land.

By the nineteenth century most slaves in the United States were native born.[32] The omission of the pronoun *this* in references to their nativities indicates the emergence both of a broader African American population and of the United States as the proper place of settlers' agentive belonging, through which they asserted slaves' objectified belonging. Slaveholders and traders found the phrase "country born" relevant in reference to the kinds of labor slaves could perform—as in an ad for the sale of a "valuable gang of country born NEGROES, accustomed to the culture of Rice and Cotton"[33]—or to slaves' appearance, as in an ad for a fugitive who was "African but appears like a country born, of a yellowish complexion."[34]

The givenness of "country born" slaves' presence in America registered not agentive inhabitance, but the natural growth and objectified belonging of agricultural produce or livestock. This connotation was clarified by the use in the ads of the verb *raised*, which replaced nativity's potential openness to the possibility of positive birthright with a sense of crop. Yet even when slaveholders used the verb *raised*, they sometimes augmented it with native status through which affirmative belonging could resurface. When Maryland slaveholder Levi Veirs advertised Abraham, a fugitive aged "50 or 60," he referred both to Abraham's remote birth and to Abraham's bondage history in order to speculate about Abraham's destination: "He was raised in Charles county, and formerly belonged to a Mr. Lyon in said county, and it is thought he has made for his native place."[35] Veirs's ad ironically invests Abraham's "native place" with a sense of longing that guides Abraham's presumed return there while it also denies Abraham the right to choose where he might live. Abraham's possible volitional return there endows him with affirmative, agentive, noncommodified belonging that Veirs simultaneously indexes and denies. The raising and growing of slaves distances them from settler rights-bearing inhabitation by confirming *partus sequitur ven-*

trem, which governed both slavery and livestock ownership.[36] Slavery's contribution to the "givenness" of "nonnative inhabitance" that naturalizes the settler regime was therefore immense. If the objectified belonging of slaves grew out of the land that they cultivated, settler lands could be presented as always already spontaneously supportive of settlers' property rights.

The ads served the settler property regime. They were motivated by the need to locate fugitives by denying them any geopolitical positions beyond the circumscribed nativity of objectified property that emerged in the soil they cultivated. Thus, many ads attempted to attach fugitives to small-scale locales that contrasted with settler ideology of liberating territorial expansion and lack of commitment to any particular place. In his study of North Carolina runaway ads, Freddie L. Parker shows that slaveholders referred to the counties from which over 98 percent of the fugitives he studied had fled.[37] This proportion indicates that slaveholders fortified the objectified belonging they imposed on slaves with spatial containment in the localities where the enslaved were forced to labor and whose law enforcement powers could be mobilized to capture fugitives. Settlers used the birthplaces of runaway slaves similarly to resist fugitives' agency as though such nativities could stabilize and localize them. Elie Burgee from Frederick County, Maryland, wished to capture George, who "was born in Prince George's county"; having "c[o]me away from there a small boy," Burgee speculated, George might have "made for Pennsylvania" where he may "try to pass as a freeman."[38] Slavery's order of belonging limits George's legitimate residence to Prince George's County in the past and to Frederick County in the present. Passing "as a freeman" thus depends on the fugitive's ability to forge new relations with the localities he or she chooses to inhabit beyond the confining territorialities of slavery.

Slaveholders' knowledge of slaves' nativities was at times too limited to name a particular county, yet they still used native status as a foundation of negative birthright to counter slaves' implicit reclamation of their spatial agencies. In January 1786, James Gittings Jr. of Long Green, Maryland, heard that his runaway slave Clem, who had been missing for eight months, was "seen at Bush-River," about thirteen miles east of Gittings's home. Gittings wrote that Clem had previously belonged to "Mr. Burket" in "Gunpowder-Neck," to the southeast of Long Green and a bit further south from Bush River, and identified Clem as "a native of the lower counties of this State," some eighty miles down the Bush River and Chesapeake Bay—a place that Clem might or might not have tried to reach.[39] Clem's nativity appears between Gittings's claim of ownership and details of Clem's former owner, floating uncertainly between the negative birthright that Gittings attempts to impose on Clem and Clem's defying spatial practice.

The nativities of runaway slaves are often supplemented by subsequent holdings that both stratify their subjugating attachments and enhance their negative birthright, suggesting that slaves could exploit forced mobility created by slavery to envision volitional fugitive mobilities. North Carolina blacksmith Robert Martin mentioned in an ad that his runaway slave Arthur had been "born in Maryland" and then presented Arthur's subsequent history as a chain of ownerships in North and South Carolina. At "about fourteen years of age," Arthur

> was sold to John or James M'Gill, in Wilmington, N. C.—by M'Gill to Blue—by Blue to Wm. Thomas, on Pedee, S. C.—runaway from Thomas and got back to Wilmington and passed as a free man for some time; at last was apprehended and put in gaol, sold by order of Thomas in Wilmington gaol to John M'Daniel, of South-Carolina—by M'Daniel to Night—by Night to Alexander Bell—by Bell to me.[40]

Martin presented these seven sales in no more than sixteen years (Arthur was "25 or 30 years" old when Martin placed the ad) as Arthur's official history and positioned the period in which he "passed as a free man" in Wilmington between the two major parts of that history, perhaps in hopeful anticipation of his second recapturing. Passing for free represents a deceitful assumption of positive birthright by a person that Martin portrayed as rightful possessor of nothing but the inalienable negative birthright prescribed by *partus sequitur ventrem*.

This official history follows Martin's detailed description of the marks that slaveholders' attacks left on Arthur's body, revealing the violence required to impose the stable negative birthright that Arthur defied. By contrast to the divided history of Arthur's ownership, which the dashes represent graphically, Arthur's physical description suggests a coherent tale of continuous violence and implicit resistance. This contrast symbolizes the ironic clash between Martin's explicit perspective and Arthur's tacit one because what Martin presented as bodily coherence was in fact a repeatedly injured, tortured body. Martin wrote that Arthur had "a large scar on one of his hands and has not the proper use of one of his little fingers" and that he was "much marked with the whip, has a large scar I believe on the outside of both of his thighs, which he says was occasioned by a burn, a little bow legged, his toes much drawn up as if he had worn tight shoes."[41] Arthur's reported explanation of his scar is the only glimpse the ad provides of his own point of view, an indication that he might have once shared his own version of his personal history with Martin. By confining Arthur's reported voice to the violent history that marked his body, Martin tries to obliterate Arthur's own perspective as though his body was mere object. But whereas Arthur's ownership history attempts to confirm his negative birthright, the detailed description of his scars suggests its inefficiency. Perhaps the most interesting part of this description is the metaphoric reference to the shoes that Arthur might never have worn. Martin's language suggests that Arthur's toes acquired their shape after he was born, yet the "as if" implies that Arthur might have been born with this condition. And since Martin had received Arthur following his ownership by six previous slaveholders, he might not have known what caused the condition of Arthur's toes. This detail follows references to unambiguously acquired scars and precedes references to Arthur's "dark complexion" and Maryland birth, thus linking slavery's inscriptions on Arthur's body to Arthur's ownership history.

The ad presents the negative birthright of slaves as a complex multilayered system of intrinsic and acquired conditions that form an intricate net by which Martin might have hoped to recapture Arthur. Martin ended the ad by forewarning "all persons from harbouring, carrying away or in any way keeping" Arthur, as though no part of Arthur's history suggested his ability to direct his own escape. This warning adds another layer of irony to the ad because ten months had intervened between Arthur's escape and Martin's placement of the ad. The ad is dated "August 18," 1821, while Martin specified that Arthur had fled on "the 31st of October," 1820. Martin seems to have resisted the possibility that Arthur might have supported himself during those ten months, as though Arthur's freedom could either be prescribed by white US citizens or be completely unintelligible spatially despite its temporal duration.

In contrast to Martin's ad, numerous advertisements show that slaveholders were often forced to recognize that arrivant family histories exceeded slavery's economic order and constituted communities that disrupted the logic of negative birthright. Such instances of recognition posed the strongest symbolic challenge to slavery's objectified belonging because they belied slavery's presumably successful enforcement of negative birthright. Made under symbolic duress, these instances testify to the complexity of the ads as records of slaveholders' awareness of the social structures they had to deny and destroy in order to maintain slavery. They also contrast sharply with Felix Holbrook's first petition, which claimed to represent a paradoxical community whose members lacked "property," "Wives," "Children," "City," and "Country."

For example, when James Toussiger offered a reward for his slave Charles, he informed readers of the Charleston *City Gazette* that Charles had "been seen on a Plantation, over the Charleston Bridge, belonging to the estate of John Blake." Having identified the place in slavery's institutional terms, Toussiger added that Charles had "a father" at Blake's and a "wife by the name of Peggy" "on the adjoining place." Despite his explicit positioning of Charles within a familial setting beyond the imposition of negative birthright, and although Toussiger said that the "uncommonly smart" Charles had changed his name to "Paul Cain" and "found employment" with "Mr. John Spring," Toussiger closed the ad by denying Charles (or Cain) any agentive belonging.[42] At the end of the ad, Toussiger promised to triple the award to anyone who would provide "proof to conviction of his being harbored by any white person" and thus tacitly obliterated the arrivant community that the ad otherwise affirmed. Both Toussiger and Martin privileged the agency of white harborers in order to trivialize the freedom and communities of fugitives and subject them to white authority even when such authority resisted slavery.

Sometimes slaveowners acknowledged fugitives' ties to distant communities that testified to the breadth and strength of arrivant social networks. South Carolina slaveholder Andrew Kerr placed an ad in the *New York Gazette* offering one hundred dollars to anyone who may deliver to him "a Negro Woman named Mary" and "her mulatto child Nancy," who might have embarked for New York and "may probably go" from there to their "relations living at Newport."[43] And when the pregnant Nancy and her fellow slave Betsy escaped with their toddler children Justina and Henry, their owners, Dr. Joseph Kirkland and M'Millan Campbell, believed they were not only protected by "some white man, who ha[d] inveigled them away," but also "accompanied by a very tall black Woman, sometimes called Nancy, and sometimes Mary," and her "husband, Isaac, or Henry." With their "fair children" and black companions they created a community that Kirkland and Campbell had to recognize if they wanted to capture them. Many ads include similar recognitions of slave communities and families because in order to reimpose negative birthright on recaptured fugitives, slaveholders had first to identify the affirmative attachments by which slaves freed themselves. The specter of arrivants' agentive belonging was thus always potentially available not only to those who defied negative birthright but also to those who sought to enforce it.

Yet two ads by Maryland slaveholder Benjamin Penn show that slaveholders sometimes denied the significance of slaves' family ties even when such denials prevented them from recapturing fugitives. In April 1810, Penn offered a hundred-dollar reward for the delivery of a fugitive who "call[ed] himself Moses Brisco." Penn stated that Brisco had a "father and mother living in the city of Baltimore" who might have helped their son get away, especially as Brisco's "father," who "follows something of the shipping business," might have helped his son "get on board some vessel and go to sea."[44] Eighteen months later Penn advertised Moses Brisco again, with the reward reduced to fifty dollars, and stated that Brisco's father "no doubt harbors his said son, and probably furnished him with a free pass." Although the younger Brisco "has frequently been seen in Baltimore since he absconded," Penn had not been able to obtain him for at least a couple of months.[45] The ad suggests that fugitives' resettlement projects bordered on the unthinkable for slaveholders. Penn acknowledged Brisco's emotional ties to his parents—a constitutive element of his agentive belonging—only after receiving information on Brisco's life in Baltimore. This recognition devalued Brisco for Penn because it undermined his objectified belonging.

Slaveholders' recognition of their slaves' agentive belonging sometimes triggered renewed efforts to objectify them. In 1766, New Jersey slaveowner Philip Kearny placed an ad for Violet, who had escaped four years earlier and who, he suspected, was "some where in *Maryland*, *Virginia*, or *North-Carolina*." Following her 1762 escape, Violet was jailed as a suspected fugitive in Frederick Town, Maryland, and explained that she had escaped because, although she was born free, Kearney had bought her as slave for life. Violet broke out of jail and four years later Kearney still argued that her free birth was "only an invention of hers." Early in his ad Kearney stated that Violet "was born in *New-Jersey*," as though this information substantiated his claim of her negative birthright. Yet Kearney was certain that she "will make her Escape if taken, unless great Care is taken to secure her."[46] The ad emphasizes the long-term, continuous violence of struggles over negative and positive birthrights.

While we cannot know whether Violet claimed a specific birthplace to prove her right to freedom, some African Americans did so as though such claims supported their inherent entitlement to liberty. In March 1813 a "mulatto man, who calls himself Samuel Johnson," was brought to Maryland's Somerset County jail as a suspected fugitive. Johnson used his birthplace to support his claimed freedom. The county sheriff, William Waller, wrote that Johnson claimed he "was born in Fauquier County, Virginia, and had obtained a certificate of his freedom from the Clerk of said county, but got destroyed by getting it wet in his pocket."[47] Two orders of political legitimacy clashed in Johnson's claims—one contingent upon perishable documentation and another validated by personal historical perception. The former was vulnerable to slavery's objectified belonging, as Johnson's experience shows, while the latter could be rendered unintelligible by it.

Like Johnson, a man identified as "Peter" by Alexandria County jailor Andrew Rounsavell claimed to be free by naming his birthplace as New York City, from which he said he had moved to Virginia "about twelve years ago." Jailed on July 16, 1820, Peter seems to have been imprisoned for over a month, because ads requesting his "owner" to "come, prove property, pay charges, and take him away" ran as late as August 28. Whether such owner existed or whether Peter was freeborn, an owner's failure to claim him meant that he would probably be sold into slavery or, in Rounsavell's words, "disposed of as the law directs."[48] Thus, once free blacks were captured on suspicion of being fugitives, settlers exploited their own constructions of arrivants' rights claims to practically doom them to slavery. In other words, slaveholders had to render arrivants' claimed negative belonging and positive birthright unintelligible in order to legitimize slavery.

Peter's fate might have been similar to the history of John Davis, who was purchased "at the Sherrif's Auction" by Maryland slaveholder Anthony Mann. In 1808, Mann publicized Davis's escape and warned readers of the *American and Commercial Daily Advertiser* that although Davis "ran away some years ago from Virginia where he was born," he may "allege, as he has heretofore done, that he is a free man, and a native of New York."[49] Slaveholders, law enforcement agents, and arrivants alike referred to specific places of birth to validate claims for negative birthrights and agentive belonging and, by doing so, contributed to the growing significance of birthplace in the construction and denial of liberties in the early republic.

I end this section and prepare for the next by considering a later episode. By 1840, emancipation in the British Caribbean had blurred distinctions between slavery and freedom because Caribbean origins could suddenly signal entitlement to freedom. New Orleans' Second Municipality Council was alarmed to learn that British consul John Crawford had been issuing freedom certificates to local blacks. They argued that Crawford prepared "three different certificates of freedom" for Ben Savage, "one of them stating that he was born in New York; another that he was born in Pennsylvania; and a third, that he was a native of the West Indies." The authorities were "certain from the man's peculiar accent that he belonged to one of the slave states." Such objectified belonging would have verified their claim for his negative birthright and invalidated Savage's attempts to rewrite his history. They sought to remove Crawford from office because he seemed "as dangerous as . . . the most active abolitionist."[50] Savage's accent symbolized an undeniable nativity that circumscribed his options at a time when Caribbean emancipation led US settlers to fortify the boundaries that demarcated free and slave spatialities.

Crawford's simultaneous provision of three mutually exclusive nativities signifying freedom was counterproductive because the authenticity of birthplace depends on its irreproducibility. But the clash it created between British and US utilizations of nativity echoed earlier British dismissals of US birth certificates. As the next section shows, during the impressment crisis British officials refused to respect the birth certificates that "American magistrates, at home, and consuls, abroad" had issued to US sailors in order to prevent their impressment into the British navy. Regularly "dismiss[ing]" such documents as "frauds bought and sold by conniving sailors," British officials—as the New Orleans council members—refused to accept the claims of those whom they sought to confine to negative birthright.

Settlers' Struggle against English Birthright

The press-gangs that executed the British navy's impressment policy searched US merchant vessels for native-born British subjects and forced them to serve in Britain's navy in order to replenish manpower and deter deserters. They applied the title *native-born British subject* inclusively to anyone born within Britain's expanding royal realm and anyone who had resided in loyal British colonies long enough to be considered a de facto naturalized British subject. These principles legalized the impressment of naturalized US citizens, and British officials justified this policy by claiming that no subject could voluntarily alienate his or her birthright allegiance to the monarch. The British slogan for this policy, "once a Briton, always a Briton," turned subjects' involuntary birthplaces into their political fates. Since impressment involved forced labor and uprootedness, it represented a form of negative birthright that could be compared to slavery. Thus, impressment emerged as a site where settlers could examine and contest the extent to which negative birthright could be imposed on them. Alan Taylor writes that the British "asserted the superiority of their empire over the new republic" by arguing that "the subject was permanent but the citizen fungible."[51] Conversely, anti-impressment writers interpreted fungibility as a source of volition in order to claim that alienable citizenship was a superior form of affiliation because it was grounded in freedom rather than in compulsory allegiance.

Impressment threatened to strip self-nativized settlers of their rights-bearing subjectivities, and by protesting it, naturalized US citizens scrutinized the meanings of nativity and freedom. These protests centralize the significance of England's feudalist legacies for the early republic and show that American exceptionalism became the condition of possibility for settlers' articulations of their rights independently of British law. Anti-impressment politicians and writers argued that positive birthright allowed individuals to alienate themselves from governments they no longer wished to obey and to join voluntary political associations.[52] This argument meant that almost any form of attachment—and particularly those inflected by the spatial or geopolitical affiliations that stable inhabitation produced—could be viewed as a threat to individual liberties. Immediate kinship relations were the only order of attachment that seemed immune to feudalist subjugation.

Prior to the Revolutionary War, the settler establishment accepted impressment as a matter of course. Otis, who compared forced taxation to slavery, also used a slavery analogy to justify the policy of impressment. Whereas Otis defined the right not to be taxed without one's consent as "part of a British subject[']s birth-right, and as inherent and perpetual, as the duty of allegiance" (RBC 92), he used impressment as evidence of settlers' worthy contribution to Britain's effort in the Seven Years' War. "[T]he flower of *our* youth," he wrote, "were annually pressed by ten thousands into the service, and there treated but little better . . . than hewers of wood and drawers of water" (RBC 88)—a biblical phrase that was synonymous with slaves.[53] In this analogy, settlers' sacrifice of their freedom for the British Empire supports Otis's argument (and Franklin's earlier similar one) that in return for promoting Britain's interests, settlers gain more privileges than do English subjects who remain in England. The form of slavery that was associated with impressment thus signified the patriotic pole of the native's semantic range.

The Declaration of Independence denounced impressment and listed it among George III's crimes only because it forced rebellious settlers to fight against their "countrymen" during the Revolutionary War. It took a few decades of jingoistic propaganda to delegitimize impressment as powerfully as revolutionary discourse had rejected taxation without representation, and this rhetorical project succeeded because it represented inalienable geopolitical attachment as a fundamental threat to natural rights. Settlers' willingness to accept treatment that seemed "but little better" than slavery depended on the empire's geopolitical aspirations and the theories of territorial attachment that supported them. Settlers' pride in impressment withered as they sought to detach their rights from Britain. They started to view territorial attachment primarily as a tool of confinement and associated it with the legacy of negative birthright at the same time that arrivant petitions argued that freedom had to be rooted spatially to be meaningful. Anti-impressment discourse provided US citizens with an opportunity to distance themselves from feudalist constructs and represent the settler colonial project as a liberating mechanism unparalleled by European traditions of territorial attachment.

An anonymous anti-impressment piece published in the Maryland *Republican Advocate* in 1802 contrasted Britain's purported enslavement of its native subjects with the US protection of citizens' natural right to freedom. The piece extolled the "Rights and Privileges of the American citizen" as surpassing those of "[t]he Russian," who is "contented if he can barely subsist"; "the peasantry of the German Empire," who are "slave[s]" in a "corrupted feudal system"; and "[t]he Italians, the Swiss, the French, and the Spanish," who all "groan under the oppression of iron-hearted masters."[54] Finally the writer asserted that "Britons, who so barbarously enslave others, are themselves the worst of slaves" and hailed the United States as an exceptional "*land of genuine freedom*." This optimistic assertion of spatialized liberty was undermined by a brief adjacent report of an attempted slave kidnapping; written in apparently the same voice, the piece claimed that "[n]othing . . . is more degrading to any people, particularly one boasting of its freedom, than for them to connive at or to suffer unprincipled men to traffic in human flesh."[55] But as anti-impressment thought developed, it conflated territorial attachment with slavery and threatened to undermine the myth that American land facilitated settlers' liberty. The idea of voluntary migration that constitutes the settler helped solve this paradox and entrenched settlers' positions as quintessential rights-bearing subjects at the expense of arrivants' and Indigenous peoples' rights claims. So as arrivants looked to permanent settlement as a means of becoming rights-bearing subjects, settlers emphasized the need to keep moving in order to remain free.

The 1806 pamphlet *Observations on the Impressment of American Seamen*, signed by "A Citizen of Baltimore," illustrated the dramatic shift in settler perceptions of impressment from revolutionary acceptance to early republican rejection. Creating a tacit analogy between impressment and the Middle Passage, the writer quoted Congressman James Elliot (Vermont) as saying that "the groans of our impressed fellow citizens mingle with the murmurs of every gale from the ocean,"[56] and he elaborated on this Middle Passage imagery by invoking the families of the impressed. Arguing that all US seamen faced "perpetual danger" of impressment, he wrote that no "father," "husband," "brother," or "child, on whom perhaps an helpless family depends" could "be sure that he will escape in this general scene of oppression and injustice" (*OI* 40). Portraying immediate family relations as the most significant form of attachment, the writer asked any unmoved reader to "suppose, that he hears the heartfelt shrieks of the miserable wife piercing his ears, and entreating him in accents of rage and despair, to restore to her her impressed husband, the father of her children." He further asked his readers to "view, in imagination, the aged and helpless parent, in accents of sinking woe, misery and distress, bewailing the loss of a dutiful and beloved son" (*OI* 41). By focusing on the violated families of the impressed, anti-impressment writers decontextualized abolitionist rhetoric and portrayed settlers rather than slaves as those whose natural rights were at risk.

The equations of British allegiance with slavery and of impressed seamen with the enslaved illustrate the contrastive roles of kinship and spatial attachments in each of these discourses. Holbrook's first petition presented the denial of slave families as the elementary building block of the deterritorialized disenfranchisement through which objectified belonging operated. But whereas Holbrook's petitions tended to portray space as a necessary condition for freedom, anti-impressment writers expressed consistent suspicion of any spatial attachment that extended to multigenerational communities such as those whose loss Holbrook bemoaned. While contemporaneous critiques of slavery emphasized the sanctity of both African families and communities, the *Observations*' advocacy of portable positive birthright that could not be bound by inalienable allegiance questioned the value of permanent community. To refute Blackstone's assertion that "universal law" tied "natural born subject[s]" inalienably to their "prince" *OI* 12), the "Citizen of Baltimore" argued that Locke had refuted governments' right "to prohibit the emigration of their subjects and citizens" (*OI* 14). He portrayed inalienable allegiance as a feudalist form of slavery by contrasting the right to expatriation as "the law of Nature and of Nature's God" with the "feudal system" by which England "chained men to the soil on which they were born; and converted the bulk of mankind into the villeins, or slaves of a lord, or superior" (*OI* 20).

Whereas arrivant petitions focused their quests for freedom on resettlement that would forge new communal spatial and political relations, the *Observations* writer presented expatriation as freedom from belonging that tacitly rejected the freedom to create new political associations, which was highlighted in arrivant petitions. He argued that the right to expatriation was a natural universal condition that applied equally to those "born under constituted and ancient politics" and to those "born in the woods, amongst the unconfined inhabitants that run loose in them." The elevation of expatriation to the level of a foundational, natural, universal right responds to what the writer presented as the British argument that "the right of expatriation never existed but in the imagination of modern innovators" (*OI* 10). This powerful expression of settler colonial ideology emphasizes settlers' freedom from the imperial history that spawns them and applies the same freedom from belonging to Indigenous peoples by referring to those "born in the woods." In this fantasy, anyone can become a rights-bearing subject if only they are willing to desert their place of inhabitation and sociopolitical relations. From this perspective, resettlement is antithetical to human freedom because it envisions freedom as rooted in spatial communal belonging. The writer emphasized that individual volition necessarily overrode the choice of "our fathers or progenitors" to "bound up themselves and their posterity to perpetual subjection to the government" (*OI* 17).

These distinctions between slavery and freedom are premised on the idea that as rights-bearing subjects settlers cannot be bound by any order of belonging because attachment is always dangerously close to feudalist negative birthright. Citizenship constituted the liberty of the rights-bearing subject, and the writer distinguished it from feudalist "fealty" that "rests upon *lands*" and from "allegiance," a "territorial tenure" representing "[a] badge of inferiority" and "servitude" that is therefore "repulsive." In contrast to "fealty" and "allegiance," he wrote that "citizenship" had "arisen from the dissolution of the feudal system" and comprised "a "communicable" "political tie" that served as "the charter of equality" and "freedom" (*OI* 21, 22). The *Observations* exposes the inherent paradoxes of settler colonialism whose condition of possibility threatens its ideological imperative to represent its project as always already tied to settled land.

A few days into the War of 1812, the Charleston *City Gazette* published an anonymous opinion piece that advocated the virtues of expatriation by contrasting US citizenship with slavery. "To deny the natural freedom of man," the *Gazette* proclaimed, "is to say that all sojourners, since Eve eat [*sic*] the apple, were runaways and vagabonds." The distinction between settlers as free, migrating, rights-bearing subjects and fugitive slaves enabled settlers to protect the institution of slavery while defining the settler state as the quintessential bastion of liberty and the naturalized settler as the ultimate symbol of voluntary membership. Therefore, although settlers naturalized their rights claims by presenting themselves as America's new natives, they also had to maintain faith in potential future travels to support their freedom. Territorial expansion—whether or not any particular settler used it to start a new life elsewhere—helped solve the paradoxes of settler freedom. The national ethos of this piece reserves "the right of removal" or "the right of migration"[57] exclusively for the settler and denies it to the enslaved, shedding light on the radicalism of Revolutionary-era arrivant petitions that insisted on the right to define settled inhabitation and the spatial attachments it created as essential for agentive belonging and freedom.

This distinction was facilitated by the gap between the expansive nativities of settlers and the circumscribed ones of slaves. On July 4, 1812, following the declaration of war, comptroller of the Treasury Richard Rush integrated these ideas in a congressional oration rejecting the "poor definition of country which would limit us to an occupancy of the same little piece of earth!"[58] Rush tied his anti-British rhetoric to slavery and Manifest Destiny (*avant la lettre*) and offered "the African slave trade" as the only historical equivalent of impressment. He supported this claim by applying the abolitionist imagery of torn families to impressment and limited his critique of slavery implicitly to that banned trade rather than to domestic enslavement. He asserted that impressment was "worse" than US slavery because "the African is only made to work under the lash of a task-master, whereas the citizen of the United States thus enslaved, receives also the lash . . . and is moreover exposed to the bitter fate of fighting against . . . his own countrymen" or "his own immediate kindred" (RR 96).

This functional description of slavery deprives slaves not only of social or political membership but also of spatial belonging. The "citizen," by contrast, enjoys membership in various sociopolitical scales—the state, its community of citizens, and the family—as the national community compensates for loss of attachment to land at the same time that the "African" is denied such attachment without the right to expatriation. Rush discussed circumscribed nativity in terms of the British navy's demand to inspect sailors' birth certificates during vessel searches. Implying that the demand attempted to impose circumscribed nativities on people whose freedom rested on the settler colonial ethos of transferable nativity, Rush protested the "insolent indignity" by which "a freeborn American must be made to prove his nativity" or "be held forever a slave!" He treated Britain's scrutiny of US sailors' nativities as a preliminary stage of enslavement and protested the British demand that "a free born American . . . establish the identity that binds him to his parents, to his blood, to his native land," as though the problem was not impressment but these binding ties (RR 96).

The distrust of territorial attachment in anti-impressment discourse clashes dramatically with settlers' simultaneous claims for their exclusive, axiomatic, and absolute ownership of colonized Indigenous peoples' homelands. Although Rush implied that citizens must be free of binding attachment to land, he clarified that "*men* are the property of the *nation*" and concluded the oration with a proto–Manifest Destiny promise of the peaceful liberties the war will usher in. "[F]rom the ocean to the mountains, from the mountains to the farthest west . . . the view, on all sides," he stated, would ensure the "pleasure" and "future destinies of our happy land" (RR 97). Rush thus resolved the conflict between the two political poles of spatial attachment—circumscribed nativity and positive birthright—by presenting the territorial expansion of the settler state as antidote to the circumscription of nativity that threatened to impose negative birthright on settlers.

This chapter juxtaposed the dilemmas of arrivant belonging with the anxieties of settlers regarding spatial attachments in order to show that the relations between enslaved and free blacks' freedom discourses and Eurocentric natural rights is far more complex than mere imitation. The vast theoretical distance between settlers' and arrivants' perceptions of the relations between space and freedom demands a clearer positioning of enslaved and free blacks as significant contributors to theories of liberty and rights and specifically to their sense that nativity-affirming settlement is essential for producing rights-bearing subjects. However, the unstable spatial coordinates of these theories also suggest that we should not portray them only as elements of settler political thought. In contrast to arrivant aspirations for settled inhabitation, Rush's text clarifies that settlers' suspicions of spatial attachment required territorial expansion that enabled them to imagine a potentially unbound citizenship. The next chapter focuses more closely on settlers' territorial expansion by exploring Indigenous peoples' attempts to protect their lands from the expanding settler regime during the first decade of US treaties with Indigenous polities. In these formative years of US rights discourse, settlers' perceptions of freedom clashed with both arrivant and Indigenous rights claims. Whereas this chapter centralized rights claims that treated space primarily hypothetically, the next focuses on negotiations over physical lands and the human relations and possibilities that they could support. This is also a transition from arrivant resettlement visions that sought to redefine the meanings of settlers' presence on Indigenous peoples' lands to Indigenous peoples' perceptions of the political practices that those lands could support. The relations between freedom, alienability, and inalienability that I began to discuss in this chapter intensify in the next as I examine US Indian policies that center the national liberty ethos on the concept of inalienable national soil.

[4]

UNSETTLING BIRTHRIGHTS

ENSLAVED AND FREE BLACKS asserted their rights in the face of a settler regime that denied their agentive geopolitical positions. Even though Felix Holbrook, Prince Hall, and other black petitioners had framed their rights claims within imperial parameters, as chapter 3 showed, settlers dismissed them because they viewed forced migration, exile, and enslavement as conditions that forever deprived their victims of meaningful political volition. By contrast, settlers had to recognize Indigenous political thought even when such recognition tacitly undermined the imperial order that settlers wished to naturalize. Whereas in New England settler colonial expansion and proliferation at Indigenous peoples' expense enabled settlers to dismiss the Mohegan rights discourse discussed in chapter 2, early US officials could not afford to ignore militarily powerful Indigenous polities whose homelands the United States claimed to have received from England by the Treaty of Paris (1783). Incapable of possessing these lands by force, the United States cooperated with Indigenous geopolitical practices, however partially, dishonestly, or unwillingly. These cooperations exposed clashing geopolitical visions and rights theories.

Consequently, in the aftermath of the Revolutionary War, the United States found itself in the midst of discrepant international arenas grounded in incompatible geopolitical systems. It sought admission into a Eurocentric Westphalian order of mutually exclusive jurisdictions validated by spatial objectification, under which it claimed sovereignty over Indigenous peoples' homelands and over arrivants. Under Eurocentric political norms the United States imagined its sovereignty as axiomatic, exclusive, and absolute. However, the Indigenous polities whose lands the United States wished to settle comprised a flexible international network in which spatial practices and kinship relations complemented each other and maintained a precarious interdependent environment that operated through forms of participatory decentralized governance. Members of this international system alternately fought the United States, treated with it, and invited it to join their political arenas. The boundaries between these international spheres were in flux not only because of the discrepancies between settler and Indigenous geopolitics, but also because England, France, and Spain maintained diplomatic and commercial relations with Indigenous peoples despite assertions by the United States of its exclusive sovereignty over Indians in territories it claimed as its own.[1]

The United States approached both arenas with treaty initiatives in order to position itself within the Westphalian order of mutually exclusive sovereign states and thereby legitimize its claims to the homelands of Indigenous polities.[2] Treaties between the United States and European powers were based on mutual recognition of each party's exclusive sovereignty, but the treaties that the United States dictated to Indigenous polities in this period were predicated on a fundamental negation of Indigenous geopolitics. They served US efforts to secure Indigenous legitimation of settler sovereignty over Indigenous homelands, and they did so paradoxically by declaring Indigenous peoples as subordinate to the United States. Many treaties of the period thus began by stating that the United States "give[s] peace" to the Indigenous polity that it claimed to "receive" into its "protection."[3] The major purpose of the treaties, as far as the United States was concerned, was to assert sovereignty over Indigenous polities and their lands.

Between 1783 and 1795—the first dozen years of the US's internationally recognized existence by Eurocentric standards—these processes unfolded over a broad region that stretched from the Great Lakes through the Ohio River valley to emerging states such as Pennsylvania, Kentucky, Virginia, the Carolinas, and Georgia. Across these spaces the United States confronted concrete paradoxes that shattered its claimed sovereignty because Indigenous polities' orchestrations of political relations often left US officials wondering how to grasp difficulties that the settler regime wished simply to obliterate. Historians explain these processes by showing how Indigenous political adjustments and revisions in light of the realities of colonial powers significantly shaped early American history.[4]

Indigenous peoples could shape this history thanks primarily to their flexible, cooperative international networks in resistance to settler expansion. This chapter focuses on one such system, which the United States called the northwestern confederacy and whose Indigenous spokespersons sometimes identified as the United Indian Nations, as well as on some of its member polities. Drawing on older histories of cooperation and kinship relations, Gregory Evans Dowd notes that "between 1779 and 1781, most of the Indians between the [Great] lakes and the gulf [of Mexico] had united in their opposition to the United States."[5] By 1783, their confederacy linked some "thirty-five native nations," including Anishnaabe, Cherokee, Delaware, Haudenosaunee, Mahican, Miami, Mississauga, Munsee, Muscogee, Nanticoke, Odawa, Piankashaw, Potawatomi, Shawnee, and Wendat peoples who joined on various occasions and parted on others in order to protect their lands more effectively.[6]

The northwestern confederacy's contribution to Indigenous rights theories was immense because it utilized its diverse members' political philosophies in concerted efforts to formulate unsettlement solutions to settler colonial threats. Lisa Brooks explains that the "confederated nations were willing to share space with their [US] American 'brothers,'" but this willingness depended on an overarching logic of unsettlement because "they were *un*willing to share in a European system that constructed them as unequal inhabitants of a colonial environment."[7] Unsettlement was often accompanied by resettlement, as chapter 2 shows, but it differed from arrivant resettlement projects in its attitude toward the imperial order. Whereas arrivant rights-theorists often sought to rearrange that order from within, many articulations of Indigenous ones focused on replacing it with the interdependent precarity, flexibility, and agency that characterized Indigenous kinship relations and spatial practices.

Indigenous politics created what Robert A. Williams defines as "human solidarity where we regard others as our relatives" within kinship networks that require ongoing efforts to seek and restore balance over a broad spectrum of human and environmental relations.[8] Daniel Heath Justice explains that the "kinship with other humans and the rest of creation" that founds such politics constitutes a "dynamic" process that is "ever in motion."[9] He distinguishes the Westphalian nation-state—constituted through the "erasure of kinship bonds" and their replacement with loyalty to the "economic and political authority" of "a monolithic and coercive state"—from Indigenous nationhood. Heath argues that the latter is predicated on "an understanding of common social interdependence" because "a web of kinship rights *and* responsibilities" connects "the People, the land, and the cosmos."[10] The northwestern confederacy extended such principles to a larger framework of a "dish with one spoon" of which all its participants could partake, which Lisa Brooks reads as "a geographic-social configuration and a political concept that . . . depended on recognizing equality and building consensus among all nations who ate from the dish, a joining of minds that would enable the political system to mirror the geographic one."[11]

In the period studied here, the northwestern confederacy and some of its constituent parts tried to mobilize these principles toward radical unsettlement projects that would enable Indigenous peoples to maintain their political networks in a land transformed by settler colonialism. These unsettlement proposals profoundly critiqued settler geopolitics. They resisted settler colonialism and invited settler to modify their own formulations of the relations between spatial attachment and freedom. US negotiations with Indigenous polities thus occurred in the double context of settler expansionism and Indigenous unsettling initiatives. US officials mobilized cartography and Eurocentric political thought to support their claims for the settler regime's exclusive, axiomatic, absolute sovereignty. Cartography—often represented in these negotiations through the official map that William McMurray, assistant geographer to the United States, published in 1784—enabled the United States to assert its presumably internationally legitimate borders that turned Indigenous homelands into settlers' inalienable national soil.[12] Through this usage, McMurray's map exposed the political functions of cartography. As Mishuana Goeman argues, its presentations at treaty councils attempted to "exert political control by manipulating the representation of space into a language of normativity."[13] McMurray's map showed the new nation bounded by the Atlantic, the Saint Lawrence River, the Great Lakes, the Mississippi, and the Floridas (see map 1). Indigenous spokespersons critiqued the land surveys and maps that settlers saw as indispensable legitimizing tools for their regime, because cartographic technologies were facilitated by and constitutive of spatial objectification and commodification that threatened to dispossess Indigenous polities and obliterate their spatial practices. If, as Lisa Brooks argues, the Indigenous polities with whom the United States treated in this period understood "the political system" as one that should "mirror the geographic one," then cartography's objectification of space figured the subjugation of the polities whose homelands were surveyed and mapped.

This chapter explores constructions of rights and freedoms through the interactions of divergent geopolitical perspectives, spatial practices, and perceptions of native status in the 1785 negotiations over Cherokee lands in Hopewell (present-day Clemson, South Carolina) and in the decade-long struggle over the Ohio River valley. In both regions, Indigenous polities formulated plans to unsettle the US regime in order to create multiple sovereignties that will enable them to maintain and develop their political aspirations within Indigenous homelands.[14] Through these historical processes, settlers revised their understandings of spatial attachment and in/alienability. Whereas chapter 3 shows that impressment—and English negative birthright legacies more broadly—led settlers to associate spatial attachment with subjugation, negotiations with Indigenous peoples facilitated—or so the United States hoped—the territorial expansion that settlers perceived as a mode of liberation from confining spatial attachment. However, in asserting their rights to

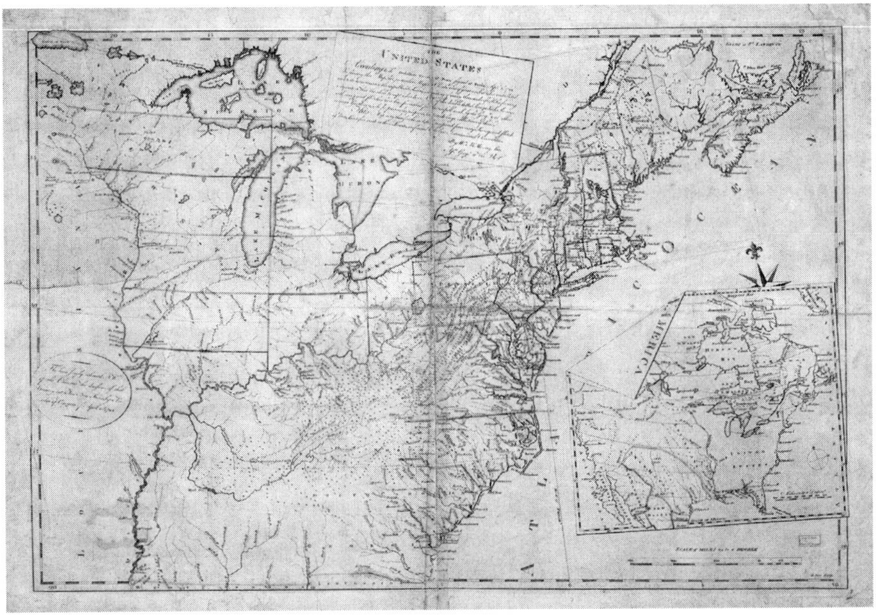

William McMurray's map of the United States, 1784. William McMurray and Robert Scot, "The United States according to the definitive treaty of peace signed at Paris Sept. 3d. 1783" (n.p., 1784), Library of Congress, Geography and Map Division.

Indigenous peoples' homelands, settlers attempted to enhance their genocidal dispossession of Indigenous peoples. US officials imagined national space as the nation's body in order to naturalize settler expansion and replace the subjugating connotations of spatial belonging with a sense of vital organic necessity.[15] They conflated the somatic and territorial traditions from which English birthright emerged and translated them into naturalized settler colonial holism that could not tolerate Indigenous unsettlement projects.

These ideas resulted in two central doctrines of US Indian affairs—impossibility and allotment—which operationalized the cartographic claims that McMurray's map represented by turning the presumed exclusivity and absolute, axiomatic validity of settler sovereignty into normative imperatives. In studies of US-Indian relations, impossibility and allotment usually refer to later processes by which the settler regime retrospectively defended its claimed axiomatic sovereignty. This temporal framework facilitates representations of settler sovereignty as the threshold from which political and legal relations ensue and to which they must conform. However, early US-Indigenous negotiations show that both doctrines were indispensable founding mechanisms of US sovereignty. Indigenous polities anticipated and responded to settlers' impossibility and allotment initiatives with unsettlement possibilities, which are the focus of this chapter.

The texts analyzed in this chapter are drawn mostly from records of treaty negotiations. These records may seem unlikely sources for such analysis because the treaties that Indigenous polities signed were often written by US officials before negotiations even began. Then, following elaborate, sometimes prolonged, and often difficult negotiations, US officials dictated the prewritten treaties to their signatories. Therefore, the signed treaties obliterated the complex negotiation process that made their signing possible. Scott Richard Lyons looks for agency in the act of signing treaties and analyzes the x-marks with which Indigenous peoples did so as ambiguous symbols of "consent in the context of coercion," where the "little choice" one has between signing and not signing represents "Indian agency" under settler dictates.[16] But the records of negotiations that preceded these acts—as well as records of failed attempts to begin negotiations, or of Indigenous peoples' resistance to treaties—constitute far richer sources for studying Indigenous agency in the context of US-Indian relations because they comprise multivocal, elaborate discussions of political philosophies and interests. These records provide explicit Indigenous theorizations of unsettling resistance to the settler regime and multiple instances of what Audra Simpson calls Indigenous "refusal" of settler authority.[17] The negotiations opened up possibilities that the treaties sought to obliterate, and they show how Indigenous peoples required the United States to accommodate the very Indigenous political protocols that the treaties tried to annul.[18]

This chapter thus centralizes the political possibilities that the treaties were meant to annihilate and shows how the late eighteenth-century US records of Indian affairs may undermine the belatedness thesis (see introduction). Whereas Goeman writes that the "imaginable geographies" developed by contemporary Native American women writers "will open up new possibilities and inaugurate new and vital meanings," treaty records show the longer histories of a broad range of geopolitical possibilities.[19] My analysis begins with the doctrines of impossibility and allotment through which the settler regime tried to annihilate such possibilities and perpetuate Indigenous dispossession. By tracing these doctrines to their early articulations this chapter shows how settlers produced Indigenous dispossession in order to repudiate Indigenous unsettlement initiatives. Then, I discuss settlers' use of cartography, by which they hoped to actualize their sovereignty claims. Against this backdrop, the rest of the chapter analyzes Indigenous unsettling geopolitics, beginning with a discussion of embodied spatial practices in contrast to settlers' cartographic assumptions. Next, I explore the significance that Indigenous spokespersons accorded to North American births as foundations of political relations. The chapter concludes with an analysis of the incompatible systems of im/possibilities that treaty negotiations reveal and of Indigenous uses of loss as an element of geopolitical renewal.

Impossibility and Allotment

The doctrine of impossibility erupted into US public discourse following the decision of Supreme Court Justice Ruth Bader Ginsburg in *City of Sherrill v. Oneida Indian Nation* (2005). The case concerned the Oneida Nation's reassertion of sovereignty over seventeen thousand acres it had purchased out of its original six-million-acre homeland—and within its historic three-hundred-thousand-acre reservation, of which the settler regime had defrauded the Oneida in the early nineteenth century. Although the Oneida had previously been barred from taking their case to court, Ginsburg argued that the two hundred years that had elapsed between original dispossession and Oneida legal action proved that the Oneida had implicitly acquiesced to settler possession of its "historic reservation." She justified her ruling against the Oneida by invoking fear that the Oneida might "initiat[e] a new generation of litigation to free" lands from the "regulatory controls that protect all landowners in the area," which would eventually result in a "checkerboard of alternating state and tribal jurisdiction in New York State" that would undermine settler governance. This scenario raised the specter of the Oneida's potential piecemeal recovery of sovereignty over their original homeland, which comprises about one-sixth of the present area of New York State. Ginsburg's metaphoric use of "new generation" also encapsulated anxiety over Native American population growth and political renewal that would frustrate US genocidal policies. Thus, Ginsburg asserted the doctrine of impossibility in the face of an unsettlement threat that seemed potentially to endanger the entire United States.[20]

Scholars agree that the doctrine of impossibility harkens to the founding of settler territorial authority. Mark Rifkin writes that the case's "dialectic of 'impossibility' and 'acquiescence' . . . lies at the heart of U.S. imperialism in the antebellum period," which promoted "the inherent coherence and contiguity of national geography."[21] Kevin Bruyneel similarly locates the doctrine of impossibility within an "affirmation of colonial rule" that must reject "overlapping U.S.-indigenous jurisdictions at the behest of the indigenous party" and explains the function of settler temporality in producing the lateness of Indigenous claims. In Ginsburg's decision, he says, arguments regarding the time that had elapsed (presumably between initial land loss and subsequent legal action) represented not "*chronological* time" but the construction of Indigenous sovereignty as incompatible with US modernity.[22]

Legal scholar Kathryn E. Fort places Ginsburg's use of impossibility within a broader judicial process that effectively "end[ed] more than thirty years of modern Indian land claims litigation," so that Indigenous peoples can no longer mobilize legal action to claim lands. Fort explains that Ginsburg's application of the impossibility doctrine "does not comport with any historical understanding" of that doctrine. In its original usage, this doctrine protects contracting parties when factors beyond their control prevent them from fulfilling their contractual obligations. Fort highlights the contrast between the function of pre-Ginsburgian impossibility as an "equity doctrine" and Ginsburg's distortion of that doctrine into a mechanism of dispossession.[23]

In 2005 Ginsburg merely provided legal authorization for a practice that has structured US Indian policy from its inception. That practice was constitutive of settler axiomatic sovereignty and served settlers' arguments that no part of the settler state could be unsettled to protect the rights of Indigenous peoples even if the United States (or any of its constituent states or former colonies) infringed those rights in order to create what eventually became inalienable national space. In the late eighteenth century the impossibility doctrine functioned within a different power dynamic than its 2005 reincarnation because Indigenous polities wielded considerable military power. Power dynamics are central here because, in both incarnations, impossibility enabled the United States to present itself implicitly as powerless—not simply because it chose not to remove settlers from Indigenous lands, but because it claimed that it *could not do so*. Such powerlessness portrays settlers as the innocent victims of predatory Indigenous peoples and thus supports settlers' disavowal of the foundational violence of settlement. In 1785, the Cherokee Beloved Man of Chota (whom settlers called Tassel) commented ironically on settler powerlessness when US commissioners used the impossibility doctrine to deny his request to remove settlers who encroached on Cherokee land. After the commissioners said that the settlers were "too numerous for us to engage to remove [them]," Tassel asked rhetorically, "Are Congress, who conquered the King of Great Britain, unable to remove those people?"[24] The rhetorical powerlessness that Tassel critiqued was essential in establishing the absolute validity of axiomatic settler sovereignty. It presented this sovereignty as so strong that even the settler regime could not undo it. This is the logic of inalienable national soil that reifies the settler nation as a holistic body that cannot be violated.

Both impossibility and allotment enabled the United States to actualize its sovereignty claims and thereby ensure that settler invasion of Indigenous polities' lands would be, as Patrick Wolfe argues, a permanent "structure" rather than a fleeting "event."[25] Allotment is a better-known mechanism of settler sovereignty because the 1887 Dawes Act implemented it on a massive scale, by which the United States converted reservation lands into eventually alienable plots of private property and dispossessed Native polities of 65 percent of their reservation lands.[26] Allotment and impossibility combine to present the same settler regime that prevents Indigenous peoples from initiating legal action to recover dispossessed lands as the only power that can legitimize Indian landholding. In the early years of US-Indian relations, the settler regime insisted that land grants from the United States were the only intelligible source of Indigenous peoples' landholding. This settler fantasy derives from the impossibility doctrine and supports it. Thus, allotment is a function of impossibility that constituted the United States as the sole legitimate source of Indigenous peoples' lands and rights. Both doctrines construct Indigenous land rights as always already extinguishable and Indigenous homelands as always already alienable. In the early republic these processes were visualized and concretized through cartography, which the next section discusses.

Maps

On November 22, 1785, US commissioners Benjamin Hawkins, Andrew Pickens, Joseph Martin, and Laughlin McIntosh opened negotiations with the Cherokee in order to gain Cherokee recognition of axiomatic US sovereignty, obtain Cherokee acceptance of settler claims for part of their homeland, redeem captured US citizens and slaves held by Cherokees, and end Cherokee resistance to settler expansion. Cherokee negotiators wanted the United States to end encroachments, remove settlers, compensate for lands of which settlers had dispossessed them fraudulently, return Cherokee prisoners, and protect traders who served Cherokee communities. The commissioners began by presenting McMurray's map, which reflects settlers' willful oblivion of Indigenous homelands. The map reduces the Cherokee, for example, to temporary, replaceable names of landscape features such as the "Tennessee or Cherokee R[iver]" and "Cherokee or Broad R[iver]." The commissioners introduced the map by stating that "Congress is now the sovereign of all our country, which we now point out to you on the map." They promised that the United States "want[s] none of your lands, or any thing else which belongs to you," and proposed "to enter into articles of a treaty perfectly equal, and conformable to what we now tell you" (*NASPIA* 6:49). McMurray's map thus functioned as the irrefutable foundation of settler sovereignty. Armed with it, settlers redefined the scope and meanings of political relations in the area it charted.

Martin Brückner discusses McMurray's map as a prominent national artifact, drawing on Benedict Anderson's analysis of maps as "one of the first examples showing the nation as a pure sign and logo." Anderson writes that the "map-as-logo" substitutes earlier cartographic "explanatory glosses" on specific spatial features with a visual symbol of the nation as complete insular space, and he bases this argument on Thongchai Winichakul's study of the geographic construction of the "geo-body of a nation."[27] This scholarly genealogy shows that national sovereignty is modeled on the presumably inalienable body of the possessive individual. Winichakul, Anderson, and Brückner present these cartographic constructs as novelties of national and imperial formations and, indeed, when US commissioners used McMurray's map to negotiate treaties with Indigenous peoples they hoped it would visualize a new geopolitical order by asserting "the *new* change of sovereignty" and claiming that Congress was "*now* the sovereign" whom they expected the Cherokee to acknowledge (*NASPIA* 6:49 [my italics]). The United States used McMurray's map in early treaties in order to obtain Indigenous peoples' legitimation of the territorial coherence of what was in reality an assortment of partially overlapping, shifting networks of relationships among Indigenous polities and the various European powers that interacted with those networks. It was not even a "checkerboard," to use Ginsburg's term, because established settlements were few and far between over much of the vast distances that McMurray's map depicted.

The Cherokee negotiators who looked at McMurray's map responded to the claims it represented by emphasizing the value of Aboriginal spatial attachment and the conditions on which settlers could inhabit Indigenous lands. James Madison and Arthur Coody rendered the words of Tassel, who was the first to respond, thus: "I am made of this earth, on which the great man above placed me, to possess it." Tassel insisted that a supreme being "made" the "land we are now on . . . for us to subsist upon," and added, "You must know the red people are the aborigines of this land, and that it is but a few years since the white people found it out." Tassel anchored his claim on his nativity by representing himself as "the first stock, . . . a native of this land" on which "the white people are now living . . . as our friends" (*NASPIA* 6:49). Tassel's recurrent usage of "this earth" and "this land"—or, rather, of the Cherokee words that Madison and Coody rendered through these pronomial phrases—differs from slaveholders' usage of "this country born," which signified objectified belonging by birth (chapter 3). Tassel's phrase "this land" evoked not simply the Cherokee homeland that McMurray's map tried to obliterate, but more specifically the land "we were fighting for, during the late contest." The commissioners understood that Tassel referred to Hopewell, Pickens's plantation where negotiations took place "in sight of Seneca," a Cherokee town destroyed in the Revolutionary War, which the commissioners described as "at present a waste." The Cherokee had lost that part of their homeland in a 1777 treaty that Tassel said he was "compelled" to sign and for which he was seeking compensation (*NASPIA* 6:49).[28]

Embedded in the Cherokee history of the particular place of negotiations, and representing an old narrative that he "had in [his] mind for many years," Tassel's argument counters the commissioners' emphases of novelty with a political logic that nurtures legitimacy over time within a familiar place of multigenerational inhabitation (*NASPIA* 6:49). Tassel presents an unambiguous model of entitlement rooted in attachment to the soil that must be maintained actively and invites US citizens to participate in this geopolitical order as "friends" who can enter "this land" only as equals because conquest would shatter the interdependent relations that sustain it. Tassel's multifaceted expression of indigeneity highlights this political logic that approximates Lisa Brooks's analysis of the common pot: generative process that makes Indigenous peoples part of the land ("I am made of this earth"; "a native of this land"), priority that facilitates their responsibilities for the land ("the red people are the aborigines of this land"; "I am of the first stock"), and divine design that sanctions these relations ("placed me, to possess it," "made it for us"). To borrow Brooks's analysis of a speech that the northwestern confederacy would deliver to the United States a year later, and which I discuss below, Tassel implied that "indigeneity was a stronger claim than conquest" and thus suggested that his oral representation of the land was more valid than McMurray's map.[29] By insisting that "the commissioners kn[e]w" what indigeneity meant, Tassel forced them to respect his geopolitical vision (*NASPIA* 6:49).[30]

Settlers distorted such articulations of Indigenous spatial attachment by imagining Indigenous peoples' alienation from the land in order to emphasize the inalienability of the settler territorial regime. In a period when newspapers rarely published Indigenous peoples' words or perspectives, but mentioned Indians primarily in reports of hostilities or signed treaties (rather than negotiations), Tassel's speech was covered in the *Baltimore Journal and Maryland Advertiser*. The anonymous writer who reported it replaced Tassel's assertion of political right to the land with an image of exotic noble savage roaming over *terra nullius*. Omitting Tassel's name, the writer identified him as a Cherokee "head warrior" who said that "God made the red people of this earth, and placed them on the same to live, and we must know they were the first on this ground. They were the natives, who on former times could range about the country without restraint."[31]

The writer adhered to Tassel's construction of indigeneity as generative process, priority, and divine design, but augmented it with words (attributed to Tassel) that negated the geopolitical logic of Tassel's speech. The resulting text portrays Indigenous land as always already alienated from Native peoples. It subjects Tassel's worldview to a logic similar to that which the writer of the *Observations on the Impressment of American Seamen* would express two decades later (chapter 3)—that freedom, measured by the right to migrate voluntarily, extends equally to those "born under constituted and ancient politics" and those "born in the woods, amongst the unconfined inhabitants that run loose in them."[32] This formulation defines positive birthright as liberation from spatial attachment both in Lockean civil society and in its state-of-nature predecessor in order to disavow the violent dispossession through which settler colonialism establishes its sovereignty. However, while anti-impressment writers referred to Indians (and slaves) metaphorically, land policies required settlers to distinguish their inalienable rights from the alienability they attributed to Indigenous claims. Consequently, inalienable settler territory depended on alienable Indigenous homelands. The anonymous report of Tassel's Hopewell speeches elided Tassel's requests that the commissioners remove settlers who encroached on Cherokee lands and replaced it with Tassel's call for friendship as though the Indigenous geopolitical world that Tassel invited settlers to enter was an utterly unintelligible construct. The writer stated that Tassel "wished that those [settlers] who now possessed what was once theirs [the Cherokee's] would be united in friendship" although "the Cherokees had been induced to give up much land" and "what was still their own was settled against their consent."[33]

Tassel's geopolitical theory resisted US attempts to divide the Cherokee homeland cartographically into lands they had lost to settlers and those that the United States wished to "allot" them. During this period the United States sought consistently to consolidate its sovereignty by "allot[ing]" lands to Indigenous peoples as though those lands had always already been the undisputed property of the settler regime.[34] Francis Paul Prucha explains that the United States wanted fixed boundaries in order to facilitate its provision of land bounties to Revolutionary War veterans, but boundaries were no less significant for alienating Indigenous lands and translating them into inalienable national soil.[35] Bruyneel argues that boundaries represent "the central dilemma for indigenous politics in the United States," and he defines "U.S.-indigenous politics" as a struggle between "an American effort to solidify inherently contingent boundaries and an indigenous effort to work on and across these boundaries, drawing on and exposing their contingency to gain the fullest possible expression of political identity, agency, and autonomy."[36] Treaty negotiation records demonstrate that both efforts were grounded in perceptions of in/alienability.

In Hopewell, commissioners used boundaries and allotment to make settled land the inalienable property of the settler state, thus enacting the doctrine of impossibility. The history of in/alienability, freedom, and attachment that allotment signifies was formulated as a national US project in post-1783 treaty councils. The commissioners told the Cherokees that they wanted "none of your lands" because under McMurray's map they imagined themselves as allotting rather than purchasing Indian lands. Allotment entrenched the inalienability of US soil, because the prevalent assumption that Indians would soon disappear convinced settlers that allotted grants would necessarily revert back to the United States.[37] Thus, US Indian policy represented Indian title to land as always already extinguishable and ready to be vested exclusively and inalienably in the United States.

McMurray's map constructs the inalienability of settler territory through simultaneously imaginary and axiomatic boundaries. "The lines singly coloured N.W. of the Ohio," its caption reads, "are the divisions of that Country into Ten New States, by a Resolve of Congress of April 23.d 1784." This prospective cartography is only one facet of the map's fictitious borders. The map keys longitudinal lines to the "Merd.n of PHILAD.A" (then the seat of the federal government) and measures distances by a "SCALE OF MILES 69 to a DEGREE," as though such lines can force space into a calculable objectivity that would erase the physical relatedness that makes "friendship" a meaningful geopolitical term in Tassel's speech. McMurray's map supported the settler state in ways that straddled figurative and literal expressions of axiomatic sovereignty claims; it was based on multiple surveys by settlers who encroached on Indigenous lands in order to prepare them for the settlements that the map's internal boundaries visualized.[38] McMurray acknowledged those surveys under the map's title, and presented them as evidence of its accuracy: "what contributed most to its accuracy, were the unpublished Surveys, co[n]sisting of many thousands of Miles." Therefore, he described his map as "composed from every Survey, and Sketch of Note, heretofore made in these Limits."[39] McMurray used inclusivity as a tool for establishing comprehensive authority, and therefore, ironically, he could not discriminate inaccurate "*Sketch*[es]" from presumably complete "*Survey*[s]."

The paradox of indiscriminatory inclusion may explain why the commissioners were not satisfied with McMurray's map. They asked Tassel to produce a map of "the boundary of your country, particularly to the northward and eastward," so they could all "agree upon the bounds of the lands, we mean to allot to you" (*NASPIA* 6:51). Tassel resisted because, as he clarified, settler boundaries rested on encroachments that allotment merely confirmed. He complained that Judge Richard Henderson had swindled the Cherokee of Kentucky by forging the signature of the late Oconestoto (and possibly also that of Attacullaculla). In response, the commissioners argued that since Henderson, Oconestoto, and Attacullaculla could not settle the matter, as they were now dead, the fraudulent boundary had to be validated. Their arguments were similar to those that Ginsburg would make in 2005 in citing the parties' deaths, the time that had "elapsed since the date of the deed," and the fact that "the country [has already been] settled, on the faith of the deed." Based on these conditions they claimed they could not "do anything" regarding Tassel's complaint and said he "must therefore be content with it, as if you had actually sold it, and point out your claim exclusive of this land." Tassel agreed to "say nothing more about Kentucky, although it is justly ours," thereby reiterating his claims while surrendering to the commissioners' demands (*NASPIA* 6:51). Following several similar exchanges of Cherokee protest and commissioner pressure, Tassel and Tuskegatahee produced a map of the Cherokee nation's eastern boundary (see map 2).[40]

This version of Tassel and Tuskegatahee's map is a "copy" in several senses. First, Tassel delayed its production in tacit protest of the commissioners' attempt to force him to validate their spatial discourse; then, the commissioners clarified that Congress would not intervene in ending "the encroachments you complain of, if they do exist," unless they provide a map; and when Tassel, Tuskegatahee, and their fellow negotiators eventually produced it, they used the commissioners' "paper" and "pencil" (*NASPIA* 6:51–52).[41] US officials "copied" that penciled map (see map 2). In penciling their map, the Cherokee negotiators were compelled to acknowledge US cartographic discourse, which enabled the commissioners to credit themselves with having "establish[ed] the boundary" (*NASPIA* 6:47). This process was shaped by the discrepancy between primarily oral Native maps, which "are formed in the human interaction with the land" as "a record of the events that give it meaning," and the detached, abstract, and objectified space of European cartography, which, in Mark Warhus's words, produces "a static landscape."[42] Goeman's analysis of "storied maps," based on the "stories that accompany the landscape" rather than on cartographic practice, suggests that Tassel's indigeneity speech, discussed above, was a more meaningful Cherokee map—one in which, as Lisa Brooks writes, "the political system mirror[s] the geographic one."[43] Tassel noted this discrepancy by following his indigeneity statement with an oral map, one that described the land on which settlers have encroached, and he intensified his critique of settler cartography by complaining that settlers' surveying activities would lead to further encroachments. He said that North Carolina and Virginia settlers "have even marked the lands on the bank of the river near the town where I live; and from thence, down in the fork of the Tennessee and Holston" (*NASPIA* 6:49).

Keenly aware of cartography's role in the dispossession of Indigenous

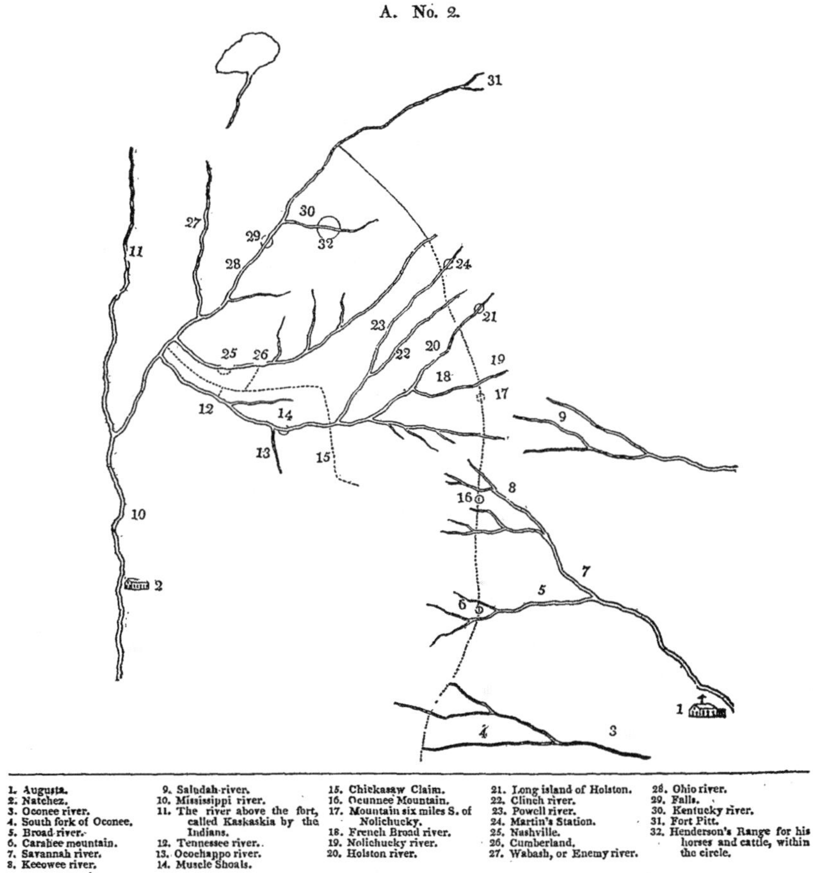

Congress's copy of Tassel and Tuskegatahee's map of the northern and eastern boundaries of the Cherokee Nation, November 28, 1785. "A. no. 2," *The New American State Papers: Indian Affairs* (Wilmington, DE: Scholarly Resources, 1972), 6:48.

peoples, the Cherokee negotiators must have faced great difficulties in producing the map. Yet their map does not suggest Cherokee surrender to settler interests. Although it complies with certain aspects of US cartography, their map emphasizes what Anderson calls the "explanatory glosses" that McMurray's map marginalizes. McMurray's map ensures its status as logo by presenting a circumscribed object whose shape can be memorized, but Tassel and Tuskegatahee's map marginalizes boundary lines and refuses to let them circumscribe the Cherokee nation. Its omission of Cherokee towns—the building blocks of Cherokee peoplehood—may function simultaneously as a rejection of US attempts to reduce Cherokee lands to these towns and as ironic resistance to the map's role in promoting US interests. In an attempt to resist the commissioners' demand that they mark a line next to present-day Nashville, Tennessee, where settlers had moved into lands presumably granted them by the Chickasaw, Tassel and Tuskegatahee asked the commissioners to "postpone this matter if the Chickasaws would come; it is a kind of common right in all the Indians, and they had no right of themselves to give it" (*NASPIA* 6:52). This principled resistance to land alienation highlights the multilayered belonging represented by the networked relations of the "common pot." Tassel and Tuskegatahee argued that land was inalienable not because it belonged to a single possessor whose absolute sovereignty prevented him from parting with it, but because it maintained vital relations that connected rather than separated individuals and polities. Even after agreeing to chart the map, Tassel and Tuskegatahee refused to mark another line in "the fork of French Broad river and Holston" occupied by "three thousand" settlers because they insisted that this was "a favorite spot of land," from which settlers "must be removed" (*NASPIA* 6:52).[44] Thus, while acknowledging US territorial conventions by drawing a map, Tassel and Tuskegatahee rejected settler cartography's promotion of Cherokee dispossession and resisted settler commodification and objectification of the land.

Similarly to the racial dynamics of Occom's representations of Mohegan peoplehood (chapter 2), the only uncontested common ground between the Cherokee negotiators and the commissioners seems to have been the idea that arrivants lacked any geopolitical agency. The first article of the signed treaty represented slaves as property from the perspective of the United States: "The Head-Men and Warriors of all the Cherokees shall restore all the prisoners, citizens of the United States, or subjects of their allies, to their entire liberty: They shall also restore all the Negroes, and all other property taken during the late war from the citizens."[45] The record does not indicate that the Cherokee negotiators objected to this demand. The day after they signed the treaty, Tassel seems to have referred to this issue when he told the commissioners that as they "demanded all their property and prisoners of the Cherokee," so he would require the United States to empower "Colonel Martin" to "find and get our prisoners" (*NASPIA* 6:52). The treaty's language suggests that Tassel's word(s) that the interpreters rendered as "property" included slaves, which demonstrates that Tassel accepted the reduction of slaves to chattel property. Nowota later told commissioners, "Your prisoner at Chickamoga, I will deliver you," and again the language of the treaty—which distinguishes "prisoners, citizens of the United States" from "Negroes, and all other property"—suggests that the "prisoner" he refers to was a US citizen (*NASPIA* 6:53). Slavery seems to constitute the limits of unsettlement in this instance of US-Indigenous negotiations, the point at which settler and Cherokee geopolitics converge rather than clash. This convergence indicates that Indigenous representations of embodied space—articulated most consistently in their references to handholding as an unsettling form of joint inhabitation—excluded arrivants from geopolitical considerations. The next section examines handholding and spatial embodiments as tools of unsettlement.

Embodied Spaces

The trope of handholding emphasizes the discrepancy between objectified and embodied space that was central to all negotiations discussed in this chapter. In Hopewell in 1785, Cherokee negotiators presented handholding as an alternative to war that required unsettlement. At the end of his indigeneity speech Tassel introduced Nanyehi (also known as Nancy Ward), the "beloved" "War-woman of Chota," who expressed her happiness at "hearing that there is a peace" and qualified her enthusiasm with an implicit unsettlement plan by telling the commissioners, "I hope you have now taken us by the hand in real friendship" (*NASPIA* 6:50). In Madison and Coody's English translation, the verb *taken* connotes unequal relations whereby an authoritative party leads a dependent one, but such reading of Nanyehi's words hinders us from hearing her fuller contribution to the negotiations. Daniel Heath Justice explains that Nanyehi had an "often contradictory approach toward preserving her cultural identity while adapting to the demands of the present."[46] In negotiating with US commissioners she highlighted both aspects of this role. As "War-woman" and mother of "warriors," Nanyehi could nurture war as well as peace; her reference to "real friendship" joined Tassel's perception of peaceful relations that would require settler removal and respect for Indigenous rights. She emphasized this idea by clarifying that she represented "the young warriors" whom she "raised in my town, as well as myself. They rejoice that we have peace, and we hope the chain of friendship will never more be broke (*NASPIA* 6:50)."

Scholars have traced the trope of handholding in Native diplomatic protocols to Haudenosaunee political philosophies. Williams formulated the title of his book *Linking Arms Together: American Indian Treaty Visions of Law and Peace* by using this trope, and he explains that "[f]or the Iroquois, the joining of hands described by the Deganawidah epic represented the inaugural act of a constitutional tradition of law and peace sustained by their treaty alliance."[47] Haudenosaunee scholar John Mohawk explains that "peace" in this context "was to be defined not as the simple absence of war or strife, but as the active striving of humans for the purpose of establishing universal justice."[48] Several instances of handholding in various treaty documents clarify its significance in countering settler constructions of disembodied, inalienable national soil as an axiomatic given that could be fixed on maps. Through this discrepancy the handholding trope symbolized *both* the equal relations in embodied, living space that Indigenous peoples proposed *and* the subjugating ones over objectified space that settlers wished to impose.

In 1788, after settlers had murdered Tassel, Cherokee leader Little Turkey welcomed the Continental Congress's proclamation of US commitment to the boundary established in the Treaty of Hopewell, and which promised to remove settlers from Chota, Tassel's town.[49] The Cherokee's "linguister" James Carry rendered Little Turkey's words in a letter to Richard Winn, superintendent of Indian affairs, thus: "Your talks are good, and your friendship we look on sincere, for the good of our land." Little Turkey positioned "friendship," as Tassel had done, within the space of the homeland and added that he had "seen the resolves of Congress . . . for all the white people settled on our hunting grounds to go off without loss of time." He reassured Winn that Creek leader Alexander McGillivray has also seen those documents and "will take his white brothers by the hand as we do, and hope to live in peace and friendship as long as the grass grows and the water runs" (*NASPIA* 6:56). Little Turkey complemented Nanyehi's earlier reference to the United States' "tak[ing]" of its Cherokee allies "by the hand" by using this trope of mutual relations in a land that sustains peaceful practices, in order to emphasize Cherokee and Muscogee agency. The condition for this peace was the urgent removal of invading settlers.

A similar usage of the handholding trope appeared in Joseph Brant's speech to US commissioners Benjamin Lincoln, Beverly Randolph, and Timothy Pickering in the summer of 1793. A Mohawk leader who was educated at Eleazar Wheelock's Moor's Charity School, where Joseph Johnson also studied, Brant was fully competent in English but chose to speak in his native language on behalf of the northwestern confederacy. Brant spoke at a preliminary meeting where a limited number of confederacy negotiators met the commissioners to ascertain whether their common ground was sufficient to open a general treaty council. The atmosphere was tense; both sides were ready to fight, and the preliminary meetings concerned the fate of previous treaties. The confederacy wanted to revalidate the Treaty of Fort Stanwix it had signed with Britain in 1768, which limited settler expansion to the southeast of the Ohio River. Settler encroachments had increased over two decades, and in 1785 and 1789 a number of Native negotiators had ceded lands north of the Ohio without the consent of the entire confederacy.[50]

Following these unauthorized cessions and one year prior to the Battle of Fallen Timbers, at which US forces defeated the confederacy and subsequently gained possession of lands north of the Ohio River, Brant emphasized that the handholding trope signified inclusive Indigenous politics and equal partnership between the confederacy and the settler state. "Our prospects are the fairer, because all our minds are one," he said. "Formerly, because you did not speak to us unitedly, what was done was not binding." He thus voided treaties with parts of the confederacy and alerted commissioners Lincoln, Randolph, and Pickering to the urgency of the matter. "Now," he stated, "you have an opportunity of speaking to us together; and we now take you by the hand, and lead you to the place appointed for the meeting" (*NASPIA* 4:133). Like Tassel, Nanyehi, and Little Turkey, Brant concluded his speech by giving the commissioners wampum symbolizing the unity of minds that Indigenous negotiators called "friendship." In all these instances, Indigenous leaders used the handholding trope to resist subordination and insist that local politics had to be embedded in Indigenous homelands. Handholding thus became an unsettling strategy to redefine settler colonialism within a geopolitical order that positioned spatial attachment as a foundation of freedom.

US officials listened and repeated that trope; Lincoln, Randolph, and Pickering told Brant, "take us by the hand, and lead us to the treaty" (*NASPIA* 4:137). Yet behind this reciprocating rhetoric was a genocidal usage of this trope, by which settlers tried to force Indigenous negotiators to accept axiomatic settler sovereignty and supplant their unsettlement aspirations with a reality of dispossession. When they urged defiant Indians to sign dictated treaties, commissioners told Indigenous spokespersons that their polities were in the hand of the United States, which could crush them at will. However, when US commissioners reported the negotiations in official records, they did not mention this threat because admitting it on these occasions would have disrupted the disavowal of the foundational violence on which settler sovereignty rests and by which it claims its axiomatic validity. The only references to this rhetoric that I found in US records appear in complaints by Native negotiators regarding past communications with US representatives and in a confidential letter that Jefferson wrote to Indiana Territory governor William H. Harrison years later, in 1803. Jefferson emphasized that the United States had to obtain as much Indian lands as possible, as soon as possible, and wrote that "our strength and their weakness is now so visible that they must see we have only to shut our hand to crush them."[51] The interactions of these two tropes illuminate the geopolitical discrepancies on which this chapter focuses. Indigenous negotiators used the handholding trope to signify cooperative human agency that accepted Indigenous geopolitical constructions and the spatial practices that sustained them. By contrast, the settlers who represented the United States as a hand that held Indigenous polities used somatic imagery to represent absolute settler power over Indigenous peoples. The closing, crushing hand metaphor derived from the twin doctrines of impossibility and allotment and portrayed the United States as the only geopolitical factor that would determine whether Indigenous peoples would be able to survive.

Indigenous negotiators understood this idea. In speeches they gave in Philadelphia between December 1790 and February 1791, while visiting George Washington, Seneca leaders Cornplanter, Half-Town, and Great-Tree complained that commissioners Oliver Wolcoot, Richard Butler, Arthur Lee, George Rogers Clark, and Samuel H. Parsons had compelled Indigenous polities to sign the treaties of Forts Stanwix, McIntosh, and Finney (1784–86)—some of the treaties that Brant would void in 1793. They said that these commissioners "told us that we were in your hand, and that, by closing it, you could crush us to nothing, and you demanded from us a great country, as the price of that peace which you had offered us." Critiquing settler political logic, they added that the United States operated "as if our want of strength had destroyed our rights." The distinction between might and right is a crucial aspect of interdependent geopolitical thought that requires the contribution of all parties and nurtures all regardless of their comparative strengths. By contrast, Cornplanter, Half-Town, and Great-Tree emphasized the subordinating mechanism that facilitated axiomatic US sovereignty: "our chiefs had felt your power," they said, "and were unable to contend against you, and therefore gave up that country" (*NASPIA* 4:24). Refuting the United States' right-of-conquest argument, the Senecas disassociated military strength from rights, and represented land cessions as the consequences of settler violence and in turn as a destructive geopolitical mechanism. Returning later to the image of a fatally closing US hand, they asked Washington, "Are you determined to crush us?" (*NASPIA* 4:25).

This metaphor had appeared earlier, in November 1791, when Odawa leader Egushawa critiqued the Treaty of Fort Finney (1786) in a council of the northwestern confederacy following the confederacy's military victory over US forces in the event known as St. Clair's defeat. Egushawa quoted Shawnee leader Kekewepelethe, who had tried to resist the demand by Clark, Butler, and Parsons that the Shawnee provide the United States with hostages to guarantee Indigenous compliance with the treaty.[52] Alexander McKee is believed to be the translator of Egushawa's argument that the United States demanded hostages "to insult us, because you know that we are poor, defenceless, and ignorant; and because you are, as you say, strong and mighty."[53] Egushawa analyzed US policies by emphasizing the settler regime's responsibility for the geopolitical realities it has sought to establish as axiomatic and unalterable. He said that the United States had told the confederacy "that you have all our nations within your hand; by closing which, you can crush us to death!" (*MD* 9). Egushawa stated that US commissioners had also evoked the image of the closing hand in negotiations with the Delaware (perhaps for the Treaty of Fort McIntosh, in 1785) when they had said that "*they held all our nations in their hand, by closing which they could crush us to death!*" (*MD* 13).

Kekewepelethe, to whom Egushawa referred, was present at Egushawa's speech and heard him tell a crowd of "chiefs, warriors, and friends" how Kekewepelethe had concluded his 1786 speech by laying a wampum belt "down on a map of our country, which [the commissioners] had spread before them" (*MD* 10). The map was McMurray's, and the wampum featured equal proportions of white and purple beads, which signified the two options that Kekewepelethe offered the commissioners: peace on equal terms, which the white beads represented, or war, which the purple (also described as black) beads signified.[54] By placing the wampum on the map, Kekewepelethe had indicated the insufficiency of cartographic representation. US officials might have hoped that McMurray's map would unambiguously prove settler sovereignty, but Kekewepelethe reminded them that human relations in the space it mapped could not be reduced to axioms that denied Indigenous agency. Instead of recognizing the map as the undisputed symbol of and evidence for exclusive US sovereignty, Egushawa renamed McMurray's map "a map of our country," thus mirroring Kekewepelethe's placement of his geopolitical analysis (in wampum form) on the map. According to Egushawa's report of the events, Clark had responded violently to Kekewepelethe's reinterpretation of McMurray's map, throwing the wampum belt "off, *contemptuously*, with his cane!" (*MD* 10).[55] Clark's violent removal of Kekewepelethe's wampum expressed his refusal to accept these readings and the unsettling invitations they embodied.

Egushawa's speech developed a critical cartographic literacy that condemned textually assisted dispossession and used this critique to envision unsettlement. Calling US literacy "*pen and ink witch-craft*, which they can make to speak things we never intended, or had any idea of, even an hundred years hence" (*MD* 11), Egushawa refuted US sovereignty claims over "all the lands of every nation of red men, between the frozen regions on the north, the Ohio river on the south, and Mississippi on the west, and Canada on the east." He defined "papers, writings, belts, and messages" as tools of coercion that the United States has "thrown at you, with threats" to dispossess Native polities (*MD* 8). Further, he protested manipulative US diplomacy by stating that a recent wampum brought by a US official contained no "fair or honest condition of peace" and "was only meant to cajole you, and to blind your eyes" (*MD* 19).

Rejecting US usage of both wampum and cartographic literacy, Egushawa urged his audience to engage with the land bodily by looking at it, walking on it, or imagining such practices. Through this distinction between spatial embodiment and cartographic representation, Egushawa developed a critical geopolitics that simultaneously recognized the devastating consequences of colonization and defied the US threat to "crush" Indian polities. He invited his listeners to "Look around" and "View the country which your deceased massacred relations occupied in peace, so many ages before the arrival of the *whites*." In contrast to abstract measurements and calculated distances, Egushawa offered an embodied assessment of the land that "extend[s] more than one hundred days journey along the sea coast, from north to south." He invited his listeners to "cast your eyes now, if you can, from *this* council fire, to *that* sea coast, which is a moon's march from you" and asked whether they could "see a single nation of your own colour? Do you even see a single town within this immense extent, inhabited by red men? No; you see not one!" (*MD* 7). Egushawa argued that the land could not be abstracted from its relations to the communities that inhabited it, giving it specific socio-historic-political meanings. He tacitly defined inhabitation as a structure of lived experience that operates through interactions among bodies, communities, and lands. While the imperative "Look" implies faith in the ability to visualize the land and its transformation in the wake of colonization, the qualifying "if you can" suggests that dispossession might have impaired the physical capabilities of Indigenous people, representing the reciprocities between spaces and bodies on which this geopolitical perception is based.

While Egushawa discussed the extensive region northwest of the Ohio River, other Indigenous spokespersons sometimes asked for limited portions of dispossessed homelands by similarly emphasizing the need to see the land. Settler denials of such small-scale restitutions anticipate Ginsburg's decision in *City of Sherrill v. Oneida Indian Nation*. In January 1791, Cornplanter, Half-Town, and Great-Tree asked President Washington to "Look at the land" they had given the United States at the 1784 Treaty of Fort Stanwix and said, "then turn your eyes upon what we now ask you to restore to us, and you will see that what we ask you to return is a *very little piece*." They promised that "[b]y giving it back again, you will satisfy the whole of our nation," and they concretized this promise through embodied spatial relations: "Every man of our nation will then turn his eyes away from all the other lands which we then gave up to you, and forget that our fathers ever said that they belonged to them" (*NASPIA* 4:27 [italics in original]).

The Seneca leaders distinguished Washington's calculating gaze—whose presumed indifference to spatial specificities stemmed from its focus on landed fungibility—from Seneca eyes that instead saw attachment to particular spots of land. Expressing willingness to revise the Seneca's historic understanding of its homelands, they asked Washington to reciprocate their compromise by returning a "*very little piece*" of the lands they had ceded. Washington responded by utilizing impossibility, saying he could not "disannul treaties formed by the United States" (NASPIA 4:28).

A few months later, Washington's administration sent Col. Thomas Proctor to recruit Senecas' help in negotiating with Indigenous peoples farther west. Proctor's negotiating career was brief, perhaps because he presented Seneca voices more fully than did other commissioners.[56] His detailed record reveals the role of Seneca women in geopolitical affairs. Proctor's interpreter, Horatio Jones, said these women insisted that Proctor "listen" to them because "we are *the owners of this land*—and it is ours; for it is we that plant it." As negotiations proceeded, Red Jacket represented these women and clarified that they had decided to extend Seneca help to the United States on that occasion. Emphasizing that he spoke for the women, Red Jacket presented them as arbiters of Seneca geopolitics and urged Proctor, in their names: "you must look when it is light in the morning until the setting sun, and you must reach your neck over the land, and take all the light you can, to show the danger" (NASPIA 4:49). The Seneca women thus asserted that geopolitical understanding demanded inhabitation, cultivation, and embodied spatial practice. They clarified further that such understanding required an active effort to see the land as interactive rather than objectified space. Proctor, who was more interested in property relations and used the trip to observe a "1,200 acre tract of land that [he] purchased," failed to reach his destination west of Lake Erie and ended his mission in May 1791 (NASPIA 4:35). Six months later the "danger" that the Seneca women had warned him about materialized in St. Clair's defeat.[57] In the next section I examine larger-scale unsettlement proposals that were similarly rooted in Indigenous rights theories and that were also answered by assertions of settler impossibility.

Continental Nativities

In late 1786 the northwestern confederacy, identifying itself as the United Indian Nations (UIN), sent Congress a speech that Joseph Brant had written.[58] The UIN rejected the "false treaties" that the United States had signed with parts of the confederacy (including the 1784 Treaty of Fort Stanwix that the Seneca leaders would ask Washington to reconsider, the 1785 Treaty of Fort McIntosh, and the 1786 Treaty of Fort Finney) and invited the United States to negotiate peace with the entire confederacy rather than attempt to divide and conquer it. Whereas Hawkins, Pickens, Martin, and McIntosh had in 1785 required Cherokee negotiators to chart their boundaries so the United States could "allot" Cherokee land to the tribe, a year later the UIN's unsettlement plan was based on the confederacy's offer to set its own boundary on the Ohio River. The confederacy insisted that in the wake of settler expansion the United States had to accept the reality of a divided continental international arena in which Indigenous and settler polities were equal sovereign bodies. As in the Seneca leaders' 1791 address to Washington, the confederacy was willing to accept US constructs of in/alienability within certain geographic bounds in order to ensure US respect for inalienable Indigenous homelands. At least some Cherokees participated in this initiative although they claimed no lands north of the Ohio, which indicates that multiple polities were committed to this effort to protect Indigenous geopolitics.

Expressing the geopolitical vision of "an enormous number of Native people," the speech attempted to maintain equality and justice by integrating the United States into an Indigenous social landscape embedded in kinship networks and by guaranteeing stable boundaries between the United States and the UIN that would end settler encroachments.[59] Much like the addresses by Tassel and Egushawa, the speech represented attachment to land as the foundation of freedom and clarified that settlers could enjoy their rights by forging attachments with Indigenous polities within Indigenous geopolitics. For at least the next decade Indigenous spokespersons continued to offer this unsettlement principle to settlers as an alternative to ongoing violence. Arguing that the United States and the UIN had emerged from the Revolutionary War as equal regional powers, Brant explained the confederacy's geopolitical attitude: "we thought we were entering upon a reconciliation and friendship with a set of people born on the same continent with ourselves" (*NASPIA* 4:17). In this "evolving conception of nativity," as Lisa Brooks calls it,[60] the UIN offered to accommodate US citizens within a continental order linking rights to birthplace.

The UIN's reference to the "same continent" was not unique. In June 1787, interpreters John Galphin and James Douzeazeaux helped Muscogee chiefs Hallowing King and Fat King write a letter to Congress amid violent struggles. Reminding the United States of Muscogee neutrality during the Revolutionary War, Hallowing King and Fat King recalled that when the English had tried to persuade them to fight the rebels, they had replied that the Muscogee and the rebels "were born in one land, and we were your friends and brothers, and will be to the last day, though you have not treated us as friends" (NASPIA 6:38). Such assertions of spatial ethics rooted in continental nativities highlight the efforts of Indigenous spokespersons to maintain their geopolitical world in the face of settler invasion by insisting that, within their homelands, settlers must act as their "friends" by accepting Indigenous geopolitical practices. The following year, Muscogee leader Alexander McGillivray wrote US commissioners Winn, Pickens, and George Mathews that he hoped the next session of Congress would act justly "so that we may become real friends to each other, settling on the same land, and having but one interest" (NASPIA 6:35). By using the terms *same continent*, *one land*, and *same land*, these negotiators represented the need to share the land as the inevitable result of settler colonialism, but such sharing required unsettlement that would allow settlers to integrate peacefully into Indigenous polities without supplanting them. Whereas US commissioners used boundaries to circumscribe Indian lands and dispossess Native communities, Native negotiators insisted on the integral wholeness of the continent and its Indigenous polities, undermining US efforts even as they spoke the language of boundary setting and conceded parts of their homelands.[61]

The UIN balanced the two parts of its geopolitical vision—independent sovereignties divided by a clear boundary, and joint inhabitation of the continent—by qualifying its acceptance of US citizens as people "born on the same continent" as Indigenous peoples, with a critical emphasis on priority. Brant wrote that if the United States failed to execute the UIN plan, "we . . . shall most assuredly, with our united force, be obliged to defend those rights and privileges which have been transmitted to us by our ancestors" (NASPIA 4:18). These "rights and privileges" concerned not alienable title to particular plots (as the United States defined Indian rights) but an inalienable freedom to define Indigenous geopolitics independently of settler impositions. Brant clarified that the confederacy's view of international relations was validated by a broader international arena that exceeded settler norms. He wrote that the treaty must "appear just and reasonable in the eyes of the world" beyond Eurocentric perceptions of geopolitical legitimacy (NASPIA 4:17).

The UIN speech reached Congress on July 18, 1787—five days after the passage of the Northwest Ordinance, which defined lands north of the Ohio River as the future heritable property of US citizens in disregard of the ancestrally derived "rights and privileges" through which Brant distinguished Indigenous rights from settler liberties. "Be it ordained," the ordinance reads, "that the estates . . . of . . . proprietors in the said territory dying intestate shall descend to and be distributed among their children and the descendants of a deceased child in equal parts." The ordinance reduced Indigenous rights to temporary features of the changing territory whose laws would extend into every area "in which the indian [*sic*] titles shall have been extinguished." It stipulated that the "utmost good faith shall always be observed toward the Indians," that "their lands and property shall never be taken from them without their consent," and that "in their property, rights and liberty, they never shall be invaded or disturbed, unless in just and lawful wars authorised by Congress." In place of the reciprocal relations that the UIN had offered to establish on both sides of the Ohio, the ordinance stated unilaterally that "laws founded in justice and humanity shall from time to time be made, for preventing wrongs being done to them, and for preserving peace and friendship with them."[62]

The disregard with which the settler regime has treated Indigenous geopolitics preceded the Northwest Ordinance and continues long afterwards. On August 7, 1786, several months prior to the UIN's formulation of the proposal, Congress passed the "Ordinance for the regulation of Indian Affairs," which referred to the lands that the UIN sought to protect as an administrative US "department" that replaced the previous "department" of Britain's Indian policy. And as early as October 1787, Continental Congress secretary Charles Thomson tried to expand the boundaries between the United States and Indigenous polities, instructing the governor of the Northwest Territory, Arthur St. Clair, to take "any opportunity that may offer, of extinguishing the Indian rights to the westward, as far as the river Mississippi." In July 1788, Thomson directed St. Clair to "endeavor to establish an east and west line as far north as the completion of the forty-first degree of north latitude," around present-day Akron, Ohio, and Fort Wayne, Illinois (*NASPIA* 4:18). In his report of the treaties of Forts Stanwix and McIntosh made with parts of the confederacy, St. Clair complained that "any attempt to extend the limits" might "defeat entirely the settling a peace with them" (*NASPIA* 4:19); his words proved too true in November 1791, when the UIN defeated his force.

St. Clair's admission of the limits of possibility in US-Indian negotiations was part of broader constructions of im/possibility that attended US discourses of in/alienable lands and rights. While the Northwest Ordinance reflected faith in the possibility of alienating Indigenous homelands and turning them into inalienable national soil, St. Clair's frustration marked the extent to which actual relations prohibited settler optimism regarding the cheap production of heritable inalienable national property. The next section examines the confederacy's unsettling challenges to US constructions of im/possibility in the context of in/alienable rights and lands.

Im/Possibility, Life, and Loss

Seven years and several military campaigns after the United States enacted the Northwest Ordinance, Indigenous and settler perceptions of impossibility clashed in protracted, failed preliminary negotiations between May and August 1793 (this failure led to the Battle of Fallen Timbers, in which US forces defeated the confederacy, a year later). In spring 1793, US secretary of war Henry Knox tried to dissolve the confederacy by sending commissioners Lincoln, Randolph, and Pickering to confirm cessions made by parts of it at the 1789 Treaty of Fort Harmar.[63] Early in the process the commissioners tacitly utilized the impossibility doctrine when they told Mahican leader Hendrick Aupaumut that "it may be very difficult, if not impossible" to give up lands that had already been "sold and settled" "along the Ohio." They were more open with John Graves Simcoe, lieutenant governor of Upper Canada, whom they told that "the sales and settlements of the lands over the Ohio, founded on the treaties of forts McIntosh and Harmar, render it impossible now to make that river the boundary" between the United States and the confederacy (*NASPIA* 4:128).

In rejecting the treaties of Forts Stanwix, McIntosh, Finney, and Harmar, the confederacy echoed Egushawa, saying that those who had signed them "were obliged to sign any paper that was laid before them; and it has since appeared that deeds of cession were signed by them, instead of treaties of peace" (*NASPIA* 4:140). Amid internal debates over feasible boundary lines, the confederacy decided to stick with the Ohio River boundary.[64] In rejecting this offer, US commissioners used the impossibility doctrine: "it is impossible," they said, "to make the river Ohio the boundary, between your people and the people of the United States" because "the customs of the white people," the "great expenses which attend their settling in a new country," and "the nature of their improvements" render settled lands too "valuable" and "dear . . . to them" (*NASPIA* 4:136). The commissioners used the impossibility doctrine again to end negotiations: "We . . . explicitly declared to you that it was now impossible to make the river Ohio the boundary between your lands and the lands of the United States. Your answer amounts to a declaration, that you will agree to no other boundary than the Ohio. The negotiation is therefore at an end" (*NASPIA* 4:141). This dead end stemmed from the clash of two impossibilities. The confederacy insisted that multigenerational spatial attachments created homelands whose peoples were entitled to inhabit and define the terms of their inhabitation; they agreed to delimit the area where such rights would be respected internationally, but they refused to adopt any geopolitical plan that would deny their theories of meaningful inhabitation. US understandings of impossibility also rested on inalienability, but one that was validated cartographically and economically—the twin foundations of legitimacy in Eurocentric geopolitics.

US official discourse, represented here through the commissioners who executed Knox's directives, constructed in/alienability and im/possibility as functions of property relations. Thus, before ending negotiations the commissioners tried to solve the impasse with what they presented as an exceptionally generous offer. They pressed the confederacy to confirm the Treaty of Fort Harmar in return for an unprecedented payment of "such a large sum . . . as was never given at one time, for any quantity of Indian lands, since the white people first set their foot on this island," plus an annual "large quantity" of "goods" (*NASPIA* 4:136). This proposal was part of the commissioners' effort to replace Indigenous unsettlement plans with an insistence that settlement was the only normative framework within which settler-Indian relations could develop. They defined diplomatic efforts in terms of "settling the differences between you and the United States" and used settlement as the sole determining factor of im/possibility (*NASPIA* 4:136). In the process, as this proposal clarifies, they acknowledged that settlement's history was recent, was future-oriented, and rested on a strictly possessive logic.

In response, Wendat negotiator Sâ-wâgh-da-wunk argued that Indigenous views of geopolitics also entailed their own im/possibilities. "[Y]ou have your houses and people on our land," he said; "you say you cannot move them off; and we cannot give up our land" (*NASPIA* 4:137). Confederacy spokespersons highlighted clashing impossibilities in order to clarify that Indigenous lands were not merely property that settlers bought, but complex systems of sociopolitical relations that the confederacy struggled to keep intact. Settler and Indigenous perceptions of impossibility were mutually exclusive precisely because "lands" had different meanings within each framework. Thus, any boundary line that would have facilitated Indigenous sovereignty beyond the purview of US allotment would have been unacceptable to the settler regime.

The confederacy's last word in these protracted preliminary negotiations came two weeks later, in a letter it sent the commissioners. Dated August 16, 1793, the letter offered the most elaborate critique of the US impossibility doctrine of any negotiation records of that period. Signed by "Nations. Wyandots, Seven Nations of Canada, Delawares, Shawanese, Miamies, Ottawas, Chippewas, Senecas of the Glaize, Pattawatamies, Connoys, Munsees, Nantekokies, Mohicans, Messasagoes, Creeks, Cherokees," the letter critiqued the logic of settlement by targeting its possessive value system and highlighting its structuring inequalities. It recontextualized the commissioners' economic language in order to offer a way out of clashing, mutually exclusive impossibilities. "Money, to us, is of no value," the confederacy clarified in response to the commissioners' offer of "such a large sum . . . as was never given." They added that since "no consideration whatever can induce us to sell the lands on which we get sustenance for our women and children," they would "point out a mode by which your settlers might be easily removed, and peace thereby obtained." The confederacy's assertion that it would be "eas[y]" to remove settlers addressed the feigned powerlessness that settler impossibility utilized, the poverty on which settler property and wealth were founded, and the oppressive rather than liberating aspects of the settler regime. "We know that these settlers are poor," the letter stated, "or they would never have ventured to live in a country which has been in continual trouble ever since they crossed the Ohio." Rather than as a spontaneous, heroic extension of liberty, then, the confederacy portrayed settlement as the result of desperation and called on the United States to compensate and free settlers from the hardships of settling on lands whose polities were not willing to cede:

> Divide, therefore, this large sum of money, which you have offered to us, among these people: give to each, also, a proportion of what you say you would give to us, annually, over and above this very large sum of money: and, we are persuaded, they would most readily accept of it, in lieu of the lands you sold them. (*NASPIA* 4:140)

The confederacy analyzed US expansionism as a compounded system of domestic and international injustice based on the oppression and dispossession of settlers as well as Indigenous peoples. With this analysis the confederacy countered the Northwest Ordinance's promise of equal heritable rights for US citizens at Indians' expense. Whereas the United States embedded the doctrine of impossibility in teleological, future-oriented linear improvement that portrayed national expansion as a historical inevitability necessitated by continual economic growth, the confederacy offered an alternative future that would ensure the well-being of settlers and Indigenous peoples and presented its inhabitation and spatial attachment practices as nonnegotiable sources of livelihood.

Like Egushawa and the Seneca negotiators who visited Washington, the confederacy contextualized its analysis within a long, spatially embodied history that required the commissioners to view the land. "[O]ur only demand," they wrote, "is the peaceable possession of a small part of our once great country. Look back, and review the lands from whence we have been driven to this spot. We can retreat no further, because the country behind hardly affords food for its present inhabitants; and we have therefore resolved to leave our bones in this small space to which we are now confined" (*NASPIA* 4:141).

The confederacy argued that forced migration was worse than death as it urged the commissioners to use their present location at the mouth of the Detroit River to look critically at the history and present conditions of the land they wanted to possess. Whereas McMurray's map reduced Indian nations to transient names of landscape features, the confederacy warned that the land could become settler property only if it was first converted into a Native burial ground. This imagery critiqued the transience of property relations on which the settler regime ironically established its permanence and future-oriented impossibility. Next to US economic impossibility, then, the confederacy presented an impossibility that stemmed from living conditions and the threat of genocidal dispossession.

A year later, Gen. Anthony Wayne led a US force that defeated the confederacy in the Battle of Fallen Timbers (1794). Following this battle the confederacy seemed broken both politically and militarily. Then the United States signed the Jay Treaty with Britain and the confederacy lost the aid of its British allies within what Britain recognized as the international borders of the United States. In 1795, Wayne met parts of the confederacy—the Wendat, Odawa, Anishnaabe, Potawatomi, Shawnee, Delaware, Miami, Eel River, Piankashaw, Kickapoo, and Kaskaskia—to sign the Treaty of Greenville, which gave the United States the southern two-thirds of present-day Ohio and southeastern parts of present-day Indiana. The Treaty of Greenville seemed like the logical conclusion of the confederacy's recent losses and the harbinger of uncompromised US power. The Indigenous peoples who had previously fought General Wayne now met him in council, emphasized that "misery" had reduced them to "objects of pity," and eventually ceded all the lands he demanded (*NASPIA* 4:160, 164, 166).

However, the negotiations that preceded the signing indicate that instead of simply submitting to Wayne's dictated treaty, the Indigenous signatories mobilized a more sustained effort than any previous record reveals, to frame the negotiations within an operational unsettlement project that critiqued settlers' perceptions of loss and gain. They presented loss as the experience from which the treaty council had materialized and through which unsettlement may open up a peaceful future. This argument was potentially powerful not only because it was grounded in Indigenous philosophies, but also because it showed settlers that by giving up settled lands—the very danger that the impossibility doctrine meant to prevent—they could live more securely than by clinging to their possessions. Utilizing Indigenous traditions of dealing with loss, Indigenous spokespersons tried to redefine what Wayne presented as the fixed, absolute rules of settler-Indigenous relations. Such traditions as Haudenosaunee condolence ceremonies and Anishnaabe covering of the bodies of the dead enabled them to transform grief into political action or, in Taiaiake Alfred's words, "loss into strength."[65]

Condolence gestures were performed by the Delaware Te-ta-boksh-ke, the Wendat Tarke (aka Tarhe), and the Anishnaabe Mash-i-pi-nash-i-wish, who also made an unsettlement proposal for joint inhabitation. Tarke's condolence ceremony presented Wayne with a particularly detailed vision of the conditions for decolonization and therefore also for replacing settlers' impossibilities with Indigenous geopolitical possibilities. Tarke opened his condolence ceremony by telling Wayne, "I now wipe your body clean from all blood with this white soft linen" and "do it with as much tenderness as I am capable of." He positioned Wayne as sufferer and thereby undermined settlers' binary views of victory and loss that supported settler claims for superiority over Indigenous peoples. Instead, Tarke reminded Wayne that "[w]e are both placed on this ground" and proceeded symbolically to treat Wayne's tearful "eyes," closed "ears," "stopped" "throat," and displaced "heart" so that both parties would "enjoy a clear bright day, and easily see the sun, which the Great Spirit has bestowed on us, rise and set continually" (*NASPIA* 4:162).

This ceremony elaborated on the decade-old efforts of Indigenous negotiators to persuade US officials to understand that political realities are founded in embodied experience. Tarke's focus on Wayne's emotional and physical distress positioned Indigenous peoples as healers on whom settlers must rely in order to view the world accurately. By contrast to New Age representations of this stereotype, in which the Native healer supports a settler possessive individual, Tarke's proposition requires settlers to replace their geopolitical practices.[66] Tarke then tended to the recent history of violence and particularly to the US casualties of the last war. Referring to the "bones which lie scattered of your ancient warriors, who fell in defence of the present cause," he told Wayne that "we gather all together, and bury them now; and place this white board over them, that they may never again be seen by our posterity" (*NASPIA* 4:162). This vision opposes the confederacy's earlier promise to "leave [their] bones in this small place to which we are now confined." Instead of taking the abstract injustice of settler geopolitics to its extreme, as the confederacy had done previously, here Tarke reiterated the idea that loss is not the end of historical relations but may very well mark their renewal on a more just foundation. This logic negates settlers' impossibility doctrine and the exclusive, absolute, and axiomatic sovereignty that supports it. Therefore, Tarke's representation of loss marked a way out of what settlers presented as the impossibility of unsettlement and thus could potentially undermine settlers' faith in the fixed power relations of white supremacism.

To replace settler impossibility with unsettling possibilities, negotiators—represented by Anishnaabe spokesperson Mash-i-pi-nash-i-wish—proposed equal joint inhabitation within the cosmological, political, and social framework of an Indigenous "common pot." Their contribution to the negotiations focused on human agency as the pivot of historical transformations and illuminated the possibility of envisioning decolonized futures from within conditions of presumably unambiguous defeat. Mash-i-pi-nash-i-wish used the history of French colonization to offer Wayne an unsettlement plan. "When the French formerly possessed this country," he said, "we were but one people, . . . and we now entertain the hope of enjoying the same happy relation with you, the United States." This context suggests that decolonization had to be developed by reworking the varied histories of colonial relations in order to be practicable and sustainable.

Then Mash-i-pi-nash-i-wish told Wayne that those Anishnaabe, Potawatomi, and Odawa who participated in the council felt "pleasure" at "seeing and hearing" him and that in order to extend that "pleasure" to their entire memberships Wayne must "come and live among" them. Joint inhabitation became the condition for Wayne's perceptual transformation, as Mash-i-pi-nash-i-wish promised that "you will then learn our title to that land" and "be convinced of my sincerity, and of the friendship and strength of our nations" (*NASPIA* 4:169). This promise was a tacit response to recurrent inquiries by US officials regarding which polity had a right to which parcel of land. Commissioners asked this question repeatedly in order to know whose right the United States had to "extinguish" in order to transfer title to the federal government, and Indigenous spokespersons often responded by emphasizing the discrepancy between US notions of exclusive landownership and Indigenous logics of kinship-based belonging. In responding to this question, Mash-i-pi-nash-i-wish critiqued US territorial interests by placing "possess[ion]" in the context of inclusive peoplehood and by clarifying that knowledge of land rights was situated within specific inhabitation practices. His unsettlement model opened for Wayne—and for the settler state—not the land as passive object for improvement but the ways of relating to the land that would have enabled settlers to decolonize themselves. At a time when these peoples seemed to have lost more lands than ever before, they insisted on the need to distribute and expand the epistemological frameworks through which the land could be perceived and inhabited.

Constructions of im/possibility in relation to conditions of life and death were also relevant, as the next two chapters show, for conceptualizing rights claims through references to past deaths. Whereas this chapter focused on Indigenous plans for reorganizing Indigenous-settler relations by unsettling the settler regime, the next two chapters examine arrivant and Indigenous protests of settlers' genocidal violence. Focusing on resistance to African colonization and Indian removal, respectively, chapters 5 and 6 explore arrivant and Indigenous arguments that the history preserved through the memory and remains of dead ancestors validated the spatial and geopolitical rights of arrivants and Indigenous peoples within the land that the

United States defined as its national territory. Chapter 5 focuses on African Americans' claims that the history of slavery, symbolized by the saturation of US soil by the blood of slaves, made that land their patrimony. Native graves, through which the confederacy represented the land claimed by the United States, reappear in chapter 6 not as testimonies to a lost era, but as the focal points for integrating Cherokee and Muscogee pasts, presents, and futures in resistance to the threat of removal.

[5]

ANCESTRAL BLOOD

CHAPTER 4 HIGHLIGHTED THE role of human volition and agency in shaping the geopolitical conditions of collective life. Settlers and Indigenous peoples disagreed over the modes of and purposes through which volition intervened in the creation of geopolitical realities, but by negotiating their geopolitical discrepancies both agreed that human actions could transform the world they inhabited. This agreement, as the tacit references to slaves in negotiations for the Treaty of Hopewell indicate, extended to implicit consensus among settlers and Indigenous negotiators, regarding arrivants' presumed *lack* of geopolitical volition and agency. At no point in these negotiations did either party consider that arrivants could intervene in geopolitical thought or develop geopolitical aspirations. In this sense, both seemed to endorse the logic of *partus sequitur ventrem* that was meant to exclude the enslaved from human sociality.

Under this radical exclusion from human history and agency, arrivants theorized their rights as geopolitical *necessities* that stemmed inevitably from the history of forced migrations and labor. Whereas the category "arrivant" underlines the uncertainties produced by the history of the transatlantic slave trade, the rights theories of ex-slaves and free blacks on which this chapter focuses were invested in replacing historical ambiguities with determinism that nativized them as involuntary settlers. In the nineteenth century, as the vast majority of free and enslaved blacks were born on US soil, arrivants and settlers negotiated arrivants' cultural positionings. Settlers tried to solidify the United States racially as a white political entity by planning African colonization, the project that promised to reverse the history of the transatlantic slave trade by transporting free African Americans to Africa. Advocates of African colonization, organized in 1816 as the American Colonization Society (ACS), argued that such voyages would restore a distorted natural order by returning exiles to their native land.

Opposition to African colonization drove African Americans to formulate more explicit, clearer claims to America as their native land and rightful patrimony than ever before. They revised the volitional emphasis of Locke's theory of property in order to position arrivants as the rightful heirs and proprietors of American lands.[1] In so doing, they redefined the settler contract that authorized voluntary settlers' portable positive birthrights and argued that the reduction of Africans to objects of property necessarily produced new entitlements. They thus effectively theorized an arrivant contract that nativized African Americans as settlers in America. Carole Pateman's analysis of what she defines as the settler contract—by which settler colonialism claims its right to Indigenous peoples' lands—suggests that arrivants are irrelevant for this history. In this sense, Pateman's critique of the settler contract accepts the tacit agreement between settlers and Indigenous peoples regarding arrivants' lack of geopolitical significance. In the scenario she critiques, settlers demoted Indigenous peoples to a state of nature—even when they recognized their "pre-existing social order," as treaty relations show—in order to imagine themselves as the first creators of an original political contract that constituted them as sole sovereigns of colonized Indigenous land. The settler contract, Pateman writes, "sets up new (civil) political institutions . . . that mark the beginnings of a new state" where none had previously existed.[2]

Arrivants adopted settlers' obliteration of Indigenous polities in order to claim their historically new American nativities. To do so, they undermined the centrality of the enslaved mother to the history of slavery, and with it the logic of *partus sequitur ventrem* that denied them patrimonial relations. In its place they nurtured a hitherto unrecognized, emancipatory genealogy symbolized by the blood of their enslaved ancestors, which, they claimed, saturated US soil and made it their own. Whereas *partus sequitur ventrem* attempted to reduce the enslaved mother to the producer of slaveholders' property, arrivants redefined the saturation of the soil by slaves' blood as the validation of African Americans' entitlement to US lands.

Through this process, African Americans contributed to the consolidation of what became US national space and the support this spatial construct provided for perceptions of citizens' rights. Therefore, this chapter demonstrates that arrivant geopolitics made a significant contribution to US national narratives (in addition to slaves' instrumental role in laying the material foundations of the settler regime). This contribution and its denials means that the relations between arrivant and settler geopolitics are far more complex than is often acknowledged.

African Americans who resisted African colonization (I refer to them as anticolonizationists) partially modeled their political philosophy on settlers' portable positive birthright and partly countered that model by arguing that their own expansive positive birthrights emerged in America as corollaries of transatlantic slavery. This idea helped to entrench and legitimize the settler regime, but required that the regime be resettled by integrating arrivants into its constitutive history as its indispensable builders, who were therefore its rightful beneficiaries. As in previous chapters on arrivants' rights claims, here too imperialism was the condition of possibility for their resettlement propositions. Most African Americans who resisted African colonization represented imperialism as the normative frame of historic progress and therefore did not protest the deleterious effects that African colonization would have on African Indigenous peoples. They established their US settler nativities by distancing themselves from Africans and explained that African colonization—by which arrivant missionaries were expected to civilize Africa—would create an aberrant form of imperialism because the presumably uneducated, illiterate emancipated slaves who would settle Liberia could not execute the colonizing mission.

I place this African American narrative of diasporic nativity within several contexts: the ACS rhetoric to which it responded; broader settler claims regarding the presumed danger that free blacks posed to the US body politic; white abolitionists' views of arrivant self-nativization; and the nativities of arrivants who settled in Liberia. Through these various frames the chapter argues that in anticolonizationist struggles, arrivants indirectly helped to naturalize settlers' American nativities by portraying diasporic or migrant nativities as the inevitable consequences of multigenerational inhabitation of colonized land. Although they focused on the native status of involuntary settlers who inherited slavery, the logic of this argument facilitated the portrayal of settler nativity as the inevitable consequence of colonial history. This process was supported by arrivants' contribution to the antebellum project by which diverse US regions were consolidated as coherent national soil. Thus, this chapter positions African American resistance to African colonization as an important site in the naturalization of the settler regime on Indigenous peoples' homelands. The chapter begins with the cultural contexts for African American resistance to colonization. The bulk of this chapter is dedicated to the 1820s' and 1830s' development of the major trope by which African Americans countered colonization, namely, the blood-enriched soil. The chapter also offers a glimpse of the ironic effect of Liberian colonization on Liberian settlers, whose diasporic experiences there validated portrayals of the United States as arrivants' native land. The chapter is followed by a discussion of the distinctions between ancestral blood and ancestral graves, the two respective rhetorical cores of arrivants' and Indigenous peoples' resettlement and unsettlement plans in resistance to African colonization and Indian removal.

African Colonization and American Lands

The idea of colonizing African Americans away from the United States and whitening the body politic while purging the US of slavery and ex-slaves dates at least to Thomas Jefferson's *Notes on the State of Virginia* (1787), in which Jefferson envisioned how to prevent slaves' eventual emancipation from impacting the racial makeup of the US citizenry. In 1816 this idea congealed in the establishment of the ACS, whose members portrayed African Americans as natives of Africa who had been temporarily exiled in America and who would be able to enjoy civil liberties only in Africa. ACS rhetoric portrayed African-descended people as inherently inferior to whites in order to justify both the disenfranchisement of free blacks and the putative need to remove them from the United States. ACS rhetoric centralized native status as a determinant geopolitical factor that governed the distribution of entitled belonging, while African American abolitionists resisted it by utilizing a comparable logic: that the United States was their patrimonial native land, where they were entitled by birth to equal citizenship.

Debates over African colonization pitted two diasporic nativities against each other: an African one, which settlers used to portray African Americans as prospective returnees to Africa, and an American one, which African Americans claimed in order to detach themselves from Africa and attach themselves inalienably to the United States. The ACS imposed diasporic nativity on African Americans by arguing that a remote, often partial African genealogical origin trivialized the American historical experiences of slaves and their descendants. In contrast to Equiano's diasporic indigeneity and support for early colonization in Sierra Leone (chapter 1), ACS ideology served the self-nativization of white settlers. It dismissed the flexible attachment that structures Equiano's resettlement plans and insisted instead on a strict historical teleology. And whereas Equiano's interest in Sierra Leone might have stemmed from aspirations for self-determination, the ACS devised its emigration plan with neither the consent nor the input of prospective emigrants. It hoped that free blacks would prefer Africa to disenfranchisement in the United States and that slaves would realize that emigration was their only chance for emancipation. But Equiano's vision differed also from the diasporic nativity claimed by African American abolitionists, which was predicated on their exclusive, recent American origins. They defined America as the only place where they could improve their present conditions, fulfill what they presented as their destiny, and be fully disenfranchised.

Both the ACS narrative and that of its arrivant opponents conflated native status with settlement and extolled African Americans as *settlers*—of Africa or America—and both attempted to replace the transience connoted by the term *arrivant* with the stable permanence that nativization provides settlers. Jodi A. Byrd and Shona N. Jackson have argued that arrivants were conscripted into the settler colonial dispossession that they eventually often served, and Jackson argues further that this participation was propelled by arrivants' need to indigenize themselves.[3] This chapter contributes to this analysis by examining anticolonizationist arrivants' explicit, complex engagements not only with slavery and US settler colonialism, but also with Africa. Settlers portrayed slavery as a correctable historical mistake while African American anticolonizationist rhetoric treated slavery as a fateful event—indeed, as a structure in its own right—that changed the course of history and created arrivants' diasporic nativity in the United States. Jackson shows that in the Caribbean, arrivants became native by appropriating settlers' roles, and in the Caribbean contexts she studies, that role was largely available for reappropriation due to the absence of large-scale white settler society. However, the pronounced whiteness of US settler society made such appropriation more difficult for African Americans, who therefore needed to redefine the category "settler" and promote resettlement propositions that would effectively rewrite the history and future of US settler colonialism in order to nativize themselves. Arrivant self-nativization was a resettlement project that revised the conditions of belonging to colonized land by turning the nativized arrivant into the consequence of an inevitable historical teleology in which native status functioned as reparations for slavery. This was part of a broader process whereby the ascendance of positive birthright changed the terms of nativity from the critical responses to colonialism discussed in chapters 1 and 2 to a source of settler entitlement.

The African American abolitionists whose texts I analyze envisioned the consolidation of national space and anticipated Manifest Destiny *avant la lettre* while reversing its racial logic to serve their resettlement schemes. At the heart of this narrative was a trope that figured the blood of the enslaved as a potent fertilizer of US soil. This trope suggested that slaves' blood converted American lands from unclaimed wilderness to property and thus ensured the national prosperity that the impossibility doctrine protected (chapter 4). The arrivants who created this narrative argued that their ancestors' blood enriched the soil and turned it into the patrimony of slaves and their descendants. Whereas settlers imagined Manifest Destiny as the divinely ordained expansion of white liberty, arrivants used the trope of the blood-enriched soil to redefine slavery as the source of their superior, embodied entitlement to expansive nationalized lands. Through this trope they hoped to reverse what Orlando Patterson defined as "[t]he essence of slavery," that is, "that the slave, in his social death, lives on the margin between community and chaos, life and death, the sacred and the secular."[4] The trope enabled antebellum African Americans to place their history at the spatial and symbolic heart of a unified national territory.

The trope of the blood-enriched soil revised hegemonic views of the origins of civil liberties, which reminded US citizens of their debt to the Revolutionary War soldiers whose shed blood had purchased the freedom of the living. In this conventional construction of civil rights as acquired property, voluntary sacrifice bought alienable liberties whose survival depended on citizens' nationalist commitments. For example, on the eve of the War of 1812 an opinion piece in the Charleston *City Gazette* called upon "ALL AMERICANS who sincerely love their country" to "rise" and protect "the sovereignty acquired by the precious blood of our ancestors" lest their apathy in the face of British threats cost them their liberty.[5] In 1818, a Fourth of July oration to "Vermont State Prisoners" emphasized "the blessings purchased by the blood of our venerated ancestors" and asked prisoners to "unite" and "declare" that they "love[d] and admire[d]" their government's "laws . . . even in a state penitentiary."[6] Narratives of national unity depended on voluntary consent—even when they referred to those temporarily stripped of their freedoms. The trope of the blood-enriched soil challenged these conventions by developing the idea that involuntary conditions produced stronger historical destinies.

Blood-Enriched Soil

This trope emerged at a January 1817 meeting in Philadelphia's Bethel Church of a thousand free African Americans, who protested the ACS's plan to remove them to West Africa. Prominent members of the city's black community signed the address that used the trope, including Absalom Jones, Richard Allen, James Forten, Robert Douglass, Francis Perkins, John Gloucester, Robert Gorden, James Johnson, Quamoney Clarkson, John Summersett, Randall Shepard, and Russell Parrott. Their first resolution read as follows: "Whereas our ancestors (not of choice) were the first successful cultivators of the wilds of America, we their descendants feel ourselves entitled to participate in the blessings of her luxuriant soil, which their blood and sweat manured."[7]

This statement established a new order of arrivant priority that disregarded Indigenous polities. It challenged the Eurocentric doctrine of discovery that constructed the voluntary settler as the quintessential rights-bearing subject by arguing that volition was irrelevant for belonging, patrimony, and entitlement. If anything, the address suggested, volition may hurt rather than support these endowments. In this historical narrative the "wilds of America" awaited the "blood and tears" of the enslaved, which was the only means by which they could become "luxuriant." Against the malleability of the "wilds of America," anticolonizationist rhetoric pitted the "burning sands of Africa" as spaces that remained beyond progressive history until proper European imperialists would usher them into a Eurocentric civilized international arena.[8] This sentiment was popular enough to lead James Forten—the meeting's president and a previous associate of Paul Cuffe, who had actively supported Sierra Leone's colonization—to suppress his former advocacy of African colonization.[9] By the 1840s, numerous African American writers would reproduce the trope of ancestral blood in US soil and claim that slavery's history was the irrefutable foundation of African Americans' positive birthright in the United States.

We may appreciate the trope's novel spatial intervention by considering a statement that Forten wrote in 1813, protesting Pennsylvania legislators' proposed ban on African Americans' entrance to the state. Forten worried about "the honor and dignity of our native state," writing that African Americans' "grievances" would be "light compared with the load of reproach that must be heaped upon our commonwealth" by the proposed bill. He added, "The story will fly from the north to the south, and the advocates of slavery, the traders in human blood, will smile contemptuously at the once boasted moderation and humanity of Pennsylvania!"[10] This plea for the state's "honor" presents the settler regime as a collection of distinct regions whose unification must not be affected by antiblack legislation. It responds to prevalent perceptions of the United States as an unconsolidated polity composed of disparate regional centers. Scholars have explained that the discourses of immediate abolition and Indian removal helped to cement these disorganized political entities into the consolidated national image that McMurray's map envisioned (chapter 4).[11] But whereas this scholarship often dates this process to the 1830s, anticolonizationist free blacks began using the trope of the blood-enriched soil to this effect as early as 1817.

The white settler state that emerged, as Trish Loughran argues, with President Madison's official invention of the "fiction" of "consolidated domestic space"[12] and culminated with John L. O'Sullivan's 1845 formulation of "Manifest Destiny"[13] was already questioned, redefined, and reformulated as a biracial polity in 1817, the last year of Madison's presidency. Robert S. Levine, Peter P. Hinks, and Christopher Apap discuss David Walker's creation and circulation of his *Appeal to the Coloured Citizens of the World*

(1829) as a major event in the consolidation of national space.[14] Walker helped elaborate the trope of the blood-enriched soil (which he borrowed from a letter that Richard Allen published in *Freedom's Journal* in 1827), but his predecessors, including Allen, had first developed that trope and embarked on this project earlier.

The trope of the blood-enriched soil nationalized African American rights by positing "America" as a coherent geopolitical unit against the image of a benighted "Africa" that dominated colonizationist discourse. It portrayed the blood of the enslaved—shed in various locales across the United States—as a shared element that provided national soil with the very historic coherence that slavery seemed to disrupt as it divided North from South. Africa was indispensable to this process. The 1817 Bethel Church address positioned the "savage wilds of Africa" as destinations of exile rather than of homecoming, ones that seem antithetical to the "wilds of America" that anticipate their future enrichment by slaves' blood.[15] This distinction between Africa's presumably unredeemable "savage wilds" and America's improvable "wilds" structured black anticolonizationist representations of their native status as malleable in one direction only—that which supported the imperial construction of the US settler regime. This discourse symbolically obliterated Indigenous polities—often cast as savage, barbarous, or wild in antebellum settler rhetoric—and presented American lands as either settled or in the process of settlement.

In January 1817, at the same time that the Philadelphia address first used the trope of the blood-enriched soil in opposition to African colonization, free blacks in Richmond used this logic to mobilize resistance to African colonization in support of colonization in the United States. "[W]e prefer being colonized in the most remote country of the land of our nativity," they wrote, "to being exiled to a foreign country." By distinguishing the United States as the "land of our nativity" from Africa as "a foreign country" they invested the passive verb *colonized* with agency, in contrast to *exiled*, and thereby suggested that further removal would entrench their US nativities, but only if it facilitated the expansion of the US settler regime. Through this request they negotiated their distance from white US culture by asking the United States to give them "a small portion of their territory, either on the Missouri River, or any place that may seem to them most conducive to the public good, and our future welfare."[16] The pronouns *their* and *them* refer to the United States and suggest the alienated exclusion that the proposal attempts to rectify by portraying disenfranchised blacks as new settlers who would contribute to domestic colonization efforts. Under pressure of removal they suggested that their right to US soil extended to the entire area of the nation, thus detaching their "nativity" from *partus sequitur ventrem* and attaching it instead to the expanding settler regime. To appreciate the novelty of this argument in 1817, one may recall that O'Sullivan, who would later coin the term Manifest Destiny, wrote as late as 1839 that "American patriotism is not of soil; we are not aborigines."[17] African American anticolonizationists grounded "American patriotism" in the land early on, as chapter 3 also shows, and tried to nativize themselves before white settlers embraced this project on a broad scale.

These early self-nativization projects used abolitionist metaphors as well to distinguish Africa from America. In 1818, a group of free blacks in Philadelphia joined James Forten and Russell Parrott to claim that colonization would reproduce the crimes of the Middle Passage because African Americans had now become thoroughly attached to America. They wrote that "all the heart-rending agonies which were endured by our forefathers when they were dragged into bondage from Africa will be again renewed, and with increased anguish" if they were to be expelled from the United States. "The shores of America will, like the sands of Africa, be watered by the tears of those who will be left behind," they added, implicitly arguing for an affinity between space and affect that ties people to their native land, which alone can receive their tears or blood. They stated further that "[t]hose who shall be carried away will roam childless, widowed, and alone, over the burning plains of Guinea," as though they could never be integrated into African society and space.[18] They thus established their diasporic American nativities as equal to their ancestors' pre-slavery attachment to Africa. This analogy turns slavery's history into a process that naturally produced arrivants' entitlement to settlers' positive birthright in America. Here African Americans naturalized their claimed positions as nativized settlers by engaging elaborately with settlement's violent history, as did the black abolitionists discussed in chapter 3.

The ACS responded to such claims by ventriloquizing African American voices and harnessing them to pro-colonization advocacy that tried to trivialize, refute, and redirect African American conceptualizations of belonging. Between late 1817 and early 1818, northern free black communities lost two prominent members: Paul Cuffe, an Afro-Wampanoag Quaker businessman who had supported Sierra Leone, and Episcopal minister Absalom Jones. Following their deaths, a colonizationist writer anonymously published a series, "Dialogues on the African Colony," that ventriloquized Cuffe's and Jones's voices in support of colonization.[19] Set in heaven and featuring "William Penn," "Paul Cuffe," and "Absalom Jones," the "Dialogues" urged "Africans" to become settlers in Africa lest they prove themselves "the only nation incapable of great and noble exertions." The writer, who cast "Cuffe" as a "zealous advocate" and "Jones" as a stubborn opponent of colonization, trivialized opposition to colonization by portraying it as an irrational emotional obstacle to African Americans' progress. The ventriloquized voice of "Jones" reduced anticolonizationist positions to an incoherent collection of "diversified" "feelings," "considerations," and "dispositions." Avoiding the language of rights, "Jones" supported his opposition to colonization by arguing that African Americans were finally "beginning to feel themselves at home" in the United States.[20]

In response, "Penn" simultaneously acknowledged and denied African Americans' attachment to the United States by characterizing free blacks as "aliens in their own land" and by urging them to "Return to the land of your forefathers . . . whose laws, government, honours, victories and . . . destiny you can proudly call your own."[21] The tension between the reference to the United States as "their own land" and to Africa as that which they would be able to "call [their] own" stems from the tacit problem of impure racial and civic mixtures, which African colonization would solve. The writer promised that colonization would usher in future purity by separating "America" from "Africa" as distinct historical subjects, and he portrayed colonization as a form of reparations. But instead of positioning African Americans as the recipients of reparations for slavery, "Penn" cast them as the object with which America would compensate Africa: "Those who were dragged by violence from the land of their fathers . . . now return to . . . their native home" in an act of "noble . . . reparation, which America will make to Africa for all the injuries she has done her."[22] Detached from human and civil rights, colonization constitutes a recuperative historical project that would restore a violated natural geopolitical order. The "Dialogues," like Forten and Parrott's 1818 text, exposed historic violence, but did so in order to detach it from the United States by representing the transatlantic slave trade as foreign to American history. The earlier demotion of anticolonizationist discourse to fragmented affective "considerations" becomes particularly useful because "feelings" that have yet to cohere logically cannot withstand this portrayal of colonization as a historical force decreed by heaven's residents. Consequently, "Jones" surrendered and supported colonization after his "objections" have been "refuted" and his "doubts" had been "satisfied," and he called upon "Heaven" to "speed the undertaking."[23]

The "Dialogues" formulates nativity, reparations, and alienation within a natural order that would remain a mainstay of colonizationist discourse and clash with the historical trajectory of the blood-enriched soil trope. Beyond such fictional ventriloquizing, the ACS wished to present solid evidence of African American support for colonization; in December 1826 the society boasted that two African American congregations—Baltimore's Bethel and African Churches—had decided to emigrate. The congregations' "Memorial from the Free People of Colour to the Citizens of Baltimore" imitated ACS propaganda so closely it is hard to tell whether its authors had been trying to gain the favor of ACS officials or whether such officials had doctored the statement.[24] James M. Wright states that black Baltimoreans "were induced to sign" it, and only two members of each church actually did so.[25] But the "Memorial" might have triggered the resurgence and development of the blood-enriched soil trope in the late 1820s.

ACS rhetoric displaced the taboo topic of racial mixture by using it to portray civic relations, and the "Memorial" identified its writers as "natives, and yet not citizens," who resided among "the freest people . . . in the world" but enjoyed "none of the immunities of freedom." They clarified that even had they desired to "mingle" with white US citizens, their "difference of colour," the "servitude" of "most" of their "brethren," and "the prejudices which those circumstances have naturally occasioned" would have prevented them from doing so. Like many colonizationist texts, the "Memorial" disavows settler colonial violence by representing slavery as a historic mistake or crime for which England is responsible. It portrayed African Americans as an "extraneous mass of men" whose attachment to the United States was limited to climatic adjustments. Denying any affective spatial attachment, the "Memorial" proposed that the United States may profitably replace free blacks with European immigrants, and it promised that colonization may enable unemployed white men to "provide for themselves and their families" by taking jobs held by prospective free black emigrants. While free African Americans who opposed colonization often stated that their presence in the United States was required for the abolitionist struggle, and while ACS officials often portrayed that presence as a threat to slavery, the "Memorial" stated that free blacks' "absence will accelerate the liberation of such of our brethren as are in bondage." The value of slaves "must decrease and disappear before the superior advantages of free labour," as many European immigrants would come to replace those who would leave for Liberia.[26] This memorial might have partially motivated the resurgence of the trope of the blood-enriched soil on the pages of the first African American newspaper, *Freedom's Journal*, in 1827.[27]

Ancestral Blood in Freedom's Journal

In 1827, its first year of publication, *Freedom's Journal* revived the trope of the blood-enriched soil by printing a letter that its editor, John B. Russworm, had commissioned from Richard Allen, one of the signatories to the 1817 address of Philadelphia's Bethel Church. The ACS must have spread rumors that Allen supported its cause, because Russworm had asked Allen "to contradict certain reports, of his having become a convert to the colonization scheme."[28] Allen referred to Africa as "a far country" three times in his short letter, and he used this literal exoticization to distance its historic destiny from African Americans. He stated that he could not "reconcile" himself to "the colonization of Africans in Liberia" because an "unlettered people, brought up in ignorance" like the majority of African Americans could not "convert or civilize" Africa's "Heathens" since "they themselves are neither *civilized* nor *Christianized*."[29] Ironically, the similarity between these perceptions of Africa and African Americans is precisely what makes them incompatible because in Allen's imperial geopolitics, civilizing can only proceed from discrepancy between a heathen land and civilized colonists. This idea relates indirectly to slavery's nativizing impact on African Americans, as though coerced exposure to an utterly alien system is the mechanism of historic transformation. Allen's argument crystallized antebellum perceptions of imperialism by, paradoxically, suggesting that African Americans were as heathen as Africa itself. This claim responded to the prevalent colonizationist argument that once African Americans were restored to "their ancestors' native land," they "may enjoy their unalienable rights, and prove an everlasting advantage to the natives," as Illinois Baptist minister John Clark put it in 1826.[30] Both Allen and Clark envisioned African Americans as precivilized peoples, and both argued that geopolitical conditions would facilitate their civilization, because both represented imperialism and settlement as the means for historical progress. But whereas Clark portrayed this process in terms of inevitable natural development to which African Americans would be subjected once they emigrated, Allen emphasized the paradoxical agency of their forced labor in America.

Allen used the settler ethos of immigrant contribution to the settler state in order to position arrivants as preexisting natives. "See the thousands of foreigners emigrating to America every year," he wrote, "and if there be ground sufficient for them to cultivate, and bread for them to eat; why would they wish to send the *first tillers* of the land away?" This comparison utilizes portrayals of American lands as available for agricultural settlement in order to challenge the distinction between settlers' portable positive birthright and arrivants' presumably indelible negative birthright. Allen claimed that the latter were attached foundationally to settled land and held prior, inalienable rights next to which those of voluntary settlers were necessarily inferior. This insistence on priority reproduces settler historical narratives but revises their constructions of original contract, volition, and violence.

Through this comparison Allen restored arrivants to the rank of national farmers, reproduced the Lockean denial of Native American agriculture, and replaced colonizationists' spatialization of African American rights with a temporalized argument for their prior entitlement to US soil. He enlisted slavery's history into this project by reversing the portrayal of historic responsibility that the "Memorial" offered. "We were *stolen* from our mother country and brought *here*," he wrote. "We have *tilled* the ground and made fortunes for thousands." Therefore, he protested the idea that arrivants "*who stay to till the ground must be slaves*." Having emphasized arrivants' function as settlers, Allen employed the trope of the blood-enriched soil to ground his antiracist critique of African colonization in an inevitable historical process that shifted slavery's logic of *partus sequitur ventrem* to the logic of settlers' naturalization in colonized land. "This land which we have watered with our *tears* and *our blood*, is now our *mother country*," he wrote.[31] This representation implicitly reconstituted African Americans as a patrilineal society whose maternity was confined to the national soil that they possessed naturally.

This masculinist discourse of patrimony was haunted by women's reproductive bodies, the central site of *partus sequitur ventrem*. Jennifer L. Morgan discusses slaveholders' calculations of the future gains they saw in female slaves. Morgan focuses on the fact that "*becoming* a slave" often took "place in the act of birth," explaining that "[l]egislators developed the definition of slavery within [the] very body" of the enslaved woman, and manipulated "childbirth" in an effort "to sever a black woman's hold on her humanity."[32] As Thomas D. Morris shows, *partus sequitur ventrem* had two sources: property law, where it determined the ownership of newborn calves, and bastardy law, where it was used to prevent children whose paternity was not recognized by church or state from enjoying patrilineal inheritance.[33] The dehumanizing effect of *partus sequitur ventrem* was rooted in its denial of legally recognized fathers to enslaved and free blacks. In this context, the enslaved mother figured as a source of negative birthright that anticolonizationist discourse had to repress. The enslaved mother was treated similarly to African space, which anticolonizationists often imagined as irredeemable "burning sands" from which they tried to distance themselves. By contrast, the "wilds of America" that were fertilized by slaves' "blood and tears" provided symbolic compensation both for patrilineal inheritance and for volitional agency, constitutive elements of Eurocentric freedom of which slaves were deprived. Exclusion from these orders of rights and property meant that free blacks who asserted their entitlement to US civil protection could not simply adopt Locke's influential theory of property in which "Man" mixes his labor with the soil and thereby appropriates it and its produce. By ridding Locke's theory of its condition of possibility—"Man's" voluntary choice—they inverted it and claimed that *forced* labor created the strongest foundation of entitlement and inheritance.

Locke's "Man" was "Master of himself, and *Proprietor of his own Person*, and the Actions of *Labour* of it," who could therefore not "*enslave himself* to any one."[34] In contrast to this masculinist teleology, the legalization of slavery used the enslaved to symbolize negative birthright that comprised both subjugation and presumed African savagery. This savagery was often disguised in colonizationist texts as the anticipating, long-forsaken mother of all African-descended people. Colonizationists portrayed Africa as "the land of promise to degraded thousands—the rich inheritance which God has given to tribes who have drank deep of the waters of affliction, labored and wept in a land of strangers."[35] In an 1823 piece entitled "Africa," an anonymous writer using the pen name "Homo" claimed to speak for humanity as he urged his white readers to encourage "our free blacks" to heed "the claims of their own Africa!"[36] These portrayals of Africa used a logic of historic necessity similar to that of anticolonizationist rhetoric, but attributed it to Africa's soil rather than to America's. Legal denials of property and land rights to free blacks in various US jurisdictions supported this argument.

An 1821 opinion piece in the Charleston *City Gazette* elaborated on this idea in order to distinguish free blacks from settlers—the very distinction that free blacks reworked in order to nativize themselves. The writer, who signed his piece "T. G.," identified himself as a "justice of the peace" and translated the presumed reproductive impurities of negative birthright into legal pathologies. Presuming all "Mulattoes" to "be of corrupt origin maternally," he recognized three statuses as comprising the settler regime's "civil society"—"citizens, denizens or aliens"—distinguished by their differential access to state-sanctioned "rights" and "disabilities." T. G. defined citizens as entitled to "equal privileges and immunities" including exclusive "dominion over the soil"; aliens as enjoying "incoherent and temporary rights"; and denizens as occupying a "probationary state" between them. He portrayed "free people of colour" as "a fourth class . . . of an anomalous nature—an excrescence of the body politic" that "depriv[ed] the general system of its health and vigour, and corrupt[ed] its vital functions."[37] T. G. interpreted South Carolina's 1740 slave code, which founded slavery on *partus sequitur ventrem*, as distinguishing among the rights that "Indians," "Mestizos" (i.e., "descendants of Whites and Indians"), "Sambos" ("descendants of Indians and Negroes"), and "Mulattoes" may legitimately claim. He argued that a free black mother may be "sufficient" for affirming a "coloured" person's right to freedom, but that only a "white" mother may provide such person with "rights of property." T. G. therefore portrayed the rights of free blacks as "encroachments" on settlers' civil society and suggested that free blacks endangered settlers' landed regime. He represented race—perpetuated through the black mother, whether free or enslaved—as the decisive factor blocking free blacks' entitlement to settler lands. T. G. warned white settlers against extending property rights to free blacks, as such "favours" may cause arrivant "encroachments" and might be "construed into privileges, and privileges matured to rights." He used this organic imagery to warn that if rights were to "ripen," it would be "hazardous to limit their extent, or to question their legitimacy."

Scholars have discussed the liminal positions of free and enslaved blacks as well as those of Native Americans in relation to the United States, but the focus on nativity by which arrivants claimed settler status illuminates a more specific angle of this process. Priscilla Wald discusses the US Supreme Court's (later) definitions of Indigenous and African-descended people as "neither citizens, nor aliens," who were therefore prevented from "tell[ing] their stories officially" and whose ambiguous positions undermined the settler state's founding liberal principles.[38] Edlie L. Wong studies similar ambiguities caused by slaves' travels across the boundaries between slaveholding and non-slaveholding jurisdictions.[39] By focusing on "official" stories and legal discourse, Wald and Wong's analyses pay particular attention to state formations. However, my focus on the resettlement project entailed in arrivants' claims to historic recognition and reward calls for rethinking the state. While this resettlement project does not undermine settlers' claims to Indigenous peoples' homelands, it transforms the conditions that produce settlers—and thereby the entire logic of entitlement and property that governs the settler regime. This is why some arrivants, most prominently David Walker, claimed a nativized settler status superior to that of voluntary settlers. In the process, Walker redeemed the enslaved mother from the legacy of *partus sequitur ventrem*.

Walker's Superior Proprietorship

In 1829, Walker copied Allen's letter in his *Appeal to the Coloured People of the World*, the last article of which protested African colonization, and particularly the ACS. Unlike the writers who preceded him in replacing the reproductive imagery of *partus sequitur ventrem* with the fertility of the soil, Walker employed the figure of the enslaved and free African American "mother" in his critique of slavery's destruction of families. He referred twice to "our mothers, who bore the pains of death to give us birth" and thus alluded to Eve's punishment in Genesis to emphasize the humanity of African Americans and the cruelty of US slavery.[40] This idea is reinforced through the text's multiple references to slavery's violations of family ties, both in the forced separation of family members and in the use of one family member to inflict violence on another. Following Walker's death, Maria Stewart continued his reclamation and exhortation of African American parents, especially mothers. Lamenting that "our tender babes are tainted as soon as they are born" and that "they go astray, as it were, from the womb," Stewart urged African American women to elevate the next generations: "upon your exertions almost entirely," she wrote, "depends whether the rising generation shall be anything more than we have been or not."[41] Walker and Stewart freed the black mother from *partus sequitur ventrem* by investing her with familial responsibilities. The by-product of this process was a revised order of property to supplant *partus sequitur ventrem*. However, in this substitution the enslaved mother was often marginalized, again, because it was framed by US property law, which marginalized women.

Walker's self-nativizing rhetoric that turned arrivants into settlers was based on property relations. He opened the first article of his *Appeal* by referring to blood and tears as currency that "enrich[ed]" slaveholders while the dehumanized slaves—reduced to the condition of "*brutes*"—must "go on enriching them, from one generation to another with our *blood* and our *tears*!!!!"[42] Walker repeatedly redirected the ancestral blood trope toward a sustained critique of property and reminded his readers that "*we*" "have enriched their country with our blood and tears"; he concluded that US citizens punished African Americans "for enriching them and their country."[43] Addressing the reduction of slaves to property in US law, he protested the white perception of African Americans as "an inheritance to them and theirs forever"—the logic of *partus sequitur ventrem*—and clarified that the wealth of the United States was accumulated through slavery.[44] This attack on settler property regimes addresses the construction of positive birthright as property. Legal scholar Ayelet Shachar argues that contemporary "birthright citizenship laws resemble ancient property regimes that shaped rigid and tightly regulated estate-transmission rules." She explains that "[b]irthright citizenship . . . moves down the generations like an entail form of untaxed inherited property."[45] Walker attributed a similar process to voluntary settlers and represented it as a crime by emphasizing that the slaves who were denied both citizenship and recognition as humans were the producers of that wealth.

In Walker's contemporaneous intellectual milieu, territorial birthright citizenship was associated with Jefferson's elevation of voluntary settler yeomen farmers to the idealized position of republican citizens, in contrast to disenfranchised arrivants. Jefferson defined voluntary settler "cultivators of the earth" as "the most virtuous and independent citizens" and wrote that "if a slave can have a country in this world, it must be any other in preference to that in which he is born to live and labour for another."[46] ACS rhetoric reproduced this patronizing attitude to arrivant volition in order to represent African colonization as a benevolent project. To counter his argument, anticolonizationist rhetoric—particularly that of Walker, who framed his *Appeal* by references to Jefferson—used the trope of the blood-enriched soil to replace official legalistic landholding with ideas of naturalistic inevitability in which slave labor turned US soil into the patrimony of slaves and their descendants. Walker developed the naturalistic argument of arrivant rights by using the Bible as irrefutable proof of justice's eventual global victory and recast African Americans' ancestral blood as biblical evidence for US sins. Alluding to Genesis 4:10, he asked rhetorically, "Do you think that our blood is hidden from the Lord?"[47] He answers this question in the last article of the book, stating that "[t]he Blood of our fathers who had been murdered by the whites," as well as "the groans of our Brethren, who are now held in cruel ignorance, wretchedness and slavery by them, cry aloud to the Maker of Heaven and of earth, against the whole continent of America, for redress."[48] This allusion to Genesis in the rhetorical question and its answer reinterprets biblical myths such as the voice of Abel's blood as geopolitical events in order to support the idea that the continent itself must recompense slaves and their descendants with property rights based on native status. The United States is thus extended to "the continent of America" in order to fulfill what Walker presents as its inevitable destiny.

Yet Walker referred to the "coloured people of these United States" consistently as "sons of Africa," thus developing a bifurcated nativity that organizes his intervention in the ACS's historical narrative.[49] Whereas colonizationists confined African American nativities to Africa, Walker and other African American writers temporalized their African nativities by imagining them as a unified, remote origin from which slavery detached them and then reattached them irrevocably to American spaces. This bifurcated nativity, by which arrivants' pasts are tied to Africa while their presents and futures are inseparable from the United States, becomes persuasive thanks to representations of the Middle Passage as a decisive historic break from which arrivants' American nativities ensued without erasing their African ones. In both cases, nativity served geopolitical unification, and in both it was facilitated by slavery. The transatlantic slave trade created a unified idea of Africa that made African identity possible, and slavery in America distributed Africans and their descendants over vast regions that were thereby potentially unified. As the 1818 "Dialogues on the African Colony" show, a similar geopolitical imagery of African origins enabled the ACS to portray African Americans as objects of America's reparations for Africa, and the difference between colonizationist and anticolonizationist portrayals of African origins concerned the future rather than the past. In anticolonizationist rhetoric, slavery severed time irreparably, reduced African origins to elements of the past, and supported the idea that arrivants' presents and futures were American. Walker entrenched this idea by representing African Americans as both the beneficiaries and the primary proprietors of America.

Following his reproduction of Allen's *Freedom's Journal* letter, Walker returned to the trope of the blood-enriched soil in order to link resistance to colonization with arrivants' superior proprietorship by comparison to that of white US citizens. "Let no man of us budge one step," he wrote, "and let slave-holders come to beat us from our country. America is more our country, than it is the whites—we have enriched it with our *blood and tears*." He clarified that this discussion concerned property relations by writing that "[t]he greatest riches in all America have arisen from our blood and tears:—and will they drive us from our property and homes, which we have earned with our *blood*?"[50] Walker established self-nativization by portraying settler rule as invasion—not of America's Indigenous peoples' homelands, but of the arrivants, whom he positions as the only rightful proprietors of the "country." In this scenario the invading "slaveholders" who "come" to that country to "beat" African Americans out have no legitimate claim to America, yet Walker offered to share the land with slave-holding invaders, thereby positioning nativized arrivants as generous hosts who would accept settlers into the "country" as long as these newcomers respect them. "Throw away your fears and prejudices," Walker told his white readers, "and enlighten us and treat us like men, and we will like you more than we do now hate you, and tell us now no more about colonization, for America is as much our country, as it is yours."[51] This resettlement proposition differs from the unsettlement offers of joint inhabitation discussed in chapter 4 in that it accepts settler ideology and its view of settlement as the only framework for geopolitical development. By equating settlers' and arrivants' rights, Walker clarifies that the antiracist transformation he advocates would neither threaten the settler regime nor acknowledge Indigenous peoples' rights. Throughout his *Appeal*, Walker oscillates between two evaluations of arrivants' proprietorship—as equal to or superior to that of settlers—because his model of rights and freedom is founded on settler history and property relations. The next section elaborates on the relations between arrivants, Indigenous peoples, and settlers in anticolonizationist discourse.

Arrivants, Indigenous Peoples, and Settlers

Walker died in 1830 shortly after publishing his *Appeal*. A rising "insurrectionary spirit," culminating in Nat Turner's 1831 revolt, created an unprecedented surge in ACS popularity among northern and southern whites.[52] Congress passed the Indian Removal Act in 1830, and the Cherokee Nation turned to the Supreme Court to challenge Georgia's efforts to override Cherokee sovereignty. In this climate, African American abolitionists issued resolutions that founded their rights claims more forcefully on their exclusive US nativities.[53] While arrivants argued that their ancestors' blood saturated US soil, giving them rights to the land, Indigenous peoples used the presence of their ancestors' graves in the soil to claim a precolonial Indigenous history that demanded settler respect of their rights. Ancestral blood and ancestral graves signify the different historical claims that anti-removal and anticolonization discourses developed. The blood-enriched soil forced its listeners to acknowledge an unrecognized history, one that no monuments celebrated or symbolized; it paralleled Walker's claim for disrespected yet superior black proprietorship of the United States. By contrast, ancestral graves grounded Indigenous rights in a material historical record that called for US respect for Indigenous priority and sovereignty. Ancestral graves evidence a long history of multigenerational attachment to particular places, while ancestral blood refers to a delimited history of injustice that produced inalienable attachment to an expanding spatial terrain.

In the early 1830s, some anticolonizationist African American resolutions merged the two tropes, especially in order to relate African colonization to Indian removal and thereby appeal to anti-removal, pro-colonization white audiences. The writers of those resolutions lived among primarily northern whites who supported African colonization, opposed Indian removal, and saw no conflict between these positions. Within this climate the comparison between arrivants' and Indigenous peoples' native status could potentially expose African colonization as a racist project. It was a short-lived yet politically inspiring indication that arrivant rights could be formulated from a position of support for Indigenous peoples' struggles.

In the first resolution from this period that William Lloyd Garrison printed in his *Thoughts on African Colonization* (1831), Samuel Ennals and Philip Bell claimed, "This is our home, and this our country. Beneath its sod lie the bones of our fathers: for it some of them fought, bled, and died."[54] Ennals and Bell connected their protest explicitly to the Cherokee struggle by expressing their "hope that those who have so eloquently pleaded the cause of the Indian, will at least endeavor to preserve consistency in their conduct." Despite the different historical scales of Indigenous and arrivant presence in America, and although arrivants could not claim prior inhabitation of the land, Ennals and Bell referred to manipulations of consent and coercion in order to suggest that their nativities were comparable to those of Indigenous peoples. To validate this argument, they had to discard Walker's bifurcated nativities that distinguished arrivants from Native Americans. They clarified that "we claim *this country, the place of our birth, and not Africa,* as our mother country" and protested the "Christian philanthropy" that assumed their consent to emigrate from the United States. They elaborated on the comparison between arrivants and Indigenous peoples in order to refute the colonizationist thesis that African-descended people were irredeemably inferior to whites and therefore could not integrate into US society. They argued that the "flourishing conditions," "intelligence," and "refinement" of "the Cherokees" proved that none "of the races of mankind" was "brand[ed] with inferiority." Like Walker's invitation to white settlers to share in joint proprietorship of America, this self-nativization argument was also shaped by imperial distinctions, as Ennals and Bell argued for the "civilization and refinement" of "respectable" African Americans. Based on the comparison between "respectable" arrivants and "refined" Cherokees, they argued that whites who mistrusted Georgia's declarations "that the Indians shall not be removed but '*with their own consent*'" should not "blame us if we attach the same credit to the declaration that they mean to colonize us 'only with our consent.'"[55]

In February 1831 the Georgia *Macon Telegraph* quoted Ennals and Bell's words in a brief report on "[t]he 'colored citizens of the city of New York'" who rejected African colonization. Emphasizing Ennals and Bell's critique of "Christian philanthropy," the Georgia paper quoted their claim for exclusive US nativity without mentioning their critique of Georgia's attacks on the Cherokee Nation. The *Macon Telegraph* followed this report with one on Louisiana's appointment of a "Committee to enquire into the expediency of encouraging the emigration of the free people of colour to Liberia" and another on a new law by which the Savannah City Council would impose "a tax of one hundred dollars upon every free person of color coming to that City." The *Telegraph*'s editors thus sought not only to report Ennals and Bell's claims, but to counter them. And much like anti-removal whites, pro-removal Georgia sought to separate opposition to African colonization from that which targeted Indian removal. By linking these projects, northern African Americans suggested that in order for whites to accept their claims to American birthrights, they would first need to recognize the systematic violence that facilitated the white supremacist settler regime.

Six months later in Brooklyn, Henry C. Thompson and George Hogarth issued a resolution that similarly used the Cherokee struggle as a model for claiming rights while distinguishing arrivants from Cherokees by founding African Americans' entitlement to US citizenship on their contribution to the settler project. Arguing that they were "already American citizens," Thompson and Hogarth grounded this assertion in the settler ethos by stating that "our fathers were among the first that peopled this country." They thus perpetuated the idea of *terra nullius* even as they argued that God who "has lately pleaded the Indian's cause in our land" would do so for them as well, so that settlers and arrivants would "re-echo liberty and equal rights in all parts of Columbia's soil." The references to "our land" and "Columbia's soil" in this context neutralized "the Indian's cause" in order to celebrate settler colonialism. Thompson and Hogarth also shifted the ancestral blood trope away from its connotations of entitlement that resulted from slavery by emphasizing the settler ethos in which blood served as currency for purchasing land through voluntary heroic sacrifice. Stating that "[m]any of [our ancestors] fought, and bled, and died for the gaining of her liberties," they asserted that they could not "forsake their tombs, and flee to an unknown land."[56] These "tombs," unlike the "sweat and tears" to which they also referred, suggest the permanent validity of settlement. Rejecting the ACS's portrayals of free blacks as anomalous entities endangering the body politic, Thompson and Hogarth claimed de facto US citizenship that ensured their expansive entitlement to national space, and the only terms in which they could do so were those of the settler state.[57] The next section examines the geopolitical consolidation that this discourse supported.

From Africans to Americans

The image of ancestral graves that African Americans borrowed from antiremoval discourse lost its appeal toward the late 1830s, as the Trail of Tears proved the settler regime would not respect Indigenous peoples' geopolitical rights. Having gradually abandoned the trope of ancestral graves, free blacks turned from geography to race in order to detach themselves from Africa. They replaced Walker's sense of bifurcated nativity with an unambiguous "American" one by arguing that they may be termed "colored" but not "African."[58] This process demonstrates arrivants' investment in the black/white binary as a tactic by which they naturalized their rights as nativized settlers. This process had begun earlier and was already at work in Thompson and Hogarth's use of "the sable sons of America" to whom the "friendship" of racist colonizationists was "as foreign . . . as the coast of Africa."[59] It seems to have originated in its most elaborate form in the work of Hosea Easton.

In his 1828 Thanksgiving address, Easton argued that the names "Africans" and "Ethiopians" constituted an "insult," and he framed this argument by his text's explicit endorsement of settlers' genocidal invasion of Indigenous peoples' homelands. Explaining that "the brutal conduct" of African Americans' white "fathers" made ex-slaves and free blacks "distantly related to some of the white members" of the settler state, Easton extolled early settlers as "our forefathers" who "display[ed] their superior knowledge in the use of fire arms above that of the natives" and acquired the "peaceable possession of the soil."[60] Yet Easton oscillated between viewing Native Americans as savages whose defeat enabled the settler colonial project and—when resistance to Indian removal became more vocal—as a model of struggle against a racist white regime. Nine years later, Easton's *Treatise on the Intellectual Character, and Civil and Political Condition of the Colored People of the U. States* (1837) censured settlers for the "late unholy war with the Indians, and the wicked crusade against Mexico," which he attributed to the effect of Europe's medieval past on its descendants.[61]

Easton differentiated between what he called the "natural" "prejudice" against Native Americans and the "national and personal" one against "the colored people" who were forcibly deprived of their African "birthright" and thereafter "denied [their] birthright" in the United States (*HSP* 101). While he positioned the oppression of Native Americans as a result of their self-determining "national life," he argued that the oppression of "colored people" was motivated by antiblack racism that pervaded all areas of US life despite arrivants' contribution to the settler regime (ibid.). The blood of enslaved and free blacks who fought for the United States in the Revolutionary War lay in the ground while its "incense" was "borne upward . . . to the throne of national honor," although the widows and orphans of those who sacrificed their lives for the United States shed "tears of blood" because the United States "refuse[d] to be their protector" (*HSP* 98). Easton founded his critique of the settler regime on the institutional and cultural disavowal both of such sacrifice and of the systematic racism that facilitated slavery in a liberal republican confederacy. He wrote that this disavowal resulted in the "hypocrisy of the nation" that withheld "the *inalienable rights* of one part" of its "subjects" (*HSP* 97). Easton defined "the colored people" as "American by birth and blood" and critiqued their oppression "on the ground of their complexion and blood" (*HSP* 113). "Blood" is therefore distinct from race, and perhaps superior to it, as it functions ambiguously as a category that should guarantee rights but is used instead as an excuse to infringe them. Easton explained that "there is not a drop of African blood . . . in the veins of an American born child, though black as jet," because "the blood of the parents in seasoning to this country becomes changed" (ibid). However, once this change occurred it could not be reversed, and denying these "Americans" access to US institutions would be tantamount to "murder[ing]" them (*HSP* 113–14).

Easton developed these ideas by elaborating on the reproductive aspects of geopolitical transformations and centralizing the role of the enslaved mother in this process. He explained that the "laws of nature may be crossed by the misconduct or misfortune of her who has the prospect of being a mother" and invested the enslaved mother with a particular historical role in transforming Africans into Americans. He stated that "the exposed condition of slave mothers," their "subjection to despotism and barbarity," their confinement to "narrow bounds of servile obedience," and their "irritation," "disappointment," and "physical suffering" in the face of "maiming," "flagellation," and "shrieks of woe" accounted for "the intellectual and physical inferiority of the slave population" (*HSP* 85). Thus Easton revised *partus sequitur ventrem* by using the enslaved mother as agent who involuntarily ensured the Americanization of her children in a manner that paralleled the involuntary translation of the blood of slaves' ancestors into inalienable entitlement to the soil. Such claims gradually accompanied a resurgence of the trope of the blood-enriched soil and its appropriation of slavery's history in forging the inalienable positive birthright of African-descended people in the United States.

Northern white abolitionists who had been persuaded by African Americans' anticolonizationist arguments also helped this process.[62] In 1836, Lydia Maria Child argued that it would be more appropriate to view England as the "native country" of white US citizens than to deem Africa as that of US blacks who had "no community of language or habit" with contemporaneous Africans.[63] That same year, the General Synod of the Reformed Presbyterian Church retracted its former support of the ACS and declared "[t]hat none of the native citizens of this Republic are Africans; and that they all have an equal right to their own country."[64] In a letter to his constituents in March 1837, congressman and former president John Quincy Adams responded to the gag rule by endorsing the US nativities of African Americans and protesting the thesis whereby "the native American becomes, by descent from African ancestry, an outcast of human nature."[65] A year later Joshua Leavitt, editor of the New York abolitionist newspaper *The Emancipator*, censured a report in the *New York Star* that counted "20,000 free negroes" among the city's "foreign population." Leavitt stated, "The colored people do not choose to be included among the 'foreign population'" because they are "all *native* Americans, and as proud of their birth as any of their fellow-countrymen of lighter hue."[66] Of these writers, only Child challenged settlers' attempts to nativize themselves by imagining that their ties to England had been forever severed. However, even she did so only in support of the nativized settler positions of arrivants and of the settler regime that made those positions imaginable. As had the Reformed Presbyterian Church, Adams, and Leavitt, she used arrivants' claims to entrench settlers' entitlement to the homelands of Indigenous peoples.

Anticolonizationists endorsed the category "colored" while rejecting "African" in order to present racial distinctions as irrelevant to political and civil rights. Thus, African Americans' nativization as settlers was predicated on the extension of the settler across the racial black/white divide. In other words, anticolonizationists tried to bridge the rift created by the black/white binary by representing both whites and blacks as settlers in contrast to a dispossessed Indigenous population. In March 1837, Samuel Cornish explained the title of the newspaper he edited, *The Colored American*, by claiming that "the endeared name, 'AMERICANS,'" was "a distinction more emphatically belonging to us, than [to] five-sixths of this nation." The number of enslaved and free blacks was about a sixth of the US population, so Cornish's math replaced the Constitution's reduction of each slave to "three fifths" of each "free" person with an argument for a privileged minority that developed Walker's idea of superior proprietorship. Cornish stated that "[i]n complexion, in blood and in nativity," "colored Americans" were "more exclusively 'American'" than their "white brethren." Cornish did not elaborate on this idea, but he might have founded it on prevalent geographic divisions of race that associated whiteness with Europe and identified other regions with various "colored" peoples.[67] If this is indeed the context for Cornish's claim, it demonstrates that arrivants solidified their positions as nativized settlers by appropriating representations of Native Americans, a process in which white settlers were also engaged, though in other ways.[68] Cornish suggested that this might have been the case when he denounced efforts to "rob us of our nationality and reproach us as exoticks," while he implied that Indigenous peoples were irrelevant to his revision of US politics.[69]

In a January 1839 anticolonization resolution, Philip Bell, author of an 1831 resolution who had become associated with *The Colored American*, clarified the contrast between constitutional protection and the endangered positive birthright for which African Americans struggled.[70] Bell identified a new threat that the ACS posed for free blacks when it proposed to supply vessels to African American seamen who would transport emigrants to Liberia. Urging his fellow activists to resist such temptations, Bell asserted that "our sympathies for the slave," the "love we bear our native land," and "our respect and veneration for the institutions and government of our country" functioned as "cords which bind us to our home, the soil of our birth, which has been wet by the tears and fertilized by the blood of our ancestors." He represented slavery's history as the sole foundation of a collective affect that tied African Americans to the United States, "from which, *while life lasts*, in spite of the 'oppressor's wrongs,' we will *never be seduced or driven*." Bell defined this attachment geopolitically as loyalty to the settler regime, therefore favoring aspirations for equality under settler rule over the idea of superior proprietorship. He stated, "[W]e will tell the white Americans that their country shall be our country—we will be governed by the same laws, and worship at the same altar—where they live we will live, where they die there will we be buried." Anticipating that settler violence may prevent this prospect from materializing, he imagined how the future graves of contemporaneous African Americans would manifest either the success or the failure of the settler regime in bringing about the equality he called for. He wrote that "our graves shall remain as monuments of our suffering and triumph, or of our failure and their disgrace."[71] Thus, Bell contrasted slavery's history to the history of arrivants' abolitionist struggle—suggesting that the former left no acknowledged monuments, whereas the latter would leave an indelible mark on US history. This argument indicates that forced exile and labor in themselves might have been crimes that history could not commemorate, but they necessitated agentive resistance by which those previously excluded from history now made history. This process of producing history out of exclusion explains Bell's argument that even if the American birthrights of enslaved and free blacks were denied during his lifetime, in the future their graves would testify to this disavowed history in the same manner as Indigenous graves signified during the removal crisis.

The idea that affirmative historical agency emerges out of historical exclusion and coercion reverberates in Frederick Douglass's insistence in the wake of Manifest Destiny ideology that "[a]ll the facts in [the negro's] history mark out for him a destiny, united to America and Americans."[72] In integrating the hegemonic discourse of national destiny with that of African American rights, Douglass brought one discourse about the solidification of national space to bear on the other and integrated the project that had begun a year prior to his birth with the dominant narrative of national development. Against this backdrop of the antebellum discourse of African American nativity, I now turn to examine its consequences for those who moved to Liberia under the ACS, which claimed Africa as their exclusive authentic native land. Whereas the above discussion highlighted the idea that historic wrongs produce new, unalterable realities from which novel forms of agentive belonging may spring, the next two sections discuss the opposite conceptualization of temporal and geopolitical transformations: that historic wrongs should be rectified by reasserting the ties they had severed. I discuss white US settlers' views of this issue and then move to texts that Liberian settlers wrote.

Liberia through the Eyes of White US Settlers

Colonizationists supported their argument that Africa was the exclusive native land of African Americans by highlighting Native Africans' virtues in terms they borrowed from idealized representations of settlers' encounters with Indigenous peoples in America. Their texts thus testify also to the centrality of Native Americans and the settler histories that the United States claimed as its founding myths to the development of African Americans' native status in the early nineteenth century. They drew on the tradition of the noble savage and argued that relations between Native Africans and their colonist brethren would benefit both parties. "Homo," whose 1823 piece on "Africa" called on African Americans to heed Africa's "claims" by emigrating there, wrote that "the native African is far less unfriendly to the new settler than the American Indian." To dispel fears of violent encounters, he claimed that "[i]f even among the Indians, Penn and his company were unmolested, doubtless the African will be so among his brethren." However, Homo's text, like numerous reports about such brotherhood, revealed ironically that emigrants were whitened in Liberia, as though the emigration that constituted them explicitly as settlers redefined their racial statuses. "Such is the respect in which a civilized black is held by the aborigines," he added, "that they emphatically call him a 'white man.'"[73] Below, I explore the ironic echoes of such representations in texts by Liberian settlers. Whereas anticolonizationist rhetoric represented native Africans generally as foreign heathens in need of Christian civilization, those who settled Liberia encountered unfamiliar configurations of settler-native relations. The context for this discussion is the major impact of African colonization, and resistance to it, on the sociopolitical positions of African Americans. The movement and the protests against it entrenched the redefinition of arrivants as settlers in unprecedented ways, in both the United States and Liberia, while simultaneously justifying white settler colonialism in America. Therefore, in 1830 the Massachusetts *Newburyport Herald* reported that Liberian colonists were "now as patriotic Americans as our fore-fathers were loyal subjects of the kings of England," illustrating that Liberian settlers could finally claim portable positive birthrights that originated in the United States—where they could not enjoy them.[74]

The colonizationist idea that African Americans were inherently different from white settlers despite their newly analogous positions led to the most pernicious myth that shaped Liberia's founding: that the West African climate—particularly its endemic malaria—was less harmful to blacks than to whites. Historian Antonio McDaniel shows that Liberia (the colony and later the republic) had "the highest mortality rates in accurately recorded human history" and that its disease environment was equally dangerous to all who had not spent their childhoods there.[75] Anticolonizationist abolitionists used emigrants' high mortality rates as evidence to support the claim that African Americans should be recognized as natives of America rather than Africa. In an 1831 resolution, Robert Roberts and James G. Barbadoes "readily den[ied] the assertion" that Africa's climate would be "congenial to their [African Americans'] health" because Africa was presumably their "native country." Roberts and Barbadoes asked, "What better proof do we want of its salubrity, than to know that of the numerous bodies who have embarked," many "have immediately fallen victims, on their arrival, to the pestilence usual to that place?"[76] Despite colonists' high mortality rate, colonizationists argued that Liberia's "climate" was "not materially unfavorable to the health of *colored people*, [and] far less so than to the whites," an idea they supported by representing geopolitical circumstances as the foundations of human destiny.[77] As US navy officer John B. Nicholson wrote in 1828, "It was . . . never intended, that the white man should inhabit this region of the globe—at least we know that the diseases of this climate are more fatal to him, than to the man of color."[78] Nicholson suggested that white settler colonialism in America was "intended" and that the same supreme agency "intended" exiled Africans and their descendants to return to what he presented as their home. Thus, African colonization concerned not only the deportation of free blacks, but also the reinforcement of settlers' claimed American birthrights.

The diasporic nativities of African Americans who emigrated to Liberia were fortified further by the enmity between Liberian colonists and Native Africans. Nothing breeds foreignness better than systematic protracted violence, and in Liberia conflicts began with the first land purchase by which the ACS established Liberia in Cape Mesurado in 1821. "U.S. naval officer Robert Stockton" completed the transaction by "level[ing] a pistol" at the head of "King Peter," an Indigenous leader whose homeland the ACS coveted.[79] Two years later, US newspapers reported that Native Africans explained their recent attacks on the settlement by claiming that "the land was not fairly purchased, that no grand palaver was called at the time, and that the chief who sold it had no claim to the same."[80] Other newspapers used these events to contrast the "treacherous" savagery of Native Africans, who "will not hesitate to murder the defenceless," with the civilized dignity of colonists, who have "endured . . . dangers, privations, and warfare . . . for many months past." Consequently, colonists became settler heroes who seemed "separated from the civilized world; surrounded by barbarous foes; suffering the untried influence of tropical climate; [and] destitute of the comforts" and "necessaries of life." Liberian settlers were portrayed as having "no defence but their courage, no protection but God," which entitled them to the "high commendation" and "cherished regard" of white US settlers.[81]

The serial lacks of "civilized" communication, "comforts," "necessaries," and "protection" ironically echo the description of slaves' plight in Felix

Holbrook's first petition from 1773 (see chapter 3). When Liberian colonists complained of such "destitut[ion]" in numerous letters they wrote to their former owners and ACS officials, the ACS tried often to silence such complaints. However, this report acknowledged and celebrated Liberian settlers' destitution in order to promise African Americans that in Liberia they would be able to overcome such difficulties and consequently gain the empowering spatial attachment that the ACS placed beyond their reach in the United States.[82] Wars between Liberia and Native African communities, which continued for decades, provided the context for these promises. Enthusiastic supporters imagined that Liberia would keep expanding through successful campaigns of military conquests and religious conversions until it would eventually extend to the entire continent and civilize it. This was Liberia's founding ethos; it was modeled on North American settler colonialism and Manifest Destiny, and entailed fears that Indigenous Africans would annihilate Liberia.[83] Recounting Liberia's history for white US children in her Sunday School book *The New Republic* (1850), Helen Cross wrote, "It was feared that a general conspiracy might unite the interior tribes against Liberia, and attempts be made to blot it from the coast."[84]

Even when colonists experienced peaceful relations with Native Africans, potential wars never seemed too distant, and colonizationists discussed them as an inevitable part of Liberia's development. In 1831, Liberia's colonial governor Joseph Mechlin illustrated the colony's growing "influence over the native tribes" by stating that "several have made application to be received under our protection . . . or as they express it, 'They want to be made Americans.'" He explained that the colony could not always grant these requests because the tribes' geographic distance from the colony "render[ed] it impossible for us to afford them protection, without involving ourselves in endless and ruinous disputes with the natives." Still hoping for future expansion, Mechlin promised to grant such requests "as soon as prudence shall warrant."[85] These colonizationist portrayals of Liberia and its settlers drew on the US ethos of settler colonialism as they tried to imagine an analogous yet distinctively African settler project that the United States could inspire and oversee.

American Liberians Meet African Natives

In his extended study of the complex archive of letters by nineteenth-century Liberian settlers, David Kazanjian cautions readers of these letters against reaching decisive conclusions regarding the meanings of key terms such as *return*, *freedom*, or *nativity* in these settlers' experiences.[86] However, Kazanjian also indicates that despite the polysemous constructions of such concepts, the "desire to return to the United States—either literally or in spirit, via salutations, remembrances, and even dreams—regularly punctuates the archive."[87] This desire was a constitutive element of settlers' assertions of their American nativities, which they formulated precisely when their geopolitical positions and actions seemed to prove their African nativities to colonizationists. In Kazanjian's analysis this desire highlights the "persistent unsettlement" of Liberian settlers.[88] Such desire also helped colonizationists like "Homo" identify the whiteness that was attributed to and shaped the experiences of some of Liberia's early settlers in ways that undermined the ACS's portrayals of their African nativities.

Manumitted slave-turned-colonist Peyton Skipwith strikingly expressed the ostensibly inherent hostility between colonists and Native Africans and its impact on perceptions of African Americans' nativities in a letter he sent his former master John H. Coke in 1840. He articulated his sense of foreignness in Liberia—"It is something strange to think that these people of Africa are called our ancestors"—and added that "if we have any ancestors they could not have been like these hostile tribes in this part of Africa for you may try and distill that principle and belief in them and do all you can for them and they still will be your enemy."[89] The clause "if we have any ancestors" is one of the most telling parts of this revealing letter. Skipwith suggested that colonizationist denials of African Americans' attachment to America turned them into permanent historical outcasts, or, in Patterson's words, into "genealogical isolate[s]" whose condition could not be ameliorated by manumission. Skipwith actively maintained enmity with Native Africans: "my health has been so good," he wrote, "that I took my rifle in hand to go to fight a savage King." Having "slept one night in the bush," he "took [the King's] Town the next day about 6 o'Clock," and eventually "set fire to the Town."[90] Genealogical isolation is formulated here as a condition that necessitates genocidal action, which would compensate for it. However, while white colonizationists imagined that such conquests may fortify settlers' positions as African natives, Skipwith clarified that conquest may best be explained by lack of African ancestry.

In addition to hostilities, colonist-Native relations were tainted by colonists' subjugation of Native Africans, which further distanced these communities from each other. Anticolonizationists argued that the enslavement of Native Africans proved colonization perpetuated slavery. In 1854, William Nesbit wrote that Liberian slavery was worse than its US counterpart because Native African slaves lacked food and clothing and became "the *Slave's Slave*[s]" when manumitted African American slaves subjected them to their authority.[91] The same year, Daniel H. Peterson echoed Jefferson's fear of God's future revenge for slavery when he wrote, "let us be very careful how we deal with those natives, lest we . . . incur the displeasure of the blessed Lord, and be finally driven out of that land in a more degraded condition than the present natives are at this time."[92] Native Africans thus symbolized not only a foreign population, rather than a fraternal or ancestral one, but also a negative model of African nativity from which colonists distinguished themselves. Colonists often employed the savagery/civilization binary for this purpose, referring to Native Africans as "savage"[93] and to Liberia as their "adopted"[94] and "new"[95] country rather than as their motherland.

Texts by Liberian colonists lack the organic belonging that the trope of the blood-enriched soil connoted, and they sometimes substituted violent conquest for this lack, as Skipwith's letter suggests. Even those who developed what Randall Miller calls an "African manifest destiny" did so in quite abstract terms rather than by emphasizing the concrete somatic or landed imagery that anticolonizationist writers used.[96] In 1833, James C. Minor wrote John Minor about his hopes to welcome numerous new emigrants to Liberia. Explaining that he was "trying to live a Christian's life in this dark and benighted land," he noted his anticipation of vessels that would carry "the people destined to return to the land of their forefathers." He portrayed "Africa" as a "land of freedom" not because of any of its geophysical features, but only because nowhere else could "the man of color enjoy temporal freedom." Complaining that his former neighbors from Fredericksburg, Virginia, had failed to move to Liberia, James C. Minor blamed Virginia's "laws," which "must be more favourable to the man of color than the laws of South Carolina," from which more settlers had emigrated. Throughout his letter, the United States remains the source of Liberia's existence, which in turn serves US interests. He argued that African Americans "must fulfil the saying of Thomas Jefferson: 'Let an ocean divide the white man from the man of color.' Seeking refuge in other parts of the world" would be "useless" because "this is the land of our forefathers, destined to be the home of their descendants."[97] Thus, James C. Minor represented emigrants tacitly as "genealogical isolate[s]" distinguished from their "forefathers" and "descendants" by their detachment from a "land" that they could not call home. He suggested that nativity required birth in the land one claimed as home, in line with anticolonizationist arguments.

Thus, whether they resisted African colonization in the United States or accepted it by emigrating to Liberia, African Americans constructed complex diasporic nativities that reached ironically across the Atlantic and defied colonizationist representations of timeless African geopolitical identities. Liberian settlers' recurrent longings for the United States, which set them apart from the Indigenous Africans whom colonizationists portrayed as their long lost kin, indirectly validated anticolonizationist claims for US lands. These diasporic nativities entrenched the Native/settler binary as the decisive geopolitical factor through which Liberia's history and destiny were imagined and the black/white binary as the normative framework through which arrivants perceived and rewrote US teleologies. In chapter 6, I analyze the functions of ancestral graves in Muscogee and Cherokee anti-removal discourses, which were partially analogous to the trope of ancestral blood in arrivant anticolonizationist texts. First, the interlude that follows provides broader context for understanding the juxtaposition of ancestral blood and ancestral graves not only as figures of speech, but also in their material manifestations in the genocidal projects that settlers mounted to assert their supremacy over Indigenous peoples and arrivants.

INTERLUDE

BLOOD AND GRAVES

THE TWO TROPES ANALYZED in chapters 5 and 6, respectively—ancestral blood and ancestral graves—were central, analogous figures in the partially concurrent struggles against African colonization and Indian removal. The discrepancies between the respective historical interventions that each trope performed helped entrench the two mutually exclusive binaries that set these struggles apart from each other. The trope of slaves' blood saturating an expanding US soil served arguments for the need to recognize that arrivant experiences were constitutive elements of US history. Ancestral blood flowed horizontally, suffusing an ever-growing area of expansionist national soil as its advocates appropriated that ethos for slaves and their descendants. This trope portrayed African American rights to US soil as expanding entitlements commensurate with the entire land base of the settler regime, creating an African American interiority within the United States—one that complemented rather than challenged the cartographic logic of what Benedict Anderson calls the nation's "sign and logo" (chapter 4). The abolitionists who used that trope wished to reformulate the settler colonial ethos and the category "settler" by positioning forced migration as indispensable contributor to national evolution. They sought to revise the property relations that structured the settler regime while supporting (and thereby fortifying) US-claimed sovereignty over Indigenous peoples' homelands. Therefore, their attempts to modify the geographic and historical frameworks of the settler regime emerged from the settler logic they sought to reform. By contrast, in anti-removal rhetoric, references to ancestral graves pitted Indigenous spatialities and temporalities against those of the settler regime and generated rights claims independent of, exterior to, and incompatible with US geopolitics. Whereas anticolonizationist rhetoric presented ancestral blood as flowing horizontally into the US national narrative, ancestral graves in anti-removal discourse connoted temporal continuities and spatial depths that were incompatible with settler narratives of progress and resisted the historical teleologies that supported those narratives. In referring to ancestral graves, Indigenous spokespersons and writers insisted on the Native/settler binary by presenting settler constructions of history and destiny as impositions on ongoing realities that could not be integrated into these new forms.

These discrepancies were rooted in incompatible historical material conditions and representative traditions. The trope of ancestral blood compensated for the historical marginalization of arrivants' graves. The enslaved were often interred in unmarked, unnamed burial sites, as though their lives left no impression on the world they had inhabited. Settlers interpreted the numerous monumental works that slaves built as commemorations of their own exclusive histories rather than as testaments to African American power, agency, and contribution to the settler regime. Unlike the obliterated graves of slaves, Indigenous ancestral graves have long been sites of national fascination, appropriated by settlers as symbols of the land's history and of their own imagined pasts, and this fascination has led to numerous acts of desecration and robbery. A long history of desecrations culminated in the American Antiquities Act of 1906, which authorized the "examinations, excavations, and gatherings" of "objects of antiquity" for the "benefit of reputable museums" and other "educational institutions."[1] Jack F. Trope and Walter R. Echo-Hawk estimate that "between 100,000 and 2 million deceased Native people have been dug up from their graves for storage or display by government agencies, museums, universities and tourist attractions."[2] The National Museum of the American Indian Act (1989) and the Native American Graves Protection and Repatriation Act (NAGPRA) (1990) were landmark attempts to rectify this history by respecting Indigenous peoples' histories rather than subordinating them to settlers' nationalist and scientific interests.

A resonant reminder of settlers' discrepant treatments of Indigenous and arrivant burial sites came with the discovery of and conflict over "the nation's earliest and largest African burial ground" (eventually named the African Burial Ground) in New York City.[3] In 1990, as NAGPRA was enacted to protect Native American human remains and burial sites from US institutions, the US government purchased land in New York City for a new federal office tower although government officials *knew* that the land had formerly served as a slaves' cemetery. Assuming that previous development projects had "obliterated any remains . . . within the historic bounds of the cemetery," the government acted as though slaves' graves have always already been effaced from public memory.[4] By July 1992 the excavation and improper storage of remains from 419 graves had sparked a public outcry. The company hired by the government to run the archaeological project hoped to use the remains to develop "racing methods"—a racist (pseudo) scientific motivation that resembled justifications for the treatments of human remains that NAGPRA prohibited. Racing methods analyze the racial properties that presumably distinguish human groups from one another, thus reducing human remains to objects of racialized study. As Cheryl J. La Roche and Michael L. Blakey argue, this approach "constructs an identity that is culture-less, history-less, and biologically shallow."[5] This approach, like pre-NAGPRA collections of Indigenous human remains, attempts to reduce African American historical existence to an object of settler interest.

Activists, scholars, and policymakers eventually redefined the project and secured nonracist treatment, study, and reinterment of the remains under the direction of physical anthropologist Michael L. Blakey, who had formerly worked on NAGPRA with the Native American Rights Fund—experience he used in directing the African Burial Ground project. NAGPRA attempts to rectify disavowed violent history by defining the relations between the dead and the living through the term "culturally affiliated group," which rehistoricizes relational communities that the settler state disrupted and denied. On this model, Blakey coined the phrase "descendant community" (a term that eventually entered NAGPRA discourse, further complementing the mutual relations between these two frames for engaging the past).[6] Despite these links, institutional responses to the African American past often differ markedly from post-NAGPRA treatments of Native remains, and some scholars hope to see NAGPRA extended to include African Americans, among other groups.[7] But while NAGPRA was achieved through emphases on Indigenous peoples' exteriority and sovereignty in relation to the United States, African Americans have for the most part demanded inclusion within US political structures and sought recognition of their communities' rightful positions within the national frameworks that marginalized and disenfranchised them. Thus, the African Burial Ground is today "a US National Monument, alongside Ellis Island and the Statue of Liberty,"[8] under the same internalizing mechanism that necessitated NAGPRA.

This distinction between exteriority and interiority structures the analysis of Indigenous and arrivant rights claims throughout this book and facilitates the mutual exclusivity of the Native/settler and the black/white binaries. While the ancestral blood trope is an effect of the United States' rise out of slaveholding colonization, ancestral graves manifest a history that predated colonization and that necessarily challenges the settler ethos because it is based on Indigenous geopolitical logics that are incompatible with it. Chapters 5 and 6 represent this discrepancy most clearly through the contrast between anticolonizationist and anti-removal attitudes toward US western territories. Whereas free blacks proposed to settle such territories and thereby contribute to US expansion, Cherokee and Muscogee writers and spokespersons resisted US efforts to remove them to such territories. These two positions also differ in their respective treatments of the negative birthright that the settler regime tried to impose on arrivants and Indigenous peoples. Whereas the ancestral blood trope appropriates the imposition of negative birthright in order to translate it into the source of positive birthright within the settler logic that constructed these categories, the forms of attachment and inhabitation symbolized by ancestral graves both exceed and denaturalize settler mythologies. Yet despite these significant discrepancies, both mobilized resistance to settler attempts to impose negative birthrights on arrivants and Indigenous peoples. The next chapter analyzes the functions of ancestral graves in the 1820s and 1830s.

[6]

ANCESTRAL GRAVES

THIS CHAPTER FOCUSES ON Muscogee and Cherokee struggles to liberate indigeneity from settler constructions, and particularly from the confines of settler temporalities and spatialities. During the removal crisis of the 1820s and 1830s, settlers defined Indigenous people as tenants at will, a category derived from the doctrines of impossibility and allotment discussed in chapter 4. Blackstone defined "those who receive allotments" as "tenants or vassals"—inferior to the superior landholder who allots them the lands.[1] Tenancy was a feudalist construct by which landholders allowed the landless to inhabit lands that those inhabitants could not own. It was a precarious condition that landholders could revoke at any point if they no longer wished the tenants to remain. Therefore, it is not surprising that the earliest definition of *native* in the OED—"a person born in bondage; a person born to servants, tenants, etc., and inheriting their status"—positions the tenant within the scope of negative birthright.[2] By imagining that settler benevolence allowed Indigenous peoples to inhabit their own homelands, settlers fortified their regime's exclusive, axiomatic, and absolute sovereignty. This logical continuation of the colonial legal fiction that defined the Crown as the original proprietor of Indigenous peoples' lands made impossibility and allotment seem legally valid to settlers. In December 1827, a few months after the Cherokee Nation adopted its Constitution, the Georgia legislature used this feudalist logic in declaring Cherokees to be "tenants at will" subordinate to state law.[3]

Some settlers argued that Indigenous peoples' treatments of ancestral graves proved that these peoples were savages who had no valid present or future claims to lands. For settlers, such graves often signified an outdated form of uncivilized inhabitation that had to yield to their progressivist historical teleology. For instance, pro-removal missionary Isaac McCoy wrote in 1829 that most Indians would "cling to the land of their ancestors and hover over their tombs, until forced to retire," as though forced removal was inevitable.[4] Another commentator explained that the "deeper veneration" in which Indians held "the names of their ancestors" (as opposed to the attitudes of "civilized men" toward the memory of their progenitors) was "a natural consequence of their unsophisticated state."[5] Susan M. Ryan argues that such evolutionary perceptions allowed their advocates to imagine removal as charitable policy that would protect presumably doomed societies from civilization's destructive forces.[6] In addition, evolutionary perceptions of spatial attachment—codified through ancestry and multigenerational inhabitance—helped settlers to view their own emergent American native statuses as future-oriented properties, in contrast to what they defined as Indigenous peoples' outdated, dying indigeneity. Settlers' distinctions between the temporal frames to which they attributed the evolutionary trajectories of Indigenous and settler nativities—a past-oriented frame and a future-oriented one, respectively—helped to disavow the settler regime's founding violence at the same time that the United States executed violent removal policies.

Muscogee and Cherokee resistance to removal centralized relationships to ancestral graves in historical narratives that unsettled colonial teleologies. In this context ancestral graves constituted indigeneity as a function of multigenerational spatial attachment that could not be simulated because it was grounded in specific places and supported by particular practices over time. References to ancestral graves were central to Indigenous rights claims in this era because they represented an ethos that preceded anti-removal rhetoric, exceeded its temporal and spatial scopes, and critiqued settler perceptions of the land as a fungible object that could be ushered into history only through settler territorial expansion. In contrast to settlers' expansionism, which emphasized cartographically measurable surface areas, Muscogee and Cherokee references to ancestral graves emphasized attachment to limited areas whose historical and genealogical depths facilitated extensive, multilayered temporalities over a stable, non-expansive place. And unlike settlers' efforts to interiorize Indigenous societies within what settlers viewed as their own domestic space, the temporalities through which Indigenous peoples discussed their ancestral graves supported Indigenous claims for their polities' exteriority to the settler regime. These temporalities sustained complex relations among varied pasts, the present, and aspirations for futures whose incompatibilities with settler temporalities encapsulated unsettling possibilities.

Yet references to ancestral graves in the removal era differed from the unsettlement propositions discussed in chapter 4. Whereas in the 1780s and 1790s settler negotiators had to tolerate Indigenous unsettlement proposals, the evolutionary logic that became more pronounced in the removal era enabled settlers to demote Indigenous peoples' political philosophies, from living threats to the settler regime to dying relics of a bygone era. This evolutionary logic positioned settlers as the natural successors to Indigenous peoples, as those destined to inherit Indigenous peoples' homelands because they bore an exclusive future-oriented nativity in that land. By contrast, settlers imagined Indigenous peoples' native status as a stagnant, defunct, past-oriented (pre)historic relic with no present or future significance. Cherokee spokespersons conversant with settler discourse sometimes employed this conceptual framework—ironically or earnestly—to warn of the predictable consequences of settler policies. The settler policies discussed in this chapter represented Indigenous homelands as what Priscilla Wald calls "hole[s]" in state maps that testified to the United States' failure to completely internalize Indigenous homelands.[7] Under settlers' evolutionary logic, such "holes" were to be filled by the federal government's eventual "extinguishment" of native title to the land. Georgia, for example, settled its territorial disputes with the US government by ceding its claims to western lands in return for federal promises to eventually "extinguish the Indian title" to all lands "*within* the State of Georgia."[8] The "hole" that Wald reads in Georgia's cartographic self-representation was thus constructed as a temporal problem that would be solved by settler progress.

This chapter analyzes the role of ancestral graves as central discursive elements through which Muscogee and Cherokee spokespersons and writers distinguished their nativities from emergent settler and arrivant ones. Settlers and arrivants founded their entitlements within the settler regime through the future-oriented temporality and the expansive space of national aspirations. This logic guided Manifest Destiny and the progressive emancipation that African American anticolonizationist discourse imagined, which was to be achieved by resettling the United States so that it would reward ex-slaves and their descendants and restitute what David Walker defined as their rightful inheritance. Arrivants represented ancestral blood as an expansionist locus of passive testimony to the injustice of the settler regime, which required its resettlement. Ancestral graves figured in Indigenous antiremoval discourse as sites of interactions among the living and the dead through integrated, multilayered temporalities that resisted settlers' tacit claims that indigeneity could be reproduced, simulated, and appropriated. These multilayered temporalities produced Muscogee and Cherokee lands in terms of what Mishuana Goeman represents as "shifting, layered geographies with connecting and complex histories."[9] Ancestral graves thus necessitated unsettlement because the spatial and temporal orders that conditioned their sociopolitical functions were incompatible with the extensive spatialities and exclusive temporalities by which the settler regime legitimized itself.

Many of the texts analyzed here were printed in the *Cherokee Phoenix*, which was published bilingually—in English and in the Cherokee syllabary—although English dominated its pages. The *Cherokee Phoenix*, a weekly newspaper established in 1828, had three major objectives: resistance to removal, contribution to what its editors called Cherokee civilization, and the promotion of that civilization to a non-Cherokee audience who may help in the struggle against removal. Its founding editor, Elias Boudinot, resigned after four and a half years when his views shifted in favor of removal. Although the US Supreme Court's decision in *Worcester v. Georgia* prohibited Georgia from extending its laws into Cherokee lands, US president Andrew Jackson refused to force Georgia to comply with the ruling. This conspicuous clash between judicial and executive authorities convinced white anti-removal activists that the struggle was lost, as removal seemed preferable to escalating violence. Boudinot doubted that Cherokee resistance could succeed without strong settler support, and Elijah Hicks replaced him as *Phoenix* editor in September 1832. On May 31, 1834, following recurrent financial difficulties for the paper, Hicks printed the *Phoenix*'s last issue (until its twentieth-century renewal). In 1835, Georgia confiscated the Cherokee printing press, and later that year, Boudinot signed the Treaty of New Echota that paved the way to removal.

This chapter begins with Muscogee references to ancestral graves in response to removal, which establish the central role that ancestral graves played in distinguishing the spatial and temporal frames of Muscogee geopolitics from settler political discourses. This discussion clarifies the literal significance of ancestral graves in anti-removal discourse; prior to the removal crisis, as a result of an 1826 treaty, Muscogee had already removed burial sites from lands it had ceded to the United States to lands the treaty guaranteed them. This action showed Muscogee willingness to invest its remaining land with the historical practices that ancestral graves enabled, and Muscogee used this history to resist further removal. Next, the chapter analyzes anti-removal articles from the English-language portions of the *Cherokee Phoenix*, in which Cherokee writers considered the temporal and spatial scopes of inhabitation and attachment, through relations to ancestral graves. I conclude the chapter by analyzing explicit representations of exteriority in Cherokee anti-removal discourse, expressed through the idea that if the Cherokee were forced to remove, they would rather leave the United States altogether. The texts I read below represent ancestral graves as sites of radical unsettlement, which is necessitated by the reductive and confining temporality and spatiality that the settler regime tried to impose on the Muscogee and Cherokee.

The Graves of Muscogee Ancestors

In 1829, President Jackson sent a message to the Muscogee in order to persuade them to accept the US removal policy. Jackson's message, delivered in a speech, reiterated clichés of US Indian affairs that later helped to pass the Indian Removal Act. The speech asserted absolute US political authority over the Muscogee by emphasizing the president's patronizing "love" for his "red children" and demanded that the Muscogee surrender "bad men" who "murder[ed] . . . one of [his] white children in Georgia." Jackson's speech thus presented the federal government as the shared parent of "red" and "white" subjects in order to portray Muscogee resistance to settler encroachments as a pathological disruption of kinship ties that required Muscogee and settler obedience to US law. This kinship subordinated the Muscogee to US space and history as though they had no existence beyond it. Kinship, constructed as a system of distinction, obedience, and order, was the geopolitical framework within which settlers justified removal, as Jackson argued that his "red" and "white children" were "too near each other to live in harmony." Beyond the Mississippi, Jackson promised, the Muscogee will enjoy eternal "peace and plenty."[10]

Two speeches circulated widely in settler newspapers as Muscogee responses to Jackson's message, and they began to shape settlers' public representations of Muscogee anti-removal discourse. One was a text that might have been written by Cherokee leader John Ridge, and which was published as the speech of a Muscogee elder that the text identified as Speckled Snake.[11] The other was a speech by a speaker identified as an "Elder Chief of the Creek Nation." Ancestral graves figured in these speeches and in later Muscogee texts that undermined settler spatialities and temporalities, the value systems those spatialities and temporalities supported, and the representations of Indians that Jackson's message promoted. The speech by "an aged Chief of the Creek Nation" interwove presumably distinct temporal frameworks in protest of settler dispossession of the Muscogee. The speech began with precolonial Indigenous history, moved to its colonial disruptions as "the bones of our fathers strewed the path of [settlers'] wandering," continued with the idea of genocidal disappearance, and returned to the "fields of our youth" and the ancestral "bones" that "lie by the running stream, where we sported in the days of our childhood." Colonization threatened these complex temporal relationships over limited space; as the speaker added, "When we are gone, strangers will dig [ancestral bones] up." To prevent this scenario he urged his audience, "Let us watch over the graves of our fathers by the streams of our childhood."[12] In this speech, Muscogee ancestral remains are an integral part of the land, and colonial violence endangers both.

The speech attributed to Speckled Snake was more elaborate and portrayed colonial expansion as monstrous corporeal growth that repudiated the authoritative kinship of Jackson's message. It represented early English colonization as the feeble efforts of a "little man" who depended on Indigenous hospitality when his "legs were cramped by sitting long in his big boat" and he "begged for a little land to light his fire on." Having "warmed himself before the Indian's fire, and filled himself with their hominy," the colonizer eventually became "very large"—personifying the United States' excessive territorial corporeality. The speech argues that territorial expansion results in hyperbolic geopolitical violence as the displaced colonizer takes over terrestrial space: first he "bestrode the mountains," then "his feet covered the plains and the valleys," and eventually "[h]is hands grasped the Eastern and the Western sea, and his head rested on the moon."[13] In this representation of colonization, settlers' land hunger inflates their regime that dwarfs American space by subordinating it to insatiable greed, which the text represented as outlandish, as though settler politics were not even *geo*political because their aspirations exceeded worldly interests. Monstrosity thus results from embodiments that transcend the terrestrial spatial proportions that delimit and give them meanings (chapter 4).

This overreaching, excessive, insatiable corporeality detached from worldly space portrays the settler state as an exterior imposition on Indigenous homelands. Spatial and corporeal detachment symbolize each other, as the legs and feet that dominate disparate terrains seem disconnected from the hands that reach for the ungraspable oceans and from the head that aspires to transcend the earth. This text thus represents settler history as an exploitative, consumptive order that disregards and might therefore destroy spatial relations while it reduces America to an instrumental access point for extracontinental and extraterrestrial destinations. Whereas in chapter 4, Native negotiators defined the spatial relations that constitute indigeneity and the geopolitical processes it supported through embodied perceptions of the land, here the hyperbolic human body represents colonial domination that is oblivious to the spaces it takes over. This critique of Jackson's message points to two interrelated Eurocentric constructions of degrading spatial relations: the confining spatial attachment of feudalist negative birthright, and the Lockean presupposition that land is worthless without the trade routes that make its cultivation profitable. By comparison to this portrayal of the settler regime, this text tacitly suggests that Indigenous polities operate on limited geopolitical scales, an idea it articulates through references to ancestral graves.

The text that presented Speckled Snake's speech critiqued colonialism through an argument resembling the northwestern confederacy's resolution "to leave our bones in this small space to which we are now confined" rather than agree to removal (chapter 4).[14] In both texts, graves literalize settlers' fantasies of Indian disappearance and thus help to distinguish colonial temporalities and the value systems that support them from Indigenous ones. But whereas the confederacy referred to the future graves of its living members, this text positioned existing ancestral graves as focal points of Muscogee attachment to the homeland, an urgent matter as a result of colonial encroachments. Dwarfed by the extensive geographic and cosmological scope of settler expansionist aspirations, smaller-scale Native spaces facilitate particularist communal relations. The oversized colonizer, the text claimed, "pushed the red man over the Oconee [with one foot], and with the other he trampled down the graves of his fathers, and the forests where he had so long hunted the deer."[15] As does the image of settlers' lunar aspirations, here too exaggerated corporeal size emphasizes colonial disregard of land and people.

The text identified violent dispossession with Jackson's kinship rhetoric by stating, "But our great father still loved his red children; and . . . said 'get a little farther, you are too near me.'" Borrowing Jackson's rhetoric further, it represented Muscogee resistance as the acts of "some bad men among the Muscogees," but used it ironically in reference to those who have "lingered around the graves of their ancestors, till they were crushed beneath the heavy tread of our great father." Whereas in Jackson's message, "bad men" defined Muscogee criminality under settler law, this text translated it into loyalty to ancestral graves in defiance of settler encroachment and removal pressures. Lingering, represented here as an inhabitation practice that maintains Muscogees' spatial attachment to their homeland, emphasizes ongoing reciprocal relations between the dead and the living as present and past generations nurture each other. Indigenous resistance to dispossession is expressed by the "teeth" of those "bad men" that "pierced his feet, and made him angry." The text then emphasized the disavowed violence of settler colonialism by employing the great father trope again: "Yet he continued to love his red children, and when he found them too slow in moving, he sent his great guns before him to sweep his path."[16] The "guns" stand out in contrast to the corporeal imagery that structures the text's rhetoric, and they underline the violence of what the settler regime represents as natural growth.

By contrast, the text portrayed Muscogee through mutually constitutive relations among the land (burial ground and "forest"), the graves that concretized Muscogee history in that land, and the living community that "lingered around the graves," thus maintaining Muscogee's relationship with its land and history. The extensive temporality that links the Muscogee past, present, and future within this historical framework contrasts with the insatiable, extraterrestrial spatiality that dominates settler expansion. The violent encounter between settler "heavy tread" and Indigenous "teeth" highlights these differential scales that the speech develops in order to distance the settler regime from the land it claims as its own.

This and other discussions of ancestral graves were reprinted by a settler culture obsessed with origins and eager to relegate Indigenous peoples to the past as the source of its own foundations.[17] Well before NAGPRA, this obsession led Indigenous peoples to protect their dead from the settler state, and in 1832 a Muscogee memorial to Congress positioned ancestral graves as important subjects in the struggle against removal. Under increasing settler pressures for removal, Opoethyoholo, Tuckebachee Hajo, Tuckebachee Micco, and Benjamin Marshall complained in this memorial that in the wake of the 1826 Treaty of Washington (in which they had ceded all their lands that Georgia claimed as its own[18]), they removed "the bones of our ancestors and our kindred" from the ceded lands to those the treaty guaranteed them. "[W]e derived a consolation," they wrote, "from the reflection that [the remains] were now permanently fixed upon a spot where our ashes might be permitted peaceably to mingle with theirs, and from which we could not be removed." They elaborated on the significance of ancestral graves, saying that the "value" of their homeland was "enhanced" because its "narrow compass" now "contain[s] all that endears itself to our hearts." The Muscogee representatives pointed to the incompatible scales that made the ceded lands more valuable for settlers than the land given the Muscogee in return, but they rejected the fungibility of land that organized settler territorial thought and the expansionist surface areas that undergirded it by emphasizing that the value of their new land lay in its "fixed" position on a "narrow" "spot" of land in proximity to the dead.

Like the speech attributed to Speckled Snake, this memorial represents Muscogee rejection of the imperial spatialities and temporalities that settlers tried to impose on them by soliciting Muscogee consent for removal. The memorial suggests that Muscogee existence is structured through the relations between the living and the dead who occupy the same place and interact through the shared land not simply across temporal divides, but in a way that renders the idea of temporal divide absurd and unintelligible. The memorial is a narrative of spatial attachment, detachment, and reattachment whose central argument is that time and space cannot be extracted from each other. Such extractions guide settler justifications of Indian removal, because the presumed savagery of Indigenous peoples meant that remaining in their rapidly civilizing homelands would entail the illogical endurance of uncivilized time in civilized space, while removal promised to match Indians' presumably wild temporality with wild spaces. By removing their ancestors' remains, the Muscogee suggest that settlers' spatial and temporal fungibilities had to be revised to fit the imbrications of space and time that supported Muscogee lives and deaths.

"Beneath the soil which we inhabit," Opoethyoholo, Tuckebachee Hajo, Tuckebachee Micco, and Marshall added, "lie the frail remnants of what heretofore composed the bodies of our fathers and of our children, our wives and our kindred."[19] This multigenerational population of the dead further integrates the temporal frames that constitute the Muscogee polity, as the dead and the living are connected by kinship. As in the speech attributed to Speckled Snake and in the confederacy's letter (chapter 4), graves create a value system in which spatial attachment can be neither commodified nor teleological because it facilitates complex, dynamic links between the people's past, present, and future on its homeland. Muscogee insistence that its value systems and spatial and temporal attachments were exterior to the United States thus complicates its compliance with settler pressures. Muscogee rights discourse in the removal era thus shows that events whose meaning often seems overdetermined by US logics of territorial expansion and temporal progress may yet open up possibilities for resistance. The settler regime may neither anticipate nor recognize such possibilities because they are founded on spatial and temporal logics that repudiate settler thought, but their mobilization may pierce the discursive limits of these logics. In the next section, I read references to ancestral graves in Cherokee anti-removal discourse that similarly open up unsettling and decolonizing possibilities rather than signal their foreclosures.

Ancestral Graves in Cherokee Texts

The *Phoenix* printed fewer English translations of Cherokee speech than other English content, yet these translations were crucial to its mobilization of resistance to removal because pro-removal whites argued that the majority of Cherokees would have agreed to removal had not a small white-educated, English-writing Christian elite imposed its politics on the entire Cherokee population. Such accusations might have partially motivated John Ridge (who belonged to that elite and might have authored the Speckled Snake speech) to translate the 1829 address to "the Cherokee People" by Turkey Town citizens Money Hunter, Tah-ka-ha-kee, Scattered, Kung-was-soo-laskee, Killer, Richard Ratliff Jr., Crying Snake, Resurrection, Follower, and Turnover.[20] The address explicitly contrasts settler and Cherokee perceptions of temporalities and spatialities as a means of resisting settler attempts to reduce Indigenous peoples to an ahistorical past and deny their rights to their homelands. The signatories asserted that their position was "simple and plain" and "founded on truth as handed down to us by our ancestors." Throughout the address they anticipate and refute settler views of Indians. Presenting themselves as "limited in knowledge," they suggested that such limits corresponded to their "interest" in Cherokee "well being" and to the limited bounds of the Cherokee homeland. "Our ancestors settled in this place," they wrote, defining that place as "sacred ground" where "the council-fire blazed." The correspondingly narrow bounds of the Cherokee signatories' knowledge and spatial location clarifies at the outset that foreigners can hardly assume authority over Cherokee spatiality, which facilitates a long history that began "at a period not now in our recollection." Against this background, the address critiques the settler dichotomy of savagery and civilization on which removal advocates tried to establish the historic validity and necessity of their project.

In discussing Cherokee early history, the signatories used the first-person plural to clarify that "[w]e speak of days when we lived in the hunter's state, and when our feet were swift in the track of game." This rhetoric creates a historically consistent perspective that derives from what they portray as a fixed spatial position that bridges temporal distances between ancestors, whose inhabitance of Turkey Town was presumably not threatened, and the present generation, which is urged to remove. Having rooted their opposition to removal in the continuous stability of their inhabitation of their homeland, the signatories represented settler colonialism as a sudden violent attack that threatened to detach them from it. The "flood of inconsistency" by which settlers represented Cherokees as "incapable of learning the arts of civilized life," while also treating them "in the most uncivil manner," "raged with violence over" Cherokee leaders and "swept with its waves, from under their feet, the earth, for which they had struggled for ages past." Characterization of settler colonialism as a powerful violent force also emphasizes its transience, which supports assertions of Cherokee survival and endurance. The signatories argued that settlers attempted to deny them "the light of civilization" and to force them "to retrograde to savageism" because once Cherokees become "Christians and Politicians" settlers would have to recognize their "attachment to the soil" was "strong[er]" than that of those deemed savages, and therefore, it would have been "more difficult to defraud us of the possession." They stated that their adoption of Christianity and settler political forms facilitated their resistance to settler impositions and maintenance of Cherokee spatial and temporal logics.

The address clarified that Cherokee constructions of attachment to the homeland was an ongoing temporal-spatial source of sustenance focused on a particular limited place that localized them and to which they referred familiarly as "this place," "[h]ere was sacred ground," "this spot," and "the land that had been endeared to them as an inheritance of their fathers." To this intimate relationship between people and land they contrasted settler encroachment as motivated by unilateral, insatiable "desire" that reflected settlers' detachment from the land on which they were born. They asserted that "wicked" settlers "esteemed us a nuisance, because the Great Spirit had placed our habitations in a desirable Country, and because they themselves had crossed the Big Water (the Ocean) and had become our neighbors." In representing settlers' transatlantic territorial aspirations as merely economic desire, unlike the "sacred ground" given by "the Great Spirit" and reaffirmed as "an inheritance of their fathers," the address portrays alienability as a deficient foundation of entitlement. The ironic reference to new, voluntary "neighbours" further distances settlers from the stable benevolence that characterizes Cherokee attachment to the land. Next to this distinction the argument that "Christians and Politicians" enjoy stronger "attachment to the soil" is also ironic because such strength is valid only within the settler value system that the address critiques. However, the address emphasized Turkey Town's contribution to what the signatories present as the Cherokee civilizing momentum as an inevitable consequence of settler colonialism. As "our territory diminished, and our inheritance was circumscribed to its present bounds," they "passed the strong shoals of opposition, and its mingled cruelties, to the light of civilization," and they used the language of the civilizing mission ("The sun has arisen in our moral horizon and is fast advancing to its meridian") as a focal point of their anti-removal counter-narrative: "We hereby individually set our faces to the rising sun and turn our backs to its setting."[21]

Having collapsed the dichotomous opposition between civilization and attachment through their ironic references to settler cruelty, violence, and legal discourse, the signatories used ancestral graves to root their attachment in a multidimensional temporality that comprised a past both continuous with and distinguished from their present: "As our ancestors revered the sepulchral monuments of the noble dead, we cherish the sacred spots of their repose, as they lie under hillocks of clay, that cover them from our sight." Rather than claiming direct attachment to immemorial ancestors, they clarified that their ties to the land were renewed actively with each generation. They thus historicized these ties in terms that rejected settler portrayals of Indians as stuck in irrelevant time and frustrated attempts to label them as savages.

The address implicitly contrasted visuality, by which the settler spatial order prioritized cartography's measurements of the size of alienable land, with spatial attachment to non-fungible land characterized by the ongoing nurturing of historic depth. This contrast qualifies the discourses of progress and improvement that the address invokes through visual images of light and darkness. The signatories contextualized "the light of civilization" and the "sun" in their "moral horizon" within the logic of multigenerational commitment to ancestral graves and the land in which they were embedded; in doing so, they positioned their intervention in the removal debate at a distance from settler history—a distance that was also reinforced by the address's original formulation in Cherokee and by the signatories' x-mark signatures, which occupied a liminal position between US Anglophone literacy and Cherokee sovereignty.[22]

Ridge's translation of the address stressed the incompatible conceptualizations that separate the target text from its source, particularly when he rendered the Cherokee term for the Atlantic as "the Big Water (the Ocean)." The fact that the English term "Big Water" required further gloss suggests that the nuances of this translation exceed the mere replacement of Cherokee terms with English ones; that "the Big Water" was not interchangeable with the Atlantic but derived from a value system that Ridge distinguished from settler understandings of the ocean as simultaneous barrier and bridge between Europe and America, one that symbolized the alienability of settlers' European pasts as well as their commitments to European perceptions of space and property.

The Turkey Town address and the town meeting from which it emerged were part of a larger political affirmation of the multidimensional, temporal, and spatial continuities that positioned Indigenous homelands beyond the settler state. The Cherokee Nation—represented by its elected legislative council—asserted its commitment to this process by enacting in writing "an old law" that made "death the penalty for selling any lands in treaty, without the authority of the nation."[23] The law's transcription from oral to written form parallels the move from hunting to agriculture in the Turkey Town address as both root the source of Cherokee authority in the past, whose memory and significance frame the present in which Cherokees adopt presumably European practices as means of protecting their homeland rather than as ends in themselves. The law's passage was supplemented in council by the speech of an elder named Womankiller, who used the image of ancestral graves to explain how intertwined temporalities guided Cherokee politics. "[M]en of renown . . . who now sleep in the dust," he said, had "spoke[n] the same language" as that which was now translated into written law. On this linguistic common ground that bridges the dead and the living, Womankiller represented his liminal position between past, present, and future as though he were "stand[ing] on the verge of the grave" and "bear[ing] witness" to the dead's "love of country." Womankiller asked to be "laid in the bosom of this earth we have received from our fathers who had it from the Great Being above. When I shall sleep in forgetfulness, I hope my bones will not be deserted by you."[24] The distinction between the dead's passive "forgetfulness" and the active memory required of the living shows that the living are responsible for integrating the past, present, and future. In this economy of life, death, and land, land sellers become destructive forces because they abandon this responsibility. The death penalty symbolically imposes the forgetful passivity of the dead on those who have acted irresponsibly and have thus hurt Cherokee attempts to protect the temporal and spatial relations that maintain the Cherokee Nation. The law thus distinguishes the dead whose memory protects the land from the convicted who are perceived as threatening the homeland.

Womankiller ended his speech by establishing the exteriority of Cherokee politics to the settler regime. In contrast to his firsthand knowledge of the linguistic common ground that framed the old law's new enactment, he attributed his understanding of US policy to secondhand knowledge that signified his refusal to collaborate with it. Although he was "told, that the Government of the U. States will spoil their treaties with us and sink our National Council under their feet," he stated that "it shall not be with our consent, or by the misconduct of our people." Ancestral graves symbolized this refusal and he positioned them in the same role they filled in the confederacy's letter discussed in chapter 4: "We hold [the United States] by the golden chain of friendship; made when our friendship was worth a price, and if they act the tyrant and kill us for our lands, we shall, in a state of unoffending innocence, sleep with the thousands of our departed people."[25] Here and elsewhere, graves represent the ultimate merging of the people and the land, a logic revised, affirmed, and challenged simultaneously by the Muscogee removal of graves from lands they ceded to lands the United States guaranteed them by treaty.

The removal crisis intensified tensions between two interpretations of ancestral graves that were equally foundational to representations of Indigenous peoples' struggles against settler rule in this period: the idea that the living community's well-being depended on ongoing relations with ancestral graves, and the rhetoric of imminent annihilation in which ancestral graves prophesied the doom rather than the flourishing of Indigenous polities. The latter attitude was expressed by Indigenous spokespersons and writers who warned that their peoples must not be annihilated. The elder Muscogee chief who discussed the possibility that his people would be "gone," for example, ended his speech with the hope that "the Great Spirit [may] move" Jackson's "heart," so "that he may open his ear to the voice of children, for they are sorrowful."[26] And in a letter to the *Phoenix* published two weeks prior to that piece, Cherokee writer A Chillahcullahgee from Ookillokee wrote that no "citizens" were "more attached to their country" than the Cherokees, who were therefore "not to be alarmed from our lands." Anticipating Womankiller's assertion of compliance with prior treaties even at the price of death, and using that price to refer to the value of blood in the soil as a currency that purchases entitlement, he wrote, "resistance we never intend, but with our blood will we water our land, and deposit our ashes with those of our ancestors."[27] Whereas in the African American anticolonizationist texts discussed in chapter 5 ancestral blood integrated US lands, here it is used to distinguish Cherokee lands from US claims. Such distinctions manipulate the idea of Indian disappearance in ways that express their authors' refusals to validate US geopolitics and open up resistant historical narratives instead.

A similar employment of the ancestral graves trope in the context of the logic of genocide appeared in a letter by a Cherokee named Bruce published in the *Phoenix* one week prior to A Chillahcullahgee's letter. Bruce opened his letter by distinguishing Cherokee rights from US policy; he argued that the validity of the former was independent of the latter, stating that "Whatever [Jackson] may say, or on whatever side he may be" in the controversy between Georgia and anti-removal whites, "our rights and privileges are still the same." He then analyzed the vicissitudes of settler colonial desires for the Cherokee homeland—from Britain through the United States to Georgia—in order to invalidate any claim other than those backed by the Cherokee Nation's explicit consent in treaties. Having refuted not only the argument that Georgia may legitimately extend its laws into the Cherokee Nation, but also the notion that the United States could legitimately assert Georgia's future power to do so, Bruce shifted from legal reasoning to historical analysis in which ancestral graves were central. He wrote, "If here there is no resting place for us, there is no place to which we can flee for refuge," a statement that may be read in two ways. First, it may refer to settlers' insatiable land hunger, which would pursue the Cherokee wherever they may remove. Second, it may suggest that the Cherokee homeland is the only place the Cherokee can inhabit as a polity. Either way, Bruce represented the polity's attachment to its homeland as the foundational condition of Cherokee existence.

Bruce concluded his letter by contextualizing the Cherokee struggle in the longer history of colonization and its possible future consequences. "We have done all we could to gratify the insatiable desire of Georgia," he wrote, "but she continues to persecute us because we will not, now, abandon our homes, our farms, even the dust of our forefathers." This longstanding persecution then led him to consider the prospect that the Cherokee would be "annihilated for honestly striving to improve our condition, and render ourselves and posterity happy," in which case, he declared by returning to legal terminology, the Cherokee Nation would be "innocen[t]" and its persecutors would be guilty of annihilating an Indigenous polity. This prediction asserted that Indian disappearance was no natural fate but one that, if materialized, would result directly from settler violence. Therefore, Bruce challenged the arguments of advocates for removal, according to which removal was necessary to prevent what would otherwise be inevitable disappearance. He argued instead that Indian disappearance would result from and testify to settler oppression rather than justify it. He ended the letter by imagining a post-Cherokee future that would begin "long after we shall have disappeared," when "cities may rise up where our beloved chiefs once kindled their Council fires." In that post-Cherokee era, Bruce wrote, "The finger of the historian may point to some gentle hillock where sleep in dust the last of our Chiefs—the only monument to perpetuate the memory of a brave but unfortunate tribe. The muse may strike a melancholy note—and time hush into silence the tyranny of Georgia."[28]

In this bleak scenario the land would be pregnant with the indelible remains of the Cherokee Nation, as the "gentle hillock" would embrace "the last of our Chiefs." Next to the depth and permanence symbolized by the embeddedness of Cherokee history in the soil, the "finger of the historian" and the "note" of the "muse" seem transient, superficial commentaries that would not be able to redeem the spatial and temporal frameworks that would have been annihilated with the Cherokee Nation's disappearance. The last clause of the letter is ambiguous. The obliteration of Georgia's "tyranny" may suggest either that its oppression of the Cherokees would eventually be forgotten, or that the very existence of the state would be effaced from memory. The latter reading, which suggests that Cherokee ancestral graves would outlive Georgia, supports the multiple emphases on Indigenous peoples' unparalleled attachment to their homelands as a monumental feature of Native communities that the settler state cannot reproduce. Bruce's discussion of the presumably inevitable disappearance of Indigenous peoples thus affirms Native history by engaging the central ambiguity of ancestral graves, which stems from the discrepant uses of ancestral graves in Indigenous and settler authors' texts. The power of Bruce's letter lies precisely in its ability to subvert settler logic from within, a tactic that symbolizes the Cherokee anti-removal struggle more generally, and one that other writers extended to the argument that the Cherokee Nation would do better to leave the United States altogether than to remove within its territorial control.

Imagining Exteriority

Ancestral graves functioned as material evidence that the temporal and spatial scopes that endowed Muscogee and Cherokee politics with meaning were incommensurate with settler histories and geopolitics. This incommensurability led Cherokee writers to insist that if the Cherokee were forced to leave their homeland, they would rather leave the United States. Instead of embracing removal, those who expressed this stance insisted that Cherokee survivance depended on exteriority from the United States. This argument responded to settler representations of Indigenous spaces as relics of a savage past. Such representations temporalized Indigenous spaces and suggested that these temporalized spaces could be spatialized anew only if they were transformed into US national lands. In addition, the exteriority argument responded to settlers' assumption that Indigenous peoples' survival required US intervention and supervision—as though Indigenous peoples could exist only by inhabiting settler legal categories such as domestic dependent nations or tenants at will. US promises of post-removal bliss under settler auspices affirmed that settlers viewed Indigenous peoples as tenants at will. Although the Treaty of New Echota—which Boudinot, Ridge, and other Cherokees signed against the Cherokee Nation's official position—explicitly granted the Cherokee lands west of the Mississippi "in fee simple," a landholding category that establishes independent possession, the United States emphasized its ongoing authority over these lands by expressly promising that those lands "shall, in no future time without [the Cherokee Nation's] consent, be included within the territorial limits or jurisdiction of any State or Territory."[29] The United States affirmed what it perceived as its superior sovereignty over these lands in 1907, when it established Oklahoma in Indian Territory.

The Cherokee Nation recognized that removal was a structural aspect of settler policy rather than a singular event, to draw from Patrick Wolfe's thesis on the role of invasion in settler colonialism.[30] In 1833, Cherokee Nation officials John Ross, Richard Taylor, John F. Baldridge, and Joseph Vann wrote the US secretary of war Lewis Cass to protest the settler regime's reduction of Indigenous peoples to the status of tenants at will: "[S]hould the doctrine that Indian tribes cannot exist contiguously to a white population prevail and they be compelled to remove west of the states and territories of this republic," they asked, "what is to prevent a similar removal of them from there for the same reason?"[31] Ross, Taylor, Baldridge, and Vann emphasized that the internalization of Indigenous peoples within the state was tantamount to imprisonment and depended on the goodwill of the incarcerating regime.

As the US government prepared to enact the Indian Removal bill, Cherokee anti-removal spokespersons argued that if it were to pass, Indigenous peoples would have to leave the United States behind if they wished to avoid being reduced to tenants at will. A member of the Cherokee Nation's delegation to Washington wrote Boudinot: "Let not the dark clouds which hover around our political sun, cause us to despond, and if it sets, I hope to see it rise again, if not at [New] Echota, not within the limits of the United States."[32] The writer argued that settlers—including England, Georgia's colonial administration, Washington's federal government, and Jackson's previous military office—had long recognized the Cherokee as an independent "Nation" before their recent decision to demote the Cherokees to "*subjects* of Georgia." The change in US attitude toward the Cherokee Nation—which the writer expected the Supreme Court to reverse—suggested that removal within US territories would constitute Cherokee acquiescence to US rule. The settler regime, as chapter 4 shows, translates Indigenous peoples' struggles against dispossession into "acquiescence" in order to justify its appropriation of their homelands, so resistance to removal must be framed by pronounced exteriority to settler sovereignty.

To emphasize this idea Cherokee writers insisted on the foreignness of the United States to the Cherokee Nation. On May 19, 1832, Boudinot printed a letter sent to the *Phoenix* by "A Cherokee" who argued that the "idea of a foreign government Colonizing the aboriginal inhabitants" was "entirely novel" to the Cherokee. Several months earlier, the US Supreme Court had decided in *Worcester v. Georgia* that state law could not be enforced on Cherokee land. Cherokees and their supporters expected President Jackson to enforce the decision or face impeachment, but Jackson declined to act and remained in office. Against this background, the writer, claiming to represent Cherokee public opinion, stressed that next to Jackson's policy, the promises that US presidents Washington and Jefferson had made to the Cherokee Nation "hid[e] in the archives of the principal Chiefs" and lie "in a corner of the executive Chamber, cold, like [their] author[s] to rise no more." This metaphoric burial of US-Cherokee diplomatic relations facilitated the writer's argument that the monetary value of the Cherokee homeland—the Cherokees' "only inheritance"—far surpassed any payment the United States could offer. He made and supported this claim in response to the advice of previously anti-removal northerners who now urged the Cherokee to strike a bargain for removal before the land's value depreciated.

The writer claimed not only that the "value of the Cherokee Nation can hardly be set down in numbers," but also that if "all the Negroes in the Southern States were sold in Brazil for diamonds or gold," the "proceeds of these gems would be but a pittance" of the amount required to pay for the Cherokee Nation's land. He concluded by saying that if the Cherokee must "sell out and make fortunes on the ruins of our inheritance and say the Cherokee Nation is no more," then "the Cherokees would not be unwilling to leave the United States." Next to the forgotten relics in the Cherokee "archives" and the fluctuations of value in a dispossessive settler state, the slaves seem to constitute the only stable—though depreciated—measure of monetary value. The reduction of the enslaved to movable objects thus enables the writer to underline Cherokee stability on the land, which may be respected only outside the United States. Resistance to removal may require removal, but the latter would defy US sovereignty claims even as it would accept US reductions of arrivants to property. The letter writer therefore concluded that "[i]f the force of circumstances compels [the Cherokee] to move, they wish to go where they will not see the United States again."[33]

Jackson's disregard of the Supreme Court's decision led to the collapse of the white anti-removal movement and motivated Boudinot to support removal. Boudinot resigned his editorship of the *Cherokee Phoenix* on August 1, 1832, but he continued in office until Hicks replaced him a month later. While in this liminal position, Boudinot printed an ambiguous letter from a Cherokee (who signed as "Rocky Mountain") in which the idea of Cherokee exteriority to the United States neither supported removal nor rejected it completely. "Rocky Mountain" harnessed the pre–Manifest Destiny perception of the Rocky Mountains as the "absolute limit to American expansion"[34] in order to critique settler spatialities and temporalities. The writer identified himself metaphorically as the outer limits of the United States and implied that the "very great" "attachment" he "feels for [his] natal spot" was alien to settler forms. "Rocky Mountain" established his attachment to the Cherokee homeland in embodied practice and lived experience by arguing that the "solid earth"—that "for which our ancestors have fought and bled in days past" and "for which our chiefs have recently maintained" a legal battle—provides the only "flooring" of his "little log hut." He rooted his spatial "attachment" in particular places where he "played," drank water, "bathed," and "planted" crops.[35]

The focus of the letter shuttles between the Rocky Mountains and the Cherokee Nation as two places defined by their exteriority to the United States. The writer contrasted his attachment to the Cherokee homeland with the shallow, fraudulent, presumably "deep foundations of these U. States," which "have been laid upon the anti-human policy of Europe, which issued charters to cover our lands in usurpation." He highlighted settlers' genocidal policies, temporalities, and spatial practices by arguing that US citizens have "cherished their republicanism and christianity upon the blood & smoking ruins of the Indians!" This representation of Cherokee deaths from the perspective of settlers then enables a broader consideration of settlers' genocidal dispossession of Indigenous peoples. The writer adds that the "slaughtered Indians at Muskingum" should "rise from their ashes" to confirm that the Cherokee Nation gained nothing by ceding lands, fighting settler encroachments, signing treaties, and accepting civilizing and Christianizing missions.[36]

This reference to the 1782 massacre in which US Revolutionary forces killed "ninety-six unarmed men, women, and children" in Delaware's Moravian town Gnadenhutten refutes the idea that Indigenous peoples can prevent settler violence by embracing Christianity.[37] In the late eighteenth century the massacre enhanced "the nativist cause" of Indigenous peoples who insisted on protecting their political and cultural independence, while it "stirr[ed] some protest among whites on "the eastern seaboard."[38] It became a symbol of US treachery, and "Rocky Mountain" built on this history to end his letter with a trenchant critique of US spatiality: "When we have tested the U.S. all we can," he wrote, "we will take our women and children and go to the verge of the globe, on the shores of the Pacific, and there raise up our own standard, kindle up our own council fire, & leap out of this accursed state of pupilage *under such guardians*, and make of ourselves a foreign Nation, or gloriously die in the attempt."[39]

"Rocky Mountain" portrayed removal beyond the United States as emigration to "the verge of the globe" in tacit critique of US attempts to impose legal disabilities on the Cherokee Nation in disregard of Cherokee independence of the settler regime. The "verge of the globe" thus emphasizes the limits of the US geopolitical outlook. Whereas settlers perceived the Cherokee Nation as a "hole" in Georgia's map (and thus also in that of the United States), Georgia's violent efforts to fill this hole required the Cherokee Nation to assert a more pronounced exteriority beyond the reach of the settler regime. Comparing this letter with the story of settler expansion in the Speckled Snake speech is illustrative because in both texts, relations between the United States and Indigenous polities highlight the limits of settlers' territorial control over Indigenous peoples. In both, US expansionism clashes with Muscogee and Cherokee temporalities and spatialities not merely because it seeks to take over Indigenous peoples' lands, but also because accepting US territorial rule would require the Muscogee and Cherokee to abandon the logics of their own peoplehood. Thus, these texts crystallize the difference between Indigenous and arrivant respective resistance to Indian removal and African colonization. Whereas the former rejected the imperial logic of US spatialities and temporalities, the latter sought to carve a place for itself within it.

This chapter emphasized the incompatible spatial and temporal frameworks of US removal rhetoric and the resistance that Muscogee and Cherokee spokespersons and writers mobilized against them. Whereas settler genocidal thought was founded on the idea that the demise of Indigenous peoples

—whether through wars, deaths, enslavement, or removals—vindicated the settler regime, Muscogee and Cherokee spokespersons and writers used the dead to affirm the ongoing histories of their homelands, and in doing so, invalidated settler geopolitics. I conclude this book with further reflection on the political significance of resistant geopolitics.

CONCLUSION

THROUGHOUT THIS BOOK I placed Indigenous and arrivant rights claims within the discursive contexts in which they appeared—a methodological choice that seems necessary in light of the dehistoricizing fragmentation to which settler communication networks have tried to reduce Indigenous and arrivant rights theories. As part of this contextualization I explored the historical visions that enabled these rights claims and considered their relations to settler historical thought. The settler historicity that created Manifest Destiny used a specific interpretation of native status to sanction settlers' self-nativization and to entrust settlers with exclusive ownership of US soil while fixing Indigenous peoples in an imagined past and placing arrivants beyond historic agency. Indigenous peoples resisted these attempts primarily with unsettlement initiatives that tried to replace the settler regime's temporal and spatial constraints with political configurations of time and space that would enable settlers to remain in America without the racist possessive orders that had shaped their regime. Arrivants strove to resettle that regime by reconceiving its possessive order as inclusive of African-descended people as nativized settlers.

This analysis of the potentially unsettling and resettling rights theories that Indigenous peoples and arrivants presented to settlers in the late eighteenth and early nineteenth centuries also laid bare the processes by which these interventions contributed to the mutually exclusive Native/settler and black/white binaries. The mutual exclusivities of these binaries derived from the fact that both African Americans and Native Americans protested the settler regime almost as though the other group had nothing to do with the oppressive mechanisms against which each fought. This choice often stemmed from Indigenous peoples' acceptance of settlers' perceptions of slaves as property and from African Americans' acceptance of settler's perceptions of Indigenous peoples as vanishing savages. In this sense, both Indigenous peoples and arrivants were willing to support some aspects of settler politics even as they fought against others. Whereas arrivants tended to adopt imperialism as the normative framework of historical change within which they formulated their own aspirations, Indigenous peoples who otherwise rejected this conceptualization of history tended to acquiesce to settlers' objectification of arrivants. Creating effective solidarities between these struggles would have necessitated a broader analysis of the multiple modes by which the settler regime consolidated its power.

The purpose of this book is to consider how resettlement and unsettlement critiques of settler colonial power may relate to each other beyond the political-disciplinary compartmentalizations that often keep such texts apart. Although the authors of the texts discussed here rarely aspired to solidarity, and although their unsettlement and resettlement plans did not reverse the settler impossibilities they targeted, it would be wrong to assess their efforts from perspectives that privilege the settler regime's orders of history, place, causality, and belonging. The central lesson to be learned from these texts is that these constructs are shaped by agentive, fallible human actions. Precisely because the US settler regime established its axiomatic legitimacy on doctrines of impossibility, alternatives must insist on open-ended, multiple possibilities for envisioning and experiencing the constructs by which we understand human lives.

Understanding Indigenous and arrivant contributions to the development of rights theories requires willingness to view settler spatialities and temporalities as particular configurations of human relations whose status as the normative or conventional shape of politics emerged from the specific historical circumstances that facilitated settler power. The contingency of settler thought, and its dependence on multiple, often contradictory interactions with Indigenous and arrivant politics, means that unsettlement and resettlement projects such as those examined here do not represent failed historical attempts to change an inevitable evolution of political development. In addition to historicizing these projects and the political philosophies that undergird them, we might also read them as invitations to perceive the world we inhabit and its histories beyond settler impossibilities. The historical and political value of the rights theories studied here lies in their long-term contributions to ongoing critiques of settlement's logics.

This book focuses on freedom—in the broad sense of the ability to formulate and evaluate the experiential and interpretive processes that make life meaningful—as a function of inhabitation fostered within particular historical conditions. However, the possibilities studied here are necessarily partial and limited by the scope of this book. Indigenous and arrivant writers and spokespersons who worked in the eighteenth and nineteenth centuries offered a wealth of options for reconceiving the world, its inhabitants, and the relations among them. William Apess, for example, developed what is now a famous formulation of global human relations that questioned the racist compartmentalization that undergirded Eurocentric thought. In his "An Indian's Looking-Glass for the White Man" (1833), Apess imagined the juridical gathering of all the world's peoples in order to assess their relative contributions to global humanity. "Assemble all nations together in your imagination," he urged his readers, "and then let the whites be seated among them, and then let us look for the whites, and I doubt not it would be hard finding them; for to the rest of the nations, they are still but a handful." Apess displaced imperial hierarchies and inverted their quantitative calculations in order to propose a judicial logic wherein justice would be measured by assessments of agentive actions and their impact on people's lives. "Now suppose these skins were put together," he wrote, translating "nations" into "skins" and thereby exposing the racism that drove Eurocentric geopolitics. Further, he instructed his readers to imagine that "each skin had its national crimes written upon it" and asked, "[W]hich skin do you think would have the greatest?"[1] This criminal record maintains Christian visualizations of moral capacity as well as their phenotypical applications, but Apess used these principles in order to subordinate them to the consequences of agentive human action.

Whereas Apess entrusted to his readers the power imaginatively to judge human contributions to justice and oppression, others, including some whose works I discuss here, emphasized the judgment of non-European peoples who symbolized a complete world beyond Eurocentric formulations of universality. Olaudah Equiano's proposition that slavery should be judged by "those who are called barbarians" (chapter 1) and the United Indian Nations' statement that any agreement it would reach with the United States must "appear just and reasonable in the eyes of the world" (chapter 4) insist that the world cannot be reduced to a fraction of its inhabitants and the particular modes through which they choose to inhabit it. Similarly anti-Eurocentric views animated Quobna Ottobah Cugoano's vision of a post-slavery future in which "noble Britons" would "abolish the slavery and oppression of the Africans" and be "admired by all the world."[2] Wendat chief Tarke expressed the idea that the world is cognizant of the political relations that shape it when, using a wampum belt, he illustrated to US Gen. Anthony Wayne that the benevolent impact of their negotiations should "cover the whole earth, that it may appear white, and shine all over the world" (chapter 4).[3] During the same negotiation, Anishnaabe leader Mash-i-pi-nash-i-wish told Wayne that "we will make a new world, and leave nothing on it to incommode our children" (chapter 4).[4] The worlds that these people strove to create and protect may not be redeemable or even entirely desirable today. But their perseverance in the struggles that shaped their lives can inspire revisionary propositions that may open up possibilities we have yet to anticipate. This is the ultimate purpose of this study's attempt to understand rights theories that can be neither reduced to state power, nor confined or monopolized by it.

NOTES

Introduction

1. *OED Online*, s.v. "right" (n.), accessed January 1, 2017, http://www.oed.com. This discussion excludes those definitions that focus on "position or direction" and as "opposed to left."

2. Hannah Arendt, *The Origins of Totalitarianism*, new ed. with added prefaces (San Diego, CA: Harcourt Brace & Company, 1973), 296.

3. Michel Foucault, *"Society Must Be Defended": Lectures at the Collège de France, 1975–76*, ed. Mauro Bertani and Alessandro Fontana, trans. David Macey (New York: Picador, 2003), 27, 26. Samuel Moyn's more recent history of human rights supports the historic association of rights with states, which leads him to date the emergence of human rights to the 1970s, at which time that discourse was presumably liberated from the state. Moyn, *The Last Utopia: Human Rights in History* (Cambridge, MA: Harvard University Press, 2010).

4. The term is from Daiva Stasilius and Nira Yuval-Davis, "Introduction: Beyond Dichotomies—Gender, Race, Ethnicity and Class in Settler Societies," in *Unsettling Settler Societies: Articulations of Gender, Ethnicity and Class*, ed. Daiva Stasilius and Nira Yuval-Davis (London: Sage, 1995), 1. For more recent analyses of settler claims, see Lorenzo Veracini, *Settler Colonialism: A Theoretical Overview* (London: Palgrave Macmillan, 2010); and Mark Rifkin, *Settler Common Sense: Queerness and Everyday Colonialism in the American Renaissance* (Minneapolis: University of Minnesota Press, 2014).

5. "The Complaints and Prayer of Oweneco and Ben Uncas" (1700), Ayer MS 671, Edward E. Ayer Manuscript Collection, Newberry Library, Chicago. I am grateful to Leonard Stein for transcribing this document.

6. "By the House of Representatives of the English Colony of Connecticut, second Thursday of May, 1774," in *The Public Records of the Colony of Connecticut*, ed. Charles J. Hoadly (Hartford: Case, Lockwood & Brainard, 1887), 14:347.

7. Benjamin Franklin, "A Dialogue between X, Y, and Z," *Pennsylvania Gazette*, December 18, 1755.

8. Olaudah Equiano, *The Interesting Narrative of the Life of Olaudah Equiano, the African. Written by Himself*, in *The Interesting Narrative and Other Writings*, rev. ed., ed. Vincent Carretta (New York: Penguin, 2003), 138.

9. David Walker, *David Walker's Appeal to the Coloured Citizens of the World* (1829), ed. Peter P. Hinks (University Park: Pennsylvania State University Press, 2000), 58.

10. Henry M. Morfit, Henry J. Brent, and T. D. Jones, "Memorial of the Native American Association," 25th Cong., 2d sess., doc. no. 98 (Washington, DC, January 8, 1838), 7.

11. Frederick Douglass, *Lessons of the Hour* (Baltimore: Thomas and Evan, 1894), 25.

12. Similar ambivalence marked Barack Obama's dismissal of claims that he was not

born in the United States when he posted his long-form birth certificate and said, "We do not have time for this kind of silliness." White House, Office of the Press Secretary, "Remarks by the President," April 27, 2011, http://www.whitehouse.gov/the-press-office/2011/04/27/remarks-president.

13. Foucault, *Society Must Be Defended*, 50.

14. For examples of histories of the emergence of rights discourses that seem to be founded on faith in the Eurocentric contexts of such discourses, see Barry Alan Shain, ed., *The Nature of Rights at the American Founding* (Charlottesville: University of Virginia Press, 2007); John Philip Reid, *Constitutional History of the American Revolution*, vol. 1, *The Authority of Rights* (Madison: University of Wisconsin Press, 1986); and Jack P. Greene, *The Constitutional Origins of the American Revolution* (Cambridge: Cambridge University Press, 2011). This presupposition seems to derive from a Eurocentric logic of governance and politics that links the Bible and classic Greece and Rome to European imperial and nation-building projects. For such historical accounts of the emergence of human rights, see Micheline R. Ishay, *The History of Human Rights from Ancient Times to the Globalization Era*, 2nd ed. (Berkeley: University of California Press, 2008); and Lynn Hunt, *Inventing Human Rights: A History* (New York: Norton, 2007). For a critique of this historical logic from a Eurocentric perspective, see Moyn, *The Last Utopia*.

15. See, for example, Makau Mutua, *Human Rights: A Political and Cultural Critique* (Philadelphia: University of Pennsylvania Press, 2002); and José-Manuel Barreto, ed., *Human Rights from a Third World Perspective: Critique, History and International Law* (Newcastle upon Tyne: Cambridge Scholars Publishing, 2013).

16. See Shona N. Jackson, *Creole Indigeneity: Between Myth and Nation in the Caribbean* (Minneapolis: University of Minnesota Press, 2012).

17. For an analysis of settler thought that justified both projects, see Nicholas Guyatt, "'The Outskirts of our Happiness': Race and the Lure of Colonization in the Early Republic," *Journal of American History* 95, no. 4 (2009): 986–1011.

18. On settler colonialism's eliminatory function, see Patrick Wolfe, "Settler Colonialism and the Elimination of the Native," *Journal of Genocide Research* 8, no. 4 (2006): 387–409.

19. On the logic of disappearance, see Brian W. Dippie, *The Vanishing American: White Attitudes and U.S. Indian Policy* (Middletown, CT: Wesleyan University Press, 1982); and Jean M. O'Brien, *Firsting and Lasting: Writing Indians Out of Existence in New England* (Minneapolis: University of Minnesota Press, 2010). I discuss inheritance and African American exile, respectively, in Yael Ben-zvi, "Where Did Red Go? Lewis Henry Morgan's Evolutionary Inheritance and U.S. Racial Imagination," *CR: The New Centennial Review* 7, no. 2 (2007): 201–29; and Yael Ben-zvi, "The Racial Geopolitics of Harriet Beecher Stowe's Geography Textbooks," *Legacy: A Journal of American Women Writers* 29, no. 1 (2012): 9–36.

20. Patrick Wolfe, ed., *The Settler Complex: Recuperating Binarism in Colonial Studies* (Los Angeles: American Indian Studies Center, 2016), 8, 1.

21. Jodi A. Byrd, *The Transit of Empire: Indigenous Critiques of Colonialism* (Minneapolis: University of Minnesota Press, 2011), 124–25.

22. Iyko Day, "Being or Nothingness: Indigeneity, Antiblackness, and Settler Colonial Critique," *Critical Ethnic Studies* 1, no. 2 (2015): 112.

23. Sharon P. Holland and Tiya Miles, "Afro-Native Realities," in *The World of In-*

digenous North America, ed. Robert Warrior (New York: Routledge, 2015); Tiya Miles and Sharon P. Holland, ed., *Crossing Waters, Crossing Worlds: The African Diaspora in Indian Country* (Durham: Duke University Press, 2006).

24. J. Kēhaulani Kauanui, "'A Structure, Not an Event': Settler Colonialism and Enduring Indigeneity," *Lateral* 5, no. 1 (2016), http://csalateral.org/archive/issue/5-1.

25. For the sources of *partus sequitur ventrem*, see Thomas D. Morris, "'Villeinage . . . as it existed in England, reflects but little on our subject': The Problem of the 'Sources' of Southern Slave Law," *American Journal of Legal History* 32, no. 2 (1988): esp. 108–9.

26. Saidiya Hartman, *Lose Your Mother: A Journey along the Atlantic Slave Route* (New York: Farrar, Straus and Giroux, 2007), 107.

27. Ibid., 103.

28. Veracini, *Settler Colonialism*, 75–94.

29. Peter Linebaugh and Marcus Rediker, *The Many-Headed Hydra: Sailors, Slaves, Commoners, and the Hidden History of the Revolutionary Atlantic* (London: Verso, 2000), 4, 15, 24.

30. Lisa Lowe, *The Intimacies of Four Continents* (Durham: Duke University Press, 2015).

31. Linebaugh and Rediker, *Many-Headed Hydra*, 242, 246.

32. Susan Buck-Morss, *Hegel, Haiti, and Universal History* (Pittsburgh: University of Pittsburgh Press, 2009), 132, 133.

33. Ashraf H. A. Rushdy, "The Quality of Diaspora," *Diaspora* 18, no. 3 (2009): 299.

34. Uday Singh Mehta, *Liberalism and Empire: A Study in Nineteenth-Century British Liberal Thought* (Chicago: University of Chicago Press, 1999), 4–8; Walter D. Mignolo, *The Darker Side of the Renaissance: Literacy, Territoriality, and Colonization*, 2nd ed. (Durham: Duke University Press, 2003); Walter D. Mignolo, *The Darker Side of Western Modernity: Global Futures, Decolonial Options* (Durham: Duke University Press, 2011) (Mignolo writes that he had initially planned to title the latter volume *Breaking the Western Code*, which indicates a perception of its project similar to the one I am outlining here); Lowe, *Intimacies of Four Continents*, 137–8. In another, related context, Ali Behdad analyzes the United States' "historical amnesia about its violent formation." Behdad, *A Forgetful Nation: On Immigration and Cultural Identity in the United States* (Durham: Duke University Press, 2005), xii.

35. Walter D. Mignolo, "Who Speaks for the 'Human' in Human Rights?" *Hispanic Issues On Line* 5, no. 1 (2009): 19.

36. S. James Anaya, "Indian Givers: What Indigenous Peoples Have Contributed to International Human Rights Law," *Washington University Journal of Law & Policy* 22 (2006): 107–20.

37. Ronald Niezen, *The Origins of Indigenism: Human Rights and the Politics of Identity* (Berkeley: University of California Press, 2003), 30.

38. Thus, Mignolo refers to "global futures" and Lowe concludes her book with a chapter called "Freedoms Yet to Come." Mignolo, *Darker Side of Western Modernity*; Lowe, *Intimacies of Four Continents*, 135–75.

39. Joseph Johnson, "Sunday 20th of December AD 1772," in *To Do Good to My Indian Brethren: The Writings of Joseph Johnson, 1751–1776*, ed. Laura J. Murray (Amherst: University of Massachusetts Press, 1998), 161.

40. Walker, *Appeal to the Coloured Citizens*, 61.

41. Edward Kamau Brathwaite, *The Arrivants: A New World Trilogy* (Oxford: Oxford University Press, 1973); Byrd, *Transit of Empire*, 117–46.

42. Ibid., xix.

43. "Well, muh ol' arrivance . . . is from Africa. . . . That's muh ol' arrivants family. Muh Gran'muddah an' muh gran'fadda. Well, they came out here as slavely . . . you understan'? Well, when them came now, I doan belongs to Africa, I belongs to Jamaica. I am born here." Brathwaite, *The Arrivants*, n.p.

44. Ibid., 269–70.

45. Jackson, *Creole Indigeneity.*

46. For studies of the twentieth-century category "Indigenous peoples," see S. James Anaya, *Indigenous Peoples in International Law* (Oxford: Oxford University Press, 1996); Niezen, *Origins of Indigenism*; and Karen Engle, *The Elusive Promise of Indigenous Development: Rights, Culture, Strategy* (Durham: Duke University Press, 2010). A search for the word "indigenous" in Readex's *America's Historical Newspapers Series 2, 1758–1900* yielded 3,318 results from newspaper articles published between 1750 and 1900. In many of these texts the adjective is used to qualify references to animals, plants, diseases, and human conduct. A search for the phrase "indigenous peoples" during the same period yielded two results: one from 1877 expressing the hope that Liberia's "indigenous peoples" may evangelize Africa "with the aid of foreign nations," and another referring to Alexander Von Humboldt's *A View of the Cordilleras and Monuments of the Indigenous Peoples of America*, originally published in 1810 as *Vues des Cordillères et monuments des peuples indigènes de l'Amérique*. See "Liberia," *Philadelphia Inquirer*, November 7, 1877, 2; and "Alexander Von Humboldt.—Karl Ritter," *Daily Inter Ocean*, February 23, 1889, 11.

47. In his autobiography, *A Son of the Forest* (1829), Apess wrote that he "thought it disgraceful to be called an Indian" and asserted that "the proper term which ought to be applied to our nation, to distinguish it from the rest of the human family, is that of '*Natives*'—and I humbly conceive that the natives of this country are the only people under heaven who have a just title to the name, inasmuch as we are the only people who retain the original complexion of our father Adam." William Apess, *A Son of the Forest* (1829), in *On Our Own Ground: The Complete Writings of William Apess, a Pequot*, ed. Barry O'Connell (Amherst: University of Massachusetts Press, 1992), 10. Apess's reference to "complexion" points to the Hebrew etymology of "Adam," which shares the same root with *adom* (red) and *adamah* (land). This connection was made earlier by Roger Williams, in *A Key into the Language of America* (1643), who rendered the creation story in Genesis in similar terms: "Last of all he made one Man. / Of red Earth, / And call'd him Adam, or red Earth." Williams, *A Key into the Language of America* (London: Gregory Dexter, 1643), 125.

48. Taiaiake Alfred and Jeff Corntassel, "Being Indigenous: Resurgences against Contemporary Colonialism," *Government and Opposition* 40, no. 4 (2005): 597.

49. On settlers' self-nativization, see Mahmood Mamdani, "When Does a Settler Become a Native? Reflections on the Colonial Roots of Citizenship in Equatorial and South Africa" (lecture, New Series no. 208, University of Cape Town, May 13, 1998). For Native American studies scholars who have analyzed this theme, see Philip J. Deloria, *Playing Indian* (New Haven: Yale University Press, 1998); and Shari M. Huhndorf, *Going Native: Indians in the American Cultural Imagination* (Ithaca: Cornell University Press,

2002). For the idea of settlers' aspirations to inherit Indigenous peoples' lands and lives, see Ben-zvi, "Where Did Red Go?"; and Jenny Reardon and Kim TallBear, "'Your DNA Is Our History': Genomics, Anthropology, and the Construction of Whiteness as Property," *Current Anthropology* 53, no. S5 (2012): S233–45.

For the legal history of territorial birthright citizenship, see Polly J. Price, "Natural Law and Birthright Citizenship in Calvin's Case (1608)," *Yale Journal of Law & the Humanities* 9, no. 1 (1997): 73–146.

50. Jackson, *Creole Indigeneity*, 65.

51. Sometimes people who wrote in English on certain occasions chose to use their native languages on others; one prominent example is Mohawk leader Joseph Brant, who negotiated with US officials in Mohawk as well as in spoken and written English. On July 7, 1793, Brant gave a speech in an Indigenous language (probably Mohawk) to US commissioners Benjamin Lincoln, Beverly Randolph, and Timothy Pickering. We know that Brant did not speak English on this occasion because the commissioners confirmed that they had "understood" his speech "from the interpretation." In treaty negotiations, speeches and other texts often had to travel through several languages in order to be accessible to all council attendees. The commissioners' response to Brant (spelled Brandt in US documents) on that meeting, for example, was "interpreted by Mr. Dean in the Oneida tongue, was interpreted by Captain Brandt's nephew, into the Shawanese [Shawnee] language, and from that, by another interpreter, into the language of the Chippewa nation." *The New American State Papers: Indian Affairs* (Wilmington, DE: Scholarly Resources, 1972), 4:131–32. For a discussion of the problems that attended translation in early American encounters between settlers and Indigenous peoples, see David Murray, *Forked Tongues: Speech, Writing, and Representation in North American Indian Texts* (Indianapolis: Indiana University Press, 1991).

52. Equiano's *Interesting Narrative* validates itself by repeatedly establishing its commitment to Britain's imperial projects.

53. Christopher Hager, *Word by Word: Emancipation and the Act of Writing* (Cambridge, MA: Harvard University Press, 2013), 20.

54. On settler colonialism's resistance to decolonization, see Veracini, *Settler Colonialism*, 95–116. On the demotion of Indigenous political philosophies into anthropological culture, and Indigenous resistance to this prevalent mechanism, see Audra Simpson, *Mohawk Interruptus: Political Life across the Borders of Settler States* (Durham: Duke University Press, 2014).

55. Stuart Elden, "Land, Terrain, Territory," *Progress in Human Geography* 34, no. 6 (2010): 810.

56. Anna Brickhouse, *The Unsettlement of America: Translation, Interpretation, and the Story of Don Luis de Velasco, 1560–1945* (Oxford: Oxford University Press, 2014), 2.

57. Kauanui, "'A Structure, Not an Event.'"

58. For contemporary analyses of African Americans' relations to Africa that use slavery's imperial history as the point of departure making their projects possible, see James T. Campbell, *Middle Passages: African American Journeys to Africa, 1787–2005* (New York: Penguin, 2007); and Hartman, *Lose Your Mother*.

59. Lorenzo Veracini argues that settler colonialism "obscures the conditions of its own productions." Veracini, *Settler Colonialism*, 14.

60. For discussions of spatialized history, see Vine Deloria Jr., *God Is Red* (New York:

Delta, 1973), esp. 75–89; and Keith H. Basso, *Wisdom Sits in Places: Landscape and Language among the Western Apache* (Albuquerque: University of New Mexico Press, 1996), esp. 30–34.

61. Taiaiake Alfred, *Peace, Power, Righteousness: An Indigenous Manifesto* (Don Mills, ON: Oxford University Press, 1999), 61.

62. Taiaiake Alfred, "Sovereignty," in *Sovereignty Matters: Locations of Contestation and Possibility in Indigenous Struggles for Self-Determination*, ed. Joanne Barker (Lincoln: University of Nebraska Press, 2005), 33.

63. Lisa Brooks, *The Common Pot: The Recovery of Native Space in the Northeast* (Minneapolis: University of Minnesota Press, 2008), 3–4.

64. Glen Sean Coulthard, *Red Skin, White Masks: Rejecting the Colonial Politics of Recognition* (Minneapolis: University of Minnesota Press, 2014), 60.

65. For example, Jodi A. Byrd argues that human-spatial relations are founded on perceptions of an active "land that remembers" and that "constructs kinship relations with all living beings who inhabit it," and Mishuana Goeman writes that "Indigenous peoples make place by relating both personal and communal experiences and histories to certain locations and landscapes." Goeman highlights the functions of active participation that all these scholars discuss by arguing that "maintaining these spatial relationships is one of the most important components of [Indigenous peoples'] politics and our identity." See Byrd, *Transit of Empire*, 118; and Goeman, "Land as Life: Unsettling the Logics of Containment," in *Native Studies Keywords*, ed. Stephanie Nohelani Teves, Andrea Smith, and Michelle H. Raheja (Tucson: The University of Arizona Press, 2015), 73.

66. Rashad Shabazz, *Spatializing Blackness: Architectures of Confinement and Black Masculinity in Chicago* (Urbana: University of Illinois Press, 2015), 2.

67. Thadious M. Davis, *Southscapes: Geographies of Race, Region, and Literature* (Chapel Hill: University of North Carolina Press, 2011), 7, 3.

68. Daniel Heath Justice, "'Go Away, Water!': Kinship Criticism and the Decolonial Imperative," in *Reasoning Together: The Native Critics Collective*, ed. Craig S. Womack, Daniel Heath Justice, and Christopher B. Teuton (Norman: University of Oklahoma Press, 2008), 152. As Dale Turner explains, response becomes a necessary tool of resistance as the need for Indigenous peoples "to explain" themselves "to the dominant culture arises primarily for political reasons and only secondarily from a desire to attain some kind of rich cross-cultural understanding of indigenous philosophies." Turner, *This Is Not a Peace Pipe: Towards a Critical Indigenous Philosophy* (Toronto: University of Toronto Press, 2006), 73. Jodi A. Byrd and Michael Rothberg also define indigeneity in terms of response as "an intellectual project that challenges and disrupts the logics of colonialism" and "holds the promise of rearticulating and reframing questions of place, space, movement and belonging." Byrd and Rothberg, "Between Subalternity and Indigeneity," *Interventions* 13, no. 1 (2011): 4, 3. Audra Simpson uses rearticulation and reframing in light of philosophies that preceded colonization and emphasizes the centrality of "refusal" as "a political and ethical stance" that simultaneously rejects colonial epistemologies and insists on the need for "having one's political sovereignty acknowledged and upheld" by contrast to the depoliticized, dehistoricized cultural constructions of native existence in colonial anthropology. Simpson, *Mohawk Interruptus*, 95, 11.

69. Simpson, *Mohawk Interruptus*, 219n1.

70. As Duncan Ivison, Paul Patton, and Will Sanders write, "Western political thought

is not necessarily the language of the world's indigenous peoples, although they have often been constrained to use it and there are points at which it overlaps with indigenous conceptions of what is right or just." Ivison, Patton, and Sanders, introduction to *Political Theory and the Rights of Indigenous Peoples*, ed. Duncan Ivison, Paul Patton, and Will Sanders (Cambridge: Cambridge University Press, 2000), 3.

71. Hartman, *Lose Your Mother*, 97, 98.

72. David Scott, *Conscripts of Modernity: The Tragedy of Colonial Enlightenment* (Durham: Duke University Press, 2004), 110.

73. Ibid., 119.

74. Raymond Williams, *Keywords: A Vocabulary of Culture and Society*, rev. ed. (New York: Oxford University Press, 1983), 215. Despite this double meaning, birthright citizenship has become so dominant in our perception of entitlement that scholars sometimes interpret native status as essentially privileged. Therefore, Orlando Patterson bases his influential "social death" thesis on the argument that the enslaved experienced a "loss of native status" that turned him or her into a "genealogical isolate" deprived of "all 'rights' or claims of birth." See Patterson, *Slavery and Social Death: A Comparative Study* (Cambridge, MA: Harvard University Press, 1982), 5.

75. Mahmood Mamdani, *Define and Rule: Native as Political Identity* (Cambridge, MA: Harvard University Press, 2012), 2–3.

76. *Bracton: De Legibus et Consuetudinibus Angliæ* (c.1250), trans. by Samuel E. Thorne as *Bracton on the Laws and Customs of England*, accessed January 31, 2016, http://bracton.law.harvard.edu. For interchangeable usages of these terms, see ibid., 2:30, 2:411.

77. Henrico Spelmanno [Henry Spelman], *Glossarium Archaiologicum* (London: Warren, 1664), 426. Spelman wrote in Latin, and I am grateful to Ilaria Stiller-Timor for helping me understand his text. I am referring here to Spelman's entry for "*Native tenentes*," which reads, "*Sunt (ipsi etiam liberi) qui terram tenant nativam; hoc est nativorum servitiis obnoxiam*." Stiller-Timor translates "*terram tenant nativam*" as "possessing native land." On Spelman's role in bringing the study of feudalism to England, see Susan Reynolds, *Fiefs and Vassals: The Medieval Evidence Reinterpreted* (Oxford: Oxford University Press, 1994), 7.

78. John Cowell defines "*Nativo habendo*" as "a writ that lyeth to the Shyreeue for a Lord, whose vilein claimed as his inheritance, is runne from him, for the apprehending and restoring of him to his Lord againe." Cowell, *The Interpreter: Or Booke Containing the Signification of Words* (Cambridge: John Legate, 1607), n.p. Edward Phillips similarly defines this term as "a Writ for the apprehending a Lords Bond-woman or the Villain, claimed as his Inheritance, (who in Common Law is called *Nief*) and restoring her to his Lord." Phillips, *The New World of Words, Or a General English Dictionary*, 4th ed. (Cornhill, UK: Robert Harford, 1678), n.p.

79. *OED Online*, s.v. "native" (n.), accessed March 18, 2015, http://www.oed.com.

80. Francis Plowden, *An Investigation of the Native Rights of British Subjects* (London: Baldwin, Whieldon, and Debarett, 1784), 2.

81. William Blackstone, *Commentaries on the Laws of England*, bk. 1, 1st ed. (Oxford: Clarendon, 1765), 412.

82. Karen Orren argues that "[i]f there is one generally accepted proposition about American political development, it is the absence of feudalism and the importance of that

circumstance for the hegemony of liberal thought and practice throughout the nation's history." She challenges this assumption by studying the "belated feudalism" that she associates with labor and employment patterns under post–Civil War industrialization. Orren, *Belated Feudalism: Labor, the Law, and Liberal Development in the United States* (Cambridge: Cambridge University Press, 1991), 1. Mahmood Mamdani asserts that "political theory in America tended to gel around the acknowledgement of an absence" —that of feudalism in its history. Mamdani, "Settler Colonialism: Then and Now," *Critical Inquiry* 41, no. 3 (2015): 9. Mamdani traces the feudal absence thesis to Alexis de Tocqueville's *Democracy in America* (1835), but the *Federalist Papers* and Jefferson's writings often contrast Europe's feudal past with US culture. Robert A. Williams Jr. traces feudal landholding logic to the papal authorization of Spain's rights to the lands of Indigenous peoples in America and shows how English colonization used that logic. Williams, *The American Indian in Western Legal Thought: The Discourse of Conquest* (Oxford: Oxford University Press, 1990), 21, 200, 206–9.

83. Saskia Sassen, *Territory, Authority, Rights: From Medieval to Global Assemblages*, 2nd ed. (Princeton: Princeton University Press, 2008), 108, 109. Sassen defines feudalism as a system of "increasingly decentered geography" where multiple small-scale local units of landownership-based governance prevented the development of a large-scale geopolitical center (p. 31).

84. Critical geographer Stuart Elden defines land as "a scarce resource, one whose distribution and redistribution is an important economic and political concern." Elden, "Land, Terrain, Territory," 806. He critiques Sassen's perception of territory as "a static, ahistorical concept" (pp. 808–9).

85. Elizabeth A. R. Brown, "The Tyranny of a Construct: Feudalism and Historians of Medieval Europe," *American Historical Review* 79, no. 4 (1974): 1063–88.

86. Reynolds, *Fiefs and Vassals*.

87. Kathleen Davis, *Periodization and Sovereignty: How Ideas of Feudalism and Secularization Govern the Politics of Time* (Philadelphia: University of Pennsylvania Press, 2008), 7.

88. Jennifer Greeson, "American Enlightenment: The New World and Modern Western Thought" *American Literary History* 25, no. 1 (2013): 6.

89. Stuart Elden, *The Birth of Territory* (Chicago: University of Chicago Press, 2013), 7, 17.

90. Ibid., 245.

91. Greeson, "American Enlightenment," 6.

92. On the expansion of positive birthright, see John Phillip Reid, "The Authority of Rights at the American Founding," in *The Nature of Rights at the American Founding and Beyond*, ed. Barry Alan Shain (Charlottesville: University of Virginia Press, 2007), esp. 72–75; and Craig Yirush, *Settlers, Liberty, and Empire: The Roots of Early American Political Theory, 1675–1775* (Cambridge: Cambridge University Press, 2011), 51–54.

93. Carole Pateman formulates this idea by utilizing the conventional view of America as the laboratory where European ideas could be tested. She writes that by traveling to a "terra nullius," settlers became "the natural figures of the thought experiment in the texts of political theory come to life." Whereas Pateman examines the founding myths of modern settler colonialism, Alyosha Goldstein considers present articulations of US "white settler colonialism" and argues that the "modern rights-bearing possessive individual"

was produced by the same "legal reason" that was "essential for the notions of self and property in liberal societies generally and in settler societies in particular." Pateman, "The Settler Contract," in *Contract and Domination*, edited by Carole Pateman and Charles W. Mills (Cambridge: Polity, 2007), 55; Goldstein, "Where the Nation Takes Place: Proprietary Regimes, Antistatism, and U.S. Settler Colonialism," *South Atlantic Quarterly* 107, no. 4 (2008): 834.

94. William Waller Hening, *The Statutes at Large; Being a Collection of All the Laws of Virginia, from the First Session of the Legislature, in the Year 1619* (New York: Bartow, 1823), 1:64.

95. For discussions of Powhatan's subinfeudation, see Williams, *The American Indian*, 206–8; Robert A. Williams Jr., *Linking Arms Together: American Indian Treaty Visions of Law and Peace, 1600–1800* (New York: Oxford University Press, 1997), 31–32; and Eric Cheyfitz, *The Poetics of Imperialism: Translation and Colonization from* The Tempest *to* Tarzan (Philadelphia: University of Pennsylvania Press, 1997), 59–61.

96. John Smith, *The Generall Historie of Virginia, New England, & the Summer Isles*, bk. 3 (London: Edward Blackmore, 1632), 68.

97. For analyses of the case's contribution to US citizenship, see Polly J. Price, "Natural Law and Birthright Citizenship in Calvin's Case (1608)," *Yale Journal of Law & the Humanities* 9, no. 1 (1997): 73–146; and Rogers M. Smith, *Civic Ideals: Conflicting Visions of Citizenship in U.S. History* (New Haven: Yale University Press, 1997), 40–49. On the case's significance to imperial conquest, see Williams, *The American Indian*, 199–221.

98. Edward Coke, *The Reports of Sir Edward Coke, Knt.*, vol. 4, new ed., ed. John Henry Thomas and John Farquhar Fraser (London: Joseph Butterworth and Son, 1826), part 7, p. 8. As Elden writes, feudal logic (which guided Coke in *Calvin's Case*) "lacked an articulated concept of territory." Elden, *The Birth of Territory*, 156. Working within the tradition of what Ernst Hartwig Kantorowicz called "the king's two bodies," Coke writes that "the King hath two capacities": a "natural body" that is a divine creation "subject to death" and a "politic body or capacity . . . framed by the policy of man" under which "the King is esteemed to be immortal." Coke, *The Reports*, vol. 4, part 7, p. 17. See Kantorowicz, *The King's Two Bodies: A Study in Mediaeval Political Theology* (Princeton: Princeton University Press, 1957).

99. Coke, *The Reports*, vol. 4, part 7, pp. 10, 12.

100. *An Act for the better ordering and governing of Negroes*, 1661, CO 30/2/16–26, 16, Public Record Office, Kew, UK.

101. "An Act for the Better Governing of Negroes," in *Acts, Passed in the Island of Barbados. From 1643, to 1762, Inclusive*, ed. Richard Hall and Richard Hall (London: Richard Hall, 1764), 112–13.

102. "An Act Declaring the Negro-Slaves of this Island, to be Real Estates" (1668). In *Acts Passed in the Island of Barbados. From 1643, to 1762, Inclusive*, ed. Richard Hall and Richard Hall (London: Richard Hall, 1764), 64–65. Other colonies, in the Caribbean and North America, enacted similar laws that qualified the general definition of slaves as chattel personal.

103. Kimberly K. Smith, *African American Environmental Thought: Foundations* (Lawrence: University Press of Kansas, 2007), 14.

104. The Privy Council's 1722 decision was added as a footnote to Calvin's Case by eighteenth- or nineteenth-century editors of Coke's *Reports*. See Coke, *The Reports*, vol. 4, part 7, p. 30n.

105. Carole Pateman writes that "Locke was an investor in the Royal Africa Company and in a company trading in the Bahamas. He was the first Landgrave (member of the nobility) in Carolina and was given land there. From 1668 to 1775 [*sic*; should be 1675] he worked as secretary to the Lords Proprietors of Carolina and helped draw up its constitution of 1669 (overthrown by the colonists in 1719); from 1672 to 1676 he worked for the Council on Trade, corresponding with settlers in America, and he was Commissioner for the Board of Trade and Plantations from 1695 until 1700." Pateman, "Settler Contract," 47–48. Barbara Arneil writes that Locke's theory of property was "written to justify" colonization. Arneil, *John Locke and America: The Defence of English Colonialism* (Oxford: Oxford University Press, 1996), 2. James Tully clarifies that the "Carolina" whose constitution Locke wrote comprised "most of present-day North Carolina, all of South Carolina and almost all of Georgia." Tully, *An Approach to Political Philosophy: Locke in Contexts* (Cambridge: Cambridge University Press, 1993), 143. Although twenty years separate the publication of the *Fundamental Constitutions* and that of the *Two Treatises*, the latter provided no corrective to the former. As David Armitage shows, Locke revised the *Fundamental Constitutions* and retained its slaveholding feudal structure while working on the *Two Treatises*. Armitage, "John Locke, Carolina, and the *Two Treatises of Government*," *Political Theory* 32, no. 5 (2004): 619.

106. John Locke, *Two Treatises of Government: A Critical Edition with an Introduction and Apparatus Criticus*, ed. Peter Laslett (Cambridge: Cambridge University Press, 1966), 411–12 (italics in original).

107. John Locke, "The Fundamental Constitutions of Carolina," in *The Works of John Locke, in Ten Volumes*, 10th ed. (London: T. Davison, 1801), 10:198, 180. On Locke's position as Carolina's first landgrave, see Pateman, "Settler Contract," 48.

108. The quotation is from Tully, *Approach to Political Philosophy*, 159.

109. Locke, *Two Treatises*, 302; Locke, "Fundamental Constitutions," 196. Armitage writes that "Locke himself had augmented the slaveholders' 'absolute Authority' by adding that '<power and>' in the 1669 manuscript." Armitage, "John Locke," 609. Tully writes that the colony enslaved indigenous peoples as well as Africans and sold Indians into Caribbean slavery. Tully, *Approach to Political Philosophy*, 143–44.

110. This is perhaps the most striking illustration of the mutual constitution of negative and positive birthrights in Locke's works, and it was influential enough to resonate in nineteenth-century texts. In *My Bondage and My Freedom*, Frederick Douglass echoes North Carolina judge Thomas Ruffin's 1829 assertion that "the power of the master must be absolute, to render the submission of the slave perfect" by writing that "the judgment of the master must be deemed infallible, for his power is absolute and irresponsible." *North Carolina v. Mann*, 13 N.C. 263 (1829), accessed January 28, 2016, http://www.learnnc.org/lp/editions/nchist-antebellum/4492. Frederick Douglass, *My Bondage and My Freedom* (1855), in *Autobiographies*, by Frederick Douglass, ed. Henry Louis Gates Jr. (New York: Library of America, 1994), 194.

111. Blackstone, *Commentaries*, bk. 1, 1st ed., 105, 106.

112. Ibid., 123. Blackstone qualified this statement in order to defend slaveowners' right to their former slaves' services under English contract law. In subsequent editions Blackstone emphasizes the master's rights to any contractual services the former slave might have agreed to perform. See Blackstone, *Commentaries*, bk. 1, 2nd, 3rd, and 4th ed., 127. As Edlie Wong argues, such qualifications, which translate slavery into contrac-

tual relations, justify it as a form of master-servant relations. Wong, *Neither Fugitive nor Free: Atlantic Slavery, Freedom Suits, and the Legal Culture of Travel* (New York: New York University Press, 2009), 39–42. For a classic discussion of this portion of Blackstone's text, see David Brion Davis, *The Problem of Slavery in the Age of Revolution, 1770–1823* (Ithaca: Cornell University Press, 1975), 473–86. See also James Oldham, *English Common Law in the Age of Mansfield* (Chapel Hill: University of North Carolina Press, 2004), 316.

113. The decisions are *Blankard v. Galdy* (1693) and *Smith v. Brown and Cooper* (early 1700s); quotation from *Smith v. Brown and Cooper*, 666. Blackstone cites them from William Salkeld's *Reports of Cases Adjudged in the Court of King's Bench*, vol. 2 (Philadelphia: H. C. Carey & I. Lea, 1822).

114. Despite these similarities in their interpretations, Holt distinguished between the categories "slave" and "negro" while Blackstone conflated them. On Holt's distinction between these categories, see Davis, *Problem of Slavery*, 479–80. Holt wrote that since a "negro" is not necessarily a "slave," claims for ownership over slaves should refer to them as such rather than simply as "negro." *Smith v. Brown and Cooper*, 666.

115. "Pennsylvania Assembly: Proposed Reply to the Governor," November 25, 1755, in *Votes and Proceedings of the House of Representatives, 1755–1756* (Philadelphia, 1756), accessed October 15, 2016, http://franklinpapers.org/franklin/framedVolumes.jsp?vol=6&page=238a.

116. "By the House of Representatives of the English Colony of Connecticut, second Thursday of May, 1774," in *The Public Records of the Colony of Connecticut*, ed. Charles J. Hoadly (Hartford: Case, Lockwood & Brainard, 1887), 14:347.

117. On the colonists' interest in English rights even in the Declaration of Independence, see Reid, *Constitutional History*, esp. 5–19. On the significance of Reid's work, see Greene, *Constitutional Origins*, xii–xiii.

118. On the prevalence of the slavery metaphor in revolutionary discourse, see Bernard Bailyn, *The Ideological Origins of the American Revolution* (Cambridge, MA: Harvard University Press, 1967), 232.

119. Beside Julian Boyd's annotation in the *Papers of Thomas Jefferson*, the single scholarly treatment of this proposal of which I am aware is the brief, though useful discussion in William Howard Adams, *The Paris Years of Thomas Jefferson* (New Haven: Yale University Press, 1997), 179–80. I am grateful to Thomas M. Downey, associate editor of the *Papers of Thomas Jefferson*, for this reference.

120. Thomas Jefferson to John Adams, July 28, 1785, *Founders Online*, Jefferson Papers, National Archives, accessed October 15, 2016, http://founders.archives.gov/documents/Jefferson/01-08-02-0254. Originally published in *The Papers of Thomas Jefferson*, vol. 8, *25 February–31 October 1785*, eds. Julian P. Boyd, Mina R. Bryan, and Elizabeth L. Hutter (Princeton: Princeton University Press, 1953), 315–20. Jefferson's proposal became possible thanks to two processes. First, he hoped to position the new republic as a "treaty-worthy nation" that would reflect the ideals of European powers and earn their trust in order to bolster the US economy and its integration into Europe's international arena. Second, the recent political upheavals of the Revolutionary era had rendered "the rules of the [Westphalian international] system . . . increasingly in flux." The term "treaty-worthy nation" is coined and elaborated in Eliga H. Gould, *Among the Powers of the Earth: The American Revolution and the Making of a New World Empire* (Cambridge:

Harvard University Press, 2012), Kindle edition, introduction. For the economic context, see Adams, *The Paris Years*, 160–61. The reference to the international system is from Leonard J. Sadosky, *Revolutionary Negotiations: Indians, Empires, and Diplomats in the Founding of America* (Charlottesville: University of Virginia Press, 2009), 4.

121. For the legal history of territorial birthright citizenship, see Price, "Natural Law and Birthright."

122. Jefferson to Adams, July 28, 1785, National Archives.

123. Scott Lauria Morgensen, "Indigenous Transnationalism and the AIDS Pandemic: Challenging Settler Colonialism within Global Health Governance," in *Theorizing Native Studies*, ed. Audra Simpson and Andrea Smith (Durham: Duke University Press, 2014), 189.

124. Jefferson to Adams, July 28, 1785, National Archives.

125. Jefferson had already tried to divest the category "native" of the connotations of negative birthright when he signed his *Summary View of the Rights of British America* (1774) as "a NATIVE, and MEMBER of the HOUSE of BURGESSES" and placed birth on a par with elected position. Focusing on "the united complaints of his majesty's subjects in America," the text extends the logic of positive birthright throughout the colonies. Early in the shift from colonial rights that stemmed from the sovereign monarch (chap. 2) to entitlement rooted in birth on national soil (chap. 5), Jefferson dubbed himself "native" in order to portray positive birthright as the embodiment of divinely ordained freedom. To ground positive birthright in "British America," Jefferson denies the feudal legal fiction "that all lands belong originally to the king," distances settlers from the Normans who feudalized England, and constitutes them instead as heirs of "[o]ur Saxon ancestors" and their pre-feudal liberty tradition. Thomas Jefferson, *A Summary View of the Rights of British America* (Williamsburg, VA: Clementinarind, 1774), 1, 5, 20, accessed May 5, 2013, http://www.loc.gov/rr/rarebook/guide/ra008001.html.

126. José-Manuel Barreto, "Introduction: Decolonial Strategies and Dialogue in the Human Rights Field," in *Human Rights from a Third World Perspective: Critique, History and International Law*, ed. José-Manuel Barreto (Newcastle upon Tyne, UK: Cambridge Scholars Publishing, 2013), 20.

127. See, for example, Lynn Hunt, *Inventing Human Rights: A History* (New York: Norton, 2007).

128. See Micheline R. Ishay, "What Are Human Rights? Six Historical Controversies," *Journal of Human Rights* 3, no. 3 (2004): 361. Even Samuel Moyn, who critiques this historical narrative, formulates his critique within the terms of Eurocentric history, individualism, and international relations. Moyn, *The Last Utopia*.

129. Ishay, "What Are Human Rights?," 359–60.

130. Mutua, *Human Rights*, 22, 154.

131. Barreto, "Introduction," 12, 22.

132. For Wynter's earlier works in this field, see Sylvia Wynter, "Columbus and the Poetics of the Propter Nos," *Annals of Scholarship* 8, no. 2 (1992): 251–86. For a more recent formulation, see Sylvia Wynter, "Unsettling the Coloniality of Being/Power/Truth/Freedom: Towards the Human, After Man, Its Overrepresentation—An Argument," *CR: The New Centennial Review* 3.3 (2003): 257–337. For conversations in which Wynter elaborates on these ideas, see Sylvia Wynter and Katherine McKittrick, "Unparalleled Catastrophe for Our Species? Or, to Give Humanness a Different Future: Conversations," in *Sylvia Wynter: On Being Human as Praxis*, ed. Katherine McKittrick (Durham: Duke University Press, 2015).

133. Mignolo, *Darker Side of Western Modernity*, 234–35.

134. Mignolo, "Who Speaks for the 'Human,'" 7; Walter D. Mignolo, "Geopolitics of Sensing and Knowing: On (De)Coloniality, Border Thinking and Epistemic Disobedience," *Postcolonial Studies* 14, no. 3 (2011): 276.

135. Mignolo, "Who Speaks for the 'Human,'" 7, 8.

136. Mignolo, "Geopolitics of Sensing and Knowing," 275.

Chapter 1: Equiano's Nativity

1. Olaudah Equiano, *The Interesting Narrative of the Life of Olaudah Equiano, the African. Written by Himself* (1789–94), in *The Interesting Narrative and Other Writings*, rev. ed., ed. Vincent Carretta (New York: Penguin, 2003) (hereafter cited in text as *IN*). An earlier version of this chapter appeared as "Equiano's Nativity: Negative Birthright, Indigenous Ethic, and Universal Human Rights," *Early American Literature* 48, no. 2 (2013): 399–423.

2. I retain Equiano's spelling of "Eboe." Contemporary usage includes Igbo and Ibo.

3. Carretta first published his interpretation of the findings in "Olaudah Equiano or Gustavus Vassa? New Light on an Eighteenth-Century Question of Identity," *Slavery & Abolition* 20, no. 3 (1999): 96–105; he reiterated his reading of the documents in *Equiano, the African: Biography of a Self-Made Man* (New York: Penguin, 2005). Carretta's treatment of the documents revived older questions about Equiano's nativity. Earlier qualms regarding Equiano's African nativities were voiced in Catherine Obianju Acholonu, "The Home of Olaudah Equiano—a Linguistic and Anthropological Search," *Journal of Commonwealth Literature* 22, no. 1 (1987): 5–16; and S. E. Ogude, *No Roots Here: On the Igbo Roots of Olaudah Equiano* (Ibadan, Nigeria: RELS Monographs, 1989). Prominent contributions to the debate following Carretta's findings include Paul E. Lovejoy, "Autobiography and Memory: Gustavus Vassa, alias Olaudah Equiano, the African," *Slavery & Abolition* 27, no. 3 (2006): 317–47; Vincent Carretta, "Response to Paul Lovejoy's 'Autobiography and Memory: Gustavus Vassa, alias Olaudah Equiano, the African,'" *Slavery & Abolition* 28, no. 1 (2007): 115–19; Paul E. Lovejoy, "Issues of Motivation—Vassa/Equiano and Carretta's Critique of the Evidence," *Slavery & Abolition* 28, no. 1 (2007): 121–25; Vincent Carretta, ed., "Olaudah Equiano, the South Carolinian? A Forum" (which includes works by Lovejoy, Trevor Burnard, and Jon Sensbach), *Historically Speaking* 7, no. 3 (2006); and Chima J. Korieh, ed., *Olaudah Equiano and the Igbo World* (Trenton, NJ: Africa World Press, 2009).

4. Orlando Patterson, *Slavery and Social Death: A Comparative Study* (Cambridge, MA: Harvard University Press, 1982), 5. For a review of the book's impact, see Vincent Brown, "Social Death and Political Life in the Study of Slavery," *American Historical Review* 114, no. 5 (2009): 1231–49. Brown argues that we should not view social death as "the actual condition of the enslaved," but "as a productive peril" to which slaves responded by "pursu[ing] a politics of belonging, mourning, accounting, and regeneration" (p. 1248).

5. Carretta, *Equiano, the African*, 89.

6. Cathy Davidson, "Olaudah Equiano, Written by Himself," *Novel: A Forum on Fiction* 40, no. 1/2 (2006/2007): 29; Patterson, *Slavery and Social Death*, esp. 5. Patterson identifies slavery's two other "constituent elements" as the "extremity of power" it involves and its systematic "dishonor[ing]" of slaves (pp. 2, 10).

7. Stephanie E. Smallwood, *Saltwater Slavery: A Middle Passage from Africa to American Diaspora* (Cambridge, MA: Harvard University Press, 2007), 202. In this context, Equiano's insistence on his African birth seems counterintuitive; the stigma may explain why at certain points he had preferred to represent himself as Creole.

8. For a partial mapping of these approaches, see George Boulukos, *The Grateful Slave: The Emergence of Race in Eighteenth-Century British and American Culture* (Cambridge: Cambridge University Press, 2008), 185n35.

9. The Eurocentric view of property as the foundation of society can be traced to Aristotle, who argues that private property helped create stable communities and eliminate social tensions—though he added that citizens should make their private property available to one another. Aristotle, *Politics*, trans. H. Rackham (Cambridge, MA: Harvard University Press, 1944), 85–91. As Anthony Pagden explains, "civil society was, by definition, a society based upon property, and property relations were what constituted the basis for all exchanges between men within society." Pagden, "Dispossessing the Barbarian: The Language of Spanish Thomism and the Debate over the Property Rights of the American Indians," in *The Languages of Political Theory in Early-Modern Europe*, ed. Anthony Pagden (Cambridge: Cambridge University Press, 1987), 81.

10. V. Y. Mudimbe, *The Idea of Africa* (Bloomington: Indiana University Press, 1994), 79, 81–82. On the association of Ethiopians with barbarians, see also Anthony Pagden, *The Fall of Natural Man: The American Indian and the Origins of Comparative Ethnology* (Cambridge: Cambridge University Press, 1986), 15.

11. Pagden, *Fall of Natural Man*, 16; Aristotle, *Politics*, esp. 17–31.

12. Aristotle, *Politics*, 5–7; Pagden, *Fall of Natural Man*, 24.

13. Pagden, *Fall of Natural Man*, 29.

14. John Mair quoted in Pagden, *Fall of Natural Man*, 39.

15. Paolo G. Carozza, "From Conquest to Constitution: Retrieving a Latin American Tradition of the Idea of Human Rights," *Human Rights Quarterly* 25, no. 2 (2003): 289.

16. Daniel R. Brunstetter, "Sepúlveda, Las Casas, and the Other: Exploring the Tension between Moral Universalism and Alterity," *Review of Politics* 72, no. 3 (2010): 418, 424. See also Carozza, "From Conquest to Constitution," 293.

17. Walter D. Mignolo, "Delinking: The Rhetoric of Modernity, the Logic of Coloniality and the Grammar of De-coloniality," *Cultural Studies* 21, no. 2/3 (2007): 471. Based in part on his promotion of universal rights, Las Casas has recently been recognized as a harbinger of abolitionist thought who "perceived and condemned the evil of slavery . . . long before Enlightenment theories of rights emerged." See Carozza, "From Conquest to Constitution," 293–94; and Santa Arias, "Equal Rights and Individual Freedom: Enlightenment Intellectuals and the Lascasian Apology for Black African Slavery," *Romance Quarterly* 55, no. 4 (2008): 280.

18. Brunstetter, "Sepúlveda, Las Casas, and the Other," 421–2. Las Casas defined three additional types of "barbarian": speakers of a foreign language (the term achieves its utmost relativism here); individuals (rather than groups) whose mental capacities prevent rational behavior; and those who "do not acknowledge Christ" (pp. 422–23).

19. As Boulukos writes, Equiano refuses "the terms of 'raced' identity as practiced in the colonies." Boulukos, *The Grateful Slave*, 195.

20. See Pagden, *Fall of Natural Man*, 39, 47, 52, 58.

21. Phillis Wheatley, "Letter to Samuel Hopkins, October 30, 1774," in *The Poems of*

Phillis Wheatley: Revised and Enlarged Edition, with an Additional Poem, ed. Julian D. Mason Jr. (Chapel Hill: University of North Carolina Press, 1989), 214.

22. David Kazanjian examines Wheatley's position regarding African colonization and, through this topic, shows that her and Equiano's views were too complex to allow for any simplistic contrast between them. See Kazanjian, *The Brink of Freedom: Improvising Life in the Nineteenth-Century Atlantic World* (Durham: Duke University Press, 2016), 58–65. However, their usages of the term *barbarian* do differ.

23. Jace Weaver, *That the People Might Live: Native American Literatures and Native American Community* (New York: Oxford University Press, 1997), 43.

24. Carretta challenges treatments of Equiano as a Franklinian "self-made man" on the basis of historical sequence rather than content: "since the publication in London of Equiano's autobiography preceded by decades that of Franklin's in the United States, rather than considering Equiano an African American Franklin we should more accurately call Franklin an Anglo-American Equiano." Carretta, *Equiano, the African*, xiii. Davidson states instead that "this supposed elevation of Equiano into a Franklinian self-made man misreads the psychological state of the narrator, diminishes his anguish, compromises his spiritual quest, and undercuts *The Interesting Narrative* as a political polemic. . . . [Equiano's story] is the ultimate story of the self un-made." Davidson, "Olaudah Equiano," 43–44.

25. For an analysis of Smith's narrative in terms of the possessive individual in the context of slavery, see Jennifer Rae Greeson, "The Prehistory of Possessive Individualism," *PMLA* 127, no. 4 (2012): 918–24.

26. V. Y. Mudimbe, *Liberty in African and Western Thought* (Washington, DC: Institute for Independent Education, 1988), 1, 4–5.

27. James Sidbury, *Becoming African in America: Race and Nation in the Early Black Atlantic* (Oxford: Oxford University Press, 2007), 14–15.

28. Hazel V. Carby, "Becoming Modern Racialized Subjects," *Cultural Studies* 23, no. 4 (2009): 634.

29. Stephanie E. Smallwood defines the difference between African and New World slavery by drawing on the idea of social death: while African slavery assimilated slaves into their owners' communities, New World slavery meant "absolute exclusion from *any* community." Smallwood, *Saltwater Slavery*, 30 (italics in original).

30. William Blackstone, *Commentaries on the Laws of England*, bk. 1, 4th ed. (Oxford: Clarendon, 1770), 127. This is the final version of a tortuous sentence that Blackstone kept revising over the first four editions of his book in order to limit the eventual freedom of the "slave" or "negro."

31. "An Act for the Better Governing of Negroes," August 8, 1668, in *Acts, Passed in the Island of Barbados. From 1643, to 1762, Inclusive*, ed. Richard Hall and Richard Hall (London: Richard Hall, 1764), 120.

32. Oliver Goldsmith, *A History of the Earth, and Animated Nature* (1774) (York, UK: Thomas Wilson and Son, 1808), 1:348.

33. Thomas Salmon, *Modern History: Or, the Present State of All Nations*, 3rd ed. (London, 1746), 3:9.

34. On Equiano's use of contemporaneous English literature on Africa, see Henry Louis Gates Jr., *The Signifying Monkey: A Theory of Afro-American Literary Criticism* (New York: Oxford University Press, 1988), 153. See also Carretta's extensive annotation of Equiano's references to Africa in Equiano, *Interesting Narrative*.

35. Adam Potkay develops the anti-postcolonial reading of Christianity in "History, Oratory, and God in Equiano's *Interesting Narrative*," *Eighteenth-Century Studies* 34, no. 4 (2001): esp. 608–11. For a focus on hybridity, see Helen Thomas, *Romanticism and Slave Narratives* (Cambridge: Cambridge University Press, 2000), 248.

36. Srinivas Aravamudan, "Equiano Lite," *Eighteenth-Century Studies* 34, no. 4 (2001): 615; Joanna Brooks, *American Lazarus: Religion and the Rise of African-American and Native American Literatures* (Oxford: Oxford University Press, 2003), 62, 18, 86; Eileen Razzari Elrod, *Piety and Dissent: Race, Gender, and Biblical Rhetoric in Early American Autobiography* (Amherst: University of Massachusetts Press, 2008), 67.

37. Mary Louise Pratt, "Scratches on the Face of the Country; Or, What Mr. Barrow Saw in the Land of the Bushmen," *Critical Inquiry* 12, no. 1 (1985): 120.

38. Audra Simpson, *Mohawk Interruptus: Political Life across the Borders of Settler States* (Durham: Duke University Press, 2014), 11, 34, 203n16.

39. Roxann Wheeler, *The Complexion of Race: Categories of Difference in Eighteenth-Century British Culture* (Philadelphia: University of Pennsylvania Press, 2000), 262.

40. Potkay, "History, Oratory, and God," 608.

41. For an early articulation of this view, by Vitoria, see Pagden, *Fall of Natural Man*, 32–3.

42. Hugo Grotius, *The Free Sea* (1609), ed. David Armitage, trans. Richard Hakluyt (Indianapolis: Liberty Fund, 2004), 26.

43. John Selden, *Mare Clausum: The Right and Dominion of the Sea in Two Books* (London: Andrew Kembe and Edward Thomas, 1663), 1:46, 114; 2:182, 441–42.

44. In light of these tensions, it is no wonder that David Kazanjian emphasizes Equiano's "deep distrust" of "nationally bound, terrestrial freedom," which leads him to seek "sea-bound 'honesty,'" but the *Narrative* treats both land and sea with "distrust." Kazanjian, *The Colonizing Trick: National Culture and Imperial Citizenship in Early America* (Minneapolis: University of Minnesota Press, 2003), 55. Equiano characterizes the sea polysemously as "lawful calling"; "mad career"; site of "adventures" and "pleasure"; dangerous source of livelihood; and focus of intellectual and professional interest (pp. 189, 216, 172, 166). For a reading of the symbolism of the sea in the book, see James Collins, "Passage to Slavery, Passage to Freedom: Olaudah Equiano and the Sea," *Midwest Quarterly* 47, no. 3 (2006): 209–23.

45. John Agnew, *Geopolitics: Re-Visioning World Politics*, 2nd ed. (London: Routledge, 2003), 26.

46. The *Oxford English Dictionary* states that one sense of the noun "moor"—i.e., "a piece of unenclosed waste ground; (now usually, esp. in Brit.) uncultivated ground covered with heather; a heath"—is "unique to English" and associates other senses with particular English regions, such as Somerset and Cornwall. *OED Online*, s.v. "moor" (n.), accessed May 8, 2017, http://www.oed.com.

47. Nicholas Rogers, "Caribbean Borderland: Empire, Ethnicity, and the Exotic on the Mosquito Coast," *Eighteenth-Century Life* 26, no. 3 (2002): 118. See also Christopher Apap, "Caught between Two Opinions: Africans, Europeans, and Indians in Olaudah Equiano's *Interesting Narrative*," *Comparative American Studies* 4, no. 1 (2006): 5–24. While Apap's focus seems close to mine here, he is primarily interested in a single event—an imminent Musquito conflict that Equiano prevents—in the context of hybridity rather than in issues of settlement or perceptions of the land.

48. Lisa Lowe, *The Intimacies of Four Continents* (Durham: Duke University Press, 2015), 64.

49. Kazanjian, *Brink of Freedom*, 62.

50. Virginia also gave rewards for killing "other vermine," squirrels, and crows, which were perceived as threatening crops. On such laws, see William Waller Hening, *The Statutes at Large; Being a Collection of All the Laws of Virginia, from the First Session of the Legislature, in the Year 1619* (New York: Bartow, 1823), 1:199, 328, 475; 2:87, 396; 3:42–43, 282–83; 4:89, 446.

51. Mary Louise Pratt, *Imperial Eyes: Travel Writing and Transculturation* (London: Routledge, 1992), 39, 57.

52. Renato Rosaldo, *Culture and Truth: The Remaking of Social Analysis* (Boston: Beacon Press, 1989), 69.

53. For discussions of earlier ideas (since 1771) of the potential profitability of non-enslaving commerce with Africa or its colonization, see Wheeler, *Complexion of Race*, 283; and Stephen J. Braidwood, *Black Poor and White Philanthropists: London's Blacks and the Foundations of the Sierra Leone Settlement, 1786–1791* (Liverpool: Liverpool University Press, 1994), 6–12.

54. Wheeler, *Complexion of Race*, 283; Tanya Caldwell, "'Talking Too Much English': Languages of Economy and Politics in Equiano's *The Interesting Narrative*," *Early American Literature* 34, no. 3 (1999): 265.

55. See Carretta, *Equiano, the African*, 264.

56. The letter to Hawkesbury is reprinted in Equiano, *Interesting Narrative*, 335–37, and the book's version of the proposal appears on pp. 233–35. See also *Public Advertiser*, March 31, 1788. In discussing these versions below, I note some of their differences while disregarding variations in capitalization and punctuation.

57. Equiano mentions his former position as "Commissary for the African Settlement" at Sierra Leone. Equiano, *Interesting Narrative*, 337.

58. On this point, see also Wheeler, *Complexion of Race*, 284.

59. Carretta, *Equiano, the African*, 256.

60. Vincent Carretta, "New Equiana," *Early American Literature* 44, no. 1 (2009): 152.

61. Ibid., 151.

62. John Bugg, "The Other Interesting Narrative: Olaudah Equiano's Public Book Tour," *PMLA* 121, no. 5 (2006): 1435.

63. Joanna Brooks, ed., *The Collected Writings of Samson Occom, Mohegan: Leadership and Literature in Eighteenth-Century Native America* (Oxford: Oxford University Press, 2006), 99. As Michael Elliott shows, Occom's language draws on the "New Testament metaphor" of the "fool for Christ's sake." See Elliott, "'This Indian Bait': Samson Occom and the Voice of Liminality," *Early American Literature* 29, no. 3 (1994): 246.

Chapter 2: Mohegan Native Rights

1. "The Charter of the Ancient Colony of Connecticut" (1662), in *Letters from the English kings and queens, Charles II, James II, William and Mary, Anne, George II, &c: to the governors of the Colony of Connecticut, together with the answers thereto, from 1635 to 1749*, ed. R. R. Hinman (Hartford: John B. Eldredge, 1836), 181.

2. "By the House of Representatives of the English Colony of Connecticut, second Thurs-

day of May, 1774," in *The Public Records of the Colony of Connecticut*, ed. Charles J. Hoadly (Hartford: Case, Lockwood & Brainard, 1887), 14:347.

3. This point is illustrated in Paul Joseph Grant-Costa's discussion of the difference between the 1736 Mohegan delegation to London and earlier or concurrent delegations of Iroquois, Cherokee, Creek, and Yamacraw leaders, and the different ways in which the Mohegan and Narragansett claimed equality with the English or with settlers. While other Indigenous delegations to London emphasized their members' hunting skills and local apparel, the Mohegan visitors were "[d]ressed in English clothes, speaking English, and acting English" as though they "sought not to represent the savage 'other' but claimed their stake at justice from being a part of the empire itself." The extent of such participation distinguished the Mohegan from the Narragansett, the colonies' other Indigenous ally in the Pequot War, who tried to establish its equality to settlers by submitting itself to Charles I's royal protection and law in 1644. In doing so, the Narragansett declared its sovereignty over its homeland "from time out of mind" while accepting Charles I's current supreme jurisdiction over all the lands claimed by the New England colonies. The Narragansett thus claimed equality with settlers—as subjects of the same king—rather than with England. By contrast, the Mohegan claimed its political equality with England and used that equality to oppose settler authority. Grant-Costa, "The Last Indian War in New England: The Mohegan Indians v. The Governour and Company of the Colony of Connecticut, 1703–1774" (PhD diss., Yale University, 2008), 22–24. For the historical document explaining the Narragansett position, see Adelos Gorton, *The Life and Times of Samuel Gorton* (Philadelphia, 1907), 55.

4. For this history see, for example, Lisa Brooks, *The Common Pot: The Recovery of Native Space in the Northeast* (Minneapolis: University of Minnesota Press, 2008); Mark D. Walters, "Mohegan Indians v. Connecticut (1705–1773) and the Legal Status of Aboriginal Customary Laws and Government in British North America," *Osgoode Hall Law Journal* 33, no. 4 (1995): 785–829; Wendy B. St. Jean, "Inventing Guardianship: The Mohegan Indians and Their 'Protectors,'" *New England Quarterly* 72, no. 3 (1999): 362–87; Amy E. Den Ouden, *Beyond Conquest: Native Peoples and the Struggle for History in New England* (Lincoln: University of Nebraska Press, 2005); and Craig Yirush, "Claiming the New World: Empire, Law, and Indigenous Rights in the Mohegan Case, 1704–1743." *Law and History Review* 29, no. 2 (2011): 333–73.

5. Elizabeth A. Povinelli, *The Cunning of Recognition: Indigenous Alterities and the Making of Australian Multiculturalism* (Durham: Duke University Press, 2002), 156 ("radical"); Samantha Hepburn, "Feudal Tenure and Native Title: Revising an Enduring Fiction," *Sydney Law Review* 27, no. 1 (2005): 53 ("paramount").

6. Jean M. O'Brien, *Firsting and Lasting: Writing Indians Out of Existence in New England* (Minneapolis: University of Minnesota Press, 2010).

7. The charter, Craig Yirush states, "included the Mohegans' territory" within the colony's "boundaries." Yirush, "Claiming the New World," 342.

8. See, for example, "To the Printers in the Colony of Connecticut," *Connecticut Journal*, June 22, 1770; "For the New-London Gazette," *Connecticut Gazette*, April 9, 1773; "To the Public," *Connecticut Journal*, March 25, 1774; and "The Susquehannah Case," in *The Public Records of the Colony of Connecticut*, ed. Charles J. Hoadly (Hartford: Case, Lockwood & Brainard, 1887), 14:445–60.

9. As Wendy B. St. Jean argues, Connecticut governor John Winthrop Jr. believed

that "the colony's royal charter extinguished the sachems' 'native right' to their lands." St. Jean, "Inventing Guardianship," 376.

10. L. Brooks, *The Common Pot*, 67–70; Michael Leroy Oberg, *Uncas: First of the Mohegans* (Ithaca: Cornell University Press, 2003), esp. 153–70; St. Jean, "Inventing Guardianship," 368, 374–78; Den Ouden, *Beyond Conquest*, 91–119; Yirush, "Claiming the New World," 334–73.

11. Joanna Brooks, ed., *The Collected Writings of Samson Occom, Mohegan: Leadership and Literature in Eighteenth-Century Native America* (Oxford: Oxford University Press, 2006), 104. Further references to Occom's writings are to this edition (hereafter cited in text as *CW*). Some scholars date Occom's letter and the end of the land case differently; I use Joanna Brooks's dating of the letter to 1773 because it fits the history of the land case, and I use her dating of Occom's texts throughout this chapter.

12. For an extended analysis of the phrase "poor Indians," see Laura M. Stevens, *The Poor Indians: British Missionaries, Native Americans, and Colonial Sensibility* (Philadelphia: University of Pennsylvania Press, 2004).

13. Ibid., 21. For further discussion of Occom's use of this trope, see David Murray, *Forked Tongues: Speech, Writing, and Representation in North American Indian Texts* (Bloomington: Indiana University Press, 1991), 53–55; Jace Weaver, *That the People Might Live: Native American Literatures and Native American Community* (New York: Oxford University Press, 1997), 51–53; and J. Brooks, *Collected Writings of Samson Occom*, 144.

14. Joseph Johnson, "Joseph Johnson to Gentlemen of New Haven," in *To Do Good to My Indian Brethren: The Writings of Joseph Johnson, 1751–1776*, ed. Laura J. Murray (Amherst: University of Massachusetts Press, 1998), 225. Further references to Johnson's writings are to this edition of *To Do Good* (hereafter cited in text as *TDG*).

15. Laura Murray, "Reading Joseph Johnson," in L. Murray, *To Do Good*, 23.

16. L. Brooks, *The Common Pot*, 72. The slippage I create between "rights" and "liberties" is not accidental. As James A. Hutson shows, the terms *liberty*, *right*, and *privilege* were often used interchangeably in the eighteenth century. Hutson, "The Emergence of the Modern Concept of Rights in America: The Contribution of Michel Villey," in *The Nature of Rights at the American Founding and Beyond*, ed. Barry Alan Shain (Charlottesville: University of Virginia Press, 2007), 25–63, esp. 49–50.

17. Alan Taylor, *The Civil War of 1812: American Citizens, British Subjects, Irish Rebels, and Indian Allies* (New York: Knopf, 2010), Kindle edition, introduction.

18. L. Brooks, *The Common Pot*, 226.

19. David Murray, "Letter of Instruction from Oanhekoe, Sachem of the Mohegan Indians in New England, 14 July 1703," in *Early Native Literacies in New England: A Documentary and Critical Anthology*, ed. Kristina Bross and Hilary E. Wyss (Amherst: University of Massachusetts Press, 2008), 21–27. Murray raises this idea earlier in relation to early Native texts in his *Forked Tongues*, 57.

20. John Wood Sweet, *Bodies Politic: Negotiating Race in the American North, 1730–1830* (Philadelphia: University of Pennsylvania Press, 2007), 173, 178.

21. Brad D. E. Jarvis, *The Brothertown Nation of Indians: Land Ownership and Nationalism in Early America, 1740–1840* (Lincoln: University of Nebraska Press, 2010), 4–5.

22. J. Brooks, *Collected Writings of Samson Occom*, 138–39n153.

23. William Blackstone, *Commentaries on the Laws of England*, bk. 2, 1st ed. (Oxford, 1765), 51. Blackstone repeats the same idea on p. 53.

24. Fae Korsmo, "Claiming Memory in British Columbia: Aboriginal Rights and the State," *American Indian Culture and Research Journal* 20, no. 4 (1996): 72; Taiaiake Alfred, *Peace, Power, Righteousness: An Indigenous Manifesto* (Oxford: Oxford University Press, 1999), 58.

25. Povinelli, *Cunning of Recognition*, 156.

26. Hepburn, "Feudal Tenure and Native Title," 53 (italics in original).

27. Gordon I. Bennett, "Aboriginal Title in the Common Law: A Stony Path through Feudal Doctrine," *Buffalo Law Review* 27 (1977/1978): 632.

28. *Owaneco's Transfer of His Right to the Lands around New London bounds to the Mohegan People*, March 6, 1683/84, record no. 1684.03.06.00, New England Indian Papers Series, Yale Indian Papers Project (hereafter, YIPP), accessed December 30, 2015, http://hdl.handle.net/10079/digcoll/1018181.

29. *Treaty of Hartford*, 1638, record no. 1638.09.21.00, YIPP, accessed December 30, 2015, http://hdl.handle.net/10079/digcoll/2389; *Confirmation Deed of Owaneco to Uncas' Grant to the Colony of Connecticut*, 1689, record no. 1689.06.09.00, YIPP, accessed December 30, 2015, http://hdl.handle.net/10079/digcoll/3434.

30. "The Complaints and Prayer of Oweneco and Ben Uncas" (1700), Ayer MS 671, Edward E. Ayer Manuscript Collection, Newberry Library, Chicago. I am grateful to Leonard Stein for transcribing this text.

31. L. Brooks, *The Common Pot*, 72.

32. Owaneco, "Letter of Instruction from Oanhekoe, Sachem of the Mohegan Indians in New England, 14 July 1703," in *Early Native Literacies in New England*, ed. Kristina Bross and Hilary E. Wyss (Amherst: University of Massachusetts Press, 2008), 19.

33. Mohegan's former archivist Faith Damon Davison interprets the history that Owaneco presents by hypothesizing "that [the pipe] washed up on shore from a deluged ancient Indian site which was buried underwater when the melting of the ice cap in our last ice age raised the level of the Atlantic to a point where it flooded 'Lake Connecticut' (a geologist's term for the shallow freshwater lake that became Long Island Sound) and was treasured by these Mohegans as a 'gift' from the gods." Davison, personal communication, July 10, 2013. This hypothesis would date the finding of the pipe to about 15,000 years ago. Paul Joseph Grant-Costa offers an alternative interpretation that questions Owaneco's representation of historical knowledge: that Mohegans received the pipe as a gift from their English allies. Grant-Costa bases this interpretation on the fact that the pipe was found in Saybrook, the location of early English settlement and English-Mohegan relations; however, this interpretation seems to privilege the site's colonial history over its longer-term significance for Mohegan. See Grant-Costa, "Last Indian War," 60–62.

34. Owaneco, "Letter of Instruction," 20.

35. "The Copy of a Letter from *Oanhekoe, Sachem* of the *Mohegan Indians in New-England*, to Mr. *Nicholas Hallum*," *The Present State of Europe: or, the Historical and Political Monthly Mercury* 15 (March 1704): 140 (italics in original). I am grateful to Faith Damon Davison for discussing Owaneco's pipe with me and for bringing to my attention his sending it to London.

36. Thus, as Allan Greer writes, throughout the chapter on property in the *Two Trea-*

tises, the word "America" carries negative connotations. Greer, "Commons and Enclosure in the Colonization of North America," *American Historical Review* 117, no. 2 (2012): 367.

37. John Locke, *Two Treatises of Government: A Critical Edition with an Introduction and Apparatus Criticus*, ed. Peter Laslett (Cambridge: Cambridge University Press, 1966), 319 (italics in original) (hereafter cited in text as *TT*).

38. Craig Yirush, *Settlers, Liberty, and Empire: The Roots of Early American Political Theory, 1675–1775* (Cambridge: Cambridge University Press, 2011), 128–29.

39. John Bulkley, preface to *Poetical Meditations*, by Roger Wolcott (New London: Green, 1725), xxix, xxx (italics in original).

40. Ibid., xxx, xxxi, liv, lv.

41. Ibid., xlii–xliii.

42. In *An Essay Concerning Human Understanding*, Locke describes the acquisition of knowledge as an interaction between external objects and internal reflection: "The Senses at first let in particular *Ideas*, and furnish the yet empty Cabinet: And the Mind by degrees growing familiar with some of them, they are lodged in the Memory, and Names got to them. Afterwards the Mind proceeding further, abstracts them, and by Degrees learns the use of general Names. In this manner the Mind comes to be furnish'd with *Ideas* and language, and Materials about which to exercise its discursive Faculty." Locke, *An Essay concerning Human Understanding* (1690), ed. Peter H. Nidditch (Oxford: Clarendon, 1979), 55 (hereafter cited in text as *EC*).

43. Locke also includes certain "nations . . . of the most civilized people" among such peoples. Ibid., 70.

44. Caroline Wigginton, "Extending Root and Branch: Community Regeneration in the Petitions of Samson Occom," *Studies in American Indian Literatures* 20, no. 4 (2008): 25.

45. Wigginton suggests that in addition to "charg[ing] the colonists with making the Mohegans worth nothing," Occom's use of the word "Cyphers" "points to Mohegan code language" that colonists must decipher in order to understand, and thus the petition "asserts a cultural identity that is more intelligent, more rhetorically savvy, than its audience." Wigginton, "Extending Root and Branch," 36.

46. As Lisa Brooks explains, "Sachems were responsible for ensuring that access to [tribal] resources was allocated equally among families. . . . The people indigenous to the village held the primary responsibility for maintaining the 'kettle's' environment so that it would continue to sustain them. Their sovereignty rested on this responsibility." L. Brooks, *The Common Pot*, 53. The carets around the word *unworthy*, and later in the paragraph around *us*, represent an interlineation. See J. Brooks, "Note on the Text," in J. Brooks, *Collected Writings of Samson Occom*, xix.

47. See Drew Lopenzina, *Red Ink: Native Americans Picking Up the Pen in the Colonial Period* (Albany: SUNY Press, 2012), 224–34.

48. Lisa Brooks clarifies that "although the Oneidas may not have been acquainted with Occom as an individual, they were well acquainted with the Mohegans as a nation, and Occom's entry into Iroquoia was already grounded in alliance." L. Brooks, *The Common Pot*, 88.

49. See Linford D. Fisher, *The Indian Great Awakening: Religion and the Shaping of Native Cultures in Early America* (Oxford: Oxford University Press, 2012), 147–63.

50. Quoted in James Axtell, *The European and the Indian: Essays in the Ethnohistory of Colonial North America* (New York: Oxford University Press, 1981), 98, 95. Mohegan and other scholars hold different views of Mohegan-Haudenosaunee relations. Mohegan tribal historian Melissa Jayne Fawcett traces Mohegan spatial history to a remote past in which the tribe resided in what we may call Haudenosaunee country, and this information appears on the official website of the Mohegan Tribe. See Fawcett, *The Lasting of the Mohegans*, part 1, *The Story of the Wolf People* (Uncasville, CT: Mohegan Tribe, 1995), 10, 8; Mohegan Tribe website, accessed January 24, 2016, http://www.mohegan.nsn.us/heritage/our-history. By contrast, historian Michael Leroy Oberg insists that "[n]either linguistic not archaeological data" shows that Mohegans collectively resided anywhere except "Connecticut for several centuries prior to their first contact with Europeans," and former Mohegan archivist Faith Damon Davison supports his claim. Oberg, *Uncas*, 16; Davison, personal communication, August 21, 2013.

51. See Laura J. Murray, "Pray Sir, Consider a Little: Rituals of Subordination and Strategies of Resistance in the Letters of Hezekiah Calvin and David Fowler to Eleazar Wheelock," in *Early Native American Writing: New Critical Essays*, ed. Helen Jaskoski (Cambridge: Cambridge University Press, 1996); and D. Murray, *Forked Tongues*, 49–51.

52. Samuel Kirkland, "Samuel Kirkland to Eleazar Wheelock," in L. Murray, *To Do Good*, 78, 77.

53. St. Jean concludes her article on the establishment of the guardianship system by reminding her readers, "As the Mohegans' power declined, colonists transformed the guardianship system into an instrument of colonial dominance." St. Jean, "Inventing Guardianship," 387.

54. All biblical passages refer to the King James Version.

55. Drew Lopenzina states that "in his personal writings and letters to other Natives," Johnson "never resorts to the obsequious tones adopted in his letters to whites." Lopenzina, *Red Ink*, 308.

56. Lisa Brooks defines such processes as the replacement of colonial "dismemberment" of Native lands and communities with "re-memberment." L. Brooks, *The Common Pot*, 90–100.

57. The dating is that of Joanna Brooks, who notes that in this text Occom quotes from "John Hawkesworth, James Cook, and Joseph Banks' *A New Voyage Round the World*," published in 1774. J. Brooks, *Collected Writings of Samson Occom*, 227n85.

58. Occom's inversion of Eurocentric assumptions regarding civilization and religion preceded Equiano's similar ideas, discussed in chapter 1. Equiano might have seen Occom; both men were in Britain between September 1767 and July 1768, when Occom made numerous public appearances in order to raise money for Wheelock's school. Occom and Equiano were associated with the same evangelical milieu that promoted the conversion of African-descended people and Indians. See Carretta, *Equiano, the African*, 135–75; and J. Brooks, "Chronology," in *Collected Writings of Samson Occom*, xxiii.

59. Olaudah Equiano, *The Interesting Narrative of the Life of Olaudah Equiano, the African. Written by himself* (1789–94), in *Olaudah Equiano, The Interesting Narrative and Other Writings*, rev. ed., ed. Vincent Carretta (New York: Penguin, 2003), 61.

60. In *The Collected Writings*, Joanna Brooks dates this petition tentatively to 1785, but in *Early Native Literacies* she revises its dating, suggesting that it might have been written in "April 1788." J. Brooks, "Brotherton Tribe to United States Congress," in J. Brooks,

Collected Writings of Samson Occom, 150; J. Brooks, "'This Indian World': A Petition/Origin Story from Samson Occom and the Montaukett Tribe," in *Early Native Literacies in New England: A Documentary and Critical Anthology*, ed. Kristina Bross and Hilary E. Wyss (Amherst: University of Massachusetts Press, 2008), 215.

61. J. Brooks, "Mohegan and Niantic Tribes to the Connecticut Assembly," in J. Brooks, *Collected Writings of Samson Occom*, 148n7.

62. Isaac Watts, *The Works of the Rev. Isaac Watts, D.D. in Nine Volumes* (London: Edward Baines, 1813), 9:174, 177.

63. Lopenzina, *Red Ink*, 303.

64. J. Brooks, *American Lazarus*, 69.

65. I am grateful to Carleen Mandolfo for confirming that Johnson's apostrophe seems inspired by Lamentations 1 and for pointing me to particular verses. Laura Murray writes that despite the many "biblically cadenced phrases" in that apostrophe, "particular sources have proven elusive." L. Murray, "Th[u]rsday the 17th of December AD 1772," in L. Murray, *To Do Good*, 160n*.

66. John Calvin, *Commentaries on the Prophet Jeremiah and the Lamentations*, trans. and ed. John Owen (Grand Rapids: Christian Classic Ethereal Library, 1993), PDF ebook, 5:305, http://www.ccel.org. All subsequent quotations from Calvin are from this source (hereafter cited in text as *CPJ*).

67. Lisa Brooks's entire analysis of Occom's involvement in the land case emphasizes the fact that the early alliances between Mohegan and colonists did not protect the tribe from colonial dispossession. See L. Brooks, *The Common Pot*, 51–105.

68. Prominent among such usages are references to "precious stones" (*avanim yekarot*), "precious things" (*migdanot*), "precious ointment" (*shemen tov*), and "precious in the sight of the Lord" (*yakar be'eyney adonay*).

69. "On the Memorial of Joseph Johnson, a Mohegan Indian," *Public Records of the Colony of Connecticut*, 14:314. As Laura Murray notes, the assembly's decision is "oddly dated May 1774." L. Murray, "Johnson to Connecticut Assembly," in L. Murray, *To Do Good*, 236n.

70. The name Brothertown would be given to the settlement following Johnson's death and the Revolutionary War. Since Johnson negotiated the project with Sir William Johnson in Mohawk Country, he referred to it as the "Mohawk Affair." Joseph Johnson et al., "To the Indians Concerning Oneida Lands," in L. Murray, *To Do Good*, 203.

71. Laura Murray writes that "'Yokeag,' dried corn roasted and ground, was a Mohegan staple." L. Murray, "Farmington Indians," in L. Murray, *To Do Good*, 200n.

Chapter 3: Spaces of Slavery and Freedom

1. For a database of petitions regarding slavery, see the Digital Library on American Slavery, accessed May 22, 2013, http://library.uncg.edu/slavery.

2. Gary B. Nash, *Race and Revolution* (Lanham, MD: Rowman & Littlefield, 1990), 58.

3. Ads mention other kinds of information quite consistently, including dates and places of absconding; names, physical descriptions, and ages of fugitives; rewards that slaveholders might have offered captors; and warnings against harboring fugitives. In their study of runaway ads, John Hope Franklin and Loren Schweninger state that when Louisiana slaveowners "described slaves as 'American creole,' 'American mulatto,' 'Amer-

ican negro,' they were pointing not only to their American birth but to English as their principal language." Franklin and Schweninger, *Runaway Slaves: Rebels on the Plantation* (Oxford: Oxford University Press, 1999), Kindle edition, chap. 9.

4. Veracini, *Settler Colonialism*, 82.

5. Herbert Aptheker, ed., *A Documentary History of the Negro People in the United States* (New York: Carol Publishing, 1990), 1:6 (further references to primary texts from this volume are hereafter cited in text as *DH*; all italics are in original text unless otherwise noted). On Holbrook's free status, see Douglas R. Egerton, *Death or Liberty: African Americans and Revolutionary America* (Oxford: Oxford University Press, 2009), 58.

6. Sidney Kaplan and Emma Nogrady Kaplan, *The Black Presence in the Era of the American Revolution* (Amherst: University of Massachusetts Press, 1989), 11. Douglas R. Edgerton writes that "[s]laves . . . could not help being politicized by the [rebels'] language of protest." Egerton, *Death or Liberty*, 43. Antonio T. Bly argues that slaves "adopted the revolutionary rhetoric of the day." Antonio T. Bly, introduction to *Escaping Bondage: A Documentary History of Runaway Slaves in Eighteenth-Century New England, 1700–1789*, ed. Antonio T. Bly (Lanham, MD: Lexington Books, 2012), Kindle edition.

7. Manisha Sinha, *The Slave's Cause: A History of Abolition* (New Haven: Yale University Press, 2016), 4, 41, 42.

8. Kaplan and Kaplan, *Black Presence*, 11.

9. Benjamin Rush, *Address to the Inhabitants of the British Settlements in America, upon Slave-Keeping* (Philadelphia: John Dunlap, 1773), 22–23.

10. Dorothy Porter, introduction to Part 4 of *Early Negro Writing, 1760–1837*, ed. Dorothy Porter (Boston: Beacon Press, 1971), 249.

11. James Otis, *The Rights of the British Colonies Asserted and Proved*, 3rd ed. (London: Williams and Almon, 1766), 37 (hereafter cited in text as *RBC*; all italics are in original text unless otherwise noted).

12. "Petition for freedom to Massachusetts Governor Thomas Hutchinson, His Majesty's Council, and the House of Representatives, June 1773," Collections Online, Massachusetts Historical Society, accessed May 23, 2013, http://www.masshist.org/database/558.

13. *Journal of the Honorable House of Representatives of His Majesty's Province of the Massachusetts-Bay, in New-England*, May 26–June 29, 1773, 85. The petition was referred to a committee that eventually proposed a "Bill to prevent the Importation of Negroes into this Province," but the colony's governor did not enact it into law. *Journal of the Honorable House of Representatives*, January 26–March 9, 1774, 224. See also George W. Williams, *History of the Negro Race in America from 1619 to 1880* (New York: Putnam's Sons, 1883), 1:233–37. Kaplan and Kaplan write that the request for colonial land emerged a year later, in June 1774 (*Black Presence*, 15), but the Massachusetts *Journal* lists this discussion a year earlier.

14. "Petition for freedom to Massachusetts Governor Thomas Gage, His Majesty's Council, and the House of Representatives, June 1774," Collections Online, Massachusetts Historical Society, accessed May 26, 2013, http://www.masshist.org/database/550.

15. "For the *Massachusetts Spy*," *Massachusetts Spy*, January 28, 1773, 199. Holbrook's first petition gained further publicity when it was published in a pseudonymously authored pamphlet, *The Appendix: Or, Some Observations on the Expediency of the Petition of the Africans*, by a Lover of Constitutional Liberty (Boston: E. Russell, 1773).

The pamphlet includes both the petition and a redacted version of the *Massachusetts Spy* piece. The charter's words are somewhat different: "all and every the Subjects of Us, our Heires or Successors, which shall goe to and inhabite within the saide Landes and Premisses hereby mentioned to be graunted, and every of their Children which shall happen to be borne there, or on the Seas in goeing thither, or retorning from thence, shall have and enjoy all liberties and Immunities of free and naturall Subjects within any of the Domynions of Us, our Heires or Successors, to all Intents, Constructions, and Purposes whatsoever, as if they and everie of them were borne within the Realme of England." "Charter of Massachusetts Bay 1629," *American History: From Revolution to Reconstruction and Beyond*, accessed November 1, 2016, http://www.let.rug.nl/usa.

16. "For the *Massachusetts Spy*," 199 (italics in original).

17. "Petition for freedom (manuscript copy) to the Massachusetts Council and the House of Representatives, [13] January 1777," Collections Online, Massachusetts Historical Society, accessed May 29, 2013, http://masshist.org/database/557. For the list of signatories, see Kaplan and Kaplan, *Black Presence*, 26.

18. Petition by Nero Brester, and others, *New Hampshire Gazette*, July 15, 1780, 1.

19. Ibid.

20. On Holbrook, see Randall M. Miller and John David Smith, eds., *Dictionary of Afro-American Slavery*, updated ed. (Westport: Praeger, 1997), 336. On Hall, see James Sidbury, *Becoming African in America: Race and Nation in the Early Black Atlantic* (Oxford: Oxford University Press, 2007), 74.

21. Kaplan and Kaplan, *Black Presence*, 209.

22. Joanna Brooks, *American Lazarus: Religion and the Rise of African-American and Native American Literatures* (Oxford: Oxford University Press, 2003), 116.

23. Ibid., 122.

24. Kaplan and Kaplan, *Black Presence*, 205

25. Richard S. Newman, Roy E. Finkenbine, and Douglass Mooney, "Philadelphia Emigrationist Petition, Circa 1792: An Introduction," *William and Mary Quarterly*, 3rd ser., 64, no. 1 (2007): 163.

26. For studies that use the ads as evidence for statistical information on life under slavery, see Freddie L. Parker, *Running for Freedom: Slave Runaways in North Carolina, 1775–1840* (New York: Garland, 1993); Franklin and Schweninger, *Runaway Slaves*; and Bly, introduction to *Escaping Bondage*.

27. David Waldstreicher, "Reading the Runaways: Self-Fashioning, Print Culture, and Confidence in Slavery in the Eighteenth-Century Mid-Atlantic," *William and Mary Quarterly* 56, no. 2 (1999): 243–72.

28. *Pennsylvania Gazette*, January 23, 1750, 4. For similar instances of this phrase in ads for escaped prisoners and fugitive apprentices, see the *Pennsylvania Gazette* issues of December 18, 1750 (p. 3), June 13, 1751 (p. 6), and February 25, 1752 (p. 3).

29. *City Gazette*, March 20, 1812, 1.

30. Mark Rifkin, *Settler Common Sense: Queerness and Everyday Colonialism in the American Renaissance* (Minneapolis: University of Minnesota Press, 2014), 9.

31. Ibid., 24.

32. Tom W. Shick, *Behold the Promised Land: A History of Afro-American Settler Society in Nineteenth-Century Liberia* (Baltimore: Johns Hopkins University Press, 1977), 10–11. See also Herbert S. Klein, *A Population History of the United States* (Cambridge:

Cambridge University Press, 2004), 83–85. Shick and Klein base their analyses partially on Robert William Fogel and Stanley L. Engerman's *Time on the Cross: The Economics of American Negro Slavery* (Boston: Little, Brown, 1974).

33. "A Horse and Chair for Sale," *City Gazette*, January 21, 1813. The ad's title did not refer to the slaves, yet they were listed by A. H. M'Gillivray, who placed the ad, as an additional item he intended to sell.

34. "CUFFEE ranaway," *City Gazette*, June 9, 1820, 3.

35. "Ten Dollars Reward," *Federal Republican*, January 7, 1814, 1.

36. On the sources of *partus sequitur ventrem*, see Thomas D. Morris, "'Villeinage . . . as it existed in England, reflects but little on our subject': The Problem of the 'Sources' of Southern Slave Law," *American Journal of Legal History* 32, no. 2 (1988): esp. 108–9.

37. Parker, *Running for Freedom*, 190.

38. "Twenty Dollars Reward," *Republican Gazette*, May 13, 1803, 1.

39. "TEN POUNDS REWARD," *Maryland Journal*, January 6, 1786, 3. I used a 1795 map against Google Maps to calculate the distances. "The States of Maryland and Delaware from the Latest Surveys," map (New York: D. Martin, 1795), accessed November 6, 2016, http://www.lib.utexas.edu/maps/historical/heads_of_families/txu-pclmaps-heads-of-families-maryland-and-delaware-1795.jpg.

40. "Twenty Dollars Reward," *City Gazette*, September 3, 1821, 1.

41. Ibid.

42. "Ten Dollars Reward," *City Gazette*, April 23, 1813, 1.

43. "One Hundred Dollars Reward," *New York Gazette*, April 21, 1810, 3.

44. "100 Dollars Reward," *Frederick Town Herald*, April 21, 1810, in "Beneath the Underground: The Flight to Freedom and Communities in Maryland," Maryland State Archives (hereafter, MSA), accessed July 2, 2013, http://msa.maryland.gov/megafile/msa/speccol/sc5400/sc5496/runaway_advertisements/pdf/18100421fth2.pdf.

45. "Fifty Dollars Reward," *Federal Republican*, October 28, 1811. The ad ran until December 31, 1811, but seems not to have been renewed in 1812.

46. "Five Pounds Reward," *Maryland Gazette*, April 10, 1766, MSA, accessed July 2, 2013, http://msa.maryland.gov/megafile/msa/speccol/sc5400/sc5496/runaway_advertisements/pdf/17660410mdg1.pdf.

47. "Was Committed," *Federal Republican*, March 17, 1813, 4.

48. "Was Committed," *Alexandria Herald*, July 19, 1820, 4.

49. "Ran Away," *American and Commercial Daily Advertiser*, July 5, 1808, MSA, accessed July 2, 2013, http://msa.maryland.gov/megafile/msa/speccol/sc5400/sc5496/runaway_advertisements/pdf/18080705acda1.pdf.

50. "Second Municipality Council," *Southern Patriot*, June 17, 1840, 2.

51. Taylor, *Civil War of 1812*, introduction.

52. See Gordon Wood, *The Radicalism of the American Revolution* (New York: Vintage, 1992).

53. In 1740, the influential evangelical leader George Whitefield clarified in his "Letter to the Inhabitants of Maryland, Virginia, North and South Carolina" that "hewers of wood and drawers of water" were "slaves like yours." Whitefield, *The Works of the Reverend George Whitefield* (London: Edward and Charles Dilly, 1771), 4:39. In 1766, Quaker abolitionist Anthony Benezet quoted Whitefield to remind his readers of that analogy. Benezet, *A Caution and Warning to Great Britain and Her Colonies* (Philadel-

phia: Henry Miller, 1776), 11. On the broader interracial class connotations of the phrase in Britain (and later in the United States) following the publication of the King James Bible (1611), see Peter Linebaugh and Marcus Rediker, *The Many-Headed Hydra: Sailors, Slaves, Commoners, and the Hidden History of the Revolutionary Atlantic* (London: Verso, 2000), 36–70.

54. *Republican Advocate*, December 10, 1802, 2.

55. *Republican Advocate*, December 17, 1802, 2 (italics in original).

56. A Citizen of Baltimore [pseud.], *Observations on the Impressment of American Seamen* (Baltimore: G. Dobbin & Murphy, 1806), 39 (hereafter cited in text as *OI*).

57. "Expatriation," *City Gazette*, June 23, 1812, 3.

58. Richard Rush, "An Oration, Delivered by Richard Rush, Esq. on the 4th of July, 1812," *Weekly Aurora*, July 28, 1812, 95 (hereafter cited in text as RR).

Chapter 4: Unsettling Birthrights

1. On US official discussions of Spanish, French, and British relations with Indian nations, see the report that Indian commissioners Benjamin Hawkins, Andrew Pickens, Joseph Martin, and Laughlin McIntosh submitted to secretary of war Henry Knox on December 2, 1785. *The New American State Papers: Indian Affairs* (Wilmington, DE: Scholarly Resources, 1972), 6:46–47. On Spain's relations with the Creek, Choctaw, and Chickasaw nations in the mid-1780s, see Francis Paul Prucha, *American Indian Treaties: The History of a Political Anomaly* (Berkeley: University of California Press, 1994), 9.

2. See Eliga H. Gould, *Among the Powers of the Earth: The American Revolution and the Making of a New World Empire* (Cambridge, MA: Harvard University Press, 2012).

3. See, for example, "Treaty with the Six Nations, 1784" (also known as the Treaty of Fort Stanwix), "Treaty with the Cherokee, 1785," "Treaty with the Choctaw, 1786," and "Treaty with the Chickasaw, 1786," all in *Indian Affairs: Laws and Treaties*, vol. 2, *Treaties*, comp. and ed. Charles J. Kappler (Washington, DC: Government Printing Office, 1904), accessed November 23, 2016, http://digital.library.okstate.edu/kappler/vol2/tocyr.htm.

4. For three recent studies, see Michael Witgen, *An Infinity of Nations: How the Native New World Shaped Early North America* (Philadelphia: University of Pennsylvania Press, 2012); Stephen Warren, *The Worlds the Shawnees Made: Migration and Violence in Early America* (Chapel Hill: University of North Carolina Press, 2014); and Michael McDonnell, *Masters of Empire: Great Lakes Indians and the Making of America* (New York: Hill and Wang, 2015).

5. Gregory Evans Dowd, *A Spirited Resistance: The North American Indian Struggle for Unity, 1745–1815* (Baltimore: Johns Hopkins University Press, 1993), 59. On the earlier confederation, see Colin G. Calloway, *Pen and Ink Witchcraft: Treaties and Treaty Making in American Indian History* (Oxford: Oxford University Press, 2013), Kindle edition, chap. 2. As Calloway explains, kinship terms "constituted a system of establishing the rights and obligations of the parties vis-à-vis one another and they conveyed real messages" (chap. 1). On the significance of kinship, see Robert A. Williams Jr., *Linking Arms Together: American Indian Treaty Visions of Law and Peace, 1600–1800* (New York: Oxford University Press, 1997), 71–74.

6. Alan Taylor, *The Divided Ground: Indians, Settlers, and the Northern Borderland of the American Revolution* (New York: Knopf, 2006), 116. For an analysis of the US

confederacy versus this Algonquian-Haudenosaunee one, see Richard White, *The Middle Ground: Indians, Empires, and Republics in the Great Lakes Region, 1650–1815* (Cambridge: Cambridge University Press, 1991), 413–68.

7. L. Brooks, *The Common Pot*, 122 (my italics).

8. Williams, *Linking Arms Together*, 114, 84, 70.

9. Daniel Heath Justice, "'Go Away, Water!': Kinship Criticism and the Decolonization Imperative," in *Reasoning Together: The Native Critics Collective*, ed. Craig S. Womack, Daniel Heath Justice, and Christopher B. Teuton (Norman: University of Oklahoma Press, 2008), 150.

10. Daniel Heath Justice, *Our Fire Survives the Storm: A Cherokee Literary History* (Minneapolis: University of Minnesota Press, 2006), 23–4. See also Andrea Smith, "American Studies without America: Native Feminisms and the Nation-State," *American Quarterly* 60, no. 2 (2008): 309–15.

11. L. Brooks, *The Common Pot*, 124.

12. McMurray, William, and Robert Scot, "The United States according to the definitive treaty of peace signed at Paris Sept. 3d. 1783," map (n.p., 1784), Library of Congress, accessed December 10, 2016, https://www.loc.gov/item/gm71005423/.

13. Mishuana Goeman, *Mark My Words: Native Women Mapping Our Nations* (Minneapolis: University of Minnesota Press, 2013), 18.

14. For a discussion of this idea in the context of contemporary Mohawk politics, see Audra Simpson, *Mohawk Interruptus: Political Life across the Borders of Settler States* (Durham: Duke University Press, 2014).

15. I derive this idea, which I discuss below, from Thongchai Winichakul, *Siam Mapped: A History of the Geo-Body of a Nation* (Honolulu: University of Hawai'i Press, 1994).

16. Scott Richard Lyons, *X-Marks: Native Signatures of Assent* (Minneapolis: University of Minnesota Press, 2010), 1.

17. Simpson, *Mohawk Interruptus*, 106.

18. Prucha writes that the 1794 Treaty of Canandaigua "was the last treaty with the Iroquois in which the American commissioners followed the ancient forms of the native protocol. After that the United States no longer felt bound to observe the Indian customs." But, as Prucha writes, as late as 1818, US commissioners were still bound to respect certain Indian expectations such as gift giving as a condition for signing treaties, and as late as 1851, Indian nations still practiced participatory (rather than representative) governance when "some ten thousand Indians" of the Sioux, Cheyenne, Arapaho, Crow, Assiniboine, Gros Ventre, Mandan, and Arikara came to participate in negotiations for the Treaty of Fort Lamarie. Prucha, *American Indian Treaties*, 95, 138, 238.

19. Goeman, *Mark My Words*, 39.

20. *City of Sherrill v. Oneida Indian Nation of New York* (03-855) 544 US 197 (2005), 337 F.3d 139, reversed and remanded, http://www.law.cornell.edu/supct/html/03-855.ZO.html.

21. Mark Rifkin, *Manifesting America: The Imperial Construction of U.S. National Space* (Oxford: Oxford University Press, 2009), 5.

22. Kevin Bruyneel, *The Third Space of Sovereignty: The Postcolonial Politics of U.S.-Indigenous Relations* (Minneapolis: University of Minnesota Press, 2007), 208–9.

23. Kathryn E. Fort, "Disruption and Impossibility: The New Laches and the Unfor-

tunate Resolution of the Modern Iroquois Land Claims," *Wyoming Law Review* 11, no. 2 (2011): 375–405.

24. *New American State Papers: Indian Affairs*, 6:52 (hereafter cited in text as *NASPIA*).

25. Patrick Wolfe, "Settler Colonialism and the Elimination of the Native," *Journal of Genocide Research* 8, no. 4 (2006): 388.

26. James Riding In, "Reservations," in *Encyclopedia of North American Indians*, ed. Frederick E. Hoxie (Boston: Houghton Mifflin Harcourt, 1996).

27. Benedict Anderson, *Imagined Communities: Reflections on the Origin and Spread of Nationalism*, rev. ed. (London: Verso, 1991), 175, quoted in Martin Brückner, *The Geographic Revolution in Early America: Maps, Literacy, and National Identity* (Chapel Hill: University of North Carolina Press, 2006), 134; Winichakul, *Siam Mapped*.

28. That region, including "Senekaw" and "Old Chota" (Tassel's hometown), appears on Charles C. Royce's map of Cherokee and Chickasaw land cessions, "Tennessee and Portions of Bordering States," which was published in 1887, accessed July 2, 2014, http://usgwarchives.net/maps/cessions/ilcmap54.htm.

29. L. Brooks, *The Common Pot*, 122.

30. US officials heard similar assertions of indigeneity as a condition of empowering attachment to land from other Native negotiators. Five years later when Seneca leaders Cornplanter, Half-Town, and Great-Tree came to Philadelphia to seek restitution from George Washington, Joseph Nicholson translated their words thus: "The land we live on, our fathers received from God, and they transmitted it to us, for our children, and we cannot part with it" (*NASPIA* 4:25). Referring to a particular area they had lost to Pennsylvania, they added that "Half-Town and all his people . . . grew out of this land, and their fathers' fathers grew out of it, and they cannot be persuaded to part with it" (*NASPIA* 4:27). Two years later, Odawa leader Egushawa critiqued those US officials who believed "that we red people, who grew out of the soil we hunt upon, never had any right to it; nor to any part of the country which God planted us in, more than the buffaloes which were given to us by God." *Minutes of Debates in Council on the Banks of the Ottawa River, (Commonly Called the Miamia of the Lake) November 1791, Said to be Held there by the Chiefs of the Several Indian Nations, Who Defeated the Army of the United States, on the 4th of that Month* (Philadelphia: William Young, 1792), 12.

31. "Extract of a Letter from Seneca, Nov. —, 1785," *Maryland Republican and Baltimore Advertiser*, January 17, 1786, 2.

32. A Citizen of Baltimore, *Observations on the Impressment of American Seamen* (Baltimore: G. Dobbin & Murphy, 1806), 17.

33. "Extract of a Letter from Seneca."

34. Prucha, *American Indian Treaties*, 50, 61.

35. Francis Paul Prucha, *The Great Father: The United States Government and the American Indians*, 2 vols. (Lincoln: Nebraska University Press, 1984), 43–44.

36. Bruyneel, *Third Space of Sovereignty*, 6. For an ethnographic discussion of contemporary border politics, see Simpson, *Mohawk Interruptus*, esp. chap. 5.

37. For an analysis of the settler historical logic that made such beliefs possible, see Jean M. O'Brien, *Firsting and Lasting: Writing Indians Out of Existence in New England* (Minneapolis: University of Minnesota Press, 2010). For an earlier study of disappearance, see Brian W. Dippie, *The Vanishing American: White Attitudes and U.S. Indian Policy* (Middletown, CT: Wesleyan University Press, 1982).

38. Prucha quotes George Washington's 1784 assessment of the "rage for speculating in . . . Lands on the No. West side of Ohio": settlers "roam over the Country on the Indian side of the Ohio, mark out lands, Survey, and even settle them." Prucha, *The Great Father*, 45.

39. McMurray and Scot, "United States," map, Library of Congress.

40. Tassel and Tuskegatahee worked on the map with other Cherokee negotiators; their team might have included some or all other participants at the Hopewell negotiations, of whom the record names Nanyehi, Unsuckanail, Chescoenwhee, Tuckasee, Oonanootee, and Nowota.

41. The commissioners first asked Tassel on November 23 to chart the Cherokee boundary and repeated their request the next day. He complied on November 25 (*NASPIA* 6:50–51).

42. Mark Warhus, *Another America: Native American Maps and the History of Our Land* (New York: St. Martin's Press, 1997), 3. (Warhus discusses Tassel and Tuskegatahee's map on pp. 147–50.) For a critique of Warhus's implicit relegation of Native oral maps to the past, see Goeman, *Mark My Words*, 25.

43. Goeman, *Mark My Words*, 37; L. Brooks, *The Common Pot*, 124.

44. This area lies to the east-northeast of present-day Knoxville, Tennessee. Three years later, US commissioner Richard Winn wrote Knox that the Cherokees were fighting against settlers in that area (*NASPIA* 6:33).

45. "Treaty with the Cherokee, 1785," in Kappler, *Indian Affairs*, vol. 2, accessed January 5, 2017, http://digital.library.okstate.edu/kappler/VOL2/treaties/che0008.htm.

46. Justice, *Our Fire Survives*, 41.

47. Williams, *Linking Arms Together*, 116.

48. John Mohawk, "Thoughts of Peace: The Great Law," in *Thinking in Indian: A John Mohawk Reader*, ed. José Barreiro (Golden, CO: Fulcrum, 2010), 241.

49. The proclamation of September 1, 1788, is available in the *Journals of the Continental Congress*, 34:476–79, Library of Congress, accessed June 22, 2014, http://memory.loc.gov/ammem/amlaw/lwjc.html.

50. Lisa Brooks shows that prior to meeting negotiators, Brant tried to persuade the confederacy to compromise on the Muskingum River as its boundary with the United States (and to recognize US sovereignty over some of the lands north of the Ohio), but his efforts were frustrated by British officials who promoted the Ohio River boundary in the hope of using the Native nations as a "buffer zone between Canada and the United States." L. Brooks, *The Common Pot*, 155.

51. This quotation appears in an excerpt from Jefferson's letter in Francis Paul Prucha, ed., *Documents of United States Indian Policy*, 3rd ed. (Lincoln: University of Nebraska Press, 2000), 22.

52. "Treaty with the Shawnee, 1786," in Kappler, *Indian Affairs*, vol. 2, accessed September 8, 2013, http://digital.library.okstate.edu/kappler/vol2/treaties/sha0016.htm.

53. *Minutes of Debates in Council*, 9 (hereafter cited in text as *MD*; all italics are in original text unless otherwise noted). The text identifies the speaker as "Gush-gush-a-gwa," and I am following Colin G. Calloway in calling him Egushawa. See Calloway, *Pen and Ink Witchcraft*, chap. 3.

54. Colin G. Calloway, *The American Revolution in Indian Country: Crisis and Diversity in Native American Communities* (Cambridge: Cambridge University Press, 1995),

175; Ebenezer Denny, *Military Journal of Major Ebenezer Denny: An Officer in the Revolutionary and Indian Wars* (Philadelphia: Lippincott, 1859), 73. Francis Paul Prucha states that primary sources include conflicting reports of the negotiations. Egushawa's speech indicates that Denny's account reflects what these negotiations meant for at least some Odawa and Shawnee participants. Prucha, *American Indian Treaties*, 52n25. On wampum symbolism, see Calloway, *Pen and Ink Witchcraft*, chap. 1.

55. See also Denny, *Military Journal*, 73.

56. When Proctor (whose name is spelled Procter in the record) submitted his report to secretary of war Henry Knox, he admitted to have "transgressed, in blending any matters of opinion or of observation" with "that which immediately had relation to business" (*NASPIA* 4:35).

57. For a study of St. Clair's defeat, see Colin G. Calloway, *The Victory with No Name: The Native American Defeat of the First American Army* (Oxford: Oxford University Press, 2014).

58. On Brant's authorship of the written speech, see L. Brooks, *The Common Pot*, 122.

59. Ibid., 121.

60. Ibid., 122.

61. Calloway writes that in the early republic, treaties became "instruments for transferring land to American ownership." Calloway, *Pen and Ink Witchcraft*, chap. 3.

62. "An Ordinance for the government of the territory of the United States North West of the river Ohio," July 13, 1787, *Journals of the Continental Congress*, 32:334–35, 337, 340–41, Library of Congress, accessed August 7, 2013, http://memory.loc.gov/ammem/amlaw/lwjc.html.

63. Knox instructed the commissioners to "endeavor, as far as shall be consistent with the main design of peace, to form separate contracts, or treaties, relatively to boundaries, with the several tribes to whom the lands actually belong, avoiding, as much as possible, to confirm the idea of an union, or general confederacy of all the tribes, or of any patronage of the whole over the lands of any particular tribes, or subdivisions of tribes" (*NASPIA* 4:121).

64. See L. Brooks, *The Common Pot.*

65. On Haudenosaunee condolence ceremonies, see Taiaiake Alfred, *Peace, Power, Righteousness: An Indigenous Manifesto* (Oxford: Oxford University Press, 1999), xii. On Anishnaabe covering of the dead, see Joseph Bauerkemper and Heidi Kiiwetinepinesiik Stark, "The Trans/National Terrain of Anishinaabe Law and Diplomacy," *Journal of Transnational American Studies* 4, no. 1 (2012): 1–21.

66. For an analysis of the New Age trend, see Shari M. Huhndorf, *Going Native: Indians in the American Cultural Imagination* (Ithaca: Cornell University Press, 2001).

Chapter 5: Ancestral Blood

1. By 1817, Locke's ideas and texts had been popularly influential in the United States for some time. On the function of Locke's *Second Treaties* in the Revolutionary era, see Eric Slauter, "Reading and Radicalization: Print, Politics, and the American Revolution," *Early American Studies* 8, no. 1 (2010): 5–40. Locke's works were sold in US bookstores in the early nineteenth century; in 1818, Philadelphia bookseller Abraham Small advertised his collection, including "The works of John Locke, in ten volumes, 8vo. the eleventh edition." *Franklin Gazette*, November 4, 1818, 3. In *Johnson v. M'Intosh* (1823), US Chief

Justice Marshall relied on Locke's *Two Treatises* to argue that Indians had no property in the land and therefore could not sell it directly to settlers. In 1829, newspapers reported of "Newly discovered MSS. Of Locke.—A bundle of old manuscripts has lately come into the possession of a gentleman in Boreham, in Essex, (England,) which turn out to be original letters and writings of the illustrious John Locke." *National Journal*, April 18, 1829, 3. And in 1830, newspapers advertised the publication of a new issue of the *Edinburgh Review*, which contained an article entitled "Life of John Locke." *National Journal*, March 13, 1830, 4.

2. Carole Pateman, "The Settler Contract," in Carole Pateman and Charles W. Mills, *Contract and Domination* (Cambridge: Polity, 2007), 39, 56.

3. Jodi A. Byrd, *The Transit of Empire: Indigenous Critiques of Colonialism* (Minneapolis: University of Minnesota Press, 2011); Shona N. Jackson, *Creole Indigeneity: Between Myth and Nation in the Caribbean* (Minneapolis: University of Minnesota Press, 2011).

4. Orlando Patterson, *Slavery and Social Death: A Comparative Study* (Cambridge, MA: Harvard University Press, 1982), 51.

5. "Montgomery: Communication," *City Gazette*, May 30, 1812.

6. "Moral Department," *Vermont Republican*, August 3, 1818, 4.

7. James Forten et al., "A Voice from Philadelphia," reprinted in William Lloyd Garrison, *Thoughts on African Colonization; Or, An Impartial Exhibition of the Doctrines, Principles and Purposes of the American Colonization Society. Together with the Resolutions, Addresses and Remonstrances of the Free People of Color* (Boston: Garrison and Knapp, 1832), 2:9. Some of these names are spelled differently in different sources; I am using Garrison's spellings.

8. References to Africa's sands as inhospitable and sometimes "burning" spaces appeared in numerous early nineteenth-century newspaper articles and poems.

9. See James Oliver Horton and Lois E. Horton, *In Hope of Liberty: Culture, Community, and Protest among Northern Free Blacks, 1700–1860* (New York: Oxford University Press, 1997), 187–88, 306n29.

10. James Forten, "A Late Bill before the Senate of Pennsylvania" (1813), in *Negro Orators and Their Orations*, ed. Carter G. Woodson (1925; repr. New York: Russell and Russell, 1969), 47.

11. Trish Loughran argues that during the 1830s white abolitionists began circulating textual and other commodities that "proved" that "the North, the South, and the West were one." Loughran, *The Republic in Print: Print Culture in the Age of U.S. Nation Building, 1770–1870* (New York: Columbia University Press, 2007), 328. Jennifer Rae Greeson similarly locates this process in 1830s abolitionist and temperance print culture that linked crime and prostitution in the North to slavery in the South. Greeson, *Our South: Geographic Fantasy and the Rise of National Literature* (Cambridge, MA: Harvard University Press, 2012), Kindle edition, chap. 5. David Waldstreicher attributes a similar role to the ACS: "No voluntary association, even in that great age of voluntary associations, ever had a more auspicious, or a more national, beginning." Waldstreicher, *In the Midst of Perpetual Fetes: The Making of American Nationalism, 1776–1820* (Chapel Hill: University of North Carolina Press, 1997), 302. Mark Rifkin attributes this process to the systematic dispossession of Indians that—increasingly since 1830—"foreclos[ed] countervailing political geographies" and validated the "insistence . . . on the inherent coherence and contiguity of national geography." Rifkin, *Manifesting America: The Im-*

perial Construction of U.S. National Space (New York: Oxford University Press, 2009), 4, 5. And Christopher Apap states that both Indian removal and African colonization "insured that such groups did not gain even a fractional voice within a republic that was beginning to cement its national mythologies." Apap, "'Let No Man of Us Budge One Step': David Walker and the Rhetoric of African American Emplacement," *Early American Literature* 46, no. 2 (2011): 326.

12. Loughran, *Republic in Print*, 304.

13. O'Sullivan developed the racial-spatial focus of Manifest Destiny in his 1839 essay "The Great Nation of Futurity." As Robert W. Johannsen writes, O'Sullivan "provided a catchphrase for a concept that was as old as the nation itself, even older," and thus "exerted an influence beyond measure on generations of historians, politicians, polemicists, and writers of all sorts." Johannsen, "The Meaning of Manifest Destiny," in *Manifest Destiny and Empire: American Antebellum Expansionism*, ed. Sam W. Haynes and Christopher Morris (Arlington: Texas A&M University Press, 1997), 9.

14. Robert S. Levine, *Dislocating Race and Nation: Episodes in Nineteenth-Century American Literary Nationalism* (Chapel Hill: University of North Carolina Press, 2008), Kindle edition, chap. 2; Peter P. Hinks, *To Awaken My Afflicted Brethren: David Walker and the Problem of Antebellum Slave Resistance* (University Park: Pennsylvania State University Press, 1997), 91–93; Apap, "'Let No Man of Us Budge One Step.'"

15. Forten et al., "Voice from Philadelphia," 2:9.

16. William Bowler et al., "Meeting of Free People of Colour," *Christian Herald*, March 1, 1817, 364–65, reprinted in Garrison, *Thoughts on African Colonization*, 2:62–63.

17. John L. O'Sullivan, "The Great Nation of Futurity," *The United States Magazine and Democratic Review*, November 1839, 429.

18. James Forten and Russell Parrott, "To the Humane and Benevolent Inhabitants of the City and County of Philadelphia" (1818), in *Early Negro Writing, 1760–1837*, ed. Dorothy Porter (Boston: Beacon Press, 1971), 267.

19. The series of "Dialogues" was originally published in the Washington-based *Union* and was reprinted in the Philadelphia *Franklin Gazette*. David Waldstreicher attributes the "Dialogues" to ACS founder Robert Finley, probably because the text was reprinted in a book published in memory of Finley in 1819. See Waldstreicher, *Perpetual Fetes*, 306–8. However, since Finley died prior to Absalom Jones's death, he could not have written about the deceased Jones. The dialogues were reprinted in the book that commemorates Finley alongside texts by other authors. See Isaac V. Brown, *Memoirs of the Rev. Robert Finley, D.D* (New Brunswick, NJ: Terhune and Letson, 1819).

20. "Dialogues, between William Penn, Paul Cuffee, and Absalom Jones," *Franklin Gazette*, June 24, 1818, 2.

21. "Dialogues, between William Penn, Paul Cuffee, and Absalom Jones. Dialogue Second," *Franklin Gazette*, July 20, 1818, 2.

22. "Dialogues, between William Penn, Paul Cuffee, and Absalom Jones," *Franklin Gazette* August 12, 1818, 2.

23. Ibid.

24. William Cornish et al., "Memorial of the Free People of Colour," *African Repository* 2, no. 10 (1826): 295–98 (hereafter, "Memorial").

25. James M. Wright, *The Free Negro in Maryland, 1634–1860* (New York: Octagon Books, 1971), 283. Maryland did not have a particularly high rate of emigration to Li-

beria, and of the four signatories of the "Memorial," only Remus Harvey moved there between 1827–30. See "Emigrants to Liberia—Brig Nautilus's company, arrived at Monrovia February 19, 1828," *Christine's Genealogy Website*, accessed February 25, 2013, http://ccharity.com. I thank Eric Burin for referring me to this resource. Between 1820 and 1860, 328 free blacks left Maryland for Liberia, 621 left North Carolina, and 1,230 left Virginia. See Eric Burin, *Slavery and the Peculiar Solution: A History of the American Colonization Society* (Gainesville: University Press of Florida, 2005), n.p., table 1, table 5. Bettye J. Gardner writes that the city's black community held "heated discussions on the pros and cons of emigrating to Liberia, Haiti, or the West Indies," and "few of Baltimore's black population actually went to any of the places that were discussed." Gardner, "Opposition to Emigration, a Selected Letter of William Watkins (The Colored Baltimorean)," *Journal of Negro History* 67, no. 2 (1982): 155.

26. "Memorial," 295–96.

27. Hinks writes that *Freedom's Journal* was "probably begun in part as a response to the publication two years earlier of the ACS organ *African Repository*." Hinks, *My Afflicted Brethren*, 101.

28. "Letter from Bishop Allen," *Freedom's Journal*, November 2, 1827, 134, accessed March 23, 2016, http://www.wisconsinhistory.org/pdfs/la/FreedomsJournal/v1n34.pdf. The letter is reproduced in David Walker, *David Walker's Appeal to the Coloured Citizens of the World* (1829), ed. Peter P. Hinks (University Park: Pennsylvania State University Press, 2000), 52–60.

29. "Letter from Bishop Allen," 134 (italics in original).

30. John Clark, "Extract from the Circular for 1826 of the 'Friends of Humanity,'" *Edwardsville Spectator*, October 13, 1826, 1. The original full text of Clark's circular appears in *A History of the Illinois Baptists* (unpublished manuscript, n.p., n.d.), chap. 5; it can be found on *Lincoln/Net*, beginning on p. 411, accessed May 16, 2017, http://lincoln.lib.niu.edu/islandora/object/niu-lincoln:35044.

31. "Letter from Bishop Allen," 134 (italics in original).

32. Jennifer L. Morgan, *Laboring Women: Reproduction and Gender in New World Slavery* (Philadelphia: University of Pennsylvania Press, 2011), 93, 94, 105.

33. Thomas D. Morris, "'Villeinage . . . as it existed in England, reflects but little on our subject': The Problem of the 'Sources' of Southern Slave Law," *American Journal of Legal History* 32, no. 2 (1988): esp. 108–9.

34. Locke, *Two Treatises*, 316, 302 (italics in original).

35. "American Colonization Society," *Augusta Chronicle*, July 23, 1823, 2.

36. Homo [pseud.], "Africa," *Edwardsville Spectator*, October 4, 1823, 2.

37. T. G., "For the City Gazette," *City Gazette*, September 28, 1821, 2.

38. Priscilla Wald, *Constituting Americans: Cultural Anxiety and Narrative Form* (Durham: Duke University Press, 1995), 16, 19.

39. Edlie L. Wong, *Neither Fugitive nor Free: Atlantic Slavery, Freedom Suits, and the Legal Culture of Travel* (New York: New York University Press, 2009).

40. Walker, *Appeal to the Coloured Citizens*, 63. Earlier, Walker writes that visitors to the "southern and western states" of the United States "may see there a son take his mother, who bore almost the pains of death to give him birth, and by the command of a tyrant, strip her as naked as she came into the world, and apply the cow-hide to her, until she falls a victim to death in the road!" (pp. 23–24).

41. Maria W. Stewart, *America's First Black Woman Political Writer: Essays and Speeches*, ed. Marilyn Richardson (Bloomington: Indiana University Press, 1987), 35, 40, 31, 55.

42. Walker, *Appeal to the Coloured Citizens*, 9.

43. Ibid., 15, 16.

44. Ibid., 28. For a similar formulation, see p. 58.

45. Ayelet Shachar, *The Birthright Lottery: Citizenship and Global Inequality* (Cambridge, MA: Harvard University Press, 2009), 2–3.

46. Thomas Jefferson, *Notes on the State of Virginia* (1787), ed. William Peden (Chapel Hill: University of North Carolina Press, 1955), 175, 163.

47. Walker, *Appeal to the Coloured Citizens*, 42. Gen. 4:10 refers to "the voice of [Cain's] brother's blood" that "crieth unto [God] from the ground."

48. Walker, *Appeal to the Coloured Citizens*, 56n.

49. Ibid., 9, 70, 71, 74. At one point he refers to them as "sons and daughters of Africa" (p. 64n).

50. Ibid., 67.

51. Ibid., 73.

52. Hinks, *My Afflicted Brethren*, 172. On the popularity of the ACS after 1831, see Philip J. Staudenraus, *The African Colonization Movement, 1816–1865* (New York: Columbia University Press, 1961), 179. On the surge in the volume of manumission of slaves who would emigrate to Liberia in the aftermath of 1831, see James T. Campbell, *Middle Passages: African American Journeys to Africa, 1787–2005* (New York: Penguin, 2006), 62–63; and Burin, *Slavery and the Peculiar Solution*, 19. Burin shows this surge clearly in ibid., n.p., table 1.

53. Many of these resolutions were written in cooperation with Garrison, pledged their writers' support for his abolitionist paper *The Liberator*, and were printed therein; nineteen of them eventually appeared in Garrison's *Thoughts on African Colonization.*

54. Garrison, *Thoughts on African Colonization*, 2:17.

55. Ibid., 2:14–16.

56. Ibid., 2:27–28.

57. Jacob D. Richardson and Jacob G. Williams issued a similar statement in Harrisburg, PA, in October 1831. Identifying themselves as "the sable sons of America," they wrote, "[W]e object to leaving the land of our birth, as there is sufficient land in these United States, on which a colony can be established that would be far more consonant to the wishes of the colored population generally, and would be more adapted to their constitution: neither would it involve the country in such expense as would be incurred by sending them to a howling wilderness, far away from the graves of their forefathers, unknown to us in every respect, unless by geography, which few of us understand." Quoted in Garrison, *Thoughts on African Colonization*, 2:42.

58. Campbell, *Middle Passages*, 63–64.

59. Garrison, *Thoughts on African Colonization*, 2:27–28.

60. Hosea Easton, "An Address" (1828), in *To Heal the Scourge of Prejudice: The Life and Writings of Hosea Easton*, by Hosea Easton, ed. George R. Price and James Brewer Stewart (Amherst: University of Massachusetts Press, 1999), 58, 51.

61. Hosea Easton, "A Treatise on the Intellectual Character, and Civil and Political Condition of the Colored People of the U. States; and the Prejudice Exercised towards Them" (1837), in *To Heal the Scourge of Prejudice*, 72 (hereafter cited in text as *HSP*).

62. Alisse Portnoy writes that Garrison and Lydia Maria Child were persuaded by Walker to abandon their support of colonization. Portnoy, *Their Right to Speak: Women's Activism in the Indian and Slave Debates* (Cambridge, MA: Harvard University Press, 2005), 174.

63. Lydia Maria Child, *An Appeal in Favor of that Class of Americans Called Africans* (New York: John S. Taylor, 1836), 130.

64. "Anti Slavery Movements," *The Emancipator*, December 29, 1836, 137.

65. "Letters of Hon. John Quincy Adams," *The Emancipator*, June 29, 1837, 33

66. "Population of New York," *The Emancipator*, November 29, 1838, 125

67. Scientific racism popularized such ideas. For a classic analysis of scientific racism and its 1830s US practitioners, see Stephen Jay Gould, *The Mismeasure of Man* (New York: W. W. Norton, 1981), 30–72. Louis Agassiz, who was one of those practitioners, created a map that divided the world into racial regions; the map was reprinted in Josiah C. Nott and George R. Gliddon, *Types of Mankind* (Philadelphia: Lippincott, Grambo and Co., 1854), n.p.

68. See Yael Ben-zvi, "Where Did Red Go? Lewis Henry Morgan's Evolutionary Inheritance and U.S. Racial Imagination," *CR: The New Centennial Review* 7, no. 2 (2007): 201–29.

69. Samuel Cornish, "Title of This Journal," *The Colored American*, March 4, 1837.

70. For Bell's involvement in *The Colored American*, see Frankie Hutton, *The Early Black Press in America: 1827 to 1860* (Westport, CT: Greenwood, 1993), 18–19.

71. "Great Anti-Colonization Meeting in New York," *The Emancipator*, January 17, 1839, 153.

72. Frederick Douglass, *The Claims of the Negro, Ethnologically Considered* (Rochester, NY: Lee, Mann, & Co., 1854), 36.

73. Homo, "Africa."

74. "Liberia," *Newburyport Herald*, June 8, 1830, 2.

75. Antonio McDaniel, "Extreme Mortality in Nineteenth-Century Africa: The Case of Liberian Immigrants," *Demography* 29, no. 4 (1992): 582.

76. Quoted in Garrison, *Thoughts on African Colonization*, 2:19.

77. "American Colonization Society," *Edwardsville Spectator*, June 15, 1822, 2.

78. "American Colony at Liberia," *Connecticut Gazette*, April 9, 1828, 2.

79. Burin, *Slavery and the Peculiar Solution*, 141.

80. "Extract of the letter to the editors of the Boston Patriot," *City Gazette*, May 5, 1823, 2.

81. "American Colonization Society," *Augusta Chronicle*, July 23, 1823, 2.

82. Destitution is a persistent theme in most of the surviving letters published in books or online. Many of these letters expressed longings to reunite with distant friends and family members and often included quite desperate requests for supplies, tools, food, and money. The letters circulated within particular structures of power relations; most were written by less literate ex-slaves to their former masters or to ACS official. Communicational conventions within such power relations certainly dictated some of the focus on destitution, but the tones of many of these requests testify to the sense of urgency that many of the writers felt. Perhaps the earliest expression of this idea was in a letter Daniel Coker wrote his wife, who remained in the United States following his departure to Liberia, on May 26, 1820. Having asked his wife to encourage others to emigrate, Coker wrote, "[T]ell . . . every body that can do good for this people, to come as soon as possible

. . . [and] bring every thing you can for nothing you want in America, will be useless here, either to wear, to eat, or as furniture." "African Colony," *Orange County Patriot*, January 1, 1821, 2. For letters of colonists, see Randall M. Miller, ed. *"Dear Master": Letters of a Slave Family* (Ithaca: Cornell University Press, 1978); Bell I. Wiley, ed. *Slaves No More: Letters from Liberia, 1833–1869* (Lexington: University Press of Kentucky, 1980); and Liberian Letters, University of Virginia Library, accessed February 19, 2013, http://etext.lib.virginia.edu/subjects/liberia/intro.html.

83. This was, for example, Harriet Beecher Stowe's representation of Liberia. See Elizabeth Ammons, "*Uncle Tom's Cabin*, Empire, and Africa," in *Approaches to Teaching Stowe's* Uncle Tom's Cabin, ed. Elizabeth Ammons and Susan Belasco (New York: MLA, 2000), esp. 73–74; and Yael Ben-zvi, "The Racial Geopolitics of Harriet Beecher Stowe's Geography Textbooks," *Legacy: A Journal of American Women Writers* 29, no. 1 (2012): 9–36. Liberia avoided charting its ground borders until European powers forced it do so in the late nineteenth century. See Yekutiel Gershoni, "The Formation of Liberia's Boundaries: Part 1: Agreements," *Liberian Studies Journal* 17, no. 1 (1992): 25–45; and Yekutiel Gershoni, "The Formation of Liberia's Boundaries: Part 2: The Demarcation Process," *Liberian Studies Journal* 17, no. 2 (1992): 177–202.

84. Helen Cross, *The New Republic*, 2nd ed. (Boston: Massachusetts Sabbath School Society, 1851), 185.

85. "Liberia," *Daily National Journal*, April 4, 1831, 2. This article contains a letter that Mechlin wrote Elliot Cresson on February 21, 1831.

86. David Kazanjian, *The Brink of Freedom: Improvising Life in the Nineteenth-Century Atlantic World* (Durham: Duke University Press, 2016), 53, 132.

87. Ibid., 66.

88. Ibid., 77.

89. "Peyton Skipwith to John H. Coke," in Wiley, *Slaves No More*, 53.

90. Ibid., 52.

91. William Nesbit, "Four Months in Liberia: Or African Colonization Exposed" (1855), in *Liberian Dreams: Back-to-Africa Narratives from the 1850s*, ed. Wilson Jeremiah Moses (University Park: Pennsylvania State University Press, 1997), 102.

92. Daniel H. Peterson, "The Looking-Glass" (1854), in Moses, *Liberian Dreams*, 64–65. Jefferson famously wrote, "I tremble for my country when I reflect that God is just." Jefferson, *Notes on the State of Virginia*, 163.

93. See, for example, letters by Peyton Skipwith, Solomon S. Page, and Stephen Rice and Henry Smith in Wiley, *Slaves No More*, 48, 52, 66, 106, 183.

94. See, for example, letters by Henrietta Fuller McDonogh, Peter Ross and Robert Carter, and Titus Glover in ibid., 153, 157, 186.

95. See, for example, letters by George R. Ellis McDonogh, Titus Glover, and William C. Burke in ibid., 140, 181, 204.

96. Miller, *"Dear Master,"* 47.

97. James C. Minor to John Minor, February 11, 1833, in Wiley, *Slaves No More*, 16, 17.

Interlude: Blood and Graves

1. "An Act for the Preservation of American Antiquities," Pub. No. 209, 59th Cong., sess. 1 (1906), accessed September 4, 2014, http://www.legisworks.org/congress/59/session-1/publaw-209.pdf.

2. Jack F. Trope and Walter R. Echo-Hawk, "The Native American Graves Protection and Repatriation Act: Background and Legislative History," *Arizona State Law Journal* 24, no. 1 (1992): 39.

3. Cheryl J. La Roche and Michael L. Blakey, "Seizing Intellectual Power: The Dialogue at the New York African Burial Ground," *Historical Archaeology* 31, no. 3 (1997): 84.

4. Spencer P. M. Harrington, "Bones and Bureaucrats: New York's Great Cemetery Imbroglio," *Archaeology* 46, no. 2 (1993): 31; see also p. 36.

5. La Roche and Blakey, "Seizing Intellectual Power," 88–89.

6. Michael L. Blakey, "African Burial Ground Project: Paradigm for Cooperation?" *Museum International* 62, no. 1/2 (2010): 63. For subsequent uses of "descendant communities" in NAGPRA discourse, see, for example, the statement on NAGPRA by the Department of Anthropology at California State University, Sacramento: "The staff at the Archaeological Curation Facility is actively inventorying collections, consulting with tribal representatives, and other tasks necessary under the law to repatriate ancestral remains to descendant communities." "Native American Graves Protection and Repatriation Act," accessed October 20, 2014, http://www.csus.edu/anth/curation/Archaeological%20Curation%20Facility/NAGPRA.html.

7. See Gays S. McGowan and Cheryl J. La Roche, "The Ethical Dilemma Facing Conservation: Care and Treatment of Human Skeletal Remains and Mortuary Objects," *Journal of the American Institute for Conservation* 35, no. 2 (1996): 109–21, accessed October 20, 2014, http://cool.conservation-us.org/coolaic/jaic/articles/jaic35-02-003.html; and D. G. Roberts and J. F. McCarthy, "Descendant Community Partnering in the Archaeological and Bioanthropological Investigation of African-American Skeletal Populations: Two Interrelated Case Studies From Philadelphia," in *Bodies of Evidence: Reconstructing History through Skeletal Analysis*, ed. Anne L. Grauer (New York: John Wiley and Sons, 1995).

8. Blakey, "African Burial Ground Project," 62.

Chapter 6: Ancestral Graves

1. William Blackstone, *Commentaries on the Laws of England*, bk. 2, 1st ed. (Oxford: Clarendon, 1765), 50.

2. *OED Online*, s.v. "native" (n.), accessed March 18, 2015, http://www.oed.com.

3. Jeremiah Evarts, *Cherokee Removal: The "William Penn" Essays and Other Writings*, ed. Francis Paul Prucha (Knoxville: University of Tennessee Press, 1981), 242.

4. Isaac McCoy, *Remarks on the Practicability of Indian Reform, Embracing Their Colonization; With an Appendix*, 2nd ed. (New York: Gray and Bunce, 1829), 6, quoted in "From the Connecticut Observer. Remarks on Indian Reform," *Cherokee Phoenix*, March 3, 1830, 1.

5. "Governor Troup—Again," *Newburyport Herald*, August 30, 1825, 2.

6. For a discussion of McCoy's work in this context, see Susan M. Ryan, *The Grammar of Good Intentions: Race and the Antebellum Culture of Benevolence* (Ithaca: Cornell University Press, 2003), 32–41.

7. Priscilla Wald, *Constituting Americans: Cultural Anxiety and Narrative Form* (Durham: Duke University Press, 1995), 26.

8. "Georgia: Cession of Western Land Claims," in *The Territorial Papers of the United*

States, vol. 5, *The Territory of Mississippi, 1798–1817*, comp. and ed. Clarence Edwin Carter (Washington, DC: Government Printing Office, 1937), 144 (my italics), HathiTrust Digital Library, accessed December 25, 2013, http://catalog.hathitrust.org/Record/000495370.

9. Mishuana Goeman, *Mark My Words: Native Women Mapping Our Nations* (Minneapolis: University of Minnesota Press, 2013), 22.

10. "Indian Talk," *Macon Weekly Telegraph*, May 30, 1829, 87.

11. Although the speech was published as the work of "Speckled Snake," that name is not easily corroborated by other sources on Muscogee history. Historian Angie Debo suggests that the text might have been written by Ridge. Debo, *The Road to Disappearance: A History of the Creek Indians* (Norman: University of Oklahoma Press, 1941), 97.

12. "From the Lancaster (Mass.) Gazette," *Cherokee Phoenix* (hereafter, *CP*), July 22, 1829, 1.

13. "From the Savannah Mercury," *CP*, July 8, 1829, 2. *Cherokee Phoenix* editor Elias Boudinot reprinted the piece from the *Savannah Mercury*. Quotations from the *Phoenix* are based on the University of Georgia's Georgia Historic Newspapers collection, accessed May 18, 2017, http://www.galileo.usg.edu/express?link=zlgn; and Western Carolina University's (WCU) Cherokee Phoenix website, accessed May 18, 2017, http://www.wcu.edu/library/DigitalCollections/CherokeePhoenix/. In cases where parts of the *Cherokee Phoenix* texts were either illegible or mistranscribed, I corrected them by consulting additional sources; in this case, I compared the WCU version with that of the *Daily National Journal*, August 5, 1829, 3.

14. *The New American State Papers: Indian Affairs* (Wilmington, DE: Scholarly Resources, 1972), 4:141.

15. "From the Savannah Mercury," 2.

16. Ibid., 2.

17. I discuss these processes in Ben-zvi, "Where Did Red Go? Lewis Henry Morgan's Evolutionary Inheritance and U.S. Racial Imagination," *CR: The New Centennial Review* 7, no. 2 (2007): 201–29; and Ben-zvi, "National Appropriations and Cultural Evolution: The Spatial and Temporal US of Lewis Henry Morgan's Native America," *Canadian Review of American Studies* 33, no. 3 (2003): 211–29.

18. Francis Paul Prucha, *American Indian Treaties: The History of a Political Anomaly* (Berkeley: University of California Press, 1994), chap. 6.

19. Opoethyoholo, Tuckebachee Hajo, Tuckebachee Micco, and Benjamin Marshall, "Memorial of the Head Men and Warriors, of the Creek Nation of Indians," in *The New American State Papers: Indian Affairs* (Wilmington, DE: Scholarly Resources, 1972), 9:194.

20. "Coosa River, in Turkey Town, C.N. 9th February, 1829. To The Cherokee People," *CP*, March 4, 1829, 2–3.

21. The term *counternarrative* is seminal to Timothy Sweet's discussion of the function of improvement in the Cherokee struggle against removal. Sweet, *American Georgics: Economy and Environment in American Literature, 1580–1864* (Philadelphia: University of Pennsylvania Press, 2002), chap. 6.

22. For an analysis of Indian x-marks, see Scott Richard Lyons, *X-Marks: Native Signatures of Assent* (Minneapolis: University of Minnesota Press, 2010).

23. "Council," *CP*, October 28, 1829, 3.

24. Ibid.

25. Ibid.

26. "From the Lancaster (Mass.) Gazette," *CP*, July 22, 1829, 1.

27. A Chillahcullahgee, letter to the editor, *CP*, July 8, 1829, 2–3.

28. "Bruce," letter to the editor, *CP*, July 1, 1829, 2–3.

29. "Treaty with the Cherokee, 1835," in *Indian Affairs: Laws and Treaties*, vol. 2, *Treaties*, comp. and ed. Charles J. Kappler (Washington: Government Printing Office, 1904), accessed February 5, 2015, http://digital.library.okstate.edu/kappler/Vol2/treaties/che0439.htm.

30. Patrick Wolfe, "Settler Colonialism and the Elimination of the Native," *Journal of Genocide Research* 8, no. 4 (2006): 388.

31. "No. 3" [should be 5], *CP*, August 10, 1833, 3.

32. "Extract of a letter to the Editor, dated Washington City, April 26, 1830," *CP*, May 15, 1830, 3. The delegation included George Lowrey, Lewis Ross, William Hicks, Richard Taylor, Joseph Vann, and William S. Coodey, who submitted a memorial to Congress in early May. The Indian Removal Act passed later that month.

33. "A Cherokee," letter to the editor, *CP*, May 19, 1832, 2.

34. Brian W. Dippie, *The Vanishing American: White Attitudes and U.S. Indian Policy* (Middletown, CT: Wesleyan University Press, 1982), 72.

35. "Rocky Mountain," letter to the editor, *CP*, August 25, 1832, 3. The text in the scanned page in the Georgia Historic Newspapers collection is not entirely clear; I verified it against the version of the letter that was reprinted in Calvin Colton, *Tour of the American Lakes, and among the Indians of the North-West Territory in 1830: Disclosing the Character and Prospects of the Indian Race*, vol. 2:63–67 (London: Frederick Westley and A. H. Davis, 1833), accessed May 19, 2017, https://archive.org/stream/tourofamericanla02colt.

36. "Rocky Mountain," letter to the editor.

37. Gregory Evans Dowd, *A Spirited Resistance: The North American Indian Struggle for Unity, 1745–1815* (Baltimore: Johns Hopkins University Press, 1992), 86.

38. Colin G. Calloway, *The American Revolution in Indian Country: Crisis and Diversity in Native American Communities* (Cambridge: Cambridge University Press, 1995), 278; Dowd, *A Spirited Resistance*, 87.

39. "Rocky Mountain," letter to the editor (italics in original).

Conclusion

1. William Apess, "An Indian's Looking-Glass for the White Man" (1833), in *On Our Own Ground: The Complete Writings of William Apess, a Pequot*, ed. Barry O'Conell (Amherst: University of Massachusetts Press, 1992), 157.

2. Quobna Ottobah Cugoano, *Thoughts and Sentiments on the Evil of Slavery and Other Writings*, ed. Vincent Carretta (New York: Penguin, 1999), 100–1. Cugoano preceded Apess in portraying racist views as "skin deep," when he wrote that those who believed that Africans were natural slaves and "still boast of greater degrees of knowledge, than any African is entitled to" may "enjoy all the advantages of it unenvied" as their knowledge "consists only in greater share of infidelity, and that of a blacker kind than only skin deep" (p. 12).

3. *The New American State Papers: Indian Affairs* (Wilmington: Scholarly Resources, 1972), 4:162.

4. Ibid., 4:163.

BIBLIOGRAPHY

Scholarly Sources

Acholonu, Catherine Obianju. "The Home of Olaudah Equiano—a Linguistic and Anthropological Search." *Journal of Commonwealth Literature* 22, no. 1 (1987): 5–16.

Adams, William Howard. *The Paris Years of Thomas Jefferson*. New Haven: Yale University Press, 1997.

Agnew, John. *Geopolitics: Re-Visioning World Politics*. 2nd ed. London: Routledge, 2003.

Alfred, Taiaiake. *Peace, Power, Righteousness: An Indigenous Manifesto*. Don Mills, ON: Oxford University Press, 1999.

Alfred, Taiaiake. "Sovereignty." In *Sovereignty Matters: Locations of Contestation and Possibility in Indigenous Struggles for Self-Determination*, edited by Joanne Barker, 33–50. Lincoln: University of Nebraska Press, 2005.

Alfred, Taiaiake, and Jeff Corntassel. "Being Indigenous: Resurgences against Contemporary Colonialism." *Government and Opposition* 40, no. 4 (2005): 597–614.

Ammons, Elizabeth. "*Uncle Tom's Cabin*, Empire, and Africa." In *Approaches to Teaching Stowe's* Uncle Tom's Cabin, edited by Elizabeth Ammons and Susan Belasco, 68–76. New York: MLA, 2000.

Anaya, S. James. "Indian Givers: What Indigenous Peoples Have Contributed to International Human Rights Law." *Washington University Journal of Law & Policy* 22 (2006): 107–20.

Anaya, S. James. *Indigenous Peoples in International Law*. Oxford: Oxford University Press, 1996.

Anderson, Benedict. *Imagined Communities: Reflections on the Origin and Spread of Nationalism*. Rev. ed. London: Verso, 1991.

Apap, Christopher. "Caught between Two Opinions: Africans, Europeans, and Indians in Olaudah Equiano's *Interesting Narrative*." *Comparative American Studies* 4, no. 1 (2006): 5–24.

Apap, Christopher. "'Let no man of us budge one step': David Walker and the Rhetoric of African American Emplacement." *Early American Literature* 46, no. 2 (2011): 319–50.

Aravamudan, Srinivas. "Equiano Lite." *Eighteenth-Century Studies* 34, no. 4 (2001): 615–19.

Arendt, Hannah. *The Origins of Totalitarianism*. New edition with added prefaces. San Diego, CA: Harcourt Brace & Company, 1973.

Arias, Santa. "Equal Rights and Individual Freedom: Enlightenment Intellectuals and the

Lascasian Apology for Black African Slavery." *Romance Quarterly* 55, no. 4 (2008): 279–91.

Armitage, David. "John Locke, Carolina, and the *Two Treatises of Government*." *Political Theory* 32, no. 5 (2004): 602–27.

Arneil, Barbara. *John Locke and America: The Defence of English Colonialism*. Oxford: Oxford University Press, 1996.

Axtell, James. *The European and the Indian: Essays in the Ethnohistory of Colonial North America*. New York: Oxford University Press, 1981.

Bailyn, Bernard. *The Ideological Origins of the American Revolution*. Cambridge, MA: Harvard University Press, 1967.

Barreto, José-Manuel. "Introduction: Decolonial Strategies and Dialogue in the Human Rights Field." In Barreto, *Human Rights from a Third World Perspective*, 1–42.

Barreto, José-Manuel, ed. *Human Rights from a Third World Perspective: Critique, History and International Law*. Newcastle upon Tyne: Cambridge Scholars Publishing, 2013.

Basso, Keith H. *Wisdom Sits in Places: Landscape and Language among the Western Apache*. Albuquerque: University of New Mexico Press, 1996.

Bauerkemper, Joseph, and Heidi Kiiwetinepinesiik Stark. "The Trans/National Terrain of Anishinaabe Law and Diplomacy." *Journal of Transnational American Studies* 4, no. 1 (2012): 1–21.

Behdad, Ali. *A Forgetful Nation: On Immigration and Cultural Identity in the United States*. Durham: Duke University Press, 2005.

Bennett, Gordon I. "Aboriginal Title in the Common Law: A Stony Path through Feudal Doctrine." *Buffalo Law Review* 27 (1977/1978): 617–35.

Ben-zvi, Yael. "National Appropriations and Cultural Evolution: The Spatial and Temporal US of Lewis Henry Morgan's Native America." *Canadian Review of American Studies* 33, no. 3 (2003): 211–29.

Ben-zvi, Yael. "The Racial Geopolitics of Harriet Beecher Stowe's Geography Textbooks." *Legacy: A Journal of American Women Writers* 29, no. 1 (2012): 9–36.

Ben-zvi, Yael. "Where Did Red Go? Lewis Henry Morgan's Evolutionary Inheritance and U.S. Racial Imagination." *CR: The New Centennial Review* 7, no. 2 (2007): 201–29.

Blakey, Michael L. "African Burial Ground Project: Paradigm for Cooperation?" *Museum International* 62, no. 1/2 (2010): 61–68.

Bly, Antonio T. Introduction to *Escaping Bondage: A Documentary History of Runaway Slaves in Eighteenth-Century New England, 1700–1789*, edited by Antonio T. Bly. Lanham, MD: Lexington Books, 2012. Kindle edition.

Boulukos, George. *The Grateful Slave: The Emergence of Race in Eighteenth-Century British and American Culture*. Cambridge: Cambridge University Press, 2008.

Braidwood, Stephen J. *Black Poor and White Philanthropists: London's Blacks and the Foundations of the Sierra Leone Settlement, 1786–1791*. Liverpool: Liverpool University Press, 1994.

Brickhouse, Anna. *The Unsettlement of America: Translation, Interpretation, and the Story of Don Luis de Velasco, 1560–1945*. Oxford: Oxford University Press, 2014.

Brooks, Joanna. *American Lazarus: Religion and the Rise of African-American and Native-American Literatures*. Oxford: Oxford University Press, 2003.

Brooks, Joanna. "'This Indian World': A Petition/Origin Story from Samson Occom and the Montaukett Tribe." In *Early Native Literacies in New England: A Documentary and Critical Anthology*, edited by Kristina Bross and Hilary E. Wyss, 215–22. Amherst: University of Massachusetts Press, 2008.

Brooks, Lisa. *The Common Pot: The Recovery of Native Space in the Northeast.* Minneapolis: University of Minnesota Press, 2008.

Brown, Elizabeth A. R. "The Tyranny of a Construct: Feudalism and Historians of Medieval Europe." *American Historical Review* 79, no. 4 (1974): 1063–88.

Brown, Vincent. "Social Death and Political Life in the Study of Slavery." *American Historical Review* 114, no. 5 (2009): 1231–49.

Brückner, Martin. *The Geographic Revolution in Early America: Maps, Literacy, and National Identity*. Chapel Hill: University of North Carolina Press, 2006.

Brunstetter, Daniel R. "Sepúlveda, Las Casas, and the Other: Exploring the Tension between Moral Universalism and Alterity." *Review of Politics* 72, no. 3 (2010): 409–35.

Bruyneel, Kevin. *The Third Space of Sovereignty: The Postcolonial Politics of U.S.-Indigenous Relations*. Minneapolis: University of Minnesota Press, 2007.

Buck-Morss, Susan. *Hegel, Haiti, and Universal History*. Pittsburgh: University of Pittsburgh Press, 2009.

Bugg, John. "The Other Interesting Narrative: Olaudah Equiano's Public Book Tour." *PMLA* 121, no. 5 (2006): 1424–42.

Burin, Eric. *Slavery and the Peculiar Solution: A History of the American Colonization Society*. Gainesville: University Press of Florida, 2005.

Byrd, Jodi A. *The Transit of Empire: Indigenous Critiques of Colonialism.* Minneapolis: University of Minnesota Press, 2011.

Byrd, Jody A., and Michael Rothberg. "Between Subalternity and Indigeneity." *Interventions* 13, no. 1 (2011): 1–12.

Caldwell, Tanya. "'Talking Too Much English': Languages of Economy and Politics in Equiano's *The Interesting Narrative*." *Early American Literature* 34, no. 3 (1999): 263–82.

Calloway, Colin G. *The American Revolution in Indian Country: Crisis and Diversity in Native American Communities*. Cambridge: Cambridge University Press, 1995.

Calloway, Colin G. *Pen and Ink Witchcraft: Treaties and Treaty Making in American Indian History*. Oxford: Oxford University Press, 2013. Kindle edition.

Calloway, Colin G. *The Victory with No Name: The Native American Defeat of the First American Army*. Oxford: Oxford University Press, 2014.

Campbell, James T. *Middle Passages: African American Journeys to Africa, 1787–2005*. New York: Penguin, 2006.

Carby, Hazel V. "Becoming Modern Racialized Subjects." *Cultural Studies* 23, no. 4 (2009): 624–57.

Carozza, Paolo G. "From Conquest to Constitution: Retrieving a Latin American Tradition of the Idea of Human Rights." *Human Rights Quarterly* 25, no. 2 (2003): 281–313.

Carretta, Vincent. *Equiano, the African: Biography of a Self-Made Man*. New York: Penguin, 2005.

Carretta, Vincent. "Olaudah Equiano or Gustavus Vassa? New Light on an Eighteenth-Century Question of Identity." *Slavery & Abolition* 20, no. 3 (1999): 96–105.

Carretta, Vincent, ed. "Olaudah Equiano, the South Carolinian? A Forum." *Historically Speaking* 7, no. 3 (2006): 2–16.

Carretta, Vincent. "New Equiana." *Early American Literature* 44, no. 1 (2009): 147–60.

Carretta, Vincent. "Response to Paul Lovejoy's 'Autobiography and Memory: Gustavus Vassa, alias Olaudah Equiano, the African.'" *Slavery & Abolition* 28, no. 1 (2007): 115–19.

Cheyfitz, Eric. *The Poetics of Imperialism: Translation and Colonization from* The Tempest *to* Tarzan. Philadelphia: University of Pennsylvania Press, 1997.

Collins, James. "Passage to Slavery, Passage to Freedom: Olaudah Equiano and the Sea." *Midwest Quarterly* 47, no. 3 (2006): 209–23.

Coulthard, Glen Sean. *Red Skin, White Masks: Rejecting the Colonial Politics of Recognition*. Minneapolis: University of Minnesota Press, 2014.

Davidson, Cathy. "Olaudah Equiano, Written by Himself." *Novel: A Forum on Fiction* 40, no. 1/2 (2006/2007): 18–51.

Davis, David Brion. *The Problem of Slavery in the Age of Revolution, 1770–1823*. Ithaca: Cornell University Press, 1975.

Davis, Kathleen. *Periodization and Sovereignty: How Ideas of Feudalism and Secularization Govern the Politics of Time*. Philadelphia: University of Pennsylvania Press, 2008.

Davis, Thadious M. *Southscapes: Geographies of Race, Region, and Literature*. Chapel Hill: University of North Carolina Press, 2011.

Day, Iyko. "Being or Nothingness: Indigeneity, Antiblackness, and Settler Colonial Critique." *Critical Ethnic Studies* 1, no. 2 (2015): 102–21.

Debo, Angie. *The Road to Disappearance: A History of the Creek Indians*. Norman: University of Oklahoma Press, 1941.

Deloria, Philip J. *Playing Indian*. New Haven: Yale University Press, 1998.

Deloria, Vine, Jr. *God Is Red*. New York: Delta, 1973.

Den Ouden, Amy E. *Beyond Conquest: Native Peoples and the Struggle for History in New England*. Lincoln: University of Nebraska Press, 2005.

Dippie, Brian W. *The Vanishing American: White Attitudes and U.S. Indian Policy*. Middletown, CT: Wesleyan University Press, 1982.

Dowd, Gregory Evans. *A Spirited Resistance: The North American Indian Struggle for Unity, 1745–1815*. Baltimore: Johns Hopkins University Press, 1992.

Egerton, Douglas R. *Death or Liberty: African Americans and Revolutionary America*. Oxford: Oxford University Press, 2009.

Elden, Stuart. *The Birth of Territory*. Chicago: University of Chicago Press, 2013.

Elden, Stuart. "Land, Terrain, Territory." *Progress in Human Geography* 34, no. 6 (2010): 799–817.

Elliott, Michael. "'This Indian Bait': Samson Occom and the Voice of Liminality." *Early American Literature* 29, no. 3 (1994): 233–53.

Elrod, Eileen Razzari. *Piety and Dissent: Race, Gender, and Biblical Rhetoric in Early American Autobiography*. Amherst: University of Massachusetts Press, 2008.

Engle, Karen. *The Elusive Promise of Indigenous Development: Rights, Culture, Strategy*. Durham: Duke University Press, 2010.

Fawcett, Melissa Jayne. *The Lasting of the Mohegans*. Part 1, *The Story of the Wolf People*. Uncasville, CT: Mohegan Tribe, 1995.

Fisher, Linford D. *The Indian Great Awakening: Religion and the Shaping of Native Cultures in Early America*. Oxford: Oxford University Press, 2012.

Fogel, Robert William, and Stanley L. Engerman. *Time on the Cross: The Economics of American Negro Slavery*. Boston: Little, Brown, 1974.

Fort, Kathryn E. "Disruption and Impossibility: The New Laches and the Unfortunate Resolution of the Modern Iroquois Land Claims." *Wyoming Law Review* 11, no. 2 (2011): 375–405.

Foucault, Michel. *"Society Must Be Defended": Lectures at the Collège de France, 1975–76*. Edited by Mauro Bertani and Alessandro Fontana. Translated by David Macey. New York: Picador, 2003.

Franklin, John Hope, and Loren Schweninger. *Runaway Slaves: Rebels on the Plantation*. Oxford: Oxford University Press, 1999. Kindle edition.

Gardner, Bettye J. "Opposition to Emigration, a Selected Letter of William Watkins (The Colored Baltimorean)." *Journal of Negro History* 67, no. 2 (1982): 155–58.

Gates, Henry Louis, Jr. *The Signifying Monkey: A Theory of Afro-American Literary Criticism*. New York: Oxford University Press, 1988.

Gershoni, Yekutiel. "The Formation of Liberia's Boundaries: Part 1: Agreements." *Liberian Studies Journal* 17, no. 1 (1992): 25–45.

Gershoni, Yekutiel. "The Formation of Liberia's Boundaries: Part 2: The Demarcation Process." *Liberian Studies Journal* 17, no. 2 (1992): 177–202.

Goeman, Mishuana. "Land as Life: Unsettling the Logics of Containment." In *Native Studies Keywords*, edited by Stephanie Nohelani Teves, Andrea Smith, and Michelle H. Raheja, 71–89. Tucson: University of Arizona Press, 2015.

Goeman, Mishuana. *Mark My Words: Native Women Mapping Our Nations*. Minneapolis: University of Minnesota Press, 2013.

Goldstein, Alyosha. "Where the Nation Takes Place: Proprietary Regimes, Antistatism, and U.S. Settler Colonialism." *South Atlantic Quarterly* 107, no. 4 (2008): 833–861.

Gould, Eliga H. *Among the Powers of the Earth: The American Revolution and the Making of a New World Empire*. Cambridge, MA: Harvard University Press, 2012. Kindle edition.

Gould, Stephen Jay. *The Mismeasure of Man*. New York: W. W. Norton, 1981.

Grant-Costa, Paul Joseph. "The Last Indian War in New England: The Mohegan Indians v. The Governour and Company of the Colony of Connecticut, 1703–1774." PhD diss., Yale University, 2008.

Greene, Jack P. *The Constitutional Origins of the American Revolution*. Cambridge: Cambridge University Press, 2011.

Greer, Allan. "Commons and Enclosure in the Colonization of North America." *American Historical Review* 117, no. 2 (2012): 365–86.

Greeson, Jennifer. "American Enlightenment: The New World and Modern Western Thought." *American Literary History* 25, no. 1 (2013): 6–17.

Greeson, Jennifer Rae. *Our South: Geographic Fantasy and the Rise of National Literature*. Cambridge, MA: Harvard University Press, 2012. Kindle edition.

Greeson, Jennifer Rae. "The Prehistory of Possessive Individualism." *PMLA* 127, no. 4 (2012): 918–24.

Guyatt, Nicholas. "'The Outskirts of our Happiness': Race and the Lure of Colonization in the Early Republic." *Journal of American History* 95, no. 4 (2009): 986–1011.

Hager, Christopher. *Word by Word: Emancipation and the Act of Writing*. Cambridge, MA: Harvard University Press, 2013.

Harrington, Spencer P. M. "Bones and Bureaucrats: New York's Great Cemetery Imbroglio." *Archeology* 46, no. 2 (1993): 28–38.

Hartman, Saidiya. *Lose Your Mother: A Journey along the Atlantic Slave Route*. New York: Farrar, Straus and Giroux, 2007.

Hepburn, Samantha. "Feudal Tenure and Native Title: Revising an Enduring Fiction." *Sydney Law Review* 27, no. 1 (2005): 49–86.

Hinks, Peter P. *To Awaken My Afflicted Brethren: David Walker and the Problem of Antebellum Slave Resistance*. University Park: Pennsylvania State University Press, 1997.

Holland, Sharon P., and Tiya Miles. "Afro-Native Realities." In *The World of Indigenous North America*, edited by Robert Warrior, 524–48. New York: Routledge, 2015.

Horton, James Oliver, and Lois E. Horton. *In Hope of Liberty: Culture, Community, and Protest among Northern Free Blacks, 1700–1860*. New York: Oxford University Press, 1997.

Huhndorf, Shari M. *Going Native: Indians in the American Cultural Imagination*. Ithaca: Cornell University Press, 2002.

Hunt, Lynn. *Inventing Human Rights: A History*. New York: Norton, 2007.

Hutson, James A. "The Emergence of the Modern Concept of Rights in America: The Contribution of Michel Villey." In Shain, *The Nature of Rights*, 25–63.

Hutton, Frankie. *The Early Black Press in America: 1827 to 1860*. Westport, CT: Greenwood, 1993.

Ishay, Micheline R. *The History of Human Rights from Ancient Times to the Globalization Era*. 2nd ed. Berkeley: University of California Press, 2008.

Ishay, Micheline R. "What Are Human Rights? Six Historical Controversies." *Journal of Human Rights* 3, no. 3 (2004): 359–71.

Ivison, Duncan, Paul Patton, and Will Sanders. Introduction to *Political Theory and the Rights of Indigenous Peoples*, edited by Duncan Ivison, Paul Patton, and Will Sanders, 1–21. Cambridge: Cambridge University Press, 2000.

Jackson, Shona N. *Creole Indigeneity: Between Myth and Nation in the Caribbean*. Minneapolis: University of Minnesota Press, 2012.

Jarvis, Brad D. E. *The Brothertown Nation of Indians: Land Ownership and Nationalism in Early America, 1740–1840*. Lincoln: University of Nebraska Press, 2010.

Johannsen, Robert W. "The Meaning of Manifest Destiny." In *Manifest Destiny and Empire: American Antebellum Expansionism*, edited by Sam W. Haynes and Christopher Morris, 7–20. Arlington: Texas A&M University Press, 1997.

Justice, Daniel Heath. "'Go Away, Water!': Kinship Criticism and the Decolonization Imperative." In *Reasoning Together: The Native Critics Collective*, edited by Craig S. Womack, Daniel Heath Justice, and Christopher B. Teuton, 147–68. Norman: University of Oklahoma Press, 2008.

Justice, Daniel Heath. *Our Fire Survives the Storm: A Cherokee Literary History*. Minneapolis: University of Minnesota Press, 2006.

Kantorowicz, Ernst Hartwig. *The King's Two Bodies: A Study in Mediaeval Political Theology*. Princeton: Princeton University Press, 1957.

Kaplan, Sidney, and Emma Nogrady Kaplan. *The Black Presence in the Era of the American Revolution*. Amherst: University of Massachusetts Press, 1989.

Kauanui, J. Kēhaulani. "'A Structure, Not an Event': Settler Colonialism and Enduring Indigeneity." *Lateral* 5, no. 1 (2016). Accessed October 14, 2016, http://csalateral.org/archive/issue/5-1.

Kazanjian, David. *The Brink of Freedom: Improvising Life in the Nineteenth-Century Atlantic World*. Durham: Duke University Press, 2016.

Kazanjian, David. *The Colonizing Trick: National Culture and Imperial Citizenship in Early America*. Minneapolis: University of Minnesota Press, 2003.

Klein, Herbert S. *A Population History of the United States*. Cambridge: Cambridge University Press, 2004.

Korieh, Chima J., ed. *Olaudah Equiano and the Igbo World: History, Society, and Atlantic Diaspora Connections*. Trenton, NJ: Africa World Press, 2009.

Korsmo, Fae. "Claiming Memory in British Columbia: Aboriginal Rights and the State." *American Indian Culture and Research Journal* 20, no. 4 (1996): 71–90.

La Roche, Cheryl J., and Michael L. Blakey. "Seizing Intellectual Power: The Dialogue at the New York African Burial Ground." *Historical Archaeology* 31, no. 3 (1997): 84–106.

Levine, Robert S. *Dislocating Race and Nation: Episodes in Nineteenth-Century American Literary Nationalism*. Chapel Hill: University of North Carolina Press, 2008. Kindle edition.

Linebaugh, Peter, and Marcus Rediker. *The Many-Headed Hydra: Sailors, Slaves, Commoners, and the Hidden History of the Revolutionary Atlantic*. London: Verso, 2000.

Lopenzina, Drew. *Red Ink: Native Americans Picking Up the Pen in the Colonial Period*. Albany: SUNY Press, 2012.

Loughran, Trish. *The Republic in Print: Print Culture in the Age of U.S. Nation Building, 1770–1870*. New York: Columbia University Press, 2007.

Lovejoy, Paul E. "Autobiography and Memory: Gustavus Vassa, alias Olaudah Equiano, the African." *Slavery & Abolition* 27, no. 3 (2006): 317–47.

Lovejoy, Paul E. "Issues of Motivation—Vassa/Equiano and Carretta's Critique of the Evidence." *Slavery & Abolition* 28, no. 1 (2007): 121–25.

Lowe, Lisa. *The Intimacies of Four Continents*. Durham: Duke University Press, 2015.

Lyons, Scott Richard. *X-Marks: Native Signatures of Assent*. Minneapolis: University of Minnesota Press, 2010.

Mamdani, Mahmood. *Define and Rule: Native as Political Identity*. Cambridge, MA: Harvard University Press, 2012.

Mamdani, Mahmood. "Settler Colonialism: Then and Now." *Critical Inquiry* 41, no. 3 (2015): 596–614.

Mamdani, Mahmood. "When Does a Settler Become a Native? Reflections on the Colonial Roots of Citizenship in Equatorial and South Africa." Lecture, New Series no. 208, University of Cape Town, May 13, 1998.

McDaniel, Antonio. "Extreme Mortality in Nineteenth-Century Africa: The Case of Liberian Immigrants." *Demography* 29, no. 4 (1992): 581–94.

McDonnell, Michael. *Masters of Empire: Great Lakes Indians and the Making of America*. New York: Hill and Wang, 2015.

McGowan, Gays S., and Cheryl J. La Roche. "The Ethical Dilemma Facing Conservation: Care and Treatment of Human Skeletal Remains and Mortuary Objects." *Journal of the American Institute for Conservation* 35, no.2 (1996): 109–21. http://cool.conservation-us.org/coolaic/jaic/articles/jaic35-02-003.html.

Mehta, Uday Singh. *Liberalism and Empire: A Study in Nineteenth-Century British Liberal Thought*. Chicago: University of Chicago Press, 1999.

Mignolo, Walter D. *The Darker Side of the Renaissance: Literacy, Territoriality, and Colonization*. 2nd ed. Durham: Duke University Press, 2003.

Mignolo, Walter D. *The Darker Side of Western Modernity: Global Futures, Decolonial Options*. Durham: Duke University Press, 2011.

Mignolo, Walter D. "Delinking: The Rhetoric of Modernity, the Logic of Coloniality and the Grammar of De-coloniality." *Cultural Studies* 21, no. 2/3 (2007): 449–514.

Mignolo, Walter D. "Geopolitics of Sensing and Knowing: On (De)Coloniality, Border Thinking and Epistemic Disobedience." *Postcolonial Studies* 14, no. 3 (2011): 273–83.

Mignolo, Walter D. "Who Speaks for the 'Human' in Human Rights?" *Hispanic Issues On Line* 5, no. 1 (2009): 7–24.

Miles, Tiya, and Sharon P. Holland, eds. *Crossing Waters, Crossing Worlds: The African Diaspora in Indian Country*. Durham: Duke University Press, 2006.

Miller, Randall M., ed. *"Dear Master": Letters of a Slave Family*. Ithaca: Cornell University Press, 1978.

Miller, Randall M., and John David Smith, eds. *Dictionary of Afro-American Slavery*. Updated ed. Westport: Praeger, 1997.

Mohawk, John. "Thoughts of Peace: The Great Law." In *Thinking in Indian: A John Mohawk Reader*, edited by José Barreiro, 240–48. Golden, CO: Fulcrum, 2010.

Morgan, Jennifer L. *Laboring Women: Reproduction and Gender in New World Slavery*. Philadelphia: University of Pennsylvania Press, 2004.

Morgensen, Scott Lauria. "Indigenous Transnationalism and the AIDS Pandemic: Challenging Settler Colonialism within Global Health Governance." In *Theorizing Native Studies*, edited by Audra Simpson and Andrea Smith, 188–206. Durham: Duke University Press, 2014.

Morris, Thomas D. "'Villeinage . . . as it existed in England, reflects but little on our subject': The Problem of the 'Sources' of Southern Slave Law." *American Journal of Legal History* 32, no. 2 (1988): 95–137.

Moses, Wilson Jeremiah, ed. *Liberian Dreams: Back-to-Africa Narratives from the 1850s*. University Park: Pennsylvania State University Press, 1997.

Moyn, Samuel. *The Last Utopia: Human Rights in History*. Cambridge, MA: Harvard University Press, 2010.

Mudimbe, V. Y. *The Idea of Africa*. Bloomington: Indiana University Press, 1994.

Mudimbe, V. Y. *Liberty in African and Western Thought*. Washington, DC: Institute for Independent Education, 1988.

Murray, David. *Forked Tongues: Speech, Writing, and Representation in North American Indian Texts*. Bloomington: Indiana University Press, 1991.

Murray, David. "Letter of Instruction from Oanhekoe, Sachem of the Mohegan Indians in New England, 14 July 1703." In *Early Native Literacies in New England: A*

Documentary and Critical Anthology, edited by Kristina Bross and Hilary E. Wyss, 21–27. Amherst: University of Massachusetts Press, 2008.

Murray, Laura J. "Pray Sir, Consider a Little: Rituals of Subordination and Strategies of Resistance in the Letters of Hezekiah Calvin and David Fowler to Eleazar Wheelock." In *Early Native American Writing: New Critical Essays*, edited by Helen Jaskoski, 15–41. Cambridge: Cambridge University Press, 1996.

Mutua, Makau. *Human Rights: A Political and Cultural Critique*. Philadelphia: University of Pennsylvania Press, 2002.

Nash, Gary B. *Race and Revolution*. Lanham, MD: Rowman & Littlefield, 1990.

Newman, Richard S., Roy E. Finkenbine, and Douglass Mooney. "Philadelphia Emigrationist Petition, Circa 1792: An Introduction." *William and Mary Quarterly*, 3rd ser., 64, no. 1 (2007): 161–66.

Niezen, Ronald. *The Origins of Indigenism: Human Rights and the Politics of Identity*. Berkeley: University of California Press, 2003.

O'Brien, Jean M. *Firsting and Lasting: Writing Indians Out of Existence in New England*. Minneapolis: University of Minnesota Press, 2010.

Oberg, Michael Leroy. *Uncas: First of the Mohegans*. Ithaca: Cornell University Press, 2003.

Ogude, S. E. *No Roots Here: On the Igbo Roots of Olaudah Equiano*. Ibadan, Nigeria: RELS Monographs, 1989.

Oldham, James. *English Common Law in the Age of Mansfield*. Chapel Hill: University of North Carolina Press, 2004.

Orren, Karen. *Belated Feudalism: Labor, the Law, and Liberal Development in the United States*. Cambridge: Cambridge University Press, 1991.

Pagden, Anthony. "Dispossessing the Barbarian: The Language of Spanish Thomism and the Debate over the Property Rights of the American Indians." In *The Languages of Political Theory in Early-Modern Europe*, edited by Anthony Pagden, 79–98. Cambridge: Cambridge University Press, 1987.

Pagden, Anthony. *The Fall of Natural Man: The American Indian and the Origins of Comparative Ethnology*. Cambridge: Cambridge University Press, 1986.

Parker, Freddie L. *Running for Freedom: Slave Runaways in North Carolina, 1775–1840*. New York: Garland, 1993.

Pateman, Carole. "The Settler Contract." In *Contract and Domination*, by Carole Pateman and Charles W. Mills, 35–78. Cambridge: Polity, 2007.

Patterson, Orlando. *Slavery and Social Death: A Comparative Study*. Cambridge, MA: Harvard University Press, 1982.

Porter, Dorothy, ed. *Early Negro Writing, 1760–1837*. Boston: Beacon Press, 1971.

Portnoy, Alisse. *Their Right to Speak: Women's Activism in the Indian and Slave Debates*. Cambridge, MA: Harvard University Press, 2005.

Potkay, Adam. "History, Oratory, and God in Equiano's *Interesting Narrative*." *Eighteenth-Century Studies* 34, no. 4 (2001): 601–14.

Povinelli, Elizabeth A. *The Cunning of Recognition: Indigenous Alterities and the Making of Australian Multiculturalism*. Durham: Duke University Press, 2002.

Pratt, Mary Louise. *Imperial Eyes: Travel Writing and Transculturation*. London: Routledge, 1992.

Pratt, Mary Louise. "Scratches on the Face of the Country; Or, What Mr. Barrow Saw in the Land of the Bushmen." *Critical Inquiry* 12, no. 1 (1985): 119–43.

Price, Polly J. "Natural Law and Birthright Citizenship in Calvin's Case (1608)." *Yale Journal of Law and the Humanities* 9, no. 1 (1997): 73–146.

Prucha, Francis Paul. *American Indian Treaties: The History of a Political Anomaly*. Berkeley: University of California Press, 1994.

Prucha, Francis Paul. *The Great Father: The United States Government and the American Indians*. 2 vols. Lincoln: Nebraska University Press, 1984.

Reardon, Jenny, and Kim TallBear. "'Your DNA Is Our History': Genomics, Anthropology, and the Construction of Whiteness as Property." *Current Anthropology* 53, no. S5 (2012): S233–45.

Reid, John Philip. "The Authority of Rights at the American Founding." In Shain, *The Nature of Rights*, 67–115.

Reid, John Philip. *Constitutional History of the American Revolution*. Vol. 1, *The Authority of Rights*. Madison: University of Wisconsin Press, 1986.

Reynolds, Susan. *Fiefs and Vassals: The Medieval Evidence Reinterpreted*. Oxford: Oxford University Press, 1994.

Riding In, James. "Reservations." In *Encyclopedia of North American Indians*, edited by Frederick E. Hoxie, 546–49. Boston: Houghton Mifflin Harcourt, 1996.

Rifkin, Mark. *Manifesting America: The Imperial Construction of U.S. National Space*. New York: Oxford University Press, 2009.

Rifkin, Mark. *Settler Common Sense: Queerness and Everyday Colonialism in the American Renaissance*. Minneapolis: University of Minnesota Press, 2014.

Roberts, D. G., and J. F. McCarthy. "Descendant Community Partnering in the Archaeological and Bioanthropological Investigation of African-American Skeletal Populations: Two Interrelated Case Studies From Philadelphia." In *Bodies of Evidence: Reconstructing History through Skeletal Analysis*, edited by Anne L. Grauer, 19–35. New York: John Wiley and Sons, 1995.

Rogers, Nicholas. "Caribbean Borderland: Empire, Ethnicity, and the Exotic on the Mosquito Coast." *Eighteenth-Century Life* 26, no. 3 (2002): 117–38.

Rosaldo, Renato. *Culture and Truth: The Remaking of Social Analysis*. Boston: Beacon Press, 1989.

Rushdy, Ashraf H. A. "The Quality of Diaspora." *Diaspora* 18, no. 3 (2009): 287–304.

Ryan, Susan M. *The Grammar of Good Intentions: Race and the Antebellum Culture of Benevolence*. Ithaca: Cornell University Press: 2003.

Sadosky, Leonard J. *Revolutionary Negotiations: Indians, Empires, and Diplomats in the Founding of America*. Charlottesville: University of Virginia Press, 2009.

Sassen, Saskia. *Territory, Authority, Rights: From Medieval to Global Assemblages*. 2nd ed. Princeton: Princeton University Press, 2008.

Scott, David. *Conscripts of Modernity: The Tragedy of Colonial Enlightenment*. Durham: Duke University Press, 2004.

Shachar, Ayelet. "Introduction: Citizenship and the 'Right to Have Rights.'" *Citizenship Studies* 18, no. 2 (2014): 114–24.

Shachar, Ayelet. *The Birthright Lottery: Citizenship and Global Inequality*. Cambridge, MA: Harvard University Press, 2009.

Shain, Barry Alan, ed. *The Nature of Rights at the American Founding*. Charlottesville: University of Virginia Press, 2007.

Shick, Tom W. *Behold the Promised Land: A History of Afro-American Settler Society in Nineteenth-Century Liberia.* Baltimore: Johns Hopkins University Press, 1977.

Sidbury, James. *Becoming African in America: Race and Nation in the Early Black Atlantic.* Oxford: Oxford University Press, 2007.

Simpson, Audra. *Mohawk Interruptus: Political Life across the Borders of Settler States.* Durham: Duke University Press, 2014.

Sinha, Manisha. *The Slave's Cause: A History of Abolition.* New Haven: Yale University Press, 2016.

Slauter, Eric. "Reading and Radicalization: Print, Politics, and the American Revolution." *Early American Studies* 8, no. 1 (2010): 5–40.

Smallwood, Stephanie E. *Saltwater Slavery: A Middle Passage from Africa to American Diaspora.* Cambridge, MA: Harvard University Press, 2007.

Smith, Andrea. "American Studies without America: Native Feminisms and the Nation-State." *American Quarterly* 60, no. 2 (2008): 309–15.

Smith, Kimberly K. *African American Environmental Thought: Foundations.* Lawrence: University Press of Kansas, 2007.

Smith, Rogers M. *Civic Ideals: Conflicting Visions of Citizenship in U.S. History.* New Haven: Yale University Press, 1997.

St. Jean, Wendy B. "Inventing Guardianship: The Mohegan Indians and Their 'Protectors.'" *New England Quarterly* 72, no. 3 (1999): 362–87.

Stasilius, Daiva, and Nira Yuval-Davis. "Introduction: Beyond Dichotomies—Gender, Race, Ethnicity and Class in Settler Societies." In *Unsettling Settler Societies: Articulations of Gender, Ethnicity and Class*, edited by Daiva Stasilius and Nira Yuval-Davis, 1–38. London: Sage, 1995.

Staudenraus, Philip J. *The African Colonization Movement, 1816–1865.* New York: Columbia University Press, 1961.

Stevens, Laura M. *The Poor Indians: British Missionaries, Native Americans, and Colonial Sensibility.* Philadelphia: University of Pennsylvania Press, 2004.

Sweet, John Wood. *Bodies Politic: Negotiating Race in the American North, 1730–1830.* Philadelphia: University of Pennsylvania Press, 2007.

Sweet, Timothy. *American Georgics: Economy and Environment in American Literature, 1580–1864.* Philadelphia: University of Pennsylvania Press, 2002.

Taylor, Alan. *The Civil War of 1812: American Citizens, British Subjects, Irish Rebels, and Indian Allies.* New York: Knopf, 2010. Kindle edition.

Taylor, Alan. *The Divided Ground: Indians, Settlers, and the Northern Borderland of the American Revolution.* New York: Knopf, 2006.

Thomas, Helen. *Romanticism and Slave Narratives.* Cambridge: Cambridge University Press, 2000.

Trope, Jack F., and Walter R. Echo-Hawk. "The Native American Graves Protection and Repatriation Act: Background and Legislative History." *Arizona State Law Journal* 24, no. 1 (1992): 35–77.

Tully, James. *An Approach to Political Philosophy: Locke in Contexts.* Cambridge: Cambridge University Press, 1993.

Turner, Dale A. *This Is Not a Peace Pipe: Towards a Critical Indigenous Philosophy.* Toronto: University of Toronto Press, 2006.

Veracini, Lorenzo. *Settler Colonialism: A Theoretical Overview*. London: Palgrave Macmillan, 2010.

Wald, Priscilla. *Constituting Americans: Cultural Anxiety and Narrative Form*. Durham: Duke University Press, 1995.

Waldstreicher, David. *In the Midst of Perpetual Fetes: The Making of American Nationalism, 1776–1820*. Chapel Hill: University of North Carolina Press, 1997.

Waldstreicher, David. "Reading the Runaways: Self-Fashioning, Print Culture, and Confidence in Slavery in the Eighteenth-Century Mid-Atlantic." *William and Mary Quarterly* 56, no. 2 (1999): 243–72.

Walters, Mark D. "Mohegan Indians v. Connecticut (1705–1773) and the Legal Status of Aboriginal Customary Laws and Government in British North America." *Osgoode Hall Law Journal* 33, no. 4 (1995): 785–829.

Warhus, Mark. *Another America: Native American Maps and the History of Our Land*. New York: St. Martin's Press, 1997.

Warren, Stephen. *The Worlds the Shawnees Made: Migration and Violence in Early America*. Chapel Hill: University of North Carolina Press, 2014.

Weaver, Jace. *That the People Might Live: Native American Literatures and Native American Community*. New York: Oxford University Press, 1997.

Wheeler, Roxann. *The Complexion of Race: Categories of Difference in Eighteenth-Century British Culture*. Philadelphia: University of Pennsylvania Press, 2000.

White, Richard. *The Middle Ground: Indians, Empires, and Republics in the Great Lakes Region, 1650–1815*. Cambridge: Cambridge University Press, 1991.

Wigginton, Caroline. "Extending Root and Branch: Community Regeneration in the Petitions of Samson Occom." *Studies in American Indian Literatures* 20, no. 4 (2008): 24–55.

Wiley, Bell I., ed. *Slaves No More: Letters from Liberia, 1833–1869*. Lexington: University Press of Kentucky, 1980.

Williams, Raymond. *Keywords: A Vocabulary of Culture and Society*. Rev. ed. New York: Oxford University Press, 1983.

Williams, Robert A., Jr. *The American Indian in Western Legal Thought: The Discourse of Conquest*. Oxford: Oxford University Press, 1990.

Williams, Robert A., Jr. *Linking Arms Together: American Indian Treaty Visions of Law and Peace, 1600–1800*. New York: Oxford University Press, 1997.

Winichakul, Thongchai. *Siam Mapped: A History of the Geo-Body of a Nation*. Honolulu: University of Hawai'i Press, 1994.

Witgen, Michael. *An Infinity of Nations: How the Native New World Shaped Early North America*. Philadelphia: University of Pennsylvania Press, 2012.

Wolfe, Patrick. "Settler Colonialism and the Elimination of the Native." *Journal of Genocide Research* 8, no. 4 (2006): 387–409.

Wolfe, Patrick, ed. *The Settler Complex: Recuperating Binarism in Colonial Studies*. Los Angeles: American Indian Studies Center, 2016.

Wong, Edlie L. *Neither Fugitive nor Free: Atlantic Slavery, Freedom Suits, and the Legal Culture of Travel*. New York: New York University Press, 2009.

Wood, Gordon. *The Radicalism of the American Revolution*. New York: Vintage, 1992.

Wright, James M. *The Free Negro in Maryland, 1634–1860*. New York: Octagon, 1971.

Wynter, Sylvia. "Columbus and the Poetics of the Propter Nos." *Annals of Scholarship* 8, no. 2 (1992): 251–86.

Wynter, Sylvia. "Unsettling the Coloniality of Being/Power/Truth/Freedom: Towards the Human, After Man, Its Overrepresentation—An Argument." *CR: The New Centennial Review* 3, no. 3 (2003): 257–337.

Wynter, Sylvia, and Katherine McKittrick. "Unparalleled Catastrophe for Our Species? Or, to Give Humanness a Different Future: Conversations." In *Sylvia Wynter: On Being Human as Praxis*, edited by Katherine McKittrick, 9–89. Durham: Duke University Press, 2015.

Yirush, Craig. "Claiming the New World: Empire, Law, and Indigenous Rights in the Mohegan Case, 1704–1743." *Law and History Review* 29, no. 2 (2011): 333–73.

Yirush, Craig. *Settlers, Liberty, and Empire: The Roots of Early American Political Theory, 1675–1775*. Cambridge: Cambridge University Press, 2011.

Primary Sources

Albany Argus, 1821.

Alexandria Herald, 1820.

Allen, Richard, Quamoney Clarkson, Robert Douglass, James Forten, John Gloucester, Robert Gorden, James Johnson, Absalom Jones, Russell Parrott, Francis Perkins, Randall Shepherd, and John Summersett. "A Voice from Philadelphia." In Garrison, *Thoughts on African Colonization*, 2:9–10.

American and Commercial Daily Advertiser, 1808.

Anonymous. "Petition for freedom to Massachusetts Governor Thomas Gage, His Majesty's Council, and the House of Representatives, June 1774." Collections Online, Massachusetts Historical Society. Accessed May 26, 2013. http://www masshist.org/database/550.

Anonymous. "Petition for freedom to Massachusetts Governor Thomas Hutchinson, His Majesty's Council, and the House of Representatives, June 1773." Collections Online, Massachusetts Historical Society. Accessed May 23, 2013. http://www .masshist.org/database/558.

Apess, William. "An Indian's Looking-Glass for the White Man" (1833). In *On Our Own Ground: The Complete Writings of William Apess, a Pequot*, edited by Barry O'Conell, 155–61. Amherst: University of Massachusetts Press, 1992.

Apess, William. *A Son of the Forest* (1829). In *On Our Own Ground: The Complete Writings of William Apess, a Pequot*, edited by Barry O'Connell, 3–97. Amherst: University of Massachusetts Press, 1992.

Aptheker, Herbert, ed. *A Documentary History of the Negro People in the United States*. Vol. 1. New York: Carol Publishing, 1990.

Aristotle. *Politics*. Bk. 1. Translated by H. Rackham. Cambridge, MA: Harvard University Press, 1944.

Augusta Chronicle, 1823.

Benezet, Anthony. *A Caution and Warning to Great Britain and Her Colonies*. Philadelphia: Henry Miller, 1776.

Blackstone, William. *Commentaries on the Laws of England*. Bk. 1. 1st ed. Oxford: Clarendon, 1765.

Blackstone, William. *Commentaries on the Laws of England*. Bk. 1. 4th ed. Oxford: Clarendon, 1770.

Blackstone, William. *Commentaries on the Laws of England*. Bk. 2. 1st ed. Oxford: Clarendon, 1765.

Boston Post-Boy, 1745.

Boyd, Julian P., Mina R. Bryan, and Elizabeth L. Hutter, eds. *The Papers of Thomas Jefferson*. Vol. 8, *25 February–31 October 1785*. Princeton: Princeton University Press, 1953.

Bracton: De Legibus Et Consuetudinibus Angliæ (c.1250). Translated by Samuel E. Thorne as *Bracton on the Laws and Customs of England*. *Bracton Online*, Harvard Law School Library. Accessed January 31, 2016. http://bracton.law.harvard.edu.

Brathwaite, Edward Kamau. *The Arrivants: A New World Trilogy*. Oxford: Oxford University Press, 1973.

Brooks, Joanna, ed. *The Collected Writings of Samson Occom, Mohegan: Leadership and Literature in Eighteenth-Century Native America*. Oxford: Oxford University Press, 2006.

Brown, Isaac V. *Memoirs of the Rev. Robert Finley, D.D.* New Brunswick, NJ: Terhune and Letson, 1819.

Bulkley, John. Preface to *Poetical Meditations*, by Roger Wolcott, i–lvi. New London: Green, 1725.

Calvin, John. *Commentaries on the Prophet Jeremiah and the Lamentations*. Vol 5. Translated and edited by John Owen. Grand Rapids: Christian Classic Ethereal Library, 1993. PDF ebook. http://www.ccel.org.

"Charter of Massachusetts Bay 1629." *American History: From Revolution to Reconstruction and Beyond*. Accessed November 1, 2016. http://www.let.rug.nl/usa.

Cherokee Phoenix, 1828–33.

Child, Lydia Maria. *An Appeal in Favor of that Class of Americans Called Africans*. New York: John S. Taylor, 1836.

Christian Herald, 1817.

Citizen of Baltimore, A. *Observations on the Impressment of American Seamen*. Baltimore: G. Dobbin & Murphy, 1806.

City Gazette, 1812–13, 1820–23.

Clark, John. "Extract from the Circular for 1826 of the 'Friends of Humanity.'" In *A History of the Illinois Baptists*. Unpublished manuscript, n.p., n.d., 411. Accessed February 28, 2013. http://lincoln.lib.niu.edu/islandora/object/niu-lincoln:35044.

Coke, Edward. *The Reports of Sir Edward Coke, Knt.* 6 vols. New ed. Edited by John Henry Thomas and John Farquhar Fraser. London: Joseph Butterworth and Son, 1826.

Colored American, 1837.

Colton, Calvin. *Tour of the American Lakes, and among the Indians of the North-West Territory in 1830: Disclosing the Character and Prospects of the Indian Race*. Vol. 2. London: Frederick Westley and A. H. Davis, 1833. Accessed May 19, 2017. https://archive.org/stream/tourofamericanla02colt.

"The Complaints and Prayer of Oweneco and Ben Uncas" (1700). Ayer MS 671. Edward E. Ayer Manuscript Collection, Newberry Library, Chicago.

Connecticut Gazette, 1773, 1828.

Connecticut Journal, 1770, 1774.

"Coosa River, In Turkey Town, C.N. 9th February, 1829. To The Cherokee People." *Cherokee Phoenix*, March 4, 1829.

Cornish, William, Robert Cowley, James Deaver, and Remus Harvey. "Memorial of the Free People of Colour." *African Repository* vol. 2, no. 10 (1826): 293–98.

Cowell, John. *The Interpreter: Or Booke Containing the Signification of Words.* Cambridge: John Legate, 1607.

Cross, Helen. *The New Republic.* 2nd ed. Boston: Massachusetts Sabbath School Society, 1851.

Cugoano, Quobna Ottobah. *Thoughts and Sentiments on the Evil of Slavery and Other Writings.* Edited by Vincent Carretta. New York: Penguin, 1999.

Daily National Journal, 1831.

"Dialogues, between William Penn, Paul Cuffee, and Absalom Jones." *Franklin Gazette*, June 24, 1818; July 20, 1818; August 12, 1818.

Denny, Ebenezer. *Military Journal of Major Ebenezer Denny: An Officer in the Revolutionary and Indian Wars.* Philadelphia: Lippincott, 1859.

Douglass, Frederick. *Autobiographies.* Edited by Henry Louis Gates Jr. New York: Library of America, 1994.

Douglass, Frederick. *The Claims of the Negro, Ethnologically Considered.* Rochester, NY: Lee, Mann, & Co., 1854.

Douglass, Frederick. *Lessons of the Hour.* Baltimore: Thomas and Evan, 1894.

Douglass, Frederick. *My Bondage and My Freedom* (1855). In Douglass, *Autobiographies*, 103–452.

Easton, Hosea. *To Heal the Scourge of Prejudice: The Life and Writings of Hosea Easton.* Edited by George R. Price and James Brewer Stewart. Amherst: University of Massachusetts Press, 1999.

Edwardsville Spectator, 1822, 1826.

Emancipator, 1836–39.

"Emigrants to Liberia—Brig Nautilus's company, arrived at Monrovia February 19, 1828." *Christine's Genealogy Website.* Accessed February 25, 2013. http://ccharity.com.

Equiano, Olaudah. *The Interesting Narrative and Other Writings.* Rev. ed. Edited by Vincent Carretta. New York: Penguin, 2003.

Evarts, Jeremiah. *Cherokee Removal: The "William Penn" Essays and Other Writings.* Edited by Francis Paul Prucha. Knoxville: University of Tennessee Press, 1981.

Federal Republican, 1811–14.

Forten, James. "A Late Bill before the Senate of Pennsylvania" (1813). In *Negro Orators and Their Orations*, edited by Carter G. Woodson, 42–51. 1925. Reprint, New York: Russell and Russell, 1969.

Forten, James, and Russell Parrott. "To the Humane and Benevolent Inhabitants of the City and County of Philadelphia" (1818). In *Early Negro Writing, 1760–1837*, edited by Dorothy Porter, 265–68. Boston: Beacon Press, 1971.

Franklin Gazette, 1818.

Frederick Town Herald, 1810.

Freedom's Journal, 1827.

Garrison, William Lloyd. *Thoughts on African Colonization; Or, An Impartial Exhibition of the Doctrines, Principles and Purposes of the American Colonization*

Society. Together with the Resolutions, Addresses and Remonstrances of the Free People of Color. Boston: Garrison and Knapp, 1832.

"Georgia: Cession of Western Land Claims." In *The Territorial Papers of the United States*. Vol. 5, *The Territory of Mississippi, 1798–1817*, compiled and edited by Clarence Edwin Carter, 142–46. Washington, DC: Government Printing Office, 1937. HathiTrust Digital Library. Accessed December 25, 2013. http://catalog.hathitrust.org/Record/000495370.

Goldsmith, Oliver. *A History of the Earth, and Animated Nature* (1774). York, UK: Thomas Wilson and Son, 1808.

Gorton, Adelos. *The Life and Times of Samuel Gorton*. Philadelphia, 1907.

Grotius, Hugo. *The Free Sea* (1609). Edited by David Armitage. Translated by Richard Hakluyt. Indianapolis: Liberty Fund, 2004.

Hall, Prince, et al. "Petition for freedom (manuscript copy) to the Massachusetts Council and the House of Representatives, [13] January 1777." Collections Online, Massachusetts Historical Society. Accessed May 29, 2013. http://masshist.org/database/557.

Hall, Richard, and Richard Hall, eds. *Acts, Passed in the Island of Barbados. From 1643, to 1762, inclusive*. London: Richard Hall, 1764.

Hening, William Waller. *The Statutes at Large; Being a Collection of All the Laws of Virginia, from the First Session of the Legislature, in the Year 1619*. 13 vols. New York: Bartow, 1823.

Hinman, R. R., ed. *Letters from the English kings and queens, Charles II, James II, William and Mary, Anne, George II, &c: to the governors of the Colony of Connecticut, together with the answers thereto, from 1635 to 1749*. Hartford: John B. Eldredge, 1836.

Hoadly, Charles J., ed. *The Public Records of the Colony of Connecticut*. Vol. 14. Hartford: Case, Lockwood & Brainard, 1887.

Homo. "Africa." *Edwardsville Spectator*, October 4, 1823.

Jefferson, Thomas. *Notes on the State of Virginia* (1787). Edited by William Peden. Chapel Hill: University of North Carolina Press, 1955.

Jefferson, Thomas. *A Summary View of the Rights of British America*. Williamsburg, VA: Clementinarind, 1774. Accessed May 5, 2013. http://www.loc.gov/rr/rarebook/guide/ra008001.html.

Journal of the Honorable House of Representatives of His Majesty's Province of the Massachusetts-Bay, in New-England. May 26–June 29, 1773.

Kappler, Charles J., comp. and ed. *Indian Affairs: Laws and Treaties*. Vol. 2, *Treaties*. Washington, DC: Government Printing Office, 1904. Accessed February 5, 2015. http://digital.library.okstate.edu/kappler/vol2/tocyr.htm.

Locke, John. *An Essay Concerning Human Understanding* (1690). Edited by Peter H. Nidditch. Oxford: Clarendon, 1979.

Locke, John. "The Fundamental Constitutions of Carolina." In *The Works of John Locke, in Ten Volumes*. 10th ed., 10:175–99. London: T. Davison, 1801.

Locke, John. *Two Treatises of Government: A Critical Edition with an Introduction and Apparatus Criticus*. Edited by Peter Laslett. Cambridge: Cambridge University Press, 1966.

Lover of Constitutional Liberty, A. *The Appendix: Or, Some Observations on the Expediency of the Petition of the Africans*. Boston: E. Russell, 1773.

Macon Weekly Telegraph, 1829, 1831.

Maryland Gazette, 1766.

Maryland Journal, 1786.

Maryland Republican and Baltimore Advertiser, 1786.

Massachusetts Spy, 1773.

McMurray, William, and Robert Scot. "The United States according to the definitive treaty of peace signed at Paris Sept. 3d. 1783." Map. N.p., 1784. Library of Congress. Accessed December 10, 2016. https://www.loc.gov/item/gm71005423.

McCoy, Isaac. *Remarks on the Practicability of Indian Reform, Embracing Their Colonization; With an Appendix*. 2nd ed. New York: Gray and Bunce, 1829.

Minutes of Debates in Council on the Banks of the Ottawa River (Commonly Called the Miamia of the Lake) November 1791, Said to be Held there by the Chiefs of the Several Indian Nations, Who Defeated the Army of the United States, on the 4th of that Month. Philadelphia: William Young, 1792.

Morfit, Henry M., Henry J. Brent, and T. D. Jones. "Memorial of the Native American Association." 25th Cong., 2d sess. Doc. No. 98. January 8, 1838.

Murray, Laura J., ed. *To Do Good to My Indian Brethren: The Writings of Joseph Johnson, 1751–1776*. Amherst: University of Massachusetts Press, 1998.

National Journal, 1829–30.

Nesbit, William. "Four Months in Liberia: Or African Colonization Exposed" (1855). In Moses, *Liberian Dreams*, 79–126.

The New American State Papers: Indian Affairs. 13 vols. Wilmington, DE: Scholarly Resources, 1972.

Newburyport Herald, 1825, 1830.

New Hampshire Gazette, 1780.

New York Gazette, 1810.

Nott, Josiah C., and George R. Gliddon. *Types of Mankind*. Philadelphia: Lippincott, Grambo and Co., 1854.

Orange County Patriot, 1821.

O'Sullivan, John L. "The Great Nation of Futurity." *The United States Magazine and Democratic Review*, November 1839, 426–30.

Otis, James. *The Rights of the British Colonies Asserted and Proved*. 3rd ed. London: Williams and Almon, 1766.

Oweneco. "Letter of Instruction from Oanhekoe, Sachem of the Mohegan Indians in New England, 14 July 1703." In *Early Native Literacies in New England*, edited by Kristina Bross and Hilary E. Wyss, 19–20. Amherst: University of Massachusetts Press, 2008.

Owaneco's Transfer of His Right to the Lands around New London bounds to the Mohegan People. March 6, 1683/4. Record no. 1684.03.06.00. New England Indian Papers Series, Yale Indian Papers Project. Accessed December 30, 2015. http://hdl.handle.net/10079/digcoll/1018181.

Pennsylvania Gazette, 1750–52, 1756.

Peterson, Daniel H. "The Looking-Glass" (1854). In Moses, *Liberian Dreams*, 1–78.

Phillips, Edward. *The New World of Words, Or a General English Dictionary*. 4th ed. Cornhill, UK: Robert Harford, 1678.

Plowden, Francis. *An Investigation of the Native Rights of British Subjects*. London: Baldwin, Whieldon, and Debarett, 1784.

Prucha, Francis Paul, ed. *Documents of United States Indian Policy*. 3rd ed. Lincoln: University of Nebraska Press, 2000.

Public Advertiser, 1788.

Republican Gazette, 1803.

Royce, Charles C. "Tennessee and Portions of Bordering States." Map of Cherokee and Chickasaw land cessions, 1887. Accessed July 2, 2014. http://usgwarchives.net/maps/cessions/ilcmap54.htm.

Rush, Benjamin. *Address to the Inhabitants of the British Settlements in America, upon Slave-Keeping*. Philadelphia: John Dunlap, 1773.

Rush, Richard. "An Oration, Delivered by Richard Rush, Esq. on the 4th of July, 1812." *Weekly Aurora*, July 28, 1812, 95–98.

Salkeld, William. *Reports of Cases Adjudged in the Court of King's Bench*. Vol. 2. Philadelphia: H. C. Carey & I. Lea, 1822.

Salmon, Thomas. *Modern History: Or, the Present State of All Nations*. 3rd ed. Vol. 3. London, 1746.

Selden, John. *Mare Clausum: The Right and Dominion of the Sea in Two Books*. London: Andrew Kembe and Edward Thomas, 1663.

Smith, John. *The Generall Historie of Virginia, New England, & the Summer Isles*. London: Edward Blackmore, 1632.

Southern Patriot, 1840.

Spelmanno, Henrico [Henry Spelman]. *Glossarium Archaiologicum*. London: Warren, 1664.

Stewart, Maria W. *America's First Black Woman Political Writer: Essays and Speeches*. Edited by Marilyn Richardson. Bloomington: Indiana University Press, 1987.

"The Copy of a Letter from Oanhekoe, Sachem of the Mohegan Indians in New-England, to Mr. Nicholas Hallum. Written in the Indian Language, and Translated by a Sworn Interpreter in New England." *The Present State of Europe: or, the Historical and Political Monthly Mercury* 15 (March 1704): 139–40.

Tocqueville, Alexis de. *Democracy in America* (1835). A Norton Critical Edition. Edited by Isaac Kramnick. New York: Norton, 2007.

Vermont Republican, 1818.

Votes and Proceedings of the House of Representatives, 1755–1756. Philadelphia, 1756.

Walker, David. *David Walker's Appeal to the Coloured Citizens of the World* (1829). Edited by Peter P. Hinks. University Park: Pennsylvania State University Press, 2000.

Watts, Isaac. *The Works of the Rev. Isaac Watts, D.D. in Nine Volumes*. Vol. 9. London: Edward Baines, 1813.

Wheatley, Phillis. "Letter to Samuel Hopkins, October 30, 1774." In *The Poems of Phillis Wheatley: Revised and Enlarged Edition, with an Additional Poem*, edited by Julian D. Mason Jr., 213–14. Chapel Hill: University of North Carolina Press, 1989.

Whitefield, George. *The Works of the Reverend George Whitefield*. Vol. 4. London: Edward and Charles Dilly, 1771.

Williams, George W. *History of the Negro Race in America from 1619 to 1880*. New York: Putnam's Sons, 1883.

Williams, Roger. *A Key into the Language of America*. London: Gregory Dexter, 1643.

INDEX